Austin and Mabel

Austin and Mabel

The Amherst Affair & Love Letters of Austin Dickinson and Mabel Loomis Todd

Polly Longsworth

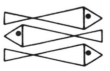

FARRAR · STRAUS · GIROUX

NEW YORK

Copyright © 1984 by Polly Longsworth
Preface copyright © 1984 by Richard B. Sewall
All rights reserved
First printing, 1984
Printed in the United States of America
Published simultaneously in Canada by Collins Publishers, Toronto
Designed by Guy Fleming
Library of Congress Cataloging in Publication Data
Dickinson, Austin, d. 1895.
Austin and Mabel.
Bibliography
Includes index.
1. Dickinson, Emily, 1830–1886. 2. Dickinson
family. 3. Dickinson, Austin, d. 1895. 4. Todd,
Mabel Loomis, 1856–1932. 5. Amherst (Mass.)—
Biography. I. Todd, Mabel Loomis, 1856–1932.
II. Longsworth, Polly. III. Title.
PS1541.Z5D47   1984   811'.4 [B]   83–20579

To the memory of my parents
KATHARINE VANKEUREN
and
CHARLES CRAMER ORMSBY

CONTENTS

ILLUSTRATIONS

P R E F A C E

by Richard B. Sewall

"No love story approaches it," wrote Mabel Todd of her own love story; and, searching the past (Antony and Cleopatra, Abélard and Héloïse, Chateaubriand and Mme Récamier), her lover Austin found "no parallel." In the course of her sober and solidly researched material, Polly Longsworth allows herself such adjectives as "absorbing," "incredible," and "unbearable." I would add "fascinating" and consider the matter still understated. Veteran novel readers will rub their eyes to remind themselves that this really happened. And since it happened close to Emily Dickinson, it is important.

Fortunately, we are prepared for this "bizarre record of human passion and tragedy," as Mrs. Longsworth calls it, by the biographical sketches that precede the letters; and judicious footnotes help us understand some important mysteries. The details of Mabel's origins and early years, the insecurity of her family's boardinghouse life, her "romantic" (Mabel's word) love for her saintly, poetic father—such matters (and more) help explain why, coming to Amherst a married woman at age twenty-five, within a little more than a year she gave herself utterly to Austin Dickinson, exactly her father's age, and himself insecure in his own marriage. We read next about Sue's (Austin's wife's) early difficulties, her orphan state, and the strained relations with the family who took her in, her longing for independence and a home of her own—all this never before so carefully documented and explaining much about her later behavior. (Thus: Mabel became a threat, not so much to Sue's romantic attachment to Austin as to the security and status she had at last managed for herself and was prepared to defend bitterly.)

[xi]

As for the men in this extraordinary situation: The outlines of Austin's character and career have been clear for some time but never so sharply and agonizingly, as we follow him step by step through what must have been, for all its ecstatic moments and spiritual fulfillments, a thirteen-year ordeal. It was a double life; for a man of his integrity, it meant constant tension, strain, anxiety. Curiously and, as Mrs. Longsworth suggests, almost ludicrously, David Todd's role seems to have been, by comparison, relaxed, even acquiescent. But as we learn more about his origins and character, even this becomes credible. It is clear that he himself knew something of the double life, before his marriage and beyond (Mabel did a little acquiescing on her own). And there was his profession and his driving ambition: to be a famous astronomer. His tragedy was not losing Mabel (he never really lost her); as his daughter Millicent told me many times, what saddened his life were three cloudy total eclipses of the sun, each one involving thousands of miles of travel and huge expense—and each one a devastating disappointment. But in between, and after, what kept him going was his work.

The same could be said of Mabel and Austin. One of the wonders that this volume makes abundantly clear is simply this: where did all the time and energy come from? No man worked harder for town and college than Austin. No woman—multitalented, brilliantly social—ever filled her days more full. Did they find ease from tension in busy-ness? And yet, according to the letters, every moment apart was a strain. Those letters! Long, passionate, well composed, and sometimes beautiful. "The awesome fervor of their love": I am more than ever convinced of it. They called it overwhelming, God-inspired, beyond any love that ever was—and yet it was doomed. "I am conscious every moment," wrote Mabel at the height of their love, "that my life is a tragedy."

And tragic it was. There is a sense of fatedness throughout this love story (the story of the Trial puts a seal on it),

[x i i]

even as the letters become most rhapsodic. Tragic to us, surely, not because we know how it turned out, but because we now have the full drama of two sensitive people who, knowing the hazards of their choice, chose between their own natures (and, as they saw Him, their God) which said Yes and the culture of their time which said No. For all the hope they cherished that someday, in some way, Fate would be kind to them, they both saw, I think, that Fate would not. They sensed a Malign Power (on the one hand, three very specific people; on the other, something in the stars) keeping them apart. Mabel sought surcease in her work; and, in a sense, it pulled her through. Austin did the same and it killed him.

Where was Emily in it all? Polly Longsworth's comment is well documented: "The Dickinson sisters not only were aware of their brother's intimacy with Mabel, they became accessory to it." An entry in Millicent Todd Bingham's diary for March 27, 1951, takes us farther:

> The effect on Emily? She was glad that Austin had found some comfort after his all but ruined life. In my mother's words, "Emily always respected real emotion."

Biased? Surely. And the words are not Emily's. But the sentiment, I think, is true. Emily hated "plated wares," and there was nothing plated about the love of Austin and Mabel. It was *real*. Mabel wrote, "We should have been born later. . . . One or two hundred years from now the world would rejoice with us." As usual, Emily never said as much; but then, she too was a century or so ahead of her time.

I

Introduction

EMILY is called in Amherst "the myth." She has not been out of her house for fifteen years. . . . She writes the strangest poems, & very remarkable ones. She is in many respects a genius. She wears always white, & has her hair arranged as was the fashion fifteen years ago when she went into retirement. She wanted me to come & sing to her, but she would not see me. She has frequently sent me flowers & poems, & we have a very pleasant friendship in that way. So last Sunday I went over there with Mr. [Austin] Dickinson. Miss Vinnie, the other sister, who does occasionally go out, told me that if I had been otherwise than a very agreeable person she would have been dreadfully tired of my name even, for she says all the members of her brother's family have so raved about me that ordinarily she would hate the sound of Mrs. Todd.

—*Mabel Loomis Todd's Journal,*

September 15, 1882

THE Sunday visit Mabel Loomis Todd first paid the Dickinson Homestead occurred on September 10, 1882, after she had lived in Amherst for a year. Austin Dickinson escorted her there to sing and play the piano for his reclusive sisters Emily and Lavinia, and his invalid mother, who died just two months later. Mabel recorded in both her diary and her journal how Emily heard her from the shadows of the hall but never appeared, instead sending in an impromptu poem; how elderly, bedridden Mrs. Edward Dickinson listened from upstairs; how

Vinnie shyly took her hands and professed fascination. "It was odd to think," Mabel wrote in her journal five days later, "as my voice rang out through the big silent house that Miss Emily in her weird white dress was outside in the shadow hearing every word. . . . When I stopped Emily sent me in a glass of rich sherry & a poem written as I sang. I know I shall see her. No one *has* seen her in all these years except her own family." The poem Emily Dickinson gave Mrs. Todd was this:

> Elysium is as far as to
> The very nearest Room
> If in that Room a Friend await
> Felicity or Doom—
>
> What fortitude the Soul contains,
> That it can so endure
> The accent of a coming Foot—
> The opening of a Door—

[#1760, ca. 1882]

Mabel believed that this tribute to anticipated momentousness was composed as Emily awaited Mabel's music and awaited, too, the coming of Mabel herself, who had so charmed Austin's family. The poem spoke to underlying circumstances that Emily only possibly divined; Mabel withheld them from her diary and journal, though by the time she wrote of the Homestead visit they were explicit. On the next evening, September 11, as Austin escorted Mrs. Todd to a whist party at his own home (the Evergreens, next door to the Homestead), the two paused in the rain and dusk, looked deeply into each other's eyes, and admitted they were in love. That night Austin wrote in his diary, "Rubicon."

Austin had been in love with Mabel for about six weeks when he confessed it. The timing between his successful presentation of Mabel to his Homestead family and that confession is too close not to recognize that they were related and that, after years of troubled marriage, Austin had taken courage from his sisters' enthusiastic reception of Mabel to make an irrevocable change in his life. His decision represented a cutting back to the roots to bloom again.

Mabel was warmly welcomed to the Homestead family bosom. A week later, she painted Emily an oil study of a flower, selecting the leafless, saprophytic Indian pipe, only to learn it was the poet's "preferred flower of life." Emily responded with a copy of her Hummingbird poem. The Homestead and its occupants remained central throughout the thirteen years that followed, that dwelling being the most constant locus of the lovers. Mabel was in it countless times—meeting Austin for assignations (usually in the dining room behind closed doors, as a servant testified), playing the piano and singing for Emily (whom she never actually saw until the poet's death in 1886), and conversing with the caustic Vinnie. The Dickinson sisters not only were aware of their brother's intimacy with Mabel, they became accessory to it. Their mother's death occurred in November 1882, only two months after Mabel's concert.

Eventually Mabel's friendship with all three Dickinson siblings drew her into the initial editing and publishing of Emily's poems, which might have gone unrecognized, then into locating and publishing the poet's extraordinary letters, which otherwise would have perished. At the same time, her inevitable estrangement from Austin's own family, living next door, provoked "the war between the houses"—the confounding literary drama that has persisted since Emily's hundreds of poems were found, after her death, in her bottom bureau drawer.

Much has been written about the poet, but the full story of her earliest presentation to the world still has not been told. It could not be told so long as the wealth of information located in Austin and Mabel's correspondence, and in related diaries and journals, was suppressed. Originally Mabel wanted to publish these letters herself, feeling certain they rivaled those of Abélard and Héloïse. "There never was such love, as his for me and mine for him," she wrote after Austin's death; and earlier, "No love story approaches it."

At least twice, about 1888 and again in 1895, after Austin's death, she set about organizing the thousand and more letters she kept collected in a pair of large tin boxes. Among her reasons for preserving them was Austin's belief that they would protect her against his family's fury should he die. "It has been my fortune to have confided to me the letters and diaries of two persons who loved so nobly, so unutterably, so endlessly that the gods themselves must have delighted to watch," Mabel wrote lyrically in her earliest introduction, which cloaked her own and Austin's identities. In 1895 she added: "As they placed these records in my hands from time to time, for safe keeping, both gave me permission, if an earthly life together were denied them, to make whatever use of the papers in a literary way I might desire."

Her quarrel with Susan Dickinson, Austin's widow, postponed Mrs. Todd's intentions until close to the end of her life. When she died in 1932, she had charged her daughter "to set the record straight," but Millicent Todd Bingham could not bring herself to expose publicly what she considered her mother's terrible sin. Mrs. Bingham wrote an otherwise reliable account of Mabel's role in editing Emily Dickinson's poems, *Ancestors' Brocades* (1945), and a later book about the Dickinson family, *Emily Dickinson's Home* (1955), but she omitted from both any mention of the love affair, thereby draining the lifeblood and the truth from her story. On the Dickinson side, Austin's widow, Susan, and his surviving child, Martha Dickinson Bianchi, had equally valid reasons for wanting to wipe the episode from memory. With possession of Emily's poems divided between the feuding families, both of which began publishing volumes of the poet's verse and versions of her life, decades of dispute ensued over the rights to the Dickinson poems.

Austin and Mabel's love letters were given to Yale University in 1968, among a large collection of Todd-Bingham family papers, in order that Professor Richard B. Sewall might incorporate the principal facts of the love affair into his two-volume *Life of Emily Dickinson* (1975). Sewall introduced the story, extracting from Austin and Mabel's correspondence the essence of what had transpired, and its effect upon Emily and those close to her, but he left for later telling a detailed account of the affair. The time has come to put into place this bizarre record of human passion and tragedy.

The Todd-Dickinson liaison was a love triangle. The apparently willing participation of Mabel's husband, David P. Todd, professor of astronomy at Amherst College, where Austin Dickinson was treasurer, is perhaps the most enigmatic element of the story, for David knew that his winsome wife's fondest dream, revealed on a scrap of paper that fell from her diary, was to become Mabel Loomis Dickinson. With divorce out of the question in that era, Mabel prayed for Sue Dickinson's demise, meanwhile taking pride in her superiority to conventional morality by her ability to love two men, then lamenting the scorn and condemnation such heresy earned her in orthodox Amherst. "God pity such love! Of one man for one woman—the mystery and the might of it," rejoiced Austin, with a pathos Mabel fully equaled.

If the love letters stood alone, as Mabel undoubtedly would have preferred, readers would encounter one prolonged "I love you," for nothing about them is more notable than their sustained passion, bearing testimony to what Sewall has called "the awesome fervor of their love." Fortunately, however, diaries, journals, and other correspondence preserved along with the love letters tie the alliance to a far more intriguing reality. This extensive documentation, which charts the considerable range of emotion, growth, and change within the union, in the end may persuade readers to the truth of Mabel's insight of 1888: "We should have been born later, that is all. One or two hundred years from now the world would rejoice with us."

1 / Mabel *and* David Todd

MABEL LOOMIS TODD was born in 1856, the year that Sue and Austin Dickinson were married, and came to Amherst, Massachusetts, soon after their twenty-fifth wedding anniversary. Alighting at the depot on a late August afternoon in 1881, she brought to the deceptively placid New England village an unusual fusion of talent, ambition, and cultivated personal charm.

At twenty-four Mabel was small and pretty, with large luminous brown eyes, a wide sensuous mouth, and softly upswept light hair. Leaning on the arm of her husband, David Peck Todd, who was returning to his alma mater to instruct in astronomy and direct the observatory, she admired the comely town that was to be her home for the next thirty-five years. Within, however, she held deep reservations about the wisdom of leaving Washington, D.C., and abandoning the promising opportunities she and David had there. He was more sanguine than she about their future at Amherst College; only much later would he bitterly regret this move, which frustrated his career and so quickly involved them both in the affairs of the Dickinson family.

Mabel Todd was a very accomplished young lady, at least by Amherst standards. She painted in oils and watercolors on canvas, wood, paper, and china; she played the piano seriously and well, and sang in a lovely, trained soprano. She was well-read, had ambitions as an author, and had had several essays published while growing up. Far from being retiring about her abilities, she put herself forward with a vivacious charm that enabled her to attract the attention of the gathering in any room she entered. In fact, she took intense pleasure in feeling all eyes turned toward her, and quite indulged her flair for arousing admiration and winning lavish praise.

At first she was bewildered by the reserve of the people David introduced her to in this village, set in an angle between the tiny Pelham and Mount Holyoke ranges, and distinguished by the presence of two collegiate institutions—Amherst College, where David was engaged, and the more recently founded Massachusetts Agricultural College. Amherst citizens were characterized by "plain living and high thinking," which, as Mrs. Todd discovered, meant that college faculty members and their wives nodded to her and David, promised to call when they had time, and turned away to their books, Bibles, and many practical duties. Having been brought up almost exclusively in boardinghouses, Mabel knew few housekeeping arts, and hated all she knew. She had left her one-and-a-half-year-old baby, Millicent, in Washington for her parents to take care of until she was more settled. Still, these differences bothered her less than the lack of gaiety and spontaneity among Amherst people, for above all Mabel loved a good time. Twenty years later, with notable hindsight, she recalled how strange it seemed in 1881,

the sad summer when Garfield was shot, and fought for his life two months, while the bulletins rose and fell—and David and I came to live in Amherst.

I can remember how the leaves turned that September, and how the western hills smothered themselves in purple lights as the sun went down—and how beautiful the village and the whole region seemed, and yet how small and circumscribed the lives of those who had always lived here. The depressed and stern-visaged Crowells—the rough and terrible, uncultivated Hitch-

cocks, the innocent and weak-minded Montagues—the severe
Seelyes, to whom cider or claret at dinner meant everlasting
doom—the tottering old Tylers, the unsmiling Henshaws, the
pompous Neills.

These were the people among whom she and David had come
to live, and Mabel was not sure at first they had made the
right choice.

One evening in early October, Mr. and Mrs. William
Austin Dickinson called at the Todds' South Pleasant Street
boardinghouse, and that visit marked Mabel's real entrance
into Amherst. Austin Dickinson, a lawyer, was the treasurer of
Amherst College and the town's leading citizen. He impressed
her at first meeting as "fine (& very remarkable) looking—&
very dignified & strong and a little odd." Having accurately
summed up the Dickinson family traits, she was more immediately attracted to Austin's wife, Susan—dark, handsome,
scintillating, and "the most of a real society person here." In
Washington Mabel had already tasted the advantages of being
taken up by an older woman of social and cultural sophistica-
tion, so she responded right away to Mrs. Dickinson's patroniz-
ing air, and appreciated her generous approbations and worldly
manner. In a very short time Sue became the center of Mabel's
universe, and her ways Mabel's ideal for things done tastefully
and well. The elegant Dickinson house, its books and paintings
and piano, and its horses and carriages, represented all that
Mabel hoped someday to possess. "I am thoroughly captivated
with her," she wrote enthusiastically of Mrs. Dickinson to her
parents, a few days after meeting her. "She does, as I supposed,
live very handsomely, & she is so easy and charming & sincere
—and she understands me completely."

At the Dickinson home on Main Street, the Evergreens,
Mabel found a touch of Washington-like society. No other
house in town indulged in such a round of musicales, whist
parties, and dancing as Sue kept going. Soon pretty, vibrant
Mrs. Todd, with her dainty figure and lively laughter, seemed

essential to the gaiety at the Evergreens, while that house in turn provided the ideal setting for the display of her many accomplishments. As autumn deepened, she played the piano there and sang, gave young Martha (Mattie) Dickinson piano lessons, and rode horseback with young Ned. She began going in and out of the Evergreens nearly every day, and was regularly included with David in Mrs. Dickinson's entertainments.

In background as well as social ambition, Susan Huntington Gilbert Dickinson and Mabel Loomis Todd were more alike than any who knew them later as mortal enemies would have suspected. Both came of modest, relatively insecure circumstances, and both, through appearance and allusion, encouraged people to believe otherwise. Having grown up in the village, Sue couldn't get away with many pretensions concerning her antecedents, though she was given to unpopular airs and duplicities. But she and Mabel managed to fool each other, at least at first,* and Mabel's foreignness to Amherst allowed certain embellishments of hers to go unchallenged. For instance, Mabel took notable pride in a New England lineage she traced through Puritan ministers to Priscilla Alden, and she did not hesitate to mention the friendships her father, Professor Eben J. Loomis, enjoyed with men of letters and science in Washington, where he was an "astronomer" associated with the U.S. Naval Observatory. References to her education at the New England

---

* Mabel was so completely taken in at first by Sue that when her parents picked up Washington gossip about Sue's cousin, the Mrs. Otis Bigelow from whom their home was purchased, Mabel disputed it. Mrs. Bigelow was a former governess who had improved her status by marrying a wealthy Washington widower, reported Mrs. Loomis. Mabel responded testily, "You did not understand me—Mrs. Dickinson is *Mrs.* Bigelow's own cousin. . . . I can hardly believe Mrs. Bigelow could have been a governess—but at all events she is far superior to her husband certainly, in education & acquirements" (MLT to her parents, October 15, 1881).

Conservatory of Music and her social connections in Washington colored her conversation. It would have been difficult to recognize which elements of her story were more tenuous than others, or that the whole was a gentle distortion, probably fabricated as much to protect herself against the perplexities of her curiously rootless girlhood as to impress others.*

For all her references to family prestige and a cosmopolitan upbringing in Washington, Mabel actually had been raised in straitened circumstances in a series of Concord, Cambridge, and Washington boardinghouses by parents who spent nearly as much time apart as together, despite strong bonds of affection. Her parents were Mary Alden Wilder and Eben Jenks Loomis, who married in July 1853, three years before the birth of Mabel, their only child, on November 10, 1856. Eben Loomis had been born on his father's farm at Morris, New York, in 1828, the fourth son of eight children of Nathan and Waite Barber Loomis. During his youth the family moved to Fairfax, Virginia, and in 1850, when Eben was a young man, his father, who practiced as a civil engineer and surveyor, became a

---

* Millicent Todd Bingham, Mabel and David Todd's only child, wrote in 1933 in an unpublished reminiscence: "One of the earliest things I can recall was a gradual awakening to the fact that both my mother and my grandmother distorted the truth, if necessary. Exaggeration, it was, rather than lying." Mrs. Bingham's own passionate regard for truth and accuracy did not prevent her from perpetuating some family illusions she was nourished on. In *Ancestors' Brocades* Mrs. Bingham writes that her mother had grown up in Washington "among distinguished scientists and men of letters," and "for two winters also she had studied at the New England Conservatory of Music in Boston" after attending Miss Liscomb's School in Georgetown, "the first Washington home of the Loomises." Mabel's father, Eben Jenks Loomis, is described in that volume as "an astronomer at the United States Naval Observatory. He was also a poet and a student of nature, a friend of Asa Gray, Henry Thoreau and Walt Whitman." Similar statements appear in the *National Encyclopedia of American Biography*, to which Mrs. Bingham supplied information about her mother. Such exaggerations misrepresent the family's position and affluence.

computer in the Cambridge, Massachusetts, office of the *American Ephemerist and Nautical Almanac*, publisher of the tables of astronomy-based computations upon which commercial and military navigation depend. About 1851 Eben and a brother followed their father to Cambridge, and after attending a mathematics course at Harvard's Lawrence Scientific School for a term, he was hired as an assistant in the Nautical Almanac Office at $500 a year.* He boarded in Cambridge at the home of another young assistant at the Office, John Wilder, whose sister Eben fell in love with, courted, and married.

A rare glimpse of Eben Loomis's youth occurs in a letter Mabel Todd's mother wrote to her in Amherst in 1884, when a Mrs. Avery was visiting nearby and planned to call on the Todds. Mrs. Loomis was eager for Mabel to convince Mrs. Avery that Eben was better than others in his family.

> Say in as few words as possible to Mrs. Avery that your father from a little child had an exquisite literary taste & love for nature & poety—and not finding the *least* congeniality among his family—spent hours—*alone*—and made nature take the place of

---

* Lawrence Scientific School was Harvard University's first graduate school, established in 1847. It provided instruction in applied science (as distinct from the pure, or "book," science taught at Harvard College), offering lectures and course work in zoology and geology under Louis Agassiz, botany under Asa Gray, and mathematics, chemistry, physiology, mineralogy, and astronomy under other prominent scientists. There is no record of Eben Loomis's enrollment in the school, but Mrs. Bingham states that her grandfather studied mathematics there. Since in early years the lectures were open to persons not enrolled at the university for a fee of five dollars per course, Loomis probably attended the twice-weekly lectures delivered by Professor Benjamin Peirce, Harvard mathematician and also computer for the Nautical Almanac Office. Taught first term, Peirce's lectures covered mathematics and astronomy, analytical and celestial mechanics, and the mechanical theory of light. Loomis's acquaintance with pioneering botanist Asa Gray probably dates from this time as well. He may have attended Gray's twenty-four-lecture course, taught second term, on structural botany and vegetable anatomy.

loved ones. To such a degree that he became an expert ornithologist and with a *few best* books such as Shakespeare, and
best classic poets—became a *critical scholar*! . . . Grandma
knows how lonely & unloved a life Eben led—before he came
to us!

This letter illustrates Mary Wilder Loomis's picturesque
prose and suggests an alien quality to Eben Loomis's upbringing. It also depicts the constant attempts made by Eben's wife,
daughter, and granddaughter to elevate his status, ostensibly
because they believed he was unappreciated by the world, but
perhaps, also, so that their own status could be raised. Much as
Eben knew about bird life and Shakespeare, he was neither an
ornithologist nor a critical scholar, any more than he was a
mathematician, scientist, astronomer, philosopher, or professor
—all titles by which his family identified him.* A self-educated,
intelligent man of forbearing manner, saintly disposition, and
handsome, ethereal appearance, Eben loved the outdoors,
esteemed the classics, and found escape from many disappointments in his life by tramping the landscape, reading extensively,
and writing high-flown verse. He had the manner of a gentleman scholar, and he read and studied and observed acutely
throughout his life, but never acquired academic training nor
achieved professional standing in any of the several vocations
he admired and emulated.

Mabel adored her father. Growing up, she leaned on his
love and wisdom and temperate guidance in ways she later
came to lean on Austin Dickinson's. She told her father, as
she later told Austin, that he "showed her her best," by which

* From girlhood Mabel addressed her letters to Professor Eben J.
Loomis. Her father's scholarly demeanor encouraged the title, and he
must have given silent assent to its use by the "men of science" among
whom he worked, for he often participated in the annual meetings of
the National Academy of Science by reading one of his poems, appearing in the program as Professor Loomis.

she meant he set spiritual aspirations and moral standards she could not provide for herself. Mabel's dependence on Eben is at least part of the explanation why she later, in a new setting and away from home, transferred feelings and needs for her father to someone like him. Eben Loomis and Austin Dickinson were the same age, and in philosophical outlook, aesthetic sensitivity, and deep, knowledgeable love of nature, much alike. Austin's nature was "lofty & spiritual beyond that of anyone I ever met, unless it is my blessed father," Mabel once said. She appreciated the "heavenly nature" of both men, and made remarkably similar journal comments about each at distinctly different times. In 1885 she wrote: "Austin & I have had a most intimate and tender relationship for more than three years— and in all that time, through all sorts of annoyances & petty trials unnumbered, he has never had even the beginning of a petulant thought to me, nor I to him." At her father's deathbed twenty-seven years later she penned: "In all my life we never had one irritable mood between us." With both men she sustained an idealized relationship that seemed to buttress needs of her own psyche.

But Austin Dickinson and Eben Loomis were very different. The former was a man of accomplishment, caught up in an active law practice and the pressing, important business affairs of his town, while the self-effacing Eben never translated his many intellectual interests and fine personal qualities into satisfying lifework. His fond dream of returning to the soil nearly materialized right after the Civil War, when he left Cambridge to sink his earnings into a partnership in a Florida cotton plantation near Jacksonville, a venture that failed within a year. Returning North nearly penniless in 1867, he found Boston enduring economic depression and could get no work. The Nautical Almanac Office had moved from Cambridge to the nation's capital to be near the U.S. Naval Observatory, and finally Eben went to Washington to take up his assistantship again. Although he always yearned for better, more lucrative employment, there was little else he was qualified to do. In the end, he held his position at the Nautical Almanac Office for fifty years.

Eben's sense of aloofness from his everyday work was shared with eleven-year-old Mabel during his first lonely winter at the capital when he wrote home to her of the daily exodus of clerks from Washington office buildings at three o'clock. "I don't like to be in the street at the same time with the crowd," he explained. "Sometimes I go to Uncle Mahlon's home and wait half an hour & then I can go home without being suspected of being a clerk." Yet for all he came to know about the stars, his remained a general clerical job. Annual reports of the Nautical Almanac Office and professional correspondence with Simon Newcomb, astronomer and superintendent of the NAO from 1877 to 1897, reveal that Eben prepared the tables of moon, star, and planet culminations from computations, copied and read endless proof of the *American Ephemeris and Nautical Almanac*, and carried out with quiet dignity the duties of the office in the absence of others. But he wasn't trained to make observations, or to do the theoretical work of the Almanac Office, which centered on establishing new, more accurate tables of constants. Although eventually he became Senior Assistant, his income was always modest. After twenty years in Washington he earned $1,600, the equivalent of a first-class clerk, a salary on which his small family always struggled to make ends meet. Though he sought supplementary income and fulfillment of his loftier dreams by writing essays and poems on nature for newspapers and periodicals, his published efforts were rarely compensated. For inspiration he looked to many admired authors, principally Shakespeare, and on his annual autumn holiday he revisited New England or took "walks" of many days' duration into the Virginia countryside, as he had had occasion to do in Massachusetts with Henry Thoreau, and at least once in Washington with Walt Whitman.* Mabel, and later Millicent, loved going on walks with Eben. His kindly patience and intimate knowledge of flora and fauna inspired their own early love for the landscape.

Mabel's mother, Mary Alden Wilder Loomis, was of a very different temperament, enjoying what her daughter once termed a "tumultuous, volcanic, enthusiastic, appreciative, happy, disappointed, prejudicial, intense, sensitive, affectionate life," the humorous aspects of which Mabel didn't always appreciate. Born in Charlton, Massachusetts, in 1831, Molly, as she was called, was the second daughter of the Reverend John Wilder and Mary Wales Fobes Jones. She grew up with an older sister, Eliza, and younger brother, John, in parishes in Concord, Massachusetts, and Marshall, Michigan, where her father, like his before him, was Congregational minister. Molly was ten when the family returned to Charlton, and twelve when her father died there, leaving her mother widowed at forty. Mrs. Wilder acquired a house in Cambridge, and apparently took in boarders to help support her children. Daughter Eliza died in 1854, when Molly was fourteen.

By the time of her marriage at twenty-two, Molly Wilder

---

* In *Ancestors' Brocades* Mrs. Bingham says of Eben Loomis: "Himself a poet as well as a man of science, he had explored with Henry Thoreau the woods and fields of Concord. He had walked in the Shenandoah Valley with Walt Whitman when the latter was a government clerk in Washington and he himself was computing stellar distances and planetary perturbations." While this story is based on family tradition, it is hard to judge from Mrs. Bingham's conceits whether Loomis's walk with either man was an isolated or regular incident. Thoreau, a dozen years older than Loomis, had been a parishioner and friend of Rev. John Wilder and, with his sisters Maria and Sophia, remained Mrs. Wilder's friend after she was widowed. Loomis and Thoreau had recognizable interests in common, and would have known each other during the decade between 1851, when Loomis came to Cambridge to live, and 1862, when Thoreau died. Whitman was employed as a clerk in the Department of the Interior in Washington when Loomis arrived in the city alone in the autumn of 1867. Whitman left in 1872. Again, their interests were compatible.

could cook and manage a household, and had developed considerable skill at embroidering, both with her needle and her tongue. She sewed exquisitely and was an effusive talker, with a vivid style that held listeners spellbound. Her pious upbringing manifested itself in strongly expressed, occasionally rigid ideas of right and wrong, and in a ready knack for quoting from the Bible, traits apparently inculcated during childhood, for as an adult she never read the Bible and only occasionally went to church. She engaged energetically in the upbringing of her adored only child, in the practicalities of household management, and in worry about the family's financial precariousness.

It is likely that concern about money was one way Molly Loomis expressed her anxieties about life, so that the endless attention to financial matters that filled her letters to Eben probably conveys an impression of tighter monetary restrictions than actually prevailed. Nevertheless, Molly did bear the responsibility for making limited ends meet on a day-to-day basis during her husband's extended Southern venture, and in general engaged more actively at the commonsense level of reality than he did. After Eben left for Florida in 1866, Molly negotiated the sale of the Wilder home and many family possessions to help finance the cotton plantation, then moved her mother and little Mabel into a Boston boardinghouse, where the three scraped pennies carefully. Since her volubility on paper was as pronounced as in person, and its flow related directly to her agitation of mind and spirit, Molly's letters to her husband during this period are crowded with her thoughts, feelings, conversations, and concerns. Her distress over Eben's foundering business investment became more acute when he was forced to find employment in Washington instead of Boston. Arguing that Eben's salary was much too small for them to live on in the capital, Molly refused to join him for over a year, although her subsequent behavior suggests that a deep reluctance to leave New England was involved. By the time she relented and moved to Washington in the fall of 1868,

Mabel was twelve and had been apart from her father for nearly three years.

The Loomises found Washington a raw, sprawling, over-grown town with muddy streets and large, elegantly planned buildings and vistas separated by vacant lots and Negro slums. The Civil War was not long over, and the capital was strug-gling to become the social, political, and intellectual center envisioned by its early planners. With no home and few furnishings of their own, the Loomises took rooms in a George-town boardinghouse and began the nomadic domestic routine they followed throughout the rest of Mabel's girlhood. During the winter months they boarded in Georgetown or Washington. From early June through late October, the hottest months of the year, Mrs. Loomis and Mabel went North to visit Grandma Wilder, who boarded in Concord. The three females then visited the Vermont mountains or the Maine or New Hampshire coast during late July and August, and returned to the environs of Boston for early fall. Eben, meanwhile, stayed at his post in the steaming city until October, when he took a month's walking trip or else joined his family in the North.

Each winter, back in Washington, the family selected a new boardinghouse, keeping at first to Georgetown, but by the mid-1870s selecting accommodations in the area northwest of the Capitol on N or O Street between 11th and 14th N.W. Washington was still small enough that they were never far from the countryside Eben loved, yet were within walking distance of the Nautical Almanac Office on 21st Street N.W. between E and F Streets. Boarding was as prudent a way of life as it was necessary for a family of small means, for in the late 1860s the Department of Public Works had grown zealous in instituting physical improvements to the city, with the result that property taxes were high and special assessments occurred regularly. School taxes also were rising, to cope with the high illiteracy rate among the thousands of black citizens who had streamed into Washington since early in the war.

Renting rooms was a common experience for those who came and went with the sittings of the legislature, and the Loomises fitted their unsettled existence unobtrusively into this pattern.

Molly Loomis looked upon her annual pilgrimage to New England as a duty, cloaking it in many folds of sacrifice. Overtly she traveled for the sake of Mabel's health, for she eyed suspiciously certain nervous tendencies in her daughter and worried constantly about illness resulting from Washington's muggy climate and primitive sanitary conditions. She also undertook her journey out of moral obligation to her mother, who was left alone in Massachusetts. Her sense of duty doubled after her brother John was murdered in 1870 in a political dispute in Kansas City, Kansas, where he had been practicing law and editing and publishing the Kansas City *Journal of Commerce*. Despite Eben's reluctance, Molly brought her much-saddened mother, nearly seventy now, to live with her in Washington. A frail, straitlaced, highly spiritual New England lady, Grandma Wilder became a fixture in the Loomis household for the next twenty-three years, during which Molly felt a compunction to leave Eben each summer to take her mother "home" to friends and relatives in Concord.

Lengthy separations didn't seem to disturb the devotion and understanding between Eben and Molly Loomis. She made no secret of her homesickness for New England, and never stopped hoping her husband eventually would find employment there, but she transposed these feelings into a fervent conviction that only in Boston could she get the bargains on fabrics and the cheap dressmaking help she needed to keep Mabel, Eben, and herself well clothed. This being one of her major responsibilities, Molly always spent her first and last weeks in Massachusetts in a frenzy of purchasing materials and refurbishing the family's summer and winter wardrobes. Details of her sewing economies, of the hours sacrificed to stitching, and the cut rate given her by a certain dressmaker, "because she pities me so," were conveyed to Eben as excuses for neglect in writing

while sewing duties absorbed her. Meanwhile, the consequences of the annual five-month abandonment lent Eben's
letters an ascetic tone. He was, as his wife often assured him, a
"kind, patient & unselfish Husband." He was also lonely and
frequently ill during the summer. He moved into a single room,
ate little, read voluminously, and worked faithfully through
the heat, his eye on his precious freedom of October, for which
he scrimped to set aside a few dollars. In addition, of course,
he accepted celibacy, though this was never mentioned; penciled
passages in the marriage manual in the Loomis library suggest
it may have been a feature of their union anyway.*

The journal Mabel began keeping when she was ten years
old reveals that she responded to her family's circumstances
with surprising resilience. By the time of her marriage in 1879,
she had called about a dozen Washington boardinghouses
home, and had spent summer after summer in a series of inex-
pensive single rented rooms shared with her mother and
grandmother. The lack of social privacy and emphasis on
keeping up appearances inherent in boardinghouse life left clear
marks on her behavior. For Mabel a public parlor or dining
room comprised a small stage which she learned to dominate

---

* Entitled *Marriage and Parentage, or The Reproductive Element in
Man as a Means to his Elevation and Happiness*, by Henry C. Wright,
this 300-page book, inscribed with Molly's name and the year of her
wedding, is a treatise in letter style advocating that men and women
"bring their sexual natures and relations under the government of
enlightened reason and tender consciences." Specifically, it encouraged
men to enjoy the "glow of life and healthful energy" resulting from
retaining certain elements in their system. Passages marked in pencil
along the book's margin, presumably by Molly, include the notions
that a man's character was improved by holding on to his powers, that
"the wife must decide how often and under what circumstances the
husband may enjoy this passionate expression of his love," and that
intercourse was properly intended for the conception of a child, and
only a selfish husband would inflict unwanted maternity upon his wife.
How the many separations between Molly and Eben related to this
prevalent mid-nineteenth-century theory can only be surmised.

with her conversational and artistic gifts. She took for granted and thoroughly enjoyed attentions accorded her as the only child of doting parents and a grandparent, and often the only child in the boardinghouse. Adulation from adults was a sustaining element of her life, for she formed few close friendships growing up, and more than once mentioned her sense that her peers didn't appreciate her.

Mabel's adolescence can be viewed in simplest terms as a process of selecting from alternative modes of behavior presented by her two very different parents, one of whom was voluble, compulsive, and down-to-earth; the other, patient, philosophical, long-suffering, and otherworldly. These differences were emphasized by the apart/together pattern that placed her mother in authority half the year and her father the other half. Whether or not her father was present, Mabel spent her first seventeen years in unusually close company with her mother, and she might easily have been overwhelmed by Molly Loomis's extravagant character traits if she had not rejected more than she accepted.* She rejected few of them fully, however. For example, spurning evidence of penny-pinching as a result of her mother's incessant economizing, Mabel still became a conscientious manager of funds, so expert at camouflaging frugality she could be severely critical of others less adept. As a cover, she adopted her father's attitude of superiority to the importance of money, consciously placing culture and accomplishment in such esteem in her own value system that her views come across as snobbish.

The roots of this perhaps pragmatic way of thinking occurred in an exchange between Mabel and her father in 1874,

---

* Later Millicent Todd, who spent long periods in the care of her grandparents while growing up, revealed some of Molly Loomis's obsessive habits: "After every trip to town she took out her coins and washed them with soap and water. She bound buttonholes with silk on new undergarments for strength. Clothing was put away for the season sewn in cloth bags, labeled endlessly with the garments' history."

the summer she was seventeen, a watershed period in her life, during which she turned to many philosophical comforts her father could provide. She was bothered at the time by her sense that Eben was overworked and underpaid, a feeling possibly exacerbated by the fun she was having that summer at the Maine seashore. She burst out in a letter of September 13, 1874: "My precious Father, I not only worship you with the tenderest love a daughter can bestow, but I admire and appreciate you above everything, and the thought that you do not have half the enjoyment & happiness in life that you deserve & that other men—bad & hateful fools—do have, nearly sets me crazy. I should like to know why it is that wicked people always have everything they want and that you, than whom there is no better man living, have comparatively nothing. I hate the injustice of things." To which Eben Loomis, who apparently had been refused a salary raise, replied: "Money is convenient, but it is not the best thing of life. . . . It is not what we *have* but what we *are* that is important; and we can be *nearly* what we choose in spite of circumstances. . . . Back & above all circumstances of wealth or poverty sits the soul, watching, growing, reticent, conscious . . . of a superiority over the small accidents of life & death." Though Mabel was too much her mother's daughter to truly believe money wasn't important, she admired her father's lofty attitude and took it for her solution too.

Her mother's obsession with domestic matters, and the overtones of self-sacrifice that accompanied it, was another area Mabel backed away from, devoting herself instead to more creative pursuits. Her father encouraged this. Once, when he feared his daughter would fall victim to the dressmaking fever that claimed his wife, and would forget to write him, he counseled sixteen-year-old Mabel: "In creating the natural woman God has his ideas of beauty; in making the artificial woman the milliner has hers. I prefer God's woman decidedly. . . . Fashions change, robes wear out, but the acquisitions of the mind are imperishable as eternity." Here was a concept that could extricate Mabel from pursuits she detested, and she seized upon self-culture as a defense against housewifery. While eschewing her mother's sewing skills, however, she formed a similarly intense love of finery and elegance, particularly in clothing, and developed a flair for improving her appearance with clever stylistic touches of her own.* But other housekeeping arts she avoided so assiduously that on her fifth wedding anniversary, when Amherst friends presented the Todds with numerous practical wooden kitchen implements, Mabel proudly described them as "objects of the most intense curiosity to me."†

The consuming occupations Mabel substituted for domestic work were writing, painting, and music, the latter being her most natural talent of the three, for she both sang and played the piano by ear remarkably well. "Mabel is begging me to take music lessons when she gets back to Georgetown," Molly wrote her husband the summer of 1872, when Mabel was

---

* "She wore beautiful lace and jewelry and she could carry it off better than anybody I ever saw and make it seem subservient," Millicent T. Bingham commented in a 1958 tape recording. An example of Mabel's eye-catching improvements to her clothing was a camel's-hair dress made for her in Washington in the spring of 1882, down the satin front panels of which she handpainted sweetpeas. She first wore it to a party at Mrs. Stearns's in Amherst, and the next day wrote David in Washington: "I was quite the center of attraction for a while, and had nearly all the gentlemen around me at once. All spoke of my magnificent painted dress." The panels of the dress can still be seen at the Amherst Historical Society, which houses numerous garments from Mrs. Todd's wardrobe.

† This scornful attitude of Mabel's toward housekeeping not only handicapped her in an era when servants had to be trained, which Mabel was ill equipped to do, it irritated many women in Amherst who felt she flaunted the ideals of womanhood by indulging in her selfish pursuits to the assumed neglect of her husband, child, and home. Millicent, as a girl, was embarrassed that her mother attended "to her 'desk things' when I thought she should have been attending to housekeeping."

fifteen, "and everybody says *she ought* to, but oh! Where is the money coming from?" Or the piano, she might have added, for Mabel's access to an instrument depended upon its availability in a given boardinghouse. The next summer she took lessons for a few weeks at the New England Conservatory of Music, and dreamed thereafter of returning there to study music when she graduated from school.*

Mabel's skills as an artist developed more slowly, partly for lack of lessons, but also for lack of someone to model herself on. In 1875 she was encouraged by a woman in her Boston boardinghouse who took lessons from May Alcott and painted careful floral studies in oils on neat black panels. Sticking closely to the natural forms she knew and loved, Mabel taught herself the techniques of painting weeds and wildflowers, and occasionally birds and butterflies, in both oil and watercolor. By 1879 she felt sufficiently authoritative to write an illustrated book, never published, on flower painting in oils. There was little that was free or imaginative about her style, but she discovered she could draw great admiration by closely imitating nature, and proceeded to do so. After her marriage, David built her a studio of her own in Washington, and still later a second one in his office quarters in Walker Hall at Amherst College, so that she had a place to give lessons and to paint the hundreds of screens, plaques, and chinaware items that decorated her home and the home of her parents, which she gave as gifts, and occasionally sold. Her greatest satisfaction as a painter came in 1889, when eminent entomologist Samuel Scudder used her study of a monarch butterfly as frontispiece for the prospectus of his *Butterflies of the Eastern United States and Canada*.

* Mabel's early affinity for the piano worked its way into a composition she wrote and sent her father in Florida when she was ten. Titled "The History of a Piano," the story concerned an instrument owned first by a lady whose husband failed in business, then by a lady who died, until the piano ended decaying in a warehouse, uncared for. The story very likely contained Mabel's own feelings of abandonment at the time.

Mabel clearly emulated her father when it came to writing, the pursuit that tied them most closely. "Is it presumptuous to say my style is improving in the direction of yours?" she inquired hopefully when she was sixteen. A few days later she announced, "I was never so happy in my life as I am now. Not from anything that happens, but because I feel in me the possibility of great things in the way of writing." This was a sense she bore all her life, so that during her girlhood she published seven essays (and wrote another twenty), and in her lifetime wrote or edited twelve published books and some two hundred articles. But Mabel had a clear enough eye for genius in writing to recognize ultimately that she herself didn't possess it. Her literary ambitions also centered on the desire "to become, & be known as, a thoroughly well-read and intellectual person," and to this end she long kept a record of all the books she read. Over the years it ranged from such girlhood favorites as Harriet Beecher Stowe's *Pink and White Tyranny* through the novels of Hawthorne, Dickens, and William Dean Howells, to volumes on interior decoration and on dress, which fascinated her. Her tastes focused most strongly on biography and letters, particularly on books about Napoleon, whom she admitted "has always been rather a hero of mine, somewhat against my better judgement," and her comments on what she admired or disliked in the notable people she read about provide clues to her growing discrimination. By 1880 the *Life and Letters of Madame Bonaparte* provoked the statement, "I thoroughly sympathize with [Madame Bonaparte] in her dislike of . . . American women & society . . . but . . . I know there *is* society here where the women are *not* all domestic, & trading is *not* the common subject of talk. We are getting to have a brilliant society in this country where gifted women may shine & reign, even if their admirers are not titled & crowned." Certainly Mabel aspired to participating in such a society. For real-life heroines she chose strong-minded, independent, literary women like Louisa May Alcott, whom she called on several times in

Boston when she was nineteen, and Sophia Thoreau, her grandmother's friend. Beyond that, her passionate dedication to "cultivating" herself drew heart from themes of improvement in the national culture and from the steady encouragement and adoration of her parents.

Perhaps no only child escapes an overdose of parental direction. "I wish it were not a sin to read the *Arabian Nights* on Sunday," she grumbled in her journal as a child. Yet she came to take most of her mother's dispensations with a grain of salt, while her father's more remote and thoughtful counsel was accepted whole. "I am trying to be more like your ideal of a young girl, & want to grow more like it every day," she told him at sixteen. Absence inevitably idealized Eben in Mabel's eyes, as her adolescent journal frequently attests. "My father is my *Ideal* of everything noble and grand. If only I can reach as high as he is," she exclaimed among the many fervent expressions of love for Eben, the fears he might die, the anguish that he went unappreciated by the world. "Tell Father I think him now as ever the one perfect man on the earth," she wrote her mother at seventeen, and as late as twenty admitted, "I have a most romantic & intense love for him, for his patience & kindness *and* altogether loveliness of character." As she grew into womanhood, her uneven assignment of parental proportion is revealed in the diminutives with which she addressed her mother ("dear little mother" or "dear child") and the expansive adjectives reserved for her father ("splendid big father").

Mabel imbibed from her mother and grandmother, however, strong pride in forebears who linked the Wilder name to John Alden and the *Mayflower*. Somehow, in her mind she blended this maternal lineage with the Alcott and Thoreau family friendships her grandmother sustained in Concord into a tradition that established her family, particularly her father, securely among New England Puritan and Transcendental intellectuals. To the many relatives on her father's side, Mabel paid little attention, although she knew all about Eben's young sister Colette, who had published poetry in the *Springfield Republican* before her early death at age twenty. In general, the Wilders were far more influential than the Loomises in Mabel's perception of herself, and she came to view her father as representative of noble men in the Wilder tradition.

For three Washington winters, beginning the autumn she turned fifteen in 1871, Mabel attended the Georgetown Female Seminary, informally known as Miss Liscomb's School. Located at 1537 I Street, N.W., it offered young ladies an ambitious program of literature, geometry, chemistry, geology, astronomy, mental philosophy, French, composition, and Spencerian Movement. Mabel was stimulated by this academic feast, and did well, despite the truncated spring and fall terms that resulted from her mother's annual travel routine.

On her journey south at the start of her senior year, Mabel found herself talking "incessantly from New York to Washington" about philosophical subjects with a Boston Universalist minister, a Dr. Miner, who sat down beside her in the car. Pleased at engaging such a learned gentleman in conversation, she took the opportunity to discuss a matter that deeply troubled her. Recently she had joined the Presbyterian Church, and already regretted it, for no clear answers to her religious perplexities were forthcoming, and she was offended by church dogma, which emphasized the wickedness in human nature and espoused a punishing God. In addition, she had a clear sense that she had displeased her father. By the time she met Dr. Miner, Mabel felt she was "acting a lie" by participating in the ritual of communion. Dr. Miner introduced her to his "enlarged views on sin," and soon she came to know her father's enlightened ideas as well.* She took further

* Eben Loomis's thoughts, which he put into a letter of June 1875, would have been known to Mabel as early as the autumn of 1873. "Don't worry yourself as to what you believe, or disbelieve. . . . No human being has a right to impose *any* belief on you. To a great extent we are *alone* with our souls, and each soul must look through the loopholes and crannies of its prison house and find out for itself its

courage from the example of Sophia Thoreau, who attended church but always left the service before communion. The following summer Mabel did likewise, wildly distressing her mother and grandmother by publicly "denying her savior," but taking heart that she was pleasing her father. Coming to feel at home only among the more radical of the Unitarians, Mabel eventually organized her churchgoing around ministers she liked or choirs in which she sang, and all her life experienced inner rage and acute social embarrassment whenever she was "caught" at church on communion Sunday, particularly in Amherst, where abstinence from the sacramental bread and wine caused comment. It was one matter in which she did not enjoy being conspicuous.

To her enormous disappointment, Mabel didn't graduate from Miss Liscomb's School. True to her mother's predictions concerning the dangers of excessive study, she succumbed to a severe illness in late February 1874, and by mid-March resigned herself to being whisked North on the first of May without finishing. Deflated by "the ignominious manner in which I quitivated," and by having her hair shaved off because so much had fallen out during her sickness, Mabel took solace that summer in writing nature essays and enjoying the pleasant social life of a coastal boardinghouse at Harpswell, Maine, on Casco Bay. Here she fell in love with the sea. Convinced it loved her back, she displayed considerable bravado at sailing upon it, her fearlessness supported more by an immunity to seasickness than good sense, for she couldn't swim. Her spirited ways attracted several young men, among them a tall blond

---

surroundings, its nature and its wants. Except so far as your temporal, personal happiness is concerned, it makes no difference what you believe. If you think there is a hell you will be unhappy from fear; but your believing it does not alter the fact that hell is the invention of vindictive human nature, and that the infinite God, having no malignity, could not form such a conception when planning the universe."

Bowdoin College teacher of mathematics and gymnastics named Fred K. Smyth, who became her first serious love interest.

Mabel's chief desire now was to spend the winter of 1874–75 in Boston, studying at the New England Conservatory of Music. When her parents consented, she and Grandma Wilder took a room together in late October at Mrs. Rahn's boardinghouse on Pinckney Street. Arranging for parlor privileges with another boarder's piano, Mabel began instrumental and voice instruction in two classes that each met twice a week and together cost her parents thirty dollars for the term. An exciting year ensued. Not only did she progress rapidly in her musical studies, attending classes, practicing several hours a day, and going to concerts and other musical events at the conservatory, she reveled in her first independence of her mother and enjoyed the stirrings of her "power" to captivate others. "The house at evening resounds with laughter & mirth, when before Grandma & I came, it was as quiet as a condensed cemetery," she reported home. And again, "I am having *lovely* times. Everybody in the house refers to me as the *centre*."

By mid-winter Mabel was anxious for permission to stay in Boston a second year, and to add harmony to her studies, though it would cost fifteen dollars more a term. Hesitation on the part of her parents brought an impassioned outburst from Mabel in the spring. "All my winter's work in music will be of no avail whatever, unless I can follow it up faithfully & scientifically for I have not a single 'show off piece,' " Mabel pleaded. "My life is nothing but beginnings. I want a specialty. . . . I shall be positively wretched if I have to stop studying music at the end of this term, for then I shall have added only one more beginning to a pointless life. . . . There is no earthly reason (or heavenly either) why I should give my music up [even] if I *should* get married, ever, & I won't if he is as poor as Job's comforter. No man can make a drudge of me. And I don't care if you haven't the money. I can teach, certainly, or sing— I will find a way."

INTRODUCTION

It wasn't just the expense of the conservatory studies or the pain of continued separation from their daughter that worried the Loomises, though these were involved. They were more concerned about Mabel's entanglement with a gentleman in her boardinghouse named Ezra Lincoln Abbott, who had fallen in love with her. Mabel didn't love "Mr. A."; in fact she was cognizant of his several deficiencies, but the romance of his devoted attentions, and his services as an escort, made him attractive to her. Neither she nor Grandma Wilder had enough sense or experience, however, to extricate Mabel from what moved rapidly toward a "conditional engagement" aided and abetted by other boarders. Mabel's assurances to her parents that she had Mr. Abbott's infatuation under control took on increasingly desperate tones as spring progressed, until in mid-May Mrs. Loomis hastened North, and after a glance at the situation summoned her husband to come take a hand. Eben's letter to Mabel following the crisis describes what happened.

May 20, 1875
Nautical Almanac Office

My dear Mabel,

During my long, lonely journey from Boston to Washington I thought over carefully every phase of the affair which called me so suddenly to you. I am rejoiced beyond measure that Mama had the forethought and good sense to send for me, for I was needed. Mr. A., while undoubtedly possessing many good qualities, is yet deficient in the one great requisite *character*. He is weak. Five years from now, with all of the efforts that he would or could make, you would be *ashamed* of him, and shame is *not* the parent of love. . . .

And now my darling, you know without my saying it that I am happy only in your happiness; if you suffer, Mama and I suffer equally with you. It is only for your good that I act as I do. I have made it not only possible but easy for you to sever entirely your intimacy with Mr. A. and you *must do it*, for I can see as clearly as with a prophet's eye the unhappiness that would follow such a marriage.

If necessary you can leave Mrs. Rahn's and go somewhere else. Mama will be the best judge of this necessity. And here I wish to make another point. Mama sometimes expresses her thoughts in a singular manner, but I have *rarely known her judgement to be wrong. . . .*

I know that you will not look on me as a "stern parent" thwarting a daughter's inclinations, as the "yellow covered" hath it, but rather as a tender father, ready to sacrifice everything for the happiness and good of his one ewe lamb, his only daughter, his brown-eyed Mabel.

I am still weary with my journey and excitement and must close now.

Goodbye my darling
from your affectionate Father
E. J. Loomis

P.S. Show this letter to Mama and ask her if she does not think I am right.

Love to Grandma & Mama
& yourself

The Loomises' intervention checked but didn't terminate the affair, for "El," as Mabel came to call Ezra Abbott in her journal, had two holds upon her interest. He appeared to be wealthy, and he had introduced her to some simple but pleasurable physical intimacies. In addition, no other suitors stepped forward. Returning to Harpswell, Maine, for the summer of 1875, Mabel found the pleasant circumstances of the preceding summer greatly altered. The handsome Fred K. Smyth now sent his signals of unspoken ardor through puzzling barriers of coolness erected by his relatives, while Mrs. Loomis was cast by fellow boarders in the role of a designing mother parading her marriageable daughter. (Molly's chagrin relieved itself in melancholy letters to Eben, one of which featured five dozen handwritten lines to a small page.) Mabel apparently was eligible for marriage. Almost nineteen, her winning prettiness and spirited intelligence made her the natural center of any gathering, and that was exactly where she most enjoyed being. By the end of her first year in Boston she was used to being made much of, and felt no self-consciousness or undue modesty. Her social inclinations developed with sureness into a steady urge to pull others toward her, so that she found herself happiest at those moments when she held individuals, whether one or several, in the spell of her animated conversation and lively charm.

In the light of her growing magnetism it is remarkable that Mabel had few real suitors. During the next couple of years she attracted and was attracted to many young men, including one other who courted, then just as inexplicably dropped her. With the exception of Mr. Abbott, however, none was seriously attentive until David Todd appeared on the scene late in 1877, and though in letters to her father during the summer of 1875 Mabel made light of her bewilderment over Fred Smyth's behavior, several journal notations indicate she had considered "Mr. S." a true contender for her hand, that she might have married him if he had persisted in wooing her. It seems likely that as far as Mabel's delightful personality and cultivated gifts took her, she was handicapped by her father's financial condition. Although pretty, accomplished, and tastefully dressed, she couldn't disguise the lack of dowry and substantial connections that would keep her from being considered an advantageous match at the social levels the Loomises aspired to.

The fact that many more men fell in love with Mabel after she was married than before suggests, too, that her personal goals may have been off-putting to young men. She was determined to devote herself to cultural pursuits and not submit to "humdrum, commonplace housewifery" in the course of marrying. Increasingly scornful of anything "commonplace," she wanted her life to be unusual, an exception to other women's lives, and even while struggling to emerge from her girlhood relationship with her parents, she guarded against compromising the freedom for self-expression her parents assured her. She looked for someone who would be as devoted as they were to her continuing development. In addition, of course, she required someone sufficiently self-effacing to tolerate the power and true end of her magnetism.

If Mabel had not gone on quietly meeting her friend Mr. Abbott for walks and talks, her second winter in Boston would have been very dull, for the initial bloom was off her experiment in independence. She felt cramped by financial restrictions that limited her enrollment at the conservatory to a single instrumental class, and she felt overprotected now by her grandmother. Her social life, dependent on invitations from other boarders or various Wilder cousins in the Boston area, barely satisfied her burgeoning convivial tastes and ambitions, and although she sang with a singing club, attended concerts and lectures, and worked industriously at painting, her aspirations for male companionship were met only by the ever-hopeful Mr. Abbott.

Early in 1876 Mabel wrote her parents that she wanted to come home the following winter. She ascribed her decision variously to need for her parents' society, ennui with being independent, and lack of money to enroll in the theory and harmony classes required for graduation from the conservatory, but her leave-taking from Boston probably was more truly related to ambitions for better social opportunities and to guilt at dallying with Mr. Abbott. When her father wrote in May, either intuitively or at a word from Grandma Wilder: "I trust your relations to Mr. Abbott are such only as a pure delicate girl might own to all the world without a blush. But I need not ask you this, for you promised me not to be intimate with him, and I have yet to learn of a broken word of yours," Mabel's immediate response betrayed her culpability. "My dear

Father," she gushed, omitting direct reference to Ezra Abbott, "You are to me what Agnes was to David Copperfield—my good angel, always keeping me away from even ordinarily commonplace standards & pointing to a summit of real, intense loftiness which is too high for me to see, away from you. . . . I believe I was born with a certain lack of something in my moral nature which can only come to me through you." Convinced she needed her father's high-minded guidance to protect her from mediocrity, Mabel now wanted only to come home. "What is a New England Conservatory diploma, or even all that it would imply, as compared with you & being with you." Her father agreed that "a winter spent in Washington will be good for you, body & mind, & I know it will be good for me."

Mabel and Washington were ready for each other. In her absence, steady improvement had affected the physical appearance and municipal services of the city. Avenues had been paved, sewers laid, sculpture and monuments erected, and buildings built or completed after wartime interruption. Social life was flourishing, with lines of distinction being drawn not only on the basis of wealth and position, but on professional and intellectual attainments and demonstrated talent as well. A young woman like Mabel could go far simply by being socially adept and culturally accomplished. The scientific community which had begun to assemble when the Smithsonian Institution was founded in 1846, and which included the scientific bureaus of the government, was responsible for the city's emerging reputation as a stimulating center for American scientific research. Eben Loomis's place on the fringe of this community gave Mabel access to lectures and social gatherings at which she met and heard the ideas of interesting people. Museums and galleries, theater and the opera, were thriving, and the liveliness of politics was in the air. In this setting Mabel quickly capitalized on her personal bloom in the two and a half years since she had last seen school and family friends.

"I am invited out a great deal and my music is considered very fine," she reported within a few weeks, as calling and being called upon began to occupy her days, and concerts, the theater, opera, and numerous whist parties, at which invariably she was asked to sing and play the piano, took her evenings. A circle of new admirers drawn by her charm and gifts buoyed Mabel's confidence in her inexplicable but tangible inner "power." As she devoted her energies to writing, painting, singing, practicing, and cultivating friends, she was aware of some genius, some greatness that she verged upon but couldn't quite identify. For lack of other explanation she linked the sensed expectation, or "presentiment," as she came to call it, to a longing beneath all surface scintillation for the appearance of the man she would marry.

As fate would have it, David Todd was first attracted to Mabel Loomis, not as the vibrant center of any gay social affair, nor by a display of her virtuosity, but because he came by the Nautical Almanac Office to borrow a telescope one wet June day in 1877 and was moved by the sight of her standing with her father in the rain wearing an old blue waterproof. David always fondly cherished his first vision of Mabel, though she retained no memory of the moment. Her journal does record, however, David's first formal call the following autumn, after she had returned from the North, on the evening of November 30. "Tonight Mr. Todd, a great friend of the Newcombs, called. He is in the Observatory, and quite charming. Evidently thoroughly at home among *young* ladies, as indeed is every man I know. They are all more or less flirts. . . . This young man is very good looking, a blond with magnificent teeth, pleasant manners, and immense, though innocent enough, powers of flirting. Well, so also have I."

David Peck Todd had lived in Washington just over two years when he began courting Mabel. He was boarding at the home of astronomer Simon Newcomb, directly across the street from lodgings the Loomises took that fall at 1325 11th Street, N.W. David was fair-haired, clean-shaven (the next summer he grew the beard and mustache he wore for four decades), and quite small, standing 5 feet 6½ inches, or three inches taller than Mabel, and weighing 135 pounds. He was a year and a half older than she, having been born March 19, 1855, on his family's farm at Lake Ridge, New York, about fifteen miles north of Ithaca on the eastern slope of Cayuga Lake. Five hundred acres of heavily wooded western New York State countryside had been homesteaded there in 1804 by David's grandfather, Josiah Todd, who came from Hamden, Connecticut, cleared farmland, and sired seven children. David's paternal grandmother, Lucretia Ingersoll Todd, was a direct descendant in the fourth generation of renowned Puritan minister Jonathan Edwards. Their youngest child was David's father, Sereno Edwards Todd, who was born on the homestead in 1820 and at the time of David's birth was building a home on his own twenty acres of the family land for his wife, his son Sereno Edwards Jr., and his daughter Naomi.

The family of David's mother, Rhoda Peck Todd, had been farmers at Greenwich, Connecticut, where Rhoda Peck was born in 1818. She moved to Lake Ridge with her parents as a girl and in 1844 married Sereno Todd, two years her junior. She named David for her youngest brother, David Peck, a graduate of Yale University, class of 1849, and subsequently a Congregational minister in a series of Massachusetts country towns.

David's father was a progressive, inventive farmer and apple grower who enjoyed developing and testing new agricultural ideas, and who had a literary bent. When David was five, his father sold the farm and moved his family to Auburn, where he worked for the duration of the Civil War for a manufacturer of agricultural machinery, farmed on a small scale, and began contributing articles to the agricultural departments of several New York newspapers. He also wrote the first of several books he published during the 1860s and '70s on agriculture and farm architecture.

In 1865 the Todds moved to Brooklyn. They joined Brooklyn's Plymouth Church, where David was baptized at age ten by its eminent minister, Henry Ward Beecher, and where seventeen-year-old Naomi, who had a lovely voice, joined the choir. The most fascinating thing about Plymouth Church in David's eyes was not Rev. Beecher but the church's huge new hand-pumped Hook and Hastings organ. He made friends with the man who pumped the bellows, and one memorable day when he was thirteen was allowed by the pumper to look inside the great instrument. Awestruck, David "fell in love with organs." He was unsure afterward whether the internal mechanism or its sound intrigued him more, but decided then and there to devote his life to organs and organ music. Fortunately, the Todds were able to acquire a second-hand Mason and Hamlin home organ, which his mother agreeably pumped for him while he pushed the pedals and learned to manipulate the stops and keys.

David remembered himself as "as shy & green & untutored a kid as ever drew breath," a boy who was happiest alone in his cellar workshop or pedaling the organ. He was embarrassed by girls, and at a tender age learned accidentally from his older brother "the very wrong things for a young boy to know" about sex.* His proudest childhood achievement was the building of a model steam engine at age fourteen. He astonished his doubting father by constructing in secret and with rough im-

---

* In an informal autobiographical essay of 1932 entitled "Re D.P.T." David revealed that as an adolescent he "knew nothing about sex and its delights, so didn't care—accidentally found out (from my brother, 5 years older) . . . I soon found that most of the other young boys I knew did likewise, so I thought it must be right. Neither father nor mother ever mentioned such matters."

plements a frictionless piston valve that permitted the flywheel of the engine to turn easily. His scholastic ability at public school earned him a four-year scholarship, one of two granted annually by the Mayor of Brooklyn, and in the fall of 1870, at age fifteen, he entered Columbia University to pursue strong interests in mathematics and astronomy. Because Columbia had no observatory, David built himself a telescope at home and began to study the moons of the planet Jupiter. His Uncle David Peck, now the minister at Sunderland, Massachusetts, and an avid amateur botanist, suggested David study astronomy at nearby Amherst College, which had an observatory. It took him a year to choose between astronomy and his passion for the organ, but in 1873 he was persuaded by his father to enter the junior class at Amherst. The college permitted him, at eighteen, to use freely the several instruments in its tiny, unheated octagonal observatory, and through the small equatorial telescope he began a series of observations on Jupiter's satellites that he would maintain for the twelve years it took the planet to orbit the sun. He also managed by many all-night vigils to witness every eclipse of the planet's moons during the next two years.

His erratic class record at Amherst indicates that, with the exception of Greek (philology intrigued him), David Todd was an indifferent student in subjects other than astronomy and mathematics. Even other sciences held little lure for him. He always claimed he had "no brains adequate to whist and botany." Nor geology either, apparently, for he confused which way the Connecticut River ran when he first arrived at Amherst, and professed never to have gotten it straight. Yet anything mechanical attracted his interest immediately, and his lifelong passion for record keeping was evidenced nowhere more clearly than in his meticulously maintained diaries, in which during college he kept careful track of the phases of the moon, hours spent in the observatory, the number of hours and minutes he slept each night, and his expenses.* By the time he graduated from Amherst in the early summer of 1875, David's introversion and proclivity for intense, independent work were set in his character. Early homesickness and the nights spent at the observatory, with compensating need for daytime sleep, made him very much a loner by his classmates' standards. He was dubbed "Professor Todd" in the pages of his yearbook and was one of only five in his forty-nine-member class who belonged to neither a fraternity nor a debating society, the chief social and intellectual outlets for the students.

His single-minded devotion to the planet Jupiter, however, drew the attention of astronomer Simon Newcomb, who may have learned of David's work through family ties that linked Newcomb's wife to the Newark, New Jersey, family that David's sister had married into. Professor Newcomb, one of six astronomers on the staff of the U.S. Naval Observatory in Washington, was an increasingly respected authority in his emerging field. He was at work revising the values of the fundamental astronomical constants from available observed data of the moon, planets, and fixed stars in order to construct more accurate planetary theories and tables. Young Todd's studies of Jupiter's eclipses were useful, and Newcomb was enough impressed with David's perseverence that he offered him an appointment as assistant on the observatory's U.S. Transit of Venus Commission, which was reducing observa-

---

* A note in David's 1874 diary suggests the care he devoted to records: "The large numbers in ink before the dates on each page indicate the no. of hours & minutes of sleep during the past night. The small nos. above & at the right—the no. hrs sleep I have to make up, allowing 8 to every 24. Blue pencil figures on the right are no. times I have been in obsy up to that time." He noted the phases of the moon by symbols, and after moving to Amherst in 1881 recorded sunspots as well. In addition, he kept track of masturbating; his diaries indicate this was a practice of the years before his marriage and of the last two decades of his life after he was institutionalized.

tions from the 1874 Transit in preparation for another that would occur in 1882. David took Professor Newcomb's letter to the east slope of the college campus and lay in deep, unmown grass looking at the spring light on the Pelham hills while he planned his future. After several hours spent thinking of the directions his life might go in, he decided to accept Newcomb's offer at eighty dollars a month.

Eventually David deeply regretted devoting his life to astronomy. At least part of the reason was the realization, too late, that his real talent lay in mechanical engineering. Through many years of teaching and eclipse-chasing on voyages that took him all over the world, David's significant contributions to his profession involved his ingenuity with mechanical techniques and devices, as in his pioneering adaptation of automatic photography processes to the recording of solar eclipses. With his ingenuity and energy he might have gone far as a mechanical engineer in an age awakening to machine technology, but when such an opportunity was his early in his career, he turned it down. In Newark in 1876, David met his contemporary Thomas Alva Edison, then a day operator for Western Union, who spent his nights playing with wires and batteries in the cellar of his Market Street office. With several electrical inventions already to his credit, Edison was looking for young colleagues of mechanical ability to join in his experiments, but couldn't lure David Todd away from astronomy. At that point David was more excited about the new 26-inch refractor at the Washington Observatory, then the largest lens in the world, than about electricity and the prospect of life in Newark.

Apparently the Todds' family life was disintegrating during the years David was a student at Amherst and beginning his career in Washington. Divorce was scandalously unmentionable at the time, and insanity nearly as much so, so it is not surprising that only the briefest suggestion of his mother's mental imbalance and his parents' separation surfaces among the voluminous Todd papers. Mrs. Todd's increasingly erratic behavior created difficulties, and later embarrassment, to her relatives for many years until she was institutionalized in 1901. But the burden of his mother's troubles fell more on David's siblings than on him during this period when his career and his courtship of Mabel Loomis were progressing. Although he confesses to being "shy and green" at times in his feelings for Mabel, the two nevertheless saw much of each other through the winter and spring of 1878, attending concerts and church together and going on long walks. By the time Mabel left for New England at the end of May, the relationship had reached a tentative, very private "understanding" that would be tested by five months' separation and the opportunity to study each other's character through correspondence.

Nearly a hundred letters were exchanged by Mabel and David between early June and late October 1978. Rereading them years later, Mabel destroyed their most intimate passages, so that parts of some letters and all of twenty-three are missing, but the remainder convey a clear impression of two very different, almost compensatory personalities moving toward union. Things Mabel intentionally revealed of herself in these letters, traits she put prettily forward to test and win David, were her passion for nature, her love of art, music and literature, her commitment to self-culture, and her social skills. ("David, if any one thing is my *'forte'* above everything else, it is the bringing together of many people, in a graceful, informal manner, and of making each one enjoy himself to the fullest extent. I can do that, I know, & make everybody want to come again— intensely.") She also spoke offhandedly but pointedly of a requirement David came to indulge as fondly as her parents did. "Mother knows that you write to me," Mabel told him, but "she almost never speaks of it at all, & when she does it is in a manner which shows that she thinks I am now capable of doing what I think right—*by myself*. It is this very freedom which is absolutely necessary to me, nor does she in the least ever wish or try to bind me in any way. She has always been like a sister to me, & is as interested (& more) in whatever concerns me than in her own life, but the dear little woman leaves me *free* to do as I like always." David, too, would permit his charming, gifted wife to pursue her many interests with all the liberty of an adored child.

Besides what she chose to reveal of her character, Mabel's three dozen extant courtship letters expose her extroverted and extremely self-centered personality. She was unusually full of herself, conveying not only complete accounts of her doings and feelings but supplying her own appreciation as well. She was, and portrayed herself as, persistently happy, a state of being she referred to as "my usual intensely cheerful outlook on life" and David dubbed her "perpetual blue sky." She had begun to believe firmly in her "right to be happy," and received confirmation, seemingly, in the four-leaf clovers she found so easily everywhere she went, and tucked in profusion into her letters and journal.

David, by contrast, disclosed murkier character traits, dwelling in his letters on his dark nature and hinting at bleak happenings in his past. Early in the correspondence he described the surreptitious theft and replacement of a key, stating, "What astounds me completely is that I am confiding [this side of myself] wholly to you w. such unwarrantable abandon and glibness—things that I wouldn't have known of me for all that I am! And yet—well, I know you don't altogether like that mixture in my character, but I've told you of it, & shall tell you as time passes slowly yet rapidly along, of many other things which will, I almost doubt not, awaken you to a more complete knowledge of what I actually am." He continued to test Mabel's capacity for accepting his hidden side, even after she assured him at one point, "I want to say one little word about that 'dreadful thing' of which you spoke in your letter. It did not take me long to make up my mind that *whatever* it may be, it cannot alter my trust in, & affection for *you*. . . . I shall certainly 'show not a sign of willingness to part' from you for *any* cause that I can imagine in that connection. Now for pleasanter subjects."

Far pleasanter for Mabel must have been the way David's career was advancing, though he wrote little about it. He had continued his work on Jupiter, in his spare time extending from 1880 to 1900 Damoiseau's Tables of the Satellites of Jupiter, from which the *Ephemeris* was prepared. In August of 1877 he identified, in the presence of Professor Newcomb and other senior astronomers at the observatory, a new satellite of Mars,* and the following spring, while not charged with the responsibility, he accurately recorded a Transit of Mercury when other observatory astronomers, with whom he competed for Simon Newcomb's attention, made errors in their calculations. David's singular achievements made him less than popular among his observatory peers, but Newcomb was sufficiently pleased that he found funds for his young protégé to make a one-man eclipse expedition to Dallas, Texas, during July and August of 1878 (the summer of the courtship letters) to observe the last solar eclipse that would be visible on the North American continent during the century. Several large expeditions went out from the Naval Observatory to stations in Colorado, where the weather was clear and where dry-plate photographs of the phenomenon were obtained. In Texas David

---

* In a conversation of the early 1930s David Todd described to his daughter how on the night of August 18, 1877, he and other astronomers at the Washington Observatory on the Potomac River viewed a new moon of Mars just found by Professor Asaph Hall. David, the last to have a turn at the telescope, moved the eyepiece of the 26-inch refractor into such a position that a micrometer screw blocked the blazing surface of the planet and allowed another, hitherto unsuspected, inner moon to become visible. This was Phobos. It later evolved when its orbit was studied that Phobos had already been measured by Hall, although he had mistaken it for a tiny star, so discovery of both moons was credited to him.

experienced cloudy conditions, yet managed to make several contacts of the eclipse from a Dallas cupola and to secure a number of observations during totality.

Just before leaving for Texas, David took and failed the mathematics examination for appointment to the U.S. Naval Observatory. On his return Newcomb appointed him instead to be his own assistant at the Nautical Almanac Office, where he was now superintendent. Part of David's duties was supervision of proofreading the *Nautical Almanac*, a vital, meticulous task. Although there is no specific evidence of disgruntlement other than the grumblings of the young observatory astronomers, Newcomb's promotion of David Todd could easily have been viewed as favoritism, for Todd was living in his home and the new appointment elevated him over several senior employees at the Almanac Office, including Eben Loomis. Yet David was well suited to his new position. He possessed energetic curiosity, painstaking determination, and fierce ambition, the latter masked by a disarmingly modest manner, but he also had a loner, secretive side that fed a seeming desire to re-create the grown-up equivalent of that triumphal moment when he had astounded his father with the secretly wrought model steam engine. There is little doubt David used his personal relationship with Simon Newcomb and his family to good advantage for a long time, until he earned Newcomb's disfavor in the mid-1880s by failing to reduce his observations from the 1882 Transit of Venus expedition; but by then he had a more useful patron in Austin Dickinson. David was probably strongly drawn to Mabel Loomis's overt aspirations for high achievement, and must have sensed that her talent for promoting her accomplishments would promote his own as well. Together over the years they created a close, enormously productive colleagueship, the reliable underpinning to their otherwise quirky marriage.*

---

* David and Mabel worked together, supported, prodded, promoted, and advised each other through countless scientific, artistic, and social

Mabel and David Todd

By the time they met again at Naomi Todd Compton's home in Newark at the end of October 1878, David and Mabel were openly declaring their love. David had had a talk with Eben, gently sounding what Mabel termed the "parental short-pocketedness," but could not determine what Mabel wanted most to hear—how her father viewed her impending liaison with David Todd. Eben had avoided mention of David in his letters to her all summer, perhaps because he had been ill, but Mabel was apprehensive about his silence. By the time she saw her father again in November, she had become engaged without consulting either parent, and the fact that there was considerable parental opposition to David didn't surface until six years later when, in a moment of anger at her mother, Mabel wrote furiously in her journal: "For years my mother appeared to be striving to make me utterly disenchanted with David—before my marriage there might have been reasonably some sense in it, as it would have been possible to prevent what seemed to her a very unequal union. But by innuendo, insinuation, open talk—everything, she continued to give vent to her prejudice against him for years after my marriage. . . . What would not my thirsty soul have given five, six years ago, for any word of kindness toward him from her. I was hungering for an understanding between them all, but I bore up without it."

This outburst, which occurred in 1885 after the Loomises learned of their daughter's relationship with Austin Dickinson, provides a glimpse of the state of affairs when the Loomises were reunited in Washington in the late autumn of 1878 and

---

endeavors. "Any other thing that you can think of to do, to outwind other women as I am outstripping other men, I shall favor," David encouraged his wife in August 1889. A decade later, when she was traveling and lecturing nearly full-time on subjects of their common experience, Mabel wrote appreciatively of David in her journal: "He is so versatile—his brain is so amazingly fertile, his work is so engrossing and his industry so unflagging that I admire him very much always, and love him dearly. . . . I think it is very rare that two persons, especially married persons, work together so well and helpfully."

Molly Loomis, as often happened, once she knew her husband's mind, began extravagantly regretting her permissiveness regarding Mabel. It isn't clear what the Loomises' objections to David Todd were. They may have had higher aspirations for their gifted daughter, or perhaps the marital and mental problems of David's parents offended them. Politics at the Nautical Almanac Office, where David now occupied a better-paid, higher-ranking position than Eben, undoubtedly played a part. Whatever the reason for the Loomises' prejudice, Mabel's determination to marry David must have been very strong, for she was coping simultaneously with a major disenchantment, one he had hinted at throughout his courtship letters and now revealed.

Mabel never identified the "dreadful thing" David told her, but may have come close to guessing a few weeks earlier when she sent him a biography of Madame Pompadour and wrote, "I am glad indeed that we do not live in such times of indiscriminate morals. Think of that place where Louis XV went to select young girls for his favorites! To me such a thing —the mere gratification of passion without the real, pure love to exalt it to holiness even—is very dreadful to contemplate. Don't you? It is only animal." David's disclosure produced in Mabel an "intense and agonizing sorrow" that for the first time in her life threatened to eclipse her incessant happiness. His diary for 1877 is curiously clipped throughout, as if to eliminate some short, regularly recurring bit of information, perhaps the record of an indiscretion or other sensitive matter. But Mabel's description of this trial as "a combination—a network of circumstances the like of which I believe no girl before me was ever called upon to bear" gives an impression that something more than a confession of "animal" was involved.

There are hints that David's relationship with the Newcomb family figured in the matter, particularly Mrs. Newcomb, whose confidant David had become, but whom Mabel disliked for being "common" and a meddler in her business. Whatever it was, Mabel's sense of trust in her fiancé was deeply under-mined. In February 1879, less than a month before her wedding, she wrote in her journal: "There are two wishes of my heart . . . the first is that David shall always love me devotedly, & be ever true to me, & the second is that I may always *trust* him implicitly. . . . May I never have reason to think I am wrong when I feel that I *can* trust him through all the long years before us." At last she rallied: "To have my darling possess clear moral sight and always follow its light is my one prayer & my answer has come—he does see clearly—he does. . . . My coming to this earth was to uplift & purify his already sweet nature."

For all her sentiments and lofty turmoil over David's morality, Mabel was no Victorian prude. David's virility and pleasure in physical intimacy were powerfully attractive to her. Marginal symbols in the daily diary she began keeping in January 1879 establish that she gave her virginity to him before the wedding ceremony. Nor does the sureness with which she later engaged in her relationship with Austin Dickinson suggest much conflict with the prevailing moral code. At the time of the wedding she may have agonized over David's chastity, but later events would demonstrate this matter was less vital to her than a deeper concern—the suspicion that it was his breeding that could not be trusted, that he might in fact have "low tastes." This fear so threatened Mabel's pride that even late in her marriage, when evidence of David's lack of discrimination was rife, Mabel continued to deny it could be true, so strong was her need to believe in her cultural superiority—for her a matter of far greater importance than fidelity.*

* For years Mabel refrained from any mention of David's philandering until in February 1890 she wrote in her journal: "Now, David & I are the pleasantest, the most cordial comrades, and we have very dear & lovely times together, but I do not think David is what might be called a monogamous animal. While I know that he loves me to the full of his

Mabel's troubles ran beneath the surface of what continued to appear an exceptionally charmed existence. In the winter season preceding her marriage, she was taken up by a Washington patroness, Mary Clemmer Ames, a wealthy widow of minor literary achievement who invited Mabel to receive with her on New Year's Day of 1879 at her Pennsylvania Avenue home and there introduced her to "scores of celebrated gentlemen." Friends filled the parlor every evening Mabel was home, and to her added pleasure, a Mr. H. R. Eliot, Washington correspondent for the *New York Evening Post*, fell in love with her and hung about with all the desperation Mr. Abbott had once exhibited. If she had any doubts that she was making an auspicious marriage, she didn't disclose them in her journal. Three days before her wedding, assessing her accomplishments with great satisfaction, she wrote: "My young-girl life has been brilliant in the extreme, & after two winters' gaiety, & 'being out,' [it] is about the right time to be married. And I have seen much of the world . . . & everybody knows about me, & I'm a favorite, & my marriage is of personal interest to many hundred

---

nature, he is not at all incapable of falling immensely in love with someone else, & having a very piquant time out of it. I do not object to that in him, but at first I used to suffer." Clues to the profligate side of David's character occur in his letters as from time to time he called upon Mabel to help arrange visits of "friends" to their home, but these involvements, at least in the years the Todds lived in Amherst, were carried on behind the mask of respectability, and his only open remarks come in a reminiscence of 1930: "But my favorite of all was Mrs. Boush. I had made up my mind at 60 (March 19, 1915) as I told you in Observatory House that morning, that I wasn't going to make love to women any more. And I kept my resolve till the day Mrs. Boush walked into the Sunshine Inn (January 1917)."

While tolerant of her husband's romances, Mabel had her limits. "I really believe he thinks I am as much interested in [a new love] as he is," she wrote in 1911, "& he always expects me to like the person especially, because he does. He is like a sweetly unmoral child. It is not in the least wrong to him, but *sometimes* I cannot quite enter in." When David's tastes took in "low-class" women, however, Mabel grew incensed. In 1911 he became involved with a "type-writer," or secretary,

dear friends. . . . I never did know what it is about me which causes people to love me so much—but there it is."

Excitement mounted on the morning of March 5, 1879, as she prepared for the simple ceremony that brought together a few friends and relatives in the 14th Street parlor (David's brother and sister were present, but not his parents). Although the service would be spoken at evening by David's uncle, the Reverend Edwards Payson Ingersoll of Brooklyn, Mabel already wore her wedding ring, for David had slipped it on her finger the night before. Nearly overwhelmed by her familiar sense of "presentiment," she penned her last lines in her girlhood journal: "I have a strong intuition that my life has really only begun as regards wonderful experiences. I *know* it will be full of romance and uncommon adventure. . . . I give my whole life to [David], but there are capacities in me, I know, which I've not yet begun to feel, & they shall be developed & filled, & he shall help me, & I shall yet *do* something which will be heard of—that I know."

---

and for the first time Mabel boiled over. She felt "furiously angry" that David "gave himself away to a fearfully common person, far below him." It was the "one thing I had always pleaded with him to spare me." Her violent reaction, which coincided with an inability to accept David's concurrent plans to join the Masons, exposed Mabel's pride at the roots, laying bare the snobbery inherent in so many of her life's actions. That David's "low tastes" contaminated her makes understandable her need for an idealized, uplifting intimacy like that with socially superior Austin Dickinson.

Torn by love for the "dear comrade," who was "absolutely blind to matters of morality," Mabel subsequently wrote, then destroyed, five pages of testimony about her marriage. Even the surviving sentences are heavily inked out (and here bracketed): "For *thirty-three* years I have absolutely refrained from putting on paper one single sentence which, under any circumstances, could ever do my [dear __?__ David any harm. I have even allowed misrepresentation] and reproach to attach to myself, to be thought [the gay] and [flirtatious one of the two;] and never a word, written or spoken, has come from me to show that I had the faintest justification for anything I have been supposed to do. If I could write out the facts it would be appalling!"

INTRODUCTION

Few of the many presentiments Mabel had in the course of her life were realized in the forms she envisioned. Most, such as the conviction that she would become Austin Dickinson's wife, or would own her own carriage, or would see Emily Dickinson, eventually occurred in sadly inverted ways.* Strong awarenesses she mistook for intuition were probably, in fact, her own very powerful wishes and desires, so intense that they took tangible form as goals she felt she inevitably would fulfill. The strongest cravings of her being she sensed not as personal ambitions but as fates that awaited her, for which she was destined by her genius. Now that she was married, how to best use her genius became her chief concern. Her diary of the summer following her wedding contains this entry: "Finished poppies. A very brilliant panel—I *think* everyone will exclaim over it. I *do* feel so much power & genius in myself, struggling for utterance in *any* way, of which these little pictures are hardly the loophole for it to peep out." It was application of her special powers that mattered now, for, as she explained to David, "It is not that I have a genius for painting, or for piano, or for writing—but it is a great, independent genius I *know*, which would give its sacred touch to a lifetime devoted exclusively to *anything*."

Mabel sensed herself a person set apart, elevated over more ordinary mortals, especially other women. While her loftiness was not far different from her father's, it was far less humble,

---

* Mabel, of course, was never Austin's wife. They considered themselves married in the sight of God, and she wore his wedding ring, but their dearest dream ended with Austin's death in 1895. The denouement of Mabel's presentiments was sometimes ludicrous. Her passion for owning her own carriage, mentioned many times over the years, was never realized. During the early Amherst years she resented Sue's public use of the Dickinson carriages in which she, Austin's true love, could only ride on back roads and hidden byways. Ironically, after her stroke in 1913, David often pulled her about the streets of town in a jinrikisha brought home from an eclipse expedition. As for seeing Emily Dickinson, although Mabel was one of ED's circle of communicants, she finally saw the poet dead in her casket in May 1886.

and there was no reverence or awe, no philosophy in what she was about. In fact, as she admitted in her journal, while she felt "deeply grateful to God . . . for I do think God must know us all personally, & do for us," she had to confess to feeling no real need of Him. Things were going swimmingly with herself in charge.

The newlyweds lived in or near the same boardinghouses as the Loomises, enjoying separate quarters but usually partaking of the same board, so that marriage enlarged rather than broke the family circle, and it signaled no shift to more practical duties or more adult responsibilities for Mabel. In fact she felt freer, if anything, to indulge herself. "[David] thinks whatever I do is just as right as my father & mother do—and that is saying a good deal," she noted in her journal. Mabel's inherent sense of herself as the center of a singularly fortunate universe was expressed nowhere more innocently than in an exchange with her mother the first summer of her marriage on the subject of absence from one's husband. Rather than feeling resigned to separations, as her mother did, Mabel opined, "The six weeks [David] has been away seem months already." This prosaic sentiment from a new bride evokes surprise only when one realizes it was not David who was away, but Mabel. She was spending Washington's hottest months visiting David's relatives in the Finger Lake region of central New York State, while he remained at the Almanac Office. From Mabel's perspective, however, David was away from her, not she from him, a significant clue to her perception of the world.

David's bride must have been an astonishing anomaly to the Todd and Peck aunts, uncles, and cousins among whom she circulated for three months that first summer of her marriage. Stoic, hardworking, good-hearted people, they toiled ceaselessly in the fields and kitchens of their prosperous farms while Mabel, untutored in simple chores, wandered in their orchards eating fruit or sat on their hillsides composing long letters to her husband. She spent the morning painting blooms from the garden and the afternoon in her "flowing white wrapper, re-clined picturesquely in [the] hammock, with pink shawl for color . . . reading *The Great German Composers*." Mabel rejoiced at being different from farmers' wives: "They work shockingly hard, whether they have 'help' or not, and notwith-standing their goodness and intelligence, it would take years of contact with culture to make genuine drawing-room disciples of them—or to get the hardness and roughness off their hands." Like astronomers' wives, whom she often criticized in the years ahead, such victims of unfortunate breeding were less to be pitied than avoided.

During this long, leisurely summer, a new facet of Mabel's genius emerged. As she sat on country porches through placid summer evenings, she amused herself and those around her with "a brilliant flow of conversation—or rather monologue—to the apparent edification of the house-hold, on all sorts of sub-jects. On several evenings I felt quite inspired in this sort of employment, and saw by the interested faces about that I was entertaining." Her ability to discourse in a fascinating manner on a great variety of topics was Mabel's most natural talent, not fully appreciated yet because it was so effortless and because she had no proper outlet. In another age her instincts and temperament might have led to a career in the theater, and though Mabel thoroughly enjoyed playing heroine in occasional Amherst theatricals, being an actress was too low a calling for serious consideration. Not until a dozen years later, when she began public lecturing, would she discover that her ability to hold an audience spellbound provided her greater pleasure and satisfaction than all her musical, artistic, and literary efforts combined.

The diaries Mabel began keeping in 1879, and would keep regularly over thirty years, are a faithful, highly reliable guide to the details of her life. Probably David influenced her to record in symbol form along the margin of these daily records the pertinent facts about her menstrual cycle and sexual activities, for her "safe" and fertile periods were of prime importance to him. The result, once the affair with Austin began, is a rare, trustworthy record of a late-nineteenth-century woman's simultaneous intimacies with two men. The symbols show that Mabel and David were familiar with the then prevalent theory that women, like other mammals, were fertile during their menstrual periods, but also could and did become pregnant during the period immediately following. Having decided to wait five years for children, the Todds were careful "to restrain ourselves from the fullness of our intercourse at all times except from fourteen days after my sickness ceased, until three before next time." Gradually such strict adherence relaxed a bit, but Mabel's code substantiates that they faithfully practiced withdrawal at all but "safe" times, a routine frustrating enough to David that over the years he planned his returns from travel to coincide with Mabel's infertile periods. She kept track of her orgasms, numbering them in sequence through each year, and only once, in the third month of marriage, did she experiment with a theory of her own that broke the regime for preventing pregnancy. The result of her experiment was that when Mabel returned from her visit to New York State in October 1879 she knew herself to be five months pregnant, a circumstance neither she nor David welcomed with much enthusiasm. As they settled in at Mrs. Stickney's on 11th Street, Mabel admitted in her journal that selfishness kept her from being totally glad. "I was not born with a very strong mother instinct in me—I have found my perfect & happy sphere in wifehood. I was *made* for a wife—for a mother, truly, *no*."

If Mabel feared the baby would be a burden, or would evict her from the childlike position she still occupied within her family, she discovered instead when her only child was born on February 5, 1880, that Molly Loomis was only too glad to assume as much care of her infant granddaughter as possible.

Mabel nursed the baby, who soon began to delight her, but otherwise experienced little interruption of her life. Family closeness was facilitated within a few weeks when Eben Loomis purchased a house on College Hill Terrace, in the northwest sector of the city along Rock Creek Park. How he afforded the house is not clear, although it involved Grandma Wilder, David, Mabel, and Millicent all paying rent to Eben, and parts of David's salary going toward the purchase of furnishings.

"A home at last! Our own home again," exclaimed Mabel. No indication she had longed for a home or treasured the memory of her early one ever appeared in her journal until this glowing intimation of what a constant dream it had been. She threw herself into decorating the house in dark Eastlake papers and rich, somber, "elegant" tones of maroon, gold, and brown. For the parlor she painted a handsome four-paneled screen of mullein, pokeberry, wild sunflowers, and thistles, which she anticipated "will bring me much notoriety," and painted as well a magnificent frieze of the four seasons around the top of her father's study. Eben at last had a small conservatory for his beloved plants, and David built Mabel a painting studio in the barn. For over a year the family of six lived comfortably together, enjoying what David would later call the "happiest days we ever had!"

Mabel was far from pleased when in June 1881 David was offered a year's position teaching astronomy and directing the observatory at Amherst. "It seems to me you should hardly dare to give up the Office place wholly," she protested, "& have no positive assurance of any Amherst position for more than a year, and that at so small a salary." But David recognized in the offer a shortcut to two of his chief ambitions—a professorship and his own observatory—and though Simon Newcomb hinted at promotion if he stayed in Washington, President Julius Seelye of Amherst spoke of an alumnus who planned to leave $300,000 for a new observatory. Encouraged that a higher salary and permanent position would be forthcoming, David finally accepted the Amherst post with the understanding he would return to the Nautical Almanac Office during vacations to finish up work with Newcomb.

Later, when the wealthy alumnus left his money elsewhere, David felt President Seelye had betrayed him. On arrival at Amherst he found himself assigned to teach three beginning divisions of mathematics in addition to astronomy, at no increase in salary, and though he shortly became involved teaching astronomy at nearby Smith College, and in 1885 designed and built the Smith observatory, funds for a new observatory at Amherst were not forthcoming for many years. It was 1904 before he was finally director of a facility he felt proud of.

When she first moved to Amherst, the narrowness of interest and experience, the devotion to piety and duty, of the faculty families and townspeople was something of a shock to Mabel. Such vestiges of Calvinism as self-abnegation and self-denial were as foreign to her nature as the musty smells, slatty beds, greasy kerosene lamps, and coarse ingrain carpets of local boardinghouses were offensive to her sensibilities. Later she would appreciate the simple, dignified traditions Amherst people had distilled from their strict heritage, and would recognize the pride invested in the modern gas lighting, piped water, and steam heat of their best hotel, the Amherst House, where the Todds lodged temporarily. But at first Mabel was a fish out of water. The faculty members she met seemed more puzzled than dazzled by her personality, and David's attention was diverted by his new duties. For solace she wandered in the beautiful New England autumn landscape, bringing back black alder, fringed gentian, and colored leaves to adorn the pair of rooms she and David finally rented in a new boardinghouse alongside the cut for the Massachusetts Central Railroad tracks on Pleasant Street. When, after several weeks' dislocation, Mabel met the Dickinsons and recognized in them her own kind, she embraced them with fervored, released joy, not fully appreciating the sources of their way of life.

Within a few weeks she was caught up in such a social whirl that she reported to her parents having "little time for anything except returning calls and going out to be amused." Life at the Dickinsons' was the key to her pleasure, but Mabel was invited to play and sing at other Amherst gatherings, and was a triumph among new friends who had heard few accomplished musicians. Soon she felt thoroughly at home at the center of attention. "If I come home utterly spoiled, conceited, vain, and proud, it will be from the flattery and compliments I labor under in this small town—which, however, are not in the least disagreeable to me," she notified her parents shortly before returning at Christmas to her daughter, Millicent, and to a Washington social scene that seemed more brilliant than usual.

In her record of that Washington visit, which lasted two months, Mabel spoke of a remarkable blossoming of her social powers: "I cannot explain it, but I feel strength & attractive power, & magnetism enough to fascinate a room full of people —which I have done, actually. . . . I have flirted outrageously with every man I have seen—but in a way which David likes to have me, too. I have simply felt as if I could attract any man to any amount. If the power is wholly bottled up I get restless & feverish like a caged eagle, but if I exercise it in the innocent ways I *do*, I am satisfied—only that I sigh for more worlds to conquer."

Amazingly, David condoned his wife's extravagant behavior, which seemed to gather momentum as she switched between Amherst and Washington several times in the ensuing year. Partly because he trusted her, partly because her flirtatiousness gave him license to pursue his own interest in attractive women, partly because he didn't know the whole of her excesses, but most of all because he worshipped his wife and wanted her to be happy, David restrained Mabel in no way, even when she engaged more deeply in her romantic friendship with Mr. Eliot, and a little later encouraged the young family physician, Dr. Eaton, who took an inordinate interest in the Loomises' health problems. The heightened velocity of her self-centered ways suggests Mabel was unconsciously seeking some restraint, such as the mature, high-minded moral guidance her father had always provided, but David was incapable of supplying it. Mabel ran as roughshod over his permissiveness as she had over her mother's. On the rare occasions when her cultivation of admirers exceeded his tolerance, David would testily insinuate that he, too, was having lovely times, or would refrain from writing until he heard a plaintive "Truly, David, you should not do this to me." But principally he indulged her, even when she played the belle among the Amherst College students, conversing and dancing with them as if she were one of the young unmarried ladies they escorted, which raised numerous eyebrows in town.* When they were alone together, David spoiled Mabel like a child, warming her clothes by the fire and dressing her in bed on cold mornings, talking baby talk with her, giving her every attention, encouraging her to spend her time doing whatever made her happiest. In her absence he kissed the floorboards she had trod, and then asked, "Do you like to have a lover of that sort—and have that lover your husband?" In Mabel's words: "He keeps me as serene & sunny

* Mabel's popularity among the students was especially evident at the commencement promenades. She described one to her mother in 1884: "The ball-books were bound in peacock plush. I had meant to stay only an hour or so, but I found my card filled for twenty-one dances immediately. I was quite surrounded for a few minutes until it was arranged, & I found myself in for all of it. However, I found after fifteen dances & a very lavish supper were over, that I was tired enough to go home— particularly as it was three o'clock. So David went around and excused me from the other six men to whom I had promised the remaining dances, & we came home." (MLT to her parents, July 5, 1884)

as a placid lake, & as happy & careless as a forest bird." About this time David fell into the lifelong habit of signing his letters *Lover/Husband/David*, later abbreviated to *L/H/D*, as if he played three separate roles in her life.

When Mabel returned to Amherst in March 1882, she discovered she had set another heart racing, that of Ned Dickinson, Austin's older son. Someone less preoccupied with herself, and perhaps less taken in by Sue, might have recognized that Ned Dickinson was different from other young men his age. Twenty years old and a sophomore at the college, Ned's childish handwriting and imitative letter style were obviously inferior to his fifteen-year-old sister, Mattie's, but Mabel seems not to have noticed anything unusual. She saw him through Sue's eyes as a graceful host, a skilled horseman, and an heir apparent encouraged by his mother to benefit from the friendship of "a brilliant accomplished married lady." Much of the social activity Sue Dickinson indulged in at the Evergreens was mounted on behalf of Ned, to make the most of what his mother knew would be the high point of his life, his college years. In addition to being slow, her son had suffered since age fifteen from periodic attacks of epilepsy, though the dread secret was kept from him by both parents. Sue made strenuous efforts to obscure and compensate for his limitations. Ned pursued a "partial course" through Amherst, received no grades, and, though a member of the class of 1884, would not graduate. Austin and Sue evidently laid at least some of the blame for Ned's problems on several attempts Sue had made to abort him during pregnancy, so that her valiant effort to simulate the friendships and experiences that should rightfully have been his can be viewed as part of a guilty charade, which Mabel did not see through quickly enough to avoid hurting Ned. The tension between Sue and Austin over Ned's condition ran deep, and was not helped by the fact that Sue was prostrated with terror during Ned's epileptic seizures, which occurred at night three or four times a year, compelling Austin to cope alone with the violent aspects of his son's illness.*

It was for heartfelt but shortsighted reasons, then, that Sue encouraged Ned to be Mabel's escort or partner whenever David was unavailable, and when he fell head over heels in love, the object of his affections was neither sorry nor unmoved. In fact, after spending April and May of 1882 in Washington while David worked at the Nautical Almanac Office, Mabel returned to Amherst in early June expressly to enjoy Ned's attentions throughout the festivities of commencement and to attend his twenty-first birthday party, for which Sue had gala plans.

Grandma Wilder and two-year-old Millicent accompanied Mabel back to Amherst, for David was detained by Professor Newcomb. Anticipating only her own pleasures, Mabel was thrown into chaotic despair when little Millicent developed

---

* Austin's diary notes Ned's epileptic seizures. His entry of April 3, 1890, indicates that he and Sue guarded their son carefully, but didn't talk with him about his condition: "Ned had attack this morning—not severe—comparatively. I was awake, & there instantly—& got a piece of pasteboard bet. his teeth, successfully so that there was no blood, & no indication that we could see afterwards that he had bitten his tongue—nothing indicating his mouth was sore. He was dull through the day, wanted to sleep—his stomach was deranged and he complained of rheumatism. He was perfectly well yesterday had [not] eaten nor done anything to account for it. Had long horseback ride yesterday. . . . Last attack before [on] Dec. 7." A description of Austin's ordeal occurs in Mabel's journal of October 18, 1891: "Austin has slept for years with his hearing on the alert for that horrible bloodcurdling cry that rings through the house, announcing the beginning of one of [Ned's] turns. Austin says he has often vaulted out of bed right over the footboard and found himself halfway upstairs before he was well awake. Sue is so terrified, afraid to go in the room with Ned, that she cowers back somewhere, and Austin sometimes, but not often, has to hold him in bed. Then, after a time it passes off, Ned never having waked or become conscious at all. The next morning he wakes as usual, with perhaps a very sore mouth, from having bitten his tongue, but otherwise all right. . . . [Austin] has never allowed [Ned] to be told or to know of these turns."

diarrhea and a tendency to cling tenaciously to her mother in the new surroundings, so that Mabel had to forgo a number of outings. After several days' acute distress at her deprivation, Mabel wrote an anguished letter home, only to find her parents more concerned about Millicent than herself. When Eben Loomis telegraphed he was coming to the rescue, Mabel came to her senses, found a young nurse, and bade her father stay in Washington.

That summer Mabel became such a regular part of the Dickinson household that she frequently joined the tea or dinner table, and once or twice a week spent the night with Mattie. For several years Austin Dickinson had held himself aloof from the social affairs of the rest of his family, occasionally entering in his diary disparaging references to "my wife's tavern" or to the high jinks of "Sue and her crowd." His distance from the family amusements registers in his surprise on returning from business in Boston the night of June 19, 1882, to find the Evergreens "illuminated for a party for Ned, he being 21. Til 1:00 a.m. a wild tear and revel, everything being turned inside out and upside down, and one dancer jamming right through a register [grilled vent in the floor]." Now through the long, lazy summer of 1882, while the Dickinsons and Todds affectionately picnicked together, went on carriage rides, camped in Shutesbury (and photographed), danced, sang, and played, Sue's elaborate scheme for Ned's happiness not only misfired but allowed a new problem to develop.

Austin appeared more regularly at the gatherings, often escorting Mabel home or insisting she sit beside him in the carriage. The two discovered congenial interests, and Mabel's admiration for Austin mounted swiftly, while her superficial feelings for Ned waned. She rejoiced at finding someone who cared as deeply as she did about nature; someone who loved the landscape, welcomed all weather, and was genuinely stirred by the chirping of August crickets; someone to whom she could safely reveal her own excessive sensibilities.

In his diary Austin began taking almost daily notice of Mabel's comings and goings through the summer of 1882. On the night of September 6 he wrote: "Sat on piazza a while in evening with Mrs. Todd waiting for the rest to come from somewhere—after a while the little man [David Todd] appeared in the darkness. Littleness not preferred." This cryptic revelation of his feelings toward David was a prelude to a crucial entry five days later. After noting on Monday, September 11, 1882, that it had been "an old fashioned rainy day," he added the single word "Rubicon." Mabel's diary of the same date bears the same word in the margin, although it appears to have been added later.

Tucked into her diary at the same place is her invitation to Mattie's whist party, held that evening, an event for which Austin came to fetch her. Instead of turning in at the Evergreens, the two had walked on beyond the Dickinson gate and looked deeply into each other's eyes, while Austin told Mabel she had more ideas that were congenial to him than anyone he had ever met. In the thirteen years to follow they both referred to the "Rubicon," or "going by the gate," as the formal beginning of their love affair. For neither of them was there ever any turning back.*

The day before the Rubicon, Austin had taken Mabel next door to the Dickinson Homestead to play and sing for his two

* Actually the Rubicon was event number 3 in the history of their early awareness, but it was the most significant. First had come a picnic Sue organized in Sunderland Park in early July, during which Mabel and Austin paused at a fence to enjoy the sunset, and momentarily clasped hands in admiration at the spectacle. Then occurred what they called "a word in a Shutesbury pew" later in the month, during a camping expedition of Sue's. It was a mutual acknowledgment, while listening to a church service, that they both loved the "chir" of crickets.

maiden sisters, Emily and Lavinia, and for his invalid mother, bedridden upstairs. As on many occasions to follow, Mabel saw only Vinnie, while "the rare, mysterious Emily listened in the quiet darkness outside." Afterwards, as already stated, Emily sent in an appreciative glass of wine and a poem, and next morning reiterated her pleasure with flowers and a note that initiated a three-and-a-half-year friendship.*

The day after the Rubicon, Mabel, David, and Millicent departed for Washington, to be gone until early November. Despite President Seelye's displeasure, David was hoping to lead one of the Naval Observatory's astronomical expeditions to photograph the December 1882 Transit of Venus. During this interval in Washington Mabel was in correspondence with every member of the Dickinson family save Vinnie, though even she confessed herself enthralled by Mabel's charms. It is apparent that Mabel's attention was far more occupied by Dickinsons than by the upcoming astronomical event, for until mid-September not a word about it had occurred in her diary or journal, although David had been preparing since early summer. Plans seemed on again, then off again. David was not chosen for one of the eight official expeditions Newcomb and the Naval Observatory sent to South America and selected stations in the United States. He then hoped to be sponsored by the trustees of the newly constructed James Lick Observatory at Mount Hamilton, California, where, at Newcomb's suggestion, a horizontal photoheliograph had been installed especially for observing this Transit. At the last minute he received word that the Lick trustees would fund him, and with

---

* Dozens of notes and attentions exchanged during the next three and a half years attest to Emily and Mabel's mutual affection, but the tie that bound them most intimately—their love for Austin—was never alluded to. The Homestead became the safest place for Mabel and Austin to meet, for by 1882 Sue rarely went there. Emily, fully aware of what was occurring in her home, rejoiced in Austin's renewed happiness and his more frequent presence, and enjoyed indirectly the gaiety and spontaneity Mabel brought to the quiet mansion.

Amherst photographer J. L. Lovell in tow, he set out from Amherst on November 10 carrying equipment that on December 6 provided 123 excellent photographs of measurable quality. David was ecstatic that the granulation of his wet plates was superior to what could be achieved by the dry plates of the other expeditions, and he fell in love with California, with the astronomers at the Lick Observatory, and with their wives. Miffed by glowing reports of Mabel's doings in Amherst with the Dickinsons, he made it plain she had missed a rare opportunity.

But Mabel never wanted to go. After considerable indecision and changes of plans, she had achieved what made her happiest—staying in Amherst alone during David's two-month absence to enjoy the rapture of her rare, intense new friendship with Austin. For the first time in her life she was unchaperoned. David moaned later, "I never should have left her," but it was already too late.

Mabel's diary and journal, and even her letters, during the weeks David was away, were full of praise for "dear Mr. Dickinson," who was "delicate beyond expression, & tender & watchful & caretaking." Such passages scarcely suggest the depth of passion that was flowing secretly between them, and was the substance of notes and letters they exchanged and of their meetings and drives together. The false pinnacle on which Mabel perched for a few weeks before David's return in early January, and only shortly before a lifelong storm with Sue broke in mid-December, is suggested by some exalted journal prose of December 11, 1882, that in tone echoes the entry made on the eve of her marriage:

> I am happy beyond measure in all my charming circumstances. My life is positively the most brilliant one I know of. I mean in its continual succession of delightful things, with almost never a cloud to dim the brightness of my sun. I am a great favorite here in Amherst. I have many callers every day— I have many letters every day. I practice & paint a great deal;

I have no care—my parlor is lovely; Millicent is perfectly well & radiantly happy [in Washington]. David has had exceptional success & is coming to me within a few days—and my admirable, noble, strong, true Mr. Dickinson is entirely devoted to me.

Quite reversing Emily Dickinson's sense of awareness, all the radii of Mabel's circumference pointed inward, toward herself as center. In her euphoria she was strangely unconcerned about the consequences of her love affair with Austin—about explaining it to David, or anticipating Sue's reaction. She hoped, of course, Sue wouldn't notice, but beyond that was lulled in her perpetual optimism, and perhaps by disclosures Austin had made concerning his marital unhappiness, into a firm "presentiment" that all would work to her advantage. Therefore, when Ned, his feelings woefully injured by what Mabel lightly termed "the tacit abandonment of our little affair," revealed to his mother what he saw happening, Mabel was both surprised and not a little frightened by Sue's resultant anger. Suddenly she needed more than the personal convictions on which her life was sustained.

Late in November 1882 she turned to her father, urging him to write her what he believed concerning the divinity of Christ. She herself doubted it, she confessed, and had always placed her religious faith in Eben. Now, however, as she substituted Austin for her father, she began to talk in religious tones about their love, and explained to Austin that he had "reawakened my almost dormant longing for God." In fact, she was quite persuaded that, in the face of all earthly conventions, God was smiling on the "rightness" of two such noble beings as herself and Austin becoming lovers.

2 / Susan *and* Austin Dickinson

OF the four key figures in the Todd-Dickinson drama, Sue Dickinson is probably the least well understood. She was a woman whose presence constantly had to be reckoned with (Mabel was not the first to discover that one ignored Susan at one's peril). Her extraordinary, bright, strong-willed, independent, but often conflicted personality had dominated Amherst for three decades before Mabel came to town, and stimulated strong reactions among her contemporaries. The pattern Mabel experienced, of being pulled into, then expelled from, Sue's orbit, was so familiar to others in Amherst that few recognized at first Sue's legitimate grounds for turning against the charming newcomer she had embraced with such enthusiasm. Most of the testimony about Sue comes from persons who had grown disenchanted with her, including her husband and her sisters-in-law. Since little remains in her own words to explain her numerous contradictions of character, certainly far less than Mabel or David or Austin left behind, it becomes essential to examine closely the materials that do survive for what they reveal of her complex personality.

Much that is known about Sue comes by way of Emily and Austin, both of whom adored her in early years, but eventually spoke or wrote of her as a woman whose magnetism concealed vindictiveness, whose intellect was self-serving and sometimes cruel, whose warmth and gaiety could mount to turbulence, and whose pleasant authority often turned rigid and controlling. She was a woman of so many facets that Emily, having idolized "Sister Sue" as a young woman, admitted to her after thirty years, "With the exception of Shakespeare, you have told me of more knowledge than anyone living—To say that sincerely is strange praise." Young Emily made Sue a goddess, and served her with aphorisms which over the years came to suggest a woman of powerful elemental warmth ("Susan fronts on the Gulf Stream"; she was "an Avalanche of Sun!"; "What depths of Domingo in that torried Spirit!"). But these extravagances met with sufficient coolness and unpredictability, and earned Emily enough bafflement and pain, that she seems never to have fathomed whether Sue was molten or granite at the core. In the end, she identified the one vast attribute her earthly idol shared with the harsh, judgmental, patriarchal God she had rejected—both were unknowable. After a quarter century's intimacy with Sue, Emily sent this poem across the stretch of lawn between their homes:

> But Susan is a Stranger yet—
> The Ones who cite her most
> Have never scaled her Haunted House
> Nor compromised her Ghost—
>
> To pity those who know her not
> Is helped by the regret
> That those who know her know her less
> The nearer her they get—
>
> [#1400, ca. 1877]

Forever enigmatic and therefore forever fascinating to Emily, who nevertheless came to keep a carefully maintained, protective distance from her, Sue hovered dominant, powerful, and potentially disruptive in Emily's awareness, a dark, explosive aspect of the life forces the poet wrestled for control.

The conundrum of Sue's identity recurs in Austin's premarital correspondence with her, a confusing assemblage of undated, roughly sequenced, highly charged, brooding drafts written during the first four years of his six-year courtship. In them Sue stands congealed at the center of a morass of feeling that Austin confesses to indulging for the first time. Unable to lead him through his emotional mire, as he somehow expected she should, equally unable to make a move on her own behalf without setting Austin's bog quaking and trembling, Sue was effectively trapped in Austin's vision of her—a highly uncooperative soul figure, the bright aspect of his innermost strivings, an investiture inevitably destined to disappoint cruelly.

Emily's and Austin's veneration of Sue tell us far more about them and what they needed Sue to be than about who and what she actually was. Listening instead to what Sue says of herself in her own girlhood letters and her few drafted reminiscences, it is possible to surmise some of the ghosts that haunted her house and to understand something of why she had by 1890 become the Power and the Great Black Mogul, in Austin and Mabel's private language. Sue's early letters illuminate her difficult childhood in Amherst, so different from the stable security the Dickinson children knew, and also reveal insecurities and fears that stemmed from several early traumas in her life.

Born Susan Huntington Gilbert on December 19, 1830, in Greenfield, Massachusetts, just twenty miles north of where Emily was born at the Dickinson Homestead nine days earlier, Sue was the youngest of seven children of Harriet Arms and Thomas Gilbert. Though both parents came of respectable Connecticut Valley families, Sue's father was a luckless tavern-keeper, his family "so poor that the neighbors had to take things in to make them comfortable," according to one contemporary. In 1832 Thomas Gilbert came to Amherst to be proprietor of the Mansion House, a tavern and livery stable on Main Street. That same year Sue's seven-year-old sister, Sophia, died, and four years later her mother succumbed to consumption at age forty-five, a tragedy that broke up the family. Susan was five at the time, and the grief, loss, fear, uncertainty, and uprooting she suffered left indelible marks upon her. All four Gilbert sisters went to Geneva, New York, to be cared for by their aunt and uncle, Sophia Arms and William Van Vranken. Nineteen-year-old Frank went west to join Sue's oldest brother, Dwight, who was already earning his living in Michigan. Five years later Sue's father died in Greenfield, at age forty-eight, reportedly of drink. He was listed an "insolvent debtor" in the county records.

The Geneva environment apparently was a happy one. Sue formed a fond attachment to her Aunt Sophia during the ten years she lived there before returning to Amherst for older girlhood. Yet a melancholy message she wrote to Dwight some dozen years after her mother's death reveals how poignantly she remembered and missed her: "I do feel so lonely at times dear brother, I [feel] so keenly the loss of a Mother's love, and influence, and that sympathy our Mother alone could give . . . I have often wished, we had Mother's [miniature] for I have quite lost her expression. I try many times to recall it, but my impressions of her face are entirely lost. The memory of her goodness will never die, for very many of her old friends often remind me of her devoted piety, and her silent, though powerful influence."

Reminders of her mother's goodness were offset, however, by stories of her father's badness. Susan left no mention of the father whom she never saw again after 1836, but since gossip of his dissoluteness and his "dying upon charity" circulated in Amherst as late as the 1880s (when the Todds picked it up), Sue undoubtedly felt the stigma of her father's disgrace when she returned to live in the village as a sixteen-year-old in 1847. Her shame and threatened self-esteem in the Amherst setting could easily explain the sense of pride she developed so strongly.

A significant piece of evidence substantiates the ne'er-do-well reputation Thomas Gilbert acquired. His father, a saddler, innkeeper, and influential citizen of Greenfield, had watched his originally promising son grow up, rise through the militia to the rank of brigadier general (he served briefly in the War of 1812), marry, and start a family. By the time Eliel Gilbert wrote his will in 1826, however, he divided his estate into five equal parts, left four of them to his four daughters, and gave Thomas's share directly to his grandchildren, Sue's brothers and sisters, appointing a legal guardian to administer the funds. The will released Thomas from nearly a thousand dollars' worth of notes and debts, and mentioned other gifts of property that had been worth another thousand. Eliel Gilbert died in 1830, and the money left to Sue and her siblings presumably helped the Van Vrankens raise their four extra daughters, and perhaps paid for Sue's two terms at Utica Female Academy in New York State when she was seventeen.

The Gilbert sisters began returning to Amherst in 1842, the year following their father's death, when Harriet, the oldest, married William Cutler, partner in the principal dry-goods store in the village. First Mary, then Martha (called Mattie), then Sue left the Van Vranken home to join Harriet in Amherst, perhaps originally coming East to help the Cutlers with the baby daughter born in 1844, then staying on to ease the lonely months when the baby died a year later. By 1847 Amherst was again "home" to all the sisters, though Mary Gilbert came and went as a schoolteacher, and Mattie Gilbert shuttled among Amherst, Geneva, and Grand Haven, Michigan, where her brothers had settled. Sue's sense of loss of a central home in which she and her siblings could be together apparently troubled her deeply as she grew up, and was particularly acute in Amherst, where she was sensitive to her position as the homeless relative of William Cutler, a brother-in-law she actively disliked.

The pattern of Sue's behavior in the years ahead indicates she made strenuous efforts to erase the past and its humiliations, and strove desperately, if unconsciously, to find the father, home, and united family that had not been hers. She tried repeatedly to escape from Amherst, where her father's reputation persisted, and also sought a more acceptable father figure (Edward Dickinson had the most irreproachable record in the region). A clue to her initial rejection of her real father is her dropping of the Gilbert name, alone among her sisters, when she became Susan Huntington Dickinson. After the death of Edward, however, she tacked to a more characteristically defiant course and reinstated her father by naming her third child Thomas Gilbert Dickinson (he was called Gilbert). A few years after that, in the summer of 1883, she and Dwight purchased land in West Cemetery and moved the graves of her father, mother, and little Sophia from their original burial spots to a site directly across the cinder path from Edward Dickinson's plot. Over the years her social posturings and the pretensions she encouraged in her two older children stimulated, rather than quelled, the village whispers about her tavern birth, and betrayed as well her deep need for superiority.

Scattered as they were, Sue's brothers and sisters were supremely important to her, especially Dwight and Mary, to whom she was temperamentally akin. These three were admired over the years for their independence, confidence, and spirit, in contrast to Frank, Harriet, and Mattie Gilbert, who were described as sweet, genial, winning, quiet, unassuming, or shy. All the Gilberts looked to Dwight as nominal head of the family (perhaps the reason he married later than any of them), but Sue went so far as to appoint him her absent father between the time she left the Van Vranken home and the time of her marriage, telling him at one point, "I look to you, dear brother . . . and find myself thinking of, and loving you as a Father." She regularly sought his long-distance counsel and approval, and he didn't disappoint her. Together with the quieter Frank, Dwight acted responsibly and generously toward all his sisters over the years, helping to meet their financial needs, and assuring each a respectable dowry at her time of marriage. Dwight's eventual success as a banker, a millionaire, and a prominent citizen of Grand Rapids (where he finally settled), a man to whom a public statue was erected at death, undoubtedly was important to Sue's own esteem during later adult life.

That Sue was striving to act braver and stronger than she really felt when she first came to Amherst at age sixteen is revealed in a fascinating essay she wrote some fifty years later about growing up in the village at mid-century.* Titled "Society in Amherst Half a Century Ago," her composition catches personalities and attitudes she encountered in the strait-laced, orthodox community about the time she returned there to live in the summer of 1847, and sheds several dramatic shafts of light upon herself. Most revealing is her candid comment that "I was habitually called a 'fraid cat' by my own family. Who sharply chid me, 'for my own good' doubtless, after the Puritan recipe, urging, 'What are you afraid of?' To which in disdain, I shot back, as any mystic, 'Oh I dont know! If I did I would not care!' " Her essay then describes two attempts she made that summer she was sixteen to prove her courage, by volunteering to "watch" all night with sick people, a village custom requiring her to sit through the night in strange, dark houses that grew increasingly eerie and frightening as the hours passed. After subjecting herself twice to the most terrifying nights of her life, she never volunteered as nurse again.†

---

* Written about 1900, the essay remained among Sue's papers at Harvard University until it was published under the title "Two Generations of Amherst Society" in *Essays on Amherst's History* (Amherst, 1978).

† It may have been these early experiences that kept Sue "cowering back," as Mabel's journal has it, when the cries of Ned's epileptic seizures disturbed the nights at the Evergreens many years later. In "Society in Amherst" Sue recounts her terror when "a series of curdling shrieks" from a young woman having a nightmare pierced the stillness. "Shaking with fright, I grasped the iron candlestick, the tallow dripping over my fingers, and fled to clutch the poor victim, who with wide staring eyes was fast in the grip of her horror. She blessed me for delivering her, but alas! nobody saved me from the most awful night of my life! I never watched again."

Sue's clear portrait of herself as a girl who was fearful but determined to prove otherwise turns on that proud response to her family's taunts. Of what was she afraid? "Oh I dont know! If I did I would not care!" Choosing to hide her fears behind disdain, she worked to overcome any self-perceived weaknesses, projecting a bravado she may have needed to face Vinnie Dickinson, Jenny Hitchcock, Emily Fowler, Abby Wood, and the other village girls who attended Amherst Academy in the fall of 1847 (at the same time Emily Dickinson attended Mount Holyoke Female Seminary). Perhaps such nerve was required to go among strangers again the following spring and autumn terms of 1848 at the Utica Female Academy, where she came alive to literature and poetry, acquired her first books, and made several friends important to her. "Susan knows no Fear," Emily once rhapsodized, possibly looking for protection from her colossus, but more probably making a very obvious statement about Sue. By the time she came back to Amherst at eighteen, her education finished, she was armed with a wit and defiance that made her appear fearless and strong to her contemporaries. The following year she became friends with Emily Dickinson, and attracted several admirers among the Amherst College students, including Austin Dickinson.

Sue's attitude toward the Amherst of her girlhood seems ambivalent. In her essay she looked back nostalgically to the single social stratum in the village, to the unaffected dress and simple pastimes of the pretty girls and pleasant college boys, but she also remembered pious, rigidly good adults among the citizens of the church, the college, and the town, repressed victims of the tense grip religion held upon the community.* Amherst could be a place of benign pastoral beauty, with fun to be found among the faculty families and college students,

* She provides a quick study of Deacon Luke Sweetser, in daily life the business partner of William Cutler, who taught a "deadly monotonous Bible class" on Sabbath noons, and "never by word or smile lent a relaxed beam of cheer or hope to the simplicities of the New Testa-

but it was also a bleak, unfriendly landscape for a young woman of buoyant, insubmissive temperament. Her feelings coalesced in a central, stark memory: "As the snow lay two or three feet on the level in those Wintry days, Amherst, with no street lighting, no trolleys, no railroads, seemed to my youthful and perverse mind, animal spirits and vigorous habit, a staring, lonely, hopeless place, enough to make angels homesick. The lugubrious sound of the church bell still rings in my Winter dreams."

Sue's situation within the Cutler household, where she did housekeeping tasks in exchange for room and board, was highly unsatisfactory to her. She chafed against being beholden to William Cutler, a joyless man whom Austin Dickinson characterized many years later as "naturally slow and cautious, more apt to see objections than advantages—the course of events never quite to his mind—finding much to condemn, little to approve outside Daniel Webster and the old Whig party." William made it plain that his wife's sisters were a charitable burden, and his condescensions persistently fed Sue's awareness of past humiliations, making her vindictive. William aroused in her the very strong-mindedness she knew he detested in women, and endless differences and contests of will between them kept the Cutler household lively. Sue wasn't alone in her contempt for William. "The same warfare with the dampers is kept up as when you were here," Mattie reported to Dwight in the late winter of 1848–49. "I have actually suffocated for the last few days. Mr. Cutler has the most intense enjoyment in stuffing the stoves and seeing us sweat."

One way Sue planned to escape the Cutlers was by making her home with her sister Mary, eight years her senior, who during the summer of 1849 was in Amherst preparing for her Sep-

---

ment. As he unfolded them via Barnes Notes, he weighed down my youthful spirit every Sunday, with his picture of myself as a rebellious sinner in the hands of an avenging God—with possible death before another dawn staring me full in the face."

tember marriage to Samuel Julius Learned, an 1845 graduate of the college. Like Mary, Julius was a teacher, and had charge of the Riddicksville Seminary in the tiny town of Sunbury, North Carolina, where the couple went to live following their wedding in the Cutler parlor. A few months later, Julius succumbed to prevalent fevers of the nearby Dismal Swamp and was forced to leave the region. He and Mary, the latter already with child, went to Dwight and Frank's home at Grand Haven, Michigan, and there on July 14, 1850, less than a month after giving birth to a daughter, Mary died. The shock and grief that suffused the Gilbert family registers in a pathetic letter that nineteen-year-old Sue wrote to Dwight on the eve of what would have been Mary's first wedding anniversary. Its set images and formal phrasing suggest the difficulty she was having making sense of the cruel blow:

My dear Brother

These sabbath nights have been sad, thoughtful hours to me, since our dear Mary was lain in her grave, for each successive Sabbath brings her image, and the scene of her burial, before me with a painful vividness and reality, and assures me but too truly, that one we have loved has passed away, and that now we are but *five*.

Just one year ago tonight you were here dearest brother. Mary too was with us, and all was bright and happy. . . . How little we thought when we stood by her side, on the morning of her marriage, that she would be first-called to the "spirit-world," or that the first anniversary of her bridal-day would come to us fraught with bitter memories and unavailing tears. At times I cannot realize that Mary is really buried from our sight. . . . I had always looked forward, with so much pleasure, to a home with Mary sometime—we had talked of it many times and promised ourselves much happiness—in living together. . . .

That Sue in this same letter expressed her keen sense of the loss of her mother, then moved on to the sentences acknowledging Dwight as her absent father, suggests what a cataclysm Mary's death was for her. Her associated thoughts reveal that Mary had been a second mother to her. Now she, too, was dead—a blow to many happy plans, an end to childhood. Donning the mourning garb she would wear for the next three years, Sue appears to have been particularly disturbed by two things—her own lack of preparedness for death and the form Mary's took. Details of the terrible event were supplied by Mattie, who had gone to Michigan to help with the new baby and had received as well Mary's last earthward look. There is little chance Sue was spared intimate acquaintance with the dark side of childbearing, which may have been responsible in great measure for her later fear of having children, an anxiety evidenced in her continual deferral of her wedding date, but even more apparent in the frigidity that marred her marriage and the several abortions she subsequently induced.

More immediately, Mary's unexpected death served as a clarion warning to Sue that she herself was not, as Mary had been, "ready to die." It appears from passages in her mournful letter to Dwight that Sue harbored a vital childhood dream, perhaps the palliative once offered a brokenhearted five-year-old, that someday she would be reunited with her mother in heaven. But she could not hope for heaven without first being "saved," a tenet that was being made patently clear that summer of 1850 by the religious revival which was sweeping New England, and since early spring had lodged a psychological maelstrom at Amherst's Congregational meetinghouses. Emily Dickinson's letters convey the power of this particular revival, for she was resisting for the second time in her life strong coercion to become a Christian, while many around her, including her father, gave over to the conversion experience. "I cant tell you *what* they have found," Emily wrote a friend during the spring, "but *they* think it is something precious. . . . It *certainly* comes from God, and I think to receive it is blessed —not that I know from *me*, but from those on whom *change* has passed. They seem so very tranquil, and their voices are kind, and gentle, and the tears fill their eyes so often, I really think I envy them."

Stress in the conversion process was placed on personal salvation, arrived at after expiation of sins and a surrendering of one's will to Christ. The sense of peace and inner happiness that Emily noted flooded an individual only after a period of soul-searching and nearly overwhelming self-abasement, but its occurrence was recognized as a sign that one was "saved." Those who could publicly testify to having "found Christ" in this manner became Christians and were admitted to member-ship in the church. They were God's Elect, who on Judgment Day would unite in heaven. Through the indigestible doses of doom, vengeance, heavy bass viol tones, and fatalistic visions of heaven and hell that were the imperfectly understood, in-herently terrifying messages of Calvinism she and other young people took in while growing up, Sue had clung to the urgency of again seeing her mother, whose presence in heaven she never doubted.* The shock and lesson of Mary's death, as well as her deep need for consolation, brought Sue into the First Congregational Church in mid-August 1850. She joined a group of seventy penitents, including her brother-in-law Wil-liam Cutler and her future father-in-law, Edward Dickinson.

Sue's pursuit of a heavenly home didn't divert her from her resolute hopes for an earthly one, a desire she mentioned

---

* The last passage of Sue's September 15, 1850, letter to Dwight spoke to this theme. "We know [Mother] was a *Christian*, and the one ab-sorbing thought was the salvation of her children. We can never know, till all secrets are revealed in the clear light of Heaven, how many fervent, heart-felt prayers she has offered at the throne of Grace, that her children might all have a share in the incorruptible inheritance beyond the grave. And is it not for each one of us to decide, whether we shall enjoy a happy reunion in Heaven with 'those not lost, but only gone before.' God grant that we may each, and all, choose that 'better portion' and one day meet, an unbroken band, in that world that knows no *change* or *death*."

persistently and with far warmer enthusiasm during the next six years than she spoke of marriage and a husband. There are three sources for knowing Sue's thoughts and feelings during the period between 1850 and 1856, when she was between the ages of nineteen and twenty-five. One is the dozen-odd letters she wrote to her brothers Dwight and Frank from the time of Mary's death until the year before her marriage to Austin in July 1856. The second is another dozen letters she wrote between 1853 and 1856 to some new friends, Reverend and Mrs. Samuel C. Bartlett of Manchester, New Hampshire, who were the sister and brother-in-law of Mary's bereaved husband, Julius Learned, with whom Sue continued to stay in touch. Sue first visited the Bartletts in March 1853, when they moved to New England from Hudson, Ohio, where Samuel Bartlett, then in his mid-thirties, had been professor of philosophy and rhetoric at Western Reserve College. He was a Dartmouth College graduate, and much later became president of that institution. Julius encouraged the friendship, for he greatly admired Sue and Mattie Gilbert. "When do you expect *Sue* to visit Manchester?" he wrote to Samuel. "You'll find her 'some punkins.'" Julius billed Sue as "handsome" and "brilliant," opinions shared by others among her contemporaries.

The third and far most elusive source of Sue's thoughts is Austin Dickinson's courtship letters and drafts, which began during the spring of 1850, a month or more before Mary Gilbert's death. Sue's letters to Austin are missing, but in several of his early letters to her, and occasionally in the scores of drafts he wrote during 1853 and 1854 while at Harvard Law School, Austin reiterated or rephrased some of Sue's words to him, providing the few rare representations of her side of their relationship. These three groups of material together contain numerous reliable clues to her aspirations and reveal quite unmistakably the cast of her mind, further borne out by her behavior during the period.

Sue's overriding wishes, mentioned several times in the letters to her brothers, were for independence and a home of her own, a pairing of dreams somewhat inappropriate at a time when women were expected to look for fulfillment of their "natural" instincts through a husband, and particularly surprising for a young woman of Sue's limited personal opportunities. Her visions didn't mention a husband or children, only financial independence and a home to which her siblings might come. Emily Dickinson managed to achieve such goals by not marrying and remaining in her family home, gaining a vast degree of freedom within her dependency on her father, but Sue had no such option. Unaware of any conflict in her ambitions, and struggling to recover lost dreams that could only have been provided by the father she never had, Sue began exploring the few routes open to her.

"So you think school-teaching won't be very profitable business for me," she wrote to Dwight the summer of 1851, when she was twenty. "Well perhaps not, but let me try once and then I'll be *easy*." By September she had secured herself a position in Mr. Robert Archer's school in Baltimore, and she rationalized to her brother, "Well Dwight I never expect to make a future teaching. If I had a Home and Parents, I never would think or trouble about it, but *now*, you know, Mat and I are dependent on Wm. for a home, and it does not seem right for us both 'to eat the bread of *idleness*.' Though I shall not amass my *thousands* here—still I am making myself a home for *one* year at least, and relieving Mr. Cutler for one year." She made so little, however, only $125 beyond room, board, and expenses, that her venture was doomed to failure even in her own eyes before she began. At most, it got her out of "plain humdrum old Amherst among the hills," where she felt confined and restless.

Part of Sue's restlessness grew out of her dependence on William Cutler, which came to crisis during the long monotonous New England winters, so that nearly every spring found her with freshly conceived plans to break away from her circumstances somehow. In January 1851, for instance, she concocted a scheme for making a trip to New York City, a project for which she had far more ingenuity than funds or opportunity ("Oh Dwight," she wailed, "I am out of my *minority* and like all heiresses I am looking about for my dowry"). Marshaling her wit, her greatest resource, she proposed to her brother, "I have a very agreeable little plan about going to N.Y. with you to hear the 'Jenny' [Lind] and have been trying to conjure up eloquence enough to give you a similar impression. It is the desire of my heart to hear the 'Nightingale' and all my friends insist that my elder brother will take me." When Dwight did not oblige by coming East from Michigan for the purpose, Sue persisted, until by early summer she had found another way to make a three-week visit to New York and New Haven. She recounted her triumph later for Dwight.

> You must know I have been on a visit to the great *Gotham*, alias New York and after such an *elbowing* as I received there, have just recovered my usual confused state. . . . I have always had an idea I should hear Jenny before she left the country, and so I started off some two or three weeks ago to realize it if possible. One of my Geneva school-mates is married and living in New York. . . . She insisted that I should come down to see her, and hear Jenny. . . . I decided to go and run the risk of bankruptcy. I went alone, and you would have laughed could you have heard the advice given, and fears expressed for my safety. . . .

Women went few places unescorted, even to church or a village lecture, so Sue's independence had indeed exerted itself to take the stage and railroad cars alone to New York. She did hear Jenny Lind sing, although she neglected to mention that the Swedish Nightingale also toured in New England during the very time she was away. Emily and Vinnie Dickinson heard her sing in Northampton on July 3, and Sue could have saved her money and stayed home had Jenny been her sole reason for traveling. Her penchant for getting her way was well set, however, and the following year when Sue, in Baltimore, requested that Dwight escort her about the city of Washington, he came.

Evidently Dwight and Frank rescued Sue from the humiliation of having to ask William Cutler for money. After the year in Baltimore she began turning to them when she needed it, always with an apology and a bit of humor to disguise her shame at having to ask. "Sometime ago, if I recollect rightly, you wrote me a letter inquiring if 'my funds were low,'" she wrote Dwight in early April 1853. "At that time my coffers were full, but *now*, alas, my poor old 'porte-monnaie' is as empty as a broken bank. . . . And now Spring is here, and my stockings are all holes, and my shoes all ditto, and my dresses all *agée*, and my bonnet 'passée' and my *teeth* all dilapidated, and like old houses, and farm fences, if put in order, and brushed over, I shall last some time and ornament the neighborhood. The question is who'll pay the Painter."

Sue was twenty-two that spring of 1853, and had some special, pressing needs. For one thing, her official three-year period of grieving for Mary was ending and she faced replacement of her all-black wardrobe. "[Susie] looks very lovely in colors—she dont wear mourning now," Emily reported to her brother at Harvard about a month after Sue had made her appeal to Dwight for funds. But in addition, in late March, after a three-year friendship full of ups and downs, Sue and Austin had secretly pledged their troth to one another. She had to begin planning, sewing, and acquiring the many things she would need to establish her own household. The engagement was known only to Emily, though no one in Amherst would have been particularly surprised, for Sue and Austin were "constantly together," as one peer commented, and Sue was obviously warmly approved of by the Dickinsons.

What did cause some stir when it got out was that Sue had surreptitiously met Austin in Boston, and even stayed overnight alone at the Revere Hotel on March 23, 1853, to see him. She accomplished this by resourcefully planning a detour through the city soon after Austin began his first term at Cambridge, when she herself was returning from her first visit to the Samuel Bartletts in Manchester. Ostensibly she took the Boston route to consult an oculist, but by prearrangement spent her hours in the city primarily with Austin and, in his words, "[we] promised ourselves to each other." Although Sue put a bold face on her excursion, she was disturbed enough by the gossip she created, and perhaps by an upset with William Cutler because she sidestepped some travel plans he had for her, that she laid her defense before Dwight a couple of weeks later, in the same letter in which she asked him for funds. By avoiding any mention of her engagement, she inadvertently emphasized what probably was a chief motive for becoming engaged—her need to extricate herself from the hopeless dependency in which she felt trapped.

> As I came home from Manchester, via Boston, my expenses were considerably increased. My reason in the main was on account of my eyes, that troubled me so much while in M. I was afraid to come home, without seeing a physician. I consulted one of the best oculists in the city. . . . They are now better, tho' I have to be very careful not using them evenings. One of my best friends while in Utica at school wrote me she should be in Boston for a few days, and I managed to meet her there, and a nice visit we had I assure you. . . . I have been feeling a little discontented this Spring that I am so dependent. It seems hardly right that I give up my time to Hattie & Wm., and have nothing but my board—looking to you and Frank for all I have, but Hattie will not let me go away to teach & really needs me, so I can do nothing but stay and be contented. I *want*, and *mean* to pay my way always, with Mr. Cutler, and not be indebted *at all* to him— and for this reason, I write for money as he never gives it to me very pleasantly—and seems to consider any little service to me a *burden.* I'm not complaining of my lot, Dwight, in the least . . . yet if I *could,* I would rather be more reliant upon my own re-

sources. I believe I *try* to do right, and who can do more? . . .
Don't laugh about this *woman's* business letter. . . .

Though she restrained herself, it was in her final phrase,
"Don't laugh about this *woman's* business letter," that Sue's
underlying despondency broke through. In its implied admission that what she really cherished was a *man's* opportunities,
and in the letter's pervading sense that she identified with her
father, the shameful burden on charity, lurks an unconscious
rejection of feminine values and roles. Her unalterable dependence on the Cutlers and other relatives, her intense
boredom with the routine of cooking, housekeeping, and mind-
ing Harriet and William's new baby,* her despair at the
prospect of spending the rest of her days in Amherst, and back
of all these a powerful, irrational determination to rid herself
of the insecurities, the humiliations that fed her helplessness,
all pushed her to take the step so many of her friends were
taking. Yet it was a woman's solution, and while she might
rejoice that the most qualified suitor in the region loved her and
would care for her as she needed and desperately wanted, it
seems likely she also felt scornful of her weakness in having to
accept the only solution available to her sex.

Sue's maintenance of secrecy about her betrothal was more
than an attempt to starve the idle chatterers of Amherst, more
than deference to Austin's having another year of law school
to complete before he could begin to earn his living, though
both were true. Her privacy seems to have masked conflict over
giving up dreams she valued—independence and the desire to
get out of Amherst—in exchange for security and a home that
would, in her mind, restore Gilbert integrity. What she went

* Dwight Gilbert Cutler was born to Harriet and William Cutler in
May 1852, shortly before Sue returned from Baltimore. "The baby
is the chief character in the household," Sue told her brother Dwight
on January 10, 1853. "His disposition is pronounced like mine, but as
it sweetens under chastisement and discipline, I presume some other
scion will claim its likeness."

through was probably as bewildering to herself as it was to Austin, who was not so much the main object of her desire as a highly eligible means to an end, and whose masculine expectations for love and the begetting of children began to rouse Sue's latent sexual anxieties as the wedding time came closer.

Another turmoil was occupying Sue at this period, an undisclosed quandary that had great bearing on her feelings about Austin. It rose out of her visit to the Bartlett family, which she had welcomed as an escape from Amherst during the late winter of 1853. Mary Bartlett was frequently ill, and as early as 1851 had proposed through Julius that Sue Gilbert come to Ohio for the winter to help with the Bartlett household, but Sue had chosen schoolteaching in Baltimore instead, so she met Julius's sister and brother-in-law for the first time when she journeyed to New Hampshire for several weeks in March 1853. "Has it occurred to you that perhaps we shall not like each other," Sue wrote to Mary a month before going. "I *really* begin almost to *fear* meeting people I have never seen, but think I shall have *courage* for the encounter when it comes." As it turned out, she fell in love with them. Her letter thanking them called their home "one green spot in this great Sahara," and contained moving testimony that she had responded deeply to all of them.

> . . . But sincerely my dear Mary, I am really lonely to go back to you and it will be the work of weeks, to get possession of a contented spirit, and my old resigned temper of mind. I loved you and Mr. Bartlett, as I have no others save my own brothers and sisters, and if I live the years of Methuselah I never shall forget the sympathy and affection I found with you—and every night and morning I thank God for it, & ask Him to bless you more abundantly than *I* ever can conceive. There was something in the atmosphere of your home just suited to my life—something so kindly and gentle (laugh at me if you will) I can't think of you all without crying like a child.

Here were people with whom Sue could risk exposing her feelings ("laugh at me if you will"), and again and again she spoke of what their home meant to her. "Whenever the world goes wrong with me, and I feel much maltreated by its occupants I resolve to take the first train for M——, for somehow I fancy that a sort of refuge from the storms," she wrote in mid-October 1853, and the following spring, having visited a second time, she assured her friends, "Your home Mary is a genuine oasis to me—even the *thought* of it refreshes me." Theirs was a home such as Sue had dreamed of but never known, a warm and charming center "of all our laughs and frolics—of all the bright speeches," in short, the model for what her own home would later be at its best.*

She had found more than a home at Manchester, however, for her response to Mr. Bartlett was particularly overwhelming. Even while visiting there the first time, she spoke so coyly of him in a letter to Austin that the latter was piqued. "And now shall I say a word in reply for Mr. Bartlett to tease you about as he hands you [it] tomorrow noon," wrote Austin huffily, "& all 'through dinner' & for 'two hours' after." Once she was home in Amherst, a number of thinly veiled expressions of ardor for Mr. Bartlett entered her letters to New Hampshire. "Kiss Eddie [the Bartletts' baby] & tell him his Auntie Sue loves him," she ended her April 1853 thank-you letter, "and kiss Mr. Bartlett too, and tell him—tell him well—everything—that

---

* Intimate glimpses of the early life Sue created in the Evergreens came years later from her dear friend and former schoolmate Kate Scott Anthon, a frequent guest during the late 1850s. "Those happy visits at your house! Those celestial evenings in the Library. The blazing *wood* fire—*Emily*—*Austin*, the music—the rampant fun—the inextinguishable laughter, the uproarious spirits of our chosen, our most congenial circle. . . ." she wrote Sue in 1906. A decade later she wrote Martha Dickinson Bianchi of "the old blissful evenings at Austin's! Rare hours, full of merriment, brilliant wit, and inexhaustible laughter. . . . Your dear Mother also—so witty & intellectual, & uncommon in every way."

there is a big niche in my heart for him, and I shall always love him—and to write me a line in your letter."

Samuel Bartlett's special hold on her became evident in a letter Sue wrote sometime later that spring, when Mary Bartlett was away partaking of a cure. Sue thanked him for a sermon she had admired and had borrowed to copy; then shyly she begged him to correspond with her, even suggesting what face to put on it. "How I wish I could have a walk with you Mr. Bartlett, now & then. I need someone who knows a '*sight*' more than I do, to lead me along—to make me know much—to make me *better*—and I have no such friend here." The proposal of a tutor/student relationship, which builds upon Bartlett's gift to Sue of two books (Charlotte Brontë's *Villette* and a copy of Tennyson's poems) while she was in Manchester, suggests that Bartlett had stirred her intellect as well as her emotions, a potent combination for a young woman whose keen wit and intelligence until then had been exercised largely through her lively intimacy with Emily Dickinson.

While a literary friendship was quite appropriate, Sue may have fantasized more, as Mary's invalidism gave her ample opportunity to do. "If I was at my own disposal I should go right to you, and establish myself 'mistress' pro-tem," Sue wrote in the summer of 1853 as she sadly refused a new invitation to live with the Bartletts the forthcoming winter. Alas, Mattie had gone West, her plans "unfixed upon," and Hattie could not spare her from Amherst. In the same letter, Sue moved directly from sympathizing with Mary's poor health into sad thoughts about the death of her own sister Mary, perhaps another train of thought she sometimes followed in fancy where the Bartletts were concerned.

Sue's relationship with Samuel Bartlett is reminiscent of Emily Dickinson's important intellectual friendship with Benjamin Franklin Newton, which Sue would have known about because of Emily's agitation when Newton died in March 1853, the very week that Sue got home from Manchester. Sue's letters and messages to Bartlett suggest more intense devotion than Emily is known to have displayed for Newton, though comparison is precluded by lack of surviving correspondence from the Dickinson-Newton friendship. However, Sue's sending of "inexpressible love" to Samuel, her gratitude for his several letters and his lines tacked onto his wife's letters, her care not to write too often lest she weary him, and her consternation at reading in the newspaper of his being offered a professorship at Dartmouth ("I was afraid if you got up there it would be the annihilation of our further intimacy"), all suggest an attachment more matched in tone to the unrequited love of Emily's "Master" letters, drafted by the poet to an unidentified recipient about 1861. Perhaps Sue's ardor for Bartlett is the key to a mysterious note she sent to Emily in the autumn of 1861:

> *Private*   I have intended to write you Emily today but the quiet has not been mine. I send you this, lest I should seem to have turned away from a kiss.
>
> If you have suffered this past Summer I am sorry. . . . *I* Emily bear a sorrow that I never uncover. If a nightingale sings with her breast against a thorn, why not *we*? When I can, I shall write.

Sue's responsiveness to Rev. Samuel Bartlett is a curious counterpoint to the extraordinary burst of feeling Austin Dickinson was releasing upon her during the spring of 1853. Austin had courted Sue for over two and a half years when they became engaged, and for that long had disguised the passion he now made known. Until shortly before their clandestine meeting at the Revere Hotel in Boston, Austin and Sue's relationship would have been termed a good friendship, for not until a discussion under a certain Amherst oak tree a month or two before Austin entered Harvard in March 1853 did the two admit to loving one another. Several times in his drafts to Sue, Austin used nearly identical words to describe the "barrier" behind which he had hidden his inner self. Once, he mentioned how desperately afraid he had been that Sue wouldn't respond to his love. "Fear that I might fail to win you was an *awful* fear," he told her. His thoughts had been more "the thoughts of a victim of Delirium Tremens than like those of a well man." But in a moment of supreme courage under the village oak he risked all, and won. For Austin the result was a tremendous release of pent-up anxiety and emotion, though he always remained conscious of the severity of the handicaps he and Sue had overcome. "We have had mighty barriers to break down," he reminded her. "Pride—doubt—lives of constraint & grandness—distrust to overcome—*habitual* distrust—a great ideal to make real—a long dream to find *not* a dream."

The best description of Austin's relationship to Sue came out of an awkward situation with her sister Mattie, whom, it has been suggested, Austin also contemplated marrying, a notion based on his kindness and devotion to her and on a long, meandering, moody letter he wrote her in the spring of 1852. Martha was a year or more older than Sue, sweeter and far more retiring ("The truth is, it is a hard matter for me to go among strangers," she told Ned Hitchcock). The sisters were sometimes called twins, probably not so much for physical likeness as for their mutual circumstances at the Cutlers', their companionableness, and their appearance together dressed in black. Both were close friends of Austin and Emily, and Austin made a point of squiring both sisters when he was in town, and of writing to both when he was away, although he wrote more fully and more frequently to Sue.

There is ample evidence to suppose that Martha fell in love with Austin during the year Sue was in Baltimore and Austin taught school in Boston. Whenever he was home Austin called on Mat, or took her driving, and at one point he sent her a bracelet of beads from Boston. During his spring vacation in 1852, Austin attended a sugaring party in Sunderland with Mattie, Emily, and others, and following it wrote the aforementioned long letter, apparently in response to something Mattie asked explanation of. It cannot be ascertained from his long-winded discursiveness, however, whether it was about his general feelings, his feelings toward her, or his feelings about joining the church she had inquired. The letter reeks of the melodramatic overtones of a favorite romantic author the Amherst young people were enjoying at the time, Ik Marvel (Donald G. Mitchell), whose style seemed to assist Austin in expressing his thoughts; yet in the end the letter told Martha next to nothing except that Austin was "drifting on—I know not whither"—through moods that constantly changed from dark to bright and back again.

During the next eight months Austin's condition apparently became more controlled. Back in Amherst, free of the hated schoolteaching, he read law all through the fall of 1852 in his father's law office, in preparation for entering Harvard the following March. Toward the end of these same eight months, he broke through the guise of devotion to both Gilbert sisters to claim Sue under the village oak. Shortly after learning this, Mattie left Amherst, her plans "unfixed upon," in Sue's words, and spent the rest of her life in Geneva. The probability that she was disappointed by Austin's declaration of love for Sue rises out of her sudden, unexplained departure, a lengthy, apologetic letter Austin wrote to her four days after his Revere Hotel meeting with Sue, and the prolonged silence Mattie maintained toward all her Amherst friends throughout the winter and spring of 1853. Austin's letter to her, dated March 27, 1853, read:

> *This* Sunday evening is not going Dear Mattie, without my writing you & I wish before I begin I might look in upon your heart just one moment & see if you still love me—"as your own brother"—if you love me tonight. If I have not yet quite exhausted all your new affection for me—as well as your pa-

tience—by my so long silence—& if I have not made you believe
me almost indifferent to the precious words of your last two
letters. . . . There's nothing that you might *not* see now dear
Mattie—for that thing that's been hidden closest for years Ire
shown you—& you^{re} not shrunk from the sight. . . . Heaven
bless you Mattie for those kind . . . words that told me you were
glad I loved Sue & she loves me. Yes, Mattie, we *do* love each
other—with a strength & a passion—unless you have sometime
felt its power—mightier than you can guess. . . .

It seems strange to me, too—does^{nt} it to you, Mattie—
that just such characters should have chosen each other to love,
that two so tall, proud, stiff people, so easily miffed, so apt to
be pert, two that could . . . stand under the "oak tree" just at
the setting of a glorious Sunday's sun & speak words—& look,
look, so cold—so bitter, as hardly the deepest hatred could have
prompted a pair as would the guiltiest wretch—& his most
wronged victim—that two who could love so well, or hate so
well—that two just such *could* not choose but love each other!—
but we *could not* Mattie.

We have loved each other a *long time*—longer than either
has guessed, but we were too proud to confess it. How we at
last broke down, I hardly know. . . . Forgive me now Mattie will
you for not writing you before. It is not because I have not
thought of you—nor because I do not love you. I *do* love you
Mattie—just as well as Emily and Vinnie . . . & you all enter
into all Sue's & my plans for the future.

If Mattie was in love with Austin, this letter must have
come close to killing her, for though Austin apologized in a
roundabout way for disguising his love for Sue, and emphasized
the brotherly nature of his affection for her, he accepted with
obvious relief her blessing on what had been achieved to some
degree at her expense. Perhaps it's not surprising that Mattie
made no answer, even after Austin wrote her twice more
inquiring about her silence. Aside from her muteness through
the spring, however, there are no signs of rupture with Sue,
so if Martha was hurt no one knew it.

If Austin long lacked courage to confess his love for Sue, Sue also had enormous trouble revealing her true feelings. Once Austin had written her, "It is a queer thing in you Sue, that the undercurrent of your feelings so clearly discernible in all your notes is never apparent in your conversation." That crucial clue to Sue, that in conversation, in the social self she presented to the world, she disguised and drew attention away from her real feelings as instinctively as a female field bird creates diversion from her defenseless chicks, was a defense of childhood, a habit grown out of her need to protect herself against fears or a sense of weakness. Yet it often led to misunderstandings with those who cared about her intensely. So hidden were her true responses, apparently, that they only appeared in what Austin termed the "undercurrent," or subliminal messages and associations of her letters.

Sue herself accounted for her "stately indifference" as distrust of anyone outside her own family. "I thank you for confiding in me," Austin wrote her in Baltimore, "so far as to tell me freely that you had no confidence in me, or anybody else, not connected to you by 'natural ties.' I am only sorry that I could not have been so excepted from that general distrust." It is hard to know whether the difference between Sue's slow acceptance of the home and friendships offered her in Amherst by the Dickinsons and the alacrity of her response to the Bartletts lies in the fact that the Bartletts were "family," related through Mary Gilbert's marriage, or is a measure of the importance to Sue of getting away from the village that sustained her distrust and low self-esteem.

Austin wasn't the only Dickinson wooing Sue. His attraction to her was strongly reinforced by the regard of his sister Emily and his father, the Honorable Edward Dickinson, both of whom participated in drawing Sue into the family. Emily was quite literally in love with her, as her letters of 1851–52, when Sue was in Baltimore, clearly attest. Sue had gone South just as impulsively and willfully as a couple of months earlier she had gone to New York to hear Jenny Lind, leaving Emily dazzled by her independence and made so lonely by her sudden departure and the rupture of their friendship that she did not write to Sue for many weeks. Withdrawal, the only defense Emily ever took against Sue (though it always dissolved at the merest approach to contriteness on Sue's part), was the attitude of a wounded lover, and Emily's letters to "dear Susie," whose kisses and comfort she sorely missed, were unmistakably love letters, more persistently and lyrically romantic than what she was writing to other friends, although they did not far exceed the nineteenth-century tolerance for intimacy between unmarried females.

Emily wrote love letters of another kind to Austin—delightful, warm, witty, playful, yet challenging weekly expositions that interpreted life (especially life with Father) to Austin, and were light and air to the homesick young man in Boston, spinning a sustaining web of devotion and interdependence between brother and sister. Austin and Sue seem to have been for Emily larger aspects of her own personality, projections of the small, restricted Emily, who felt bravest and most powerful staying at home to explore the world. In retrospect, the three together—Austin, Sue, and Emily—were a triumvirate, united at this period by inexplicable bonds of Emily's forging and seemingly tuned to some special inner frequency that even the pretty, social Vinnie and the shy, retiring Mattie, who circulated through their field, were not sensitive to. Austin and Sue were Emily's Elect.

Edward Dickinson, however, was probably the stronger if more subtle force in Sue and Austin's cleaving. He displayed unusual interest in Sue from the time they joined the church together in August 1850, a process which had been extremely difficult for him. Remote from his feelings and suspect of emotion, Squire Dickinson apparently approached the process rationally, as he did other experiences of his life, including raising his children. An incident recounted about him was that the pastor of First Church had had to chide him for trying to "come to Christ as a *lawyer*," rather than as a sinner, on his knees. Edward Dickinson so pronouncedly "leaned away from his emotions," in Emily's phrase, that occasions when he was affectively touched were momentous to him, and quite apparent to others. His conversion in 1850 had been such an instance. "I am even while I write, melted to tears at the remembrance of what we saw and felt at the working of God's spirit among us," Edward admitted to the Reverend Mr. Colton several years afterward. Emily was astounded on a subsequent occasion at her father's reaction to the July 1851 P. T. Barnum performance in which Jenny Lind sang in Northampton. "Father sat all the evening looking *mad*, and *silly*, and yet so much amused you would have *died* a-laughing." Oddly roused and confounded by his rare exposure to entertainment, he displayed a peculiar, alien embarrassment, "as if old Abraham had come to see the show, and thought it was all very well, but a little excess of *Monkey*!"

The percipient young members of his family were no less aware, then, when their father showed unaccustomed partiality for Susan Gilbert, who in her mourning attire had joined the penitents among whom he knelt. Sympathy for Sue's loss of her sister would have been felt by all in the close, unbroken Dickinson family, but her brave coping with the irrationality of death may have especially moved Edward Dickinson during his own moment of emotional susceptibility.* There is no

---

* Although Edward Dickinson's reaction to death is not known, evidence that the experience was extremely difficult for Emily and Austin makes reasonable the suspicion that it could have been momentous for their father as well. For Emily death was the "flood subject," which she explored in poem after poem with near-clinical analysis of the symptoms, emotions, and mysteries surrounding dying. Despite her efforts at comprehension, she was deeply afflicted in her fifties by the deaths of several loved ones, and her nephew Gib's death in 1883 was so debilitating, it has been mentioned as a contributing factor to her own

indication that he ever escorted another of Austin's, Emily's, or Vinnie's friends to and from their home, as he now began to do sometimes with Sue. In fact, other of their friends feared the austere squire, whereas Sue did not. Once, Mattie Gilbert jumped behind a door to avoid an encounter with him. But Sue was different. "I think Father feels that she appreciates him, better than most anybody else," reported Emily to Austin with just a trace of envy.

Edward Dickinson was intimidating. He was the leading lawyer in town, treasurer of the college, a former state legislator and member of the Governor's Council, a prominent Whig, and leader of the local Temperance Society. In 1853 he was elected to Congress for two years, and he was up to his ears in bringing the railroad to Amherst. His high moral purpose and attentiveness to duty, as familiar to urchins in the street as his stern manner and upright, black-coated figure, culminated in an egocentricity that welded the interests of the town inextricably to his own personality, causing the editor of the Northampton *Free Press* once to complain, "*Amherst*, in the mind of the chairman [of the Amherst Railroad Committee], seems to be the *hugest* and most important location on the map of the universe."

Inevitably aware and admiring of these things, Sue's eye

---

fatal illness. Austin apparently was immobilized by death, as noted on several occasions. "Austin is chilled—by Frazar's murder," Emily put it when the Stearns youth was killed at New Berne in 1862. Austin's reported behavior at the deaths of his father, his son, and his sister bears out the impression that he was close to paralysis at such times. It was Vinnie, surprisingly, who managed the family funerals with some finesse, tending to details and worrying about others, while her brother could scarcely function and her sister shut herself away in her room. Ironically, Austin was often asked to manage funerals for bereaved friends in Amherst, and probably undertook the task with difficulty. Neighbor Franklin Jameson's diary contains the July 1884 comment: "I was amazed at Mr. Dickinson's mismanagement [of Mrs. Professor Burgess's funeral], which left me in the predicament of appearing superfluous [as a bearer]."

was also caught by something else about Edward Dickinson, if one heeds her essay on Amherst at mid-century. "Luke Sweetser, Edward Dickinson and Seth Nims were invariably owners of the finest horses in the county, and one would always note the style of the two latter, as they drove through the village streets at any time sitting very erect, reins taut, and the high showy heads of their steeds refusing the senseless check or a careless hand. I never failed to turn and look after these horsemen, whenever they passed me in the street." What Sue seems to have noticed and apparently "appreciated better than most anybody else" was Edward Dickinson's hidden pride, visible to her through chinks in the fierce injunctions of conscience he wore so conspicuously, in maintaining handsome horses and a well-kept, well-driven equipage.

If she didn't know instinctively that she pleased her father-in-law-to-be, Austin assured her so in a letter of late 1853 or early 1854. "Father admired you a long time—almost ever since you came to Amherst to live. I know he'll be proud of you when we are married . . . for I believe father, Sue, is just as well satisfied in his secret heart that you are saving yourself for Austin, that you are to be the life companion & foil of the boy in whom he has watched so long & with so fond an eye—& in which centered so much of his love—& his hope— that you are to be my wife & his new child—just as well convinced of it as if we had told him." Austin was happy that Sue and his father liked each other, for he was highly aware of the hopes his father had invested in him, and cared very much about pleasing him. Still, he could scarcely have been more satisfied than Sue herself to be pleasing a father of the caliber of Edward Dickinson. She must have expressed her feelings on the matter right away, for in a letter Austin wrote her shortly after they became secretly engaged he spoke of his delight "that you are glad you are to call the 'dear name of father again on earth'—& that name you are to call *my* father— & that he will be *our* father."

In his letter to Mattie of late March 1853, Austin had blamed the pride that was a feature of both his and Sue's personalities for being the chief impediment in their courtship. He depicted a pair of lovers who could "love so well, or hate so well," locked like two warriors in a power struggle, one yielding only when the other did. Harriet Cutler may have had some sense of this when she predicted to Sue, "You & Austin will have a falling out by & by—& then if you ever do it will be an awful one." If one sorts through the scores of Austin's pencilings to Sue, it becomes apparent that his pride was the stronghold of his manliness, incorporating his notions of manhood as well as his father's expectations of him. If at times he was superior and oversensitive, so that Emily spoke of "that 'pinnacle' on which you always mount, when anybody insults you," he undoubtedly suffered from anxiety at his father's too high hopes, as well as conceit from the devotion lavished on him by adoring members of his family. To his credit, and largely out of his appreciation for Emily, Austin had considerable respect for the less rational side of himself that was loosed by what he called the "breaking down" of pride. Although he didn't always understand his feelings and emotions, so that he floundered in trying to describe them, he did not make the error of pushing what seemed senseless or soft out of his life, as his father had done, nor did he undervalue it, as Sue did.

Sue's pride was differently seated. Her experience as the youngest and most helpless of four females had been that women suffered for being weak, for being dependent, and she had come to despise qualities associated with "womanliness," holding herself proudly apart from them. Austin recognized that she was proud, and assumed, therefore, that she was like him. In the very beginning of their courtship, in fact, he had laid on her doorstep, albeit in fun, his unsigned, carefully penned version of the Narcissus myth, in which she appeared "a *pure, transparent soul,* wherein he beheld his *spirit-image* mirrored to the life, and *for* it he like the youth of old, was fired with love." At the outset, then, Austin idealized Sue as the feminine aspect of himself (although Emily was the truer candidate), and as their romance developed, perhaps sensing her basic espousal of masculine values, he persisted in believing that they saw as one, felt as one, loved as one, "as if we are almost but one person or at least exact counterparts so entirely are all our minutest, most fleeting, even yet *formless* longings disclosed to each of us in the other." By clinging to this vision of Sue as the woman in whom every facet of his own being was matched, Austin doomed himself to enormous torment, from which he began to suffer right away, later referring to his first term at Harvard as "those five months of hope & fears & doubts —those months I never wish back again."

Much as she envied his masculine opportunities, Sue was scarcely like Austin at all, so that almost anything she said or did aside from echoing his sentiments threw him into spasms of gloom. If she raised a question, responded too coolly, had an independent notion, or even if her letter was delivered late, Austin was disconcerted in a manner that couldn't have encouraged her to face him with more substantial issues. So acute was his sensitivity to criticism that he easily overreacted to Sue, who must soon have discovered that her lover seemed able to tolerate only steadfast devotion, such as he got from home. Austin's drafts indicate that he either grew sarcastic ("My last note didn't seem quite as affectionate as you all day thought it would? *didn't* it Sue? I'm *really* sorry") or, as his love intensified, became distraught when she spoke of doubts, as inevitably she must have, since she was struggling with many conflicting feelings. On one hand, Austin encouraged her to share her inmost concerns ("You are not 'weak' nor 'too womanly' in the sweet demands of your love," he once assured her, echoing her own words of distaste for such self-indulgence), but he also did his best to overcome anything that troubled her with protestations of love, so that her own tendency to bury anxieties must have been reinforced.

At one point during his second year in Cambridge, Austin dwelt on three themes of a letter he had just received from Sue.

I could take [your] first (sentence) & tell you how I want to see you too & how impatient I am for the time to come when I may— or the second—& tell you that I too think of *death*, but hardly with fear—hardly shrinkingly for there *is* no death—only a name—only a change common to all. . . . Death has but little terror for me. Love robs it of its sting, & I *am loved*—what more can earth give me? & how few have been given this? Or I could take the third—your thoughts of "your earlier childhood days before you were a woman" and that they will never come again. . . . I love the past & love to dwell in it . . . but I love the present too, & I love the future. Life is *all* beautiful to me with you to love me. . . .

The sensitive flow of Sue's thoughts from anticipation of seeing her lover, to fearsome thoughts of death and the swift-following realization that she could not retreat to childhood but had to become a woman, is drowned by Austin's overpowering insistence that love and marriage were the solution rather than the source of all such anxieties.

Austin appeared to possess the acute sensitivity needed to encourage Sue to bring her hidden, self-denigrating fears into fuller light, but actually, while he passionately believed she was the center of all his concern and tenderness, his attention was focused upon himself. In truth he was so full of himself he may have had little awareness of her feelings except as they threatened him. Several things suggest that this was so. First, it is a matter of some wonder that Austin, who in the face of frequent mention that he was pressed for time, should have written his thoughts and feelings for Sue out on scrap paper first, taking care to cross out and rewrite long ponderings that centered, curiously enough, less upon her than on himself and his own ever-fluctuating moods. In addition, he told her he had "been brought up to the idea that it was not a man's part to *show* anyone a tenderness unless in sore distress," a remark that is a leading clue to what he was about, for although he made it in reference to the demonstration of affection toward his sisters, "anyone" presumably included himself. Over the years, following his father's example, Austin had applied manly restraint from tenderness most stringently of all to himself. Yet he had desperate need for tenderness, especially when he was away from home.* Emily was able and willing to provide it, and this was the key to Austin's lifelong devotion to her, but she was his sister, so it was through Sue, his promised wife, that he now both sought tenderness and felt license to provide it for himself. "I have never *before* received *any* from any*body* —I never *would*," he told Sue. "You have shown it to me & I have received it from you—toward no other have I ever felt tenderness, & from no other would I *have* it—but what *you* have given me has bound me to you more closely than you know."

Giving way to tenderness involved for him, he told Sue more than once, a breaking down of barriers to the heart, and such breakdown, so long denied by his code of manliness, apparently inspired enough emotional confusion that he wrote his thoughts out to clarify them before sending a neat copy to Sue. The drafting process enabled him, at the same time, to keep his expressions of tenderness for himself, to quite literally pile them up on his writing table where he could see them, and

---

* Austin's homesickness, verging on depression, shows clearly in his drafts to Sue Gilbert during the years he was away teaching or attending school. Instead of making new friends, he seems everlastingly turned toward Amherst. It was an attitude both his father and grandfather expressed or exhibited in their behavior; the former only endured his Boston and Washington legislative responsibilities through his coercive sense of duty, and the latter declined into nervous breakdown and death after leaving Amherst to begin a new life in Ohio in his late fifties.

even reread them if he chose. Sue, who most certainly was "bound to Austin more closely than she knew," not only made permissible Austin's expression of his emotions, she was his appointed sounding board for tenderness toward himself. What he gave her he anticipated getting back. In moments of despair Austin feared Sue might feel she was sacrificing herself to this appointed role, might not want it or would not be made happy by it, and then he suffered agonies. "I would die today, rather than have you bound to me if I could not myself believe I was not [*sic*] the supreme object of your earthly love." Even here, however, his real concern was for himself rather than for any doubts she might be suffering, and his long emotive essays devoted to describing his love and anticipating the joy to come when they would be "one" seem oddly detached from anything real or tangible about Sue.

Part of Austin's avoidance of any reference to Sue's physical being may have been caution at arousing her fears of physical love. Among his scraps is part of a letter, apparently an early one, that euphemistically apologized and took blame for some manner of expressing love that wasn't "just up to your ideal." He desired to proceed slowly, he emphasized, to sit by Sue, hands clasped, her head on his shoulder, sharing fears and doubts "like loving, confiding *children*—as we all really are," rather than display "a little excess in [some things] that I am not quite sure will please you." How reassuring this was to Sue can't be ascertained, but a draft that appears to be of a later date tackles the subject again more directly.

Is there anything in the man relation or wife that [still] gives you sometimes gloomy thoughts—and if there is can I not say . . . that you may live just exactly as you are happiest at living, just as free from care or responsibility to me as you please—just like a girl always if so you are happiest—that I will ask nothing of you, take nothing from you, you are not the happier in giving me. . . . Don't ever be discouraged, Sue, by thinking of "a man's requirements." I ask nothing but your love—just the love you are

giving me now—& I offer in return all I am . . . without qualifications.

By late autumn 1853, Sue was quietly mentioning to a few
people close to her her plans to marry Austin, although the
Dickinson parents still apparently hadn't been told. Early in
the new year, however, in a letter of January 1854 to her
brother Frank, Sue discussed the matter in such a subdued,
unenthusiastic manner that her words contrast markedly with
the passion and commitment of Austin's letters, and may
represent an apathy Austin was encountering in his bride-to-be:

> Hattie takes care of baby—knits his stockings—makes his
> dresses—supervises his little body generally. As for me, I *sew*—
> make all the pies and cake—sweep and dust—do errands—try
> a little to make others happy—am rather useful—rather orna-
> mental, rather superfluous. Why don't you write to me Frank
> and congratulate me, that I have found someone who is going,
> by and by, to encumber himself with me? . . . I have wanted
> very much to know how you were looking on this new phase of
> my life—how, from what you know of *Austin*, you are pleased
> with my choice for I have no one else in this wide world to please,
> but you and Dwight. With *your* full approbation I am satisfied,
> no one else's opinion is cared for, a moment. I see no reason, view-
> ing the subject as I try to, without prejudice, why you won't
> like Austin and find in him all you could desire as the companion
> of your sister. He is poor and young and in the *world's* eyes
> these are great weaknesses—but he is strong, manly, resolute—
> understands human nature and will take care of me. He has not
> decided yet where to settle in business, so the where and when
> of our future home is uncertain but we shall have a cozy place
> some-where, where the long-cherished wish of my heart to have
> a home where my brothers and sisters can come, will be realized.
> I have no *extravagant* ideas of life. I expect to forego a great
> many enjoyments that wealth could procure, and that no one
> loves more than I—but I can do it very cheerfully and happily
> if the man I love well enough to marry is unable to give them
> to me. . . . I never have told [William Cutler] of my engage-

ment, and I *think* Hattie has not—and as I probably should receive no sympathy from him, I don't choose to tell him.

While Sue's motive for not telling Mr. Cutler her news
is understandable, her pleasure in such a small triumph suggests the incipient vindictiveness that accompanied her improving status. Those in Amherst who had looked down upon
her, those detractors personified by her brother-in-law, would
be properly snubbed, a satisfaction that seems to have played
some small part in things.

Sewing industriously on her trousseau through the fall
of 1853, the winter of 1854, and on into the spring, Sue still
thought of her wedding as a distant event. Her usual winter
restlessness, undoubtedly compounded by an unsettled state of
mind toward marrying, and possibly by romantic longings for
Samuel Bartlett, appears to have created merciless inner
turmoil, for which travel, for once, wasn't the cure. During the
fall of 1853, Dwight and Mattie had come East and taken Sue
with them to the World's Fair in New York. Surprisingly, she
didn't much enjoy the excursion. "I can't bear sightseeing . . ."
she told the Bartletts. "Don't think I am a fool—please understand I am a *very* intelligent young woman—only not given to
admiration 'of the works of men's hands.' " In January 1854
Julius Learned paid the Cutlers a welcome visit. With little
effort he talked Sue into joining him in Manchester for a visit
of about ten days to his sister; then he stopped back again in
February for another week at the Cutlers'. Sue thoroughly
enjoyed her second visit with the Bartletts, and her description
for them of her return to Amherst suggests her maverick state
of mind.

I suppose you are waiting with intense anxiety my dear
friends to know the result of my nocturnal departure from your
mansion. . . . I was suddenly roused [in the train] by a tap on
my shoulder from a gentleman behind me followed by the inquiry, if 'I was just from the *ball* at "Concord" '—as if it were not

bad enough to travel in the dark o' mornings, without being suspected of a night of revelry. I stared an astonished *no*, for I always pride myself on my puritanical exterior and was disgusted
that anyone should have mistaken me for a ball-room character.
Then he begged the liberty of showing me a little [mechanical]
bird about half an inch long. . . . In spite of my repellent dignity,
the old gentleman continued his attentions, wiping my window
with his gloves, that my prospect need not be obscured, looking
after my luggage at the station, and upon ascertaining from my
appearance that I was very faint, opened the window, insisted
upon taking me to the door, bought apples and cake, found out
where my home was etc. etc. . . . I was obliged to wait three or
four hours, at Palmer, as our morning train had left, and after
some deliberation as to the *propriety*, I went to the hotel and
dined with a table full of gentlemen who were evidently much
amused and perplexed at my *aloneness* and destination—but I
ate in silence and passed no doubt for a "strong-minded American
woman." With the aid of a *friend* [Austin] I reached home
safely. . . .

There are clues that Sue may have conceived some idea
of marrying Julius Learned. From her point of view it would
have been a good match. Julius already had a child, he was
sympathetic to the dangers of childbearing, and he provided
entrance into the beloved Bartlett family. Julius was prosper-
ing at Chicago, where Dwight Gilbert had set him up in the
lumber-brokering business, and his enthusiasm for that city
enticed Sue and Austin both to want to look at it as a possibility
for practicing law. By April Sue had plans to visit Mattie in
Geneva all summer, then in the fall go West to Frank and
Dwight in Michigan, and Julius in Chicago. She daringly
schemed that Austin would accompany her from Geneva.

But Austin wanted to be married in the fall. After finishing Harvard in June, he planned to take the bar examination
right away, make the trip to Chicago, have "a plain frank talk
with father" about where to set up practice, and then, in late
autumn of 1854, marry Sue. When she protested she could not

be ready, he persisted. "The 'year from next Fall' seems *pretty distant*," he wrote. "I don't quite know about it. I am sorry we are not anticipating a day less remote—*next* Fall—for I don't believe we can ever be happy again till we can no longer be separated." And again he pressed:

> I love you dearest with so fond a love—& so rare a love— and life is so short, and even tomorrow so uncertain. I cannot look forward through two long years more before we have begun under the same roof to meet together the beauties & the duties of God's richest earthly blessing—*married love.*
>
> Did you tell me Sue, you were ready whenever I could be. Will you be ready next Thanksgiving evening, if I can be? As, if I am well, I believe now I can be?

Sue may have acquiesced, for she did not start for Geneva in June as intended. But no sooner had Austin finished at Cambridge, passed the bar, and returned to Amherst in July than Susan succumbed to a serious "nervous fever" that lasted several weeks and required the services of a nurse. Her illness angered William Cutler, who was convinced she had courted disease to cause him trouble and expense. In early August, still weak, Sue left his home, with Harriet in tears behind the blinds, to make a recuperative visit to Mattie and Aunt Sophia. "I believe Hattie and Mr. Cutler think I made myself sick sewing," Sue wrote defensively to Dwight, "but I know I did not. Imprudence in other respects was the immediate cause doubtless but I have felt for a year that I was not well and whether careless or not I should have been sick. I am not willing to be censured in the matter because I know it is undeserved."

By September 1854 she continued to make good her escape, writing Dwight of her plans to go to Chicago under Austin's escort in early October, then on to visit Dwight in Grand Haven. "I suppose it will be necessary for me to return to Amherst the latter part of the Winter," she reported in resigned tones, "as Austin *now* expects our marriage to take place the following Fall [1855] and I shall need the time for preparation. I have spoken of the plan to no one but you and Hattie because all earthly plans are so *mutable*. . . . I have always felt so like a *child* the idea of really being married seems absurd enough and if the event ever occurs I think I shall experience a feeling of odd surprise."

No more of Austin's courtship letters to Sue remain, so there are no clues as to why his journey to Chicago was delayed until late December. Sue undertook her autumn trip alone, telegraphing Julius to meet her in Detroit and accompany her to Grand Haven. At Frank's home she met four-year-old Minnie, the child of Julius and Mary, and was delighted to find her as high-spirited and strong-willed as her beloved dead sister. Very like herself, in fact. Sue's affinity for the little girl seemed to release old and strongly guarded feelings. "I tell you, Dwight," she wrote her brother, "when a child's mother dies, it is a misfortune incalculable—my heart always aches for every such one."

Julius had some surprising news—first that Mary Bartlett had given birth to a daughter. Apparently unaware that Mary had even been pregnant, Sue badly concealed her displeasure at an event that may have shaken some of her fancies.

Grand Haven
Monday, Dec. 5

My dear Mary,

Great business I think, to have a feminine accession to the family at the Parsonage and not apprize Aunt Sue formally. I have half a mind not to write you a word and forswear all love for the very juvenile Miss. If I was a witch I do believe I'd glide through the keyhole this minute and pinch her nose with my invisible fingers, for her Mother's misdemeanors—bad woman. I stood aghast with astonishment, when Julius informed me. . . .

Then, when she went on to Chicago over the Christmas holidays, while Austin was in the city, Sue found that Julius was interested in a young woman whom Sue took an instant dislike to. Although Julius told Sue "he should never marry her," when he did just that the following summer, in 1855, Susan reacted as if she had been betrayed. Julius wanted to bring his wife East during August to attend his college reunion, but Sue let him know she would not receive the new Mrs. Learned at the Cutlers', and forced Julius to leave his bride with friends in nearby Lebanon, New Hampshire, while he came to Amherst alone. This odd incident seems to have interfered with Sue's relationship with the Bartlett family, for only a single letter, of a year later, remains in their correspondence, after one in which Sue lamely tried to explain to her Manchester friends her unreasonable attitude toward Julius's remarriage.

Despite its setbacks, Sue's journey West was not in vain. "[Dwight] thinks all the world of her & is disposed to let her do pretty much as she pleases now till she gets married," Julius informed his sister as Sue returned to Amherst in February 1855. That spring her brother's admiration materialized in a pre-wedding gift of five thousand dollars, and a short time later Frank also paid an old joking bet between himself and Sue by buying her fifty books of her choice. Joy at these windfalls poured into a long, blissful letter of thanks, in which Sue revealed that still another dream was coming true as well. Edward Dickinson was providing the bride and groom with their own home.

One day has passed since the reception of your letter and I almost feel this morning as if I could *never* answer it—not for lack of feeling, but rather of expressions. You must know that such a generous present would quite melt my heart and dizzy my brain and in such a state what can one say. The tears have hardly been out of my eyes since the letter came not alone for the pleasure of being the executive of five thousand dollars but also, the love and kindness that prompted the gift. . . .

Austin's plans are now definite, as he is writing you—tho' they have resulted very differently from our previously formed expectations, we are both happy in them, and hope they may strike you as pleasantly. Austin's father has over-ruled all objections to our remaining here and tho' it has been something of a sacrifice for Austin's spirit and rather of a struggle with his pre-conceived ideas, I feel satisfied that in the end it will be best and he will be fully rewarded for his filial regard. He goes into partnership on even terms with his Father, the first of June. Mr. Dickinson is fitting up the Mack house [originally the Dickinson Homestead] very handsomely for himself, and in the course of the Summer Austin will have a pleasant house in process of erection on the lot just west of that place. For the sake of going at once into our own home all complete, we have decided to defer our marriage till another Spring and *that* will give me no more time than I shall need, to prepare for housekeeping. As soon as Austin's house plan is regularly drawn, I will send it to you. It will not be a great castle, but when we get it all fixed, if you don't say it is pleasant and perfect, then I am mistaken. Won't I be proud to get you an oyster supper some cold night? Don't speak of it—it makes me too happy. Oh my brothers if you knew, or *could* know the happiness you have given me, you would feel repaid for all your years of toil and business. . . . I believe I know what *life* is—and even now, my joyous anticipations are chastened by the recollections of changes and sorrow in the past, that Time may soften, but never efface. . . .

Sue was supremely happy. Her fondest ambitions had been realized, and she had even managed to put her wedding off again, though she recognized now that that event, with its dread handmaidens, "changes and sorrow," was inevitable. Construction of the Evergreens (the first "named" house in town) began in late October 1855, about the time the E. & A. Dickinson law partnership was announced, and just as the Edward Dickinson family moved from Pleasant Street back to the renovated Dickinson Homestead, where Edward and all his children had been born. In Sue's mind there was only one more hurdle.

She had broached Austin's becoming a Christian so often

it was a sore subject. In his courtship letters Austin had "mounted his pinnacle," had tried reason and reasonableness, had resorted to sarcasm and despair, but Sue remained adamant. On the Sabbath evening of January 6, 1856, therefore, Austin read his confession of faith to the congregation of First Church. He revealed little of his inner conversion. In a rambling style reminiscent of his say-nothing letter to Mattie Gilbert of 1853, Austin came to Christ as much the lawyer as his father had, rising "as a witness recalled to the stand to state if I have any change to make in the evidence he has before given in the case in hearing." Change had occurred, Austin testified, and so recently that "my own voice indeed as I speak almost startles me. It seems as if it could *hardly be* mine—as though some other must be speaking in me—so new is the faith & experience with which it *goes* laden from me—so new is the testimony with which it is filled to the power & goodness, the constant & limitless love of our common father." That such change could have occurred in *him*, Austin argued, was sufficient proof of God's existence.

As the wedding time drew near, Sue made one more sudden move. Quite unexpectedly, in May 1856, she departed for Geneva and made new arrangements to be married in Aunt Sophia's home. "For reasons I cannot explain," she wrote Samuel Bartlett, subtly relieving him of his long-ago promise to officiate at her wedding in Amherst, "both for prudence and prolixity, it was advisable and almost an inevitable plan." The prudence in fact may have had something to do with her deteriorated friendship with the Bartletts, for in this last letter of their correspondence Sue told them, "I have felt lately that a cloud had passed over our affection—a little shadow—I wish it were not so, perhaps it is not."

On the evening of July 1, 1856, Sue and Austin were married at Oak Grove, the Van Vranken home, with all the Gilbert family present, but no Dickinsons or other Amherst friends save the minister, Professor Haven of the Amherst

College faculty. In Sue's words, it was "the millionth wedding since the world began." Years later Austin told Mabel that he "felt as if he were going to his own execution" on his wedding day. If, as he also told her, he soon found himself "woefully mistaken" in his illusions about Sue, it wouldn't have been because he was insensible, after three years of waiting, to his bride's reluctance, but only because he still cherished the hope that his love could overcome Sue's fears of matrimony.

From its outwardly auspicious but inwardly disquieting start, the marriage lasted twenty-six years, until Mabel Loomis Todd began recording in her journal and diaries her extraordinary friendship with Austin Dickinson. What happened to the union in the interim is not fully known. The wealth of information that describes the shape and direction of Sue and Austin's life together suggests little of its quality. With the exception of some letters to their friend Samuel Bowles, editor of the *Springfield Republican*, few indications remain of Sue's and Austin's sympathies for each other during the quarter century until the blossoming of the affair between Mabel and Austin suddenly served notice that in Austin's eyes his marriage to Sue was a failure. As his well-articulated feelings for her developed, Mabel came to believe strongly that "Austin has had a life which for bitter pain and disappointment can hardly be equalled by any man living."

Her journal contains in some half dozen entries written between 1883 and 1889 the gleanings of conversations in which Austin spoke directly of his disappointment in Sue, although he was loath to dwell on the dark side of his twenty-six-year experience, and could not bring himself to put into writing (as Mabel urged him to do, for her protection) the counts on which he held Sue destructive of their union. Nor would he abandon Sue and start a new life elsewhere, a risky venture Mabel was prepared to undertake. "He & his wife have not been in the least happy together," Mabel recorded shortly after the Rubicon, "although for the sake of appearances & the children, they have continued to live together." Out of charity, Austin might have preferred to leave the issue right there. What good did it do, he parried more than once, to rehearse the past when the opportunity for joy was at hand? But Mabel, much younger, less experienced, less philosophical, and intensely in love, needed a strong case to justify her radical departure from convention and to defend herself against Sue's anger and hatred, which she quickly became the target of. For her this was only the start of the argument, and over the years she enumerated the counts on which Sue was to be condemned outright. Occasionally she misconstrued what Austin told her,* but nevertheless she reported it verbatim, with a sense of shock that ensures its integrity. Austin had been made unhappy by Sue's lack of interest in sexual intimacy, by her "morbid dread of having any children," by her indulgence in acts "morally certain to do worse than alienate him from her," and by her ungoverned temper. Most startling to Mabel was the information that three or four times in the early years Sue had had babies "artificially removed," while the effort to "get rid of Ned" was so sustained that "he has always been a miserable

---

* Contrary to Mabel's conclusion, Austin's real disappointment was Sue's ambivalence toward having children, not her bearing of inferior ones. And though Mabel portrayed Austin as holding strong class feelings about Sue's "commonness," such notions rose out of her own snobbery and her lack of familiarity with earlier Amherst society, for until the changes and population influxes that followed the Civil War, the single social stratum of the village was undifferentiated. Sue not only wasn't of another social class, she was considered by her friends quite "uncommon." But Sue *was* caught out by another standard—the pervasive morality of the community. Her personal qualifications at first seemed worthy of the Dickinson measure, but as some inherent ruthlessness emerged in her nature, and her social aggrandizements became offensive to others, her father's transgressions were resurrected and held against her.

invalid, and with a decided lack of intellectual strength as well." These journal statements must be distinguished from comments Mabel made near the end of her life in a self-serving reminiscence entitled *Scurrilous but True*, which is far from reliable.* By then Mabel had suffered many years of Sue's vindictiveness, against which Austin left her oddly unprotected when he died, and she was unable to accept that Austin had ever loved Sue, or that there could have been anything in Sue worth loving.

It is doubtful that, after twenty-five years, Sue looked upon her marriage as a failure. More likely she viewed the very matters that alienated Austin as fearful challenges she had met and overcome. If she was sexually frigid in the beginning, she learned to tolerate some degree of intimacy and tenderness, for Austin's charges of physical inaccessibility were leveled at early, rather than later, behavior. In like manner, she braved her "morbid dread of having children" to have three—Ned in 1861, Mattie in 1866, and Gilbert in 1875. Nor is there mention of further abortions after Ned's birth.† In 1893 Sue wrote a long

---

* *Scurrilous but True* is the compilation of three typescripts drafted by Millicent Todd Bingham after conversations with her mother in 1932, edited by Mabel. The typescripts were preliminary exercises for *Ancestors' Brocades*, Bingham's account of her mother's role in publishing Emily Dickinson's poems and letters; they appear synthesized in Appendix II of Richard Sewall's *Life of Emily Dickinson*, Vol. 1.

† Mabel Todd's indignation over Sue's early recourses to abortion is rather curious, for Mabel herself took belladonna, morphine, and sitz baths on first suspecting she was pregnant with Millicent, actions far less free of impunity in 1879 than when Susan took her steps a quarter century earlier. Studies indicate that in the middle of the nineteenth century abortion was commonly practiced by married American-born women as one of the few practical ways of delaying or controlling the size of their family (see James Mohr, *Abortion in America*, Oxford, 1978). Not only were various readily available remedies for "women's problems" euphemistically advertised in the popular press, but doctors (presumably including the Springfield physician Sue was known to have consulted) hadn't the moral qualms or legal restrictions that developed a few decades later to deter them from performing the

essay (a "little journal," she called it) entitled "Annals of the Evergreens,"* which recapitulated the brightest moments of her marriage. Her memory for color, gesture, flavor, smell, sound, and temperature reveals Sue to have been a lively sensualist, providing at the Evergreens an appealing setting for rare friends and magnetic guests to gather at the dining table or shine far into the night before the library fire. She proudly entertained such notables as Ralph Waldo Emerson, Wendell Phillips, Frederick Law Olmsted, Henry Ward Beecher, the governor of the state, the most convivial of the college trustees, and royal intimates like Samuel Bowles, who was for her the "creator of endless perspectives."

All Sue's imagination and spirit focused on her home. She grew prizewinning flowers and arranged them daily with admirable artistry throughout the Evergreens, she served home-grown delicacies and seasonal culinary treats at her table, and her impeccable housekeeping had David Todd wiping his feet all the way from the gate to the front door. Grandma Wilder's quiet comment after visiting the Evergreens in 1882 sums up Sue's achievement: "Their house is charming beyond description, not so much for its costliness as its exquisite taste in every particular." Sue herself was a renowned and compelling element of this setting; her special style drew many accolades over the years. One knowledgeable admirer described her as "a really brilliant and highly cultivated woman of great taste and refinement, perhaps a little too aggressive, a little too sharp in wit and repartee, and a little too ambitious for social prestige, but, withal, a woman of the world in the

---

operation. The dangers from shock and infection, which easily matched the risks of childbirth, were not well known in the 1850s, and probably Sue was not alone in Amherst in employing this means of birth control.

* "Annals of the Evergreens" remained among Susan Dickinson's papers at Harvard University until published in the Amherst College alumni magazine in the spring of 1981 (Vol. 33, No. 4) under the title "Magnetic Visitors."

best sense, having a very keen and correct appreciation of what was fine and admirable." Samuel Bowles was ready to give Sue an honorary degree for her social exertions at the commencement of 1877, and even Mabel Todd admitted, despite her former idol's coldness and hauteur, that "notwithstanding all that I hear about her, I do admire her mind. And she stimulates me intellectually."

Sooner or later, many of those drawn by Sue's magnetism met with surprise. There is too much testimony from too many sources not to conclude that something in her backfired, that time after time she rejected the very adulation and warmth she attracted, and often found pleasure in small revenges. An example of her heartlessness involves the presence within the Evergreens of two orphaned adolescent girls, Anna and Clara Newman, nieces and wards of Edward Dickinson, who placed the sisters in Sue and Austin's childless home in 1858, when the girls were twelve and fifteen. Anna and Clara were parentless and homeless, as Sue once had been, but they were not indigent. Instead of being sympathetic to a situation that had caused great pain in her own life, however, Sue treated the girls like poor relations, subjecting them to small humiliations they long remembered.

Even more curious was the animosity Sue kept going with Mary Bowles, the wife of Samuel Bowles, whose friendship meant so much to the Austin Dickinsons. Bowles hinted broadly more than once that Sue's slights to Mary were distressing to him, but to no avail. Timid, dependent Mary was not a personality Sue would have tolerated easily, but the crucial if irrational reason for Sue's uncordiality, among several possibilities that suggest themselves, might have been that Mary came from Geneva, New York, and therefore was acquainted with Sue's background. It is hard to fathom otherwise why Sue, out of her love for Bowles and her awareness of his importance to Austin, would have continued to alienate his wife, but she did. It was a situation never happily resolved.

Mabel Todd was convinced Sue had mistreated Austin, whose noble, sensitive nature she was by birth too ill refined to appreciate, but as Mabel rode this theme in her journal, she planted substantial clues as to what was more probably the real source of trouble in the marriage. "[Susan] has gone her own way all these years & never tried to keep him . . ." she wrote in the fall of 1883. "The greatest joy in life lay beside her for years, & she never moved to retain it, even pushed it away from her. Now it has left her irrevocably, & she sees the awful loss & void. She has the husk, from which the soul has departed." Still later, Mabel spoke of "all that pent-up, tender spirit [of Austin's] longing for love & home & going lonesomely through fifty years, coming to me . . . so beautiful that it is real pathos, so patient that it is God-like." Sue, Mabel said still later, had gone through married life "wholly selfishly & worse," while Austin had "always kept his ideals unspotted through trials, & domestic horrors which would have turned a less sweet & sound nature into the blackest misanthropy." Judging from such statements, Sue's crime seems to have been one of un-responsiveness or indifference. She ignored Austin's feelings, while he suffered silently instead of standing up to Sue, or dealing with his own exaggerated expectations of her.

Austin's feelings were extraordinary. Even Mabel, with her unusual capacity for absorbing admiration, was over-whelmed by Austin's emotional intensity. "His love for me is perfectly amazing," she marveled in 1886. "I have read a great many stories, & I have had a good many love letters, and I have heard a good many lovers talk, but I never heard or read or imagined such a wonderful putting-into-words of so divine a love as he does to me. . . . No love story approaches it." There had been little to suggest, at early meeting, that such incipient emotionalism lay within the man. Mabel spoke of "the apathetic, careless indifference which was his leading characteristic" when she first knew him, while later an obituary would comment on his "open, frank and vigorous way" that masked "an intensity of feeling almost pathetic at times." Austin hid behind his "strong, almost bluff way with business relations" much as Emily sheltered herself within the Dickinson Homestead, extreme sensitiveness being a characteristic both Dickinsons shared. Austin could have been speaking for his sister when he said to Mabel that he had "suffered more than he can ever tell" from sensitiveness.

It isn't hard to understand how Sue easily and often injured both Austin and Emily, nor is it surprising that she chose to lavish her devotion on her home rather than on her husband, whose delicate sensibilities threatened her. In just such fashion as she gave intelligent, respectful attention to Emily's poems, but could not cope with the inordinate love that sponsored them, Sue threw herself into creating a domestic haven in lieu of dealing with the vast disorder of Austin's emotional demands. And yet, according to Mabel Todd, Austin "had a wretched life at home, in spite of the perfect house & grounds, the carriages & horses, pictures & luxuries generally." In 1885 she added, "His life has been in all *home* things a terrible failure, and a sweet home has always been his greatest desire."

Mabel almost never reproached Austin, but the reverse side of his long-suffering patience with Sue pained her. "He is so lofty—and his aims are so pure," she admired in 1886. "Those who have so bitterly injured him he forgives—and although he knows his life has been all but spoiled, yet he is ever gentle & generous in his feeling toward the spoiler." Still, she resented his kowtowing to Sue's public charade, which Mabel termed "the mockery of her marriage," and was often plagued and embarrassed by Sue's animosity, which Austin could not or did not prevent. For all his daring disregard of convention, Austin displayed an inherent fear of Sue, perhaps because of a temper that had "put Austin several times in danger of his life." An incident that suggests how Sue wielded her authority occurred in January 1885, when she decided the

Evergreens needed new wallpaper in the large central hallway that reached through both floors of the house. Ned told Mattie, "Father positively forbid anything being done. . . . Whereupon mother began to pull off the paper," and a project that disrupted the household for several weeks was under way. It may have been such confrontations as this that Austin avoided. Emily had remarked in the spring of 1883, "My brother is with us so often each Day, we almost forget that he ever passed to a wedded Home."

The relationship between Austin's inability to deal with Sue and his phenomenal shouldering of responsibility in every other facet of his life is interesting. In true Dickinson masculine style, he literally escaped into duty, encumbering himself with the burdens of others, taking on obligations to his family, his profession, his church, his village, and his college, until by the time he was fifty he had exceeded the admirable record of commitment made by his father, and by his grandfather, Samuel Fowler Dickinson. Unlike Emily, who tended her acute emotional condition as her work, Austin capitulated to the worldly demands thrust upon him and avoided the inner urgency of his feelings. Anything affecting his physical territory, that is, the two Dickinson estates, the large Dickinson meadow, the Congregational church, Amherst College, and the village of Amherst, Austin took for his affair, and as the town grew and changed after the Civil War, responding to population increases and the needs of a more pluralistic society, his depth of personal involvement and commitment to public and private concerns within the town made him indispensable to its life. As Mabel put it, by 1890, "I suppose nobody in the town could be born or married or buried, or make an investment, or buy a house-lot, or a cemetery-lot, or sell a newspaper, or build a house, or choose a profession, without you close at hand." It was, however, the impress of Austin's tender inner nature that made indelible his mark upon the village and the lives of those with whom he associated.

Efforts to institute public water, sewage, lighting, and roads kept Austin at the thick of Amherst's increasingly complicated corporate life and gave him ample opportunity over the years to express his strong aesthetic vision. He pioneered locally in landscape beautification, working long and hard to change the town common from swamp and hayfield to a handsome park, to convince the financially pressed Amherst College trustees that coveted funds should be spent on landscaping, and to create an idyllic new town cemetery, a chief passion of the last seven years of his life. Several times he brought in Frederick Law Olmsted and his botanist partner Calvert Vaux to advise on town beautification. Like them, Austin admired indigenous species. Others might bring in ornamental or curious foreign trees from Europe or the Orient, but Austin's love centered on native oaks and maples, elms and evergreens, laurel and fruit trees, with which he gradually restocked the town. Scouring the countryside in his carriage looking for specimen trees became a favorite pastime, and so strong was his personal commitment that he once apologized to Mabel, "I don't like to trust anyone with an oak," as he hurried off to Pelham to supervise workmen bringing in a tree for the college grounds.

Recent generations have paid more homage to Edward Dickinson than to Austin. Although each man in his day literally ran the town, Austin was loved as well as respected by his fellow townsmen, and examination of their achievements suggests he was, in fact, the abler of the two Dickinsons. When Austin succeeded his father as treasurer of Amherst College after thirty-seven years, he took the reins of an office that had fallen into confusion. Though the transition appeared to be a smooth one, it was not. Edward had steered the college from the discouraging debt of its founding years to institutional assets exceeding a million dollars, but for about a decade before his sudden resignation in the autumn of 1872, annual expenditures had exceeded income in a distressing manner he could not control. His reputation for honesty, uprightness, and scrupulous accountability may have led him to reach into his own pocket to make things come out right until, confounded by books that would not balance, he decided to resign his post.

Pains were taken to camouflage the confused fiscal situation for the semicentennial history of the college that Professor Tyler was writing. After some controversy Austin was finally chosen to succeed his father in late 1873, and quickly recognized that the treasurership was at the mercy of trustee appropriations the treasurer played no role in determining. He had only begun to modernize his father's outmoded bookkeeping system when Edward Dickinson died. Although his personal integrity was scarcely at stake, sadly enough Edward may have thought it was when he died.

Gradually the new treasurer and the college trustees rectified the irresponsible relationship between those who voted funds and those who accounted for them, in the process strengthening the institution and the powers of the treasurer. Especially under Julius Seelye, who was ill during his last years as president, Austin's influence and indispensability grew, until his authority and judgment pervaded nearly every aspect of running the college. By the time the Todds arrived, he was in a position to exercise considerable control over David's career. Although Professor Todd was never promoted or compensated in any way that suggests favoritism, Austin certainly influenced Seelye to keep him on the faculty, for David's eclipse-chasing greatly displeased the college president. And both town and college would have been shocked to know that for five years, from 1890 to 1895, Austin had Mabel Todd copy, in her clear handwriting, all the trustee meeting records and some of the treasurer's records, making the Todds privy to the most confidential affairs of the college during that period.

If living in her father's house is a metaphor for the confines of Emily Dickinson's father complex, living in his father's town defines Austin's entrapment, and his breakthrough into new forms of expression and power defines his real achievement. Austin "saw New Englandly" with the same steadfastness as his sister, a centrality of vision that bound him physically and psychologically to the Amherst landscape as surely as the poet was bound. His range of physical movement was only slightly broader than hers, and he was never able to shake the peculiar homesickness that tied him to the region, although one fascinating trip to the West in 1887 serves to show he tried. But while reclusiveness was a trait that brother and sister shared, Austin acted out the compulsions of heart and mind that Emily lived imaginatively, constructing a life-within-a-life for himself and Mabel out of his own highly romantic, intrinsic feeling for unified form and function.

Within the extraordinary and to some degree fantastic context of the life he and Mabel shared, the parameters of which emerge in their letters, Austin took enormous risks. By 1887 Mabel wore his wedding ring on her right hand, and during 1888 they attempted to conceive a child, an effort referred to between them as "the experiment." Austin's expedition to Kansas and New Orleans in 1887 may have been, at least in part, a scouting trip to see how life together in the West would work, for Mabel's diary indicates that she and Austin seriously contemplated leaving Amherst (with or without David Todd is not clear). None of these plans saw fruition. Instead, their affair seemed mysteriously sanctioned, or at least overlooked, by the community, and Austin's integrity among his contemporaries remained solid as a rock. In March 1890, Austin wrote Mabel: "Last evening was our annual parish meeting, where against my protest, they insisted upon putting the only outlaw of the region again at the head of parish affairs. It doesn't seem to me they can think I am very wicked—or if I am, that there is any harm in being so." So long as Austin lived, community sympathy seemed to endorse his solution to what was generally recognized as a difficult marriage to Sue.*

Consummation of Mabel and Austin's love occurred at the Homestead, Emily and Vinnie's dwelling, the evening of December 13, 1883, in the dining room, where they often met before the fire. It is confirmed by symbols in both Austin's and Mabel's diaries, and also by the existence of two small slips of paper, each bearing the same strange word, AMUASBTEILN. One of the slips was tucked into Mabel's diary at December 13, and bears that date on the reverse. The other slip was in Austin's wallet when he died. The word is composed by alternately merging the letters of Austin's and Mabel's names. The event that evening occurred with the knowledge of David Todd, who was fully aware of the depth of feeling between his wife and Austin, and had not been alienated by it. David was, and would continue to be, devoted to Austin, whom he considered his best friend. "I loved him more than any man I ever knew," he said years later.

---

* While Austin's behavior might have been overlooked by the community, Mabel's journal indicates that she endured substantial local criticism during Austin's life and afterward. Nevertheless, one looks in vain among Amherst correspondence for allusion to the Austin-Mabel affair by persons cognizant of it. Such intimate gossip was for whispered conversation, rarely trusted to written comment that might later bring embarrassment. One stray observation turns up in a letter from Mrs. John Jameson, Dickinson neighbor, to her son Frank in Washington in May 1886: "Austin has just driven in at the great gate. I have no doubt he has had a delightful drive with charming company, as the gossips say the intimacy existing between him and Mrs. Todd is as great as ever. She was at Emily's funeral dressed in black, looking haggard as if she had lost a dear friend. I hear much gossip, and that many people are leaving Mrs. T. 'alone.' It does seem a pity her fair name should be so tarnished, and such mean things said by the lower classes, as are current here."

Sue's reaction to her husband's defection, however, was scarcely so accommodating. Her grief for her little boy, Gilbert, who had recently died, and her righteous fury at Mabel developed quickly into a black martyrdom that turned her toward her two remaining children. She became intensely, almost obsessively, absorbed in Ned's and Mattie's lives, as if this compensated her for loss of control over Austin and absolved her from the humiliation Mabel inflicted. Sue feared her, Austin told Mabel in wonderment—the first woman she had ever feared. Clothed in mourning, enduring periods of fitful health, Sue fought an acrimonious battle with Austin on the homefront, and was determined that he maintain the semblance of their legal relationship. In many ways, however, she acted as if he'd moved to the next county, or even died, often reporting on his actions in letters to the children as if he were some amusing stranger. But her attitude was scarcely benign, as the potent tune to which Mabel and Austin constantly danced suggests, and her fury increased as Mabel involved herself in the publication of Emily's poems and letters.

Perhaps the best portrait of Sue's unbridled nature came from her own pen, from a scene she jubilantly depicted for Ned in the summer of 1884:

> I was roused about half past four this morning by very strange sounds—wild snortings & huffings and rushing to the window I saw Tom tearing over the grounds as fine a picture of the Scripture war-horse as I ever expect to see. Papa made one of his hasty toilets and joined Stephen who had already begun pursuit. They both approached him with *honeyed words* but Tom knew the situation, and lifted himself in superb disdain, making bolder plunges and swifter circuits of the Mansion till Papa [waved?] a pitchfork and he was obliged to make an ignoble retreat to the barn, and be led back to his stable where there was no beautiful morning for him to sniff. I shall never forget the picture—the moon just over the elms with one star

fainting in its light—the east pink with dawn—everything a little dim and shadowy, and fresh and dewy as only early morning can be, and that great splendid animal exulting in it all, *swishing* through the wet grass with head aloft, blowing and triumphing in his freedom. For a moment it seemed enough to be Tom.

If Sue had caught her own image in this momentary vision of the loosed warhorse, the postscript she added is devastating. "I am sorry to say," she told Ned, "he did no harm."

Eventually, in the pattern of his father and his grandfather, Austin's inability to extricate himself from his own human predicament seems to have brought the world he created for himself down upon him. His own words betray that the duties he ceaselessly took on grew increasingly burdensome the last five years of his life. "Exacting," "controlling," he had once called the "work that seems to fall to me on all sides," but from 1890 onward he used an idiom of encumbrance, speaking of "putting my work behind me" and "getting it out of the way." In oppressive phrases he wrote to Mabel of feeling "followed every minute," "tired and driven," "crowded," "broken in upon," and without "breathing time."

Pressured by outside responsibilities, Austin seemed equally exhausted by the incessant strain of his unresolved double life. When his heart finally stopped in the summer of 1895, he had reached no real solutions and he left behind a certain amount of chaos. The qualities for which he was most loved and admired, his originality and strength, his fine aesthetic perception and devotion to duty, were lauded by his fellow townspeople, who set up a giant boulder near his grave to acknowledge his unusual attributes. But it was the citation of the Amherst College trustees that struck closest to his likeness, and caught the spirit of the letters that follow.

"Those who knew him most intimately and met him most frequently had always a sense of refreshment & invigoration upon meeting with him, no matter how commonplace the occasion, for his own unique and vigorous personality gave to all he did and said, a turn of expression and a color of individuality as refreshing and stimulating as a breeze from the sea or the hills."

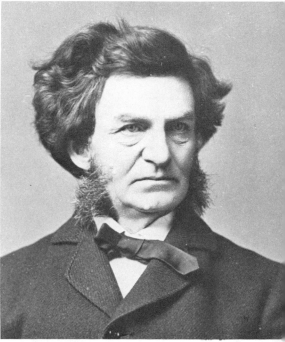

Mabel Loomis Todd in 1885 (her dress is decorated with her
hand-painted flowers); Austin Dickinson in 1890   *Yale*

The young Austin Dickinson
(1854) and Susan Gilbert
(1851), before their marriage
Yale

The young Dickinson siblings: Emily at Mount Holyoke (1847);
Austin's commencement daguerreotype (1850); and Lavinia
(*c.* 1852)

The Dickinson Homestead on Main Street, Amherst, where Emily
and Lavinia lived. Below, the Evergreens next door, where the
Austin Dickinsons lived   *Yale*

David and Mabel Todd in 1878, shortly before their marriage   *Yale*

The Todds when they lived in
Amherst. David's photo was
taken in 1884; Mabel's just
before her second trip to Japan
in 1896

An 1894 view of the Todds' house, the Dell, looking southwest across the Dickinson meadow (Austin's vegetable garden at right)   *Yale*

Caro Lovejoy Andrews about
1890. Below, Mabel's father,
Eben J. Loomis, in 1879

Yale

Mabel's mother, daughter, and grandmother about 1885. From the left:
Mary Wilder Loomis, Millicent Todd, Grandma Wilder, and Mabel

Yale

Detail from a group photo (July 1882), from the left:
Mabel Todd, Susan Dickinson holding young Gilbert, her
daughter Martha ("Mattie"), bearded David Todd in straw hat,
and Ned Dickinson with tennis racket. Bradford Hitchcock
is seated behind Ned, and William Clark in front of Mabel

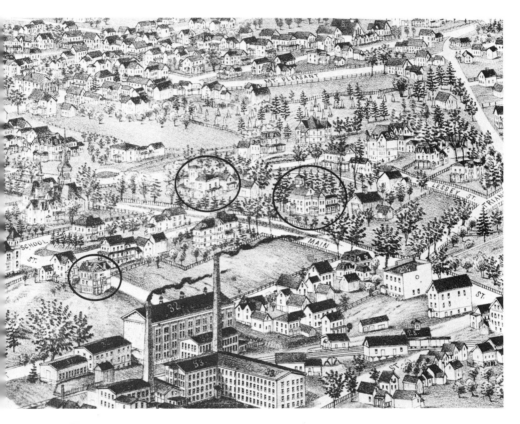

View of Amherst about 1886, showing the relative sites of the
Evergreens, to the left of the Homestead (shown above the word
"Main"), and the Dell across the Dickinson meadow on the
other side of Main Street

Ned and Mattie Dickinson, foreground; Mabel Todd and
Brad Hitchcock, in rear (summer 1882)

Lavinia Dickinson in 1896   *Jones Library, Amherst*

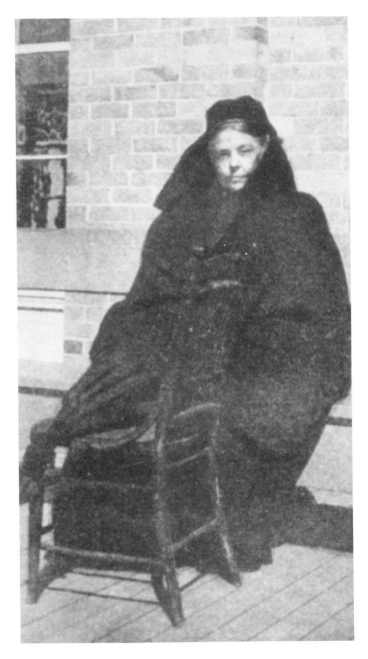

The widowed Susan Dickinson in 1897

Mabel Todd around 1900, perhaps still in
mourning for Austin　　*Yale*

Mabel and David outside Observatory House, Amherst, 1907
Yale

I I

The Letters

1

The Mutual Discovery

SELECTING from over a thousand letters that Austin and Mabel wrote each other during thirteen years was not simple. Repetitive or inconsequential letters, and dozens of notes arranging meetings or carriage drives, were easily set aside, but judicious pruning was required to avoid the sheer prolificacy of the correspondence, and yet preserve its full flavor and sacrifice none of the story. What follows represents altogether about a quarter of the collection, and delineates the budding, bloom, and maturation of an absorbing love affair. The letters are supplemented by information taken from related diaries, journals, and correspondence. It was a highly idealized love that, without the comic relief of the circumstances in which it was enacted, might make unbearable reading. The additional sources have also made it possible to arrange and date the early letters, for although Mrs. Todd had roughly organized the collection before her death, the earliest exchanges took place in intense secrecy, and a pattern emerged only through persistent sleuthing.

Austin and Mabel at first destroyed all tangible evidence of their liaison, burning many, many notes and letters soon after receiving them, until Austin began to copy Mabel's precious messages in his own hand before disposing of the originals, and slipped the copies into an outsize envelope that he gave into the keeping of his sisters. Across the envelope was scrawled this directive:

> *Vin—*
> *If anything happens to me*
> *Burn this package at once—*
> *without opening.*
> *Do this as you love me.*
>
> *W. A. Dickinson*

Later Austin added four more of Mabel's 1883 letters, two in his own hand, two in hers, to the envelope. Three other letters were copied but misfiled among his later correspondence. Mabel rather belatedly followed Austin's lead by copying short passages from sixteen of Austin's earliest letters to her, but she destroyed so many others without duplication that Austin's contribution to the early correspondence appears scantier than hers.

Letters occurring in the handwriting of the recipient rather than the sender at first created editorial confusion, as did the omission of greeting, signature, or date, among other precautions the lovers observed. Occasionally Austin noted the date he *received* a letter, and in later years Mrs. Todd supplied some dates from memory, many of them erroneous, which added to the perplexities of getting the sequence straight. Envelopes were addressed in a great variety of handwritings, and were often mailed to David Todd's name, or Vinnie Dickinson's. Most letters went through the post (even when the lovers were both in town), but hundreds were handed in person, and one or two of the earliest bear pin marks—the result of Mrs. Todd's carrying them inside her dress until she could safely deliver them. In addition, intimate love letters co-existed with a more formal "cover" correspondence written during the same months passions were flaming. These conventional epistles, designed to throw David or Sue off the scent, often held a secret note inside, just as newspapers or books innocently exchanged in the street often concealed a written message.

While the lovers conscientiously avoided mentioning names or events that could betray them if a letter went astray, circumstantial details inevitably crept in to provide the clues that, with the aid of Austin's and Mabel's diaries, helped establish dates for many of the early letters. In the correspondence that follows, a date appearing in brackets has been established through such documentary sources. In cases where interior evidence, tone, or Mrs. Todd's arrangement suggests only a likely date, approximation is indicated. Unless otherwise noted, all letters were written in Amherst. Those of Mabel's that were copied in Austin's handwriting are identified by a V; early passages of Austin's transcribed by Mrs. Todd are marked by an X.

A carefully composed bouquet of subtle sentiments and Spencerian swirl mailed from Washington, D.C., five weeks after the "Rubicon" of September 11, 1882, makes up Mabel's first surviving letter to Austin. Soon afterward the Todds returned to Amherst for the autumn, David departed for his three-month Transit of Venus expedition, and Austin and Mabel, love notes flying thick and fast, began to play a dangerous game under Sue Dickinson's nose. For over a year, until consummation of the affair in December 1883, the letters track the lovers' undeviating path through complications and acts of fate that might have deterred anyone less certain of self-destiny than Mabel or less threatened by despair than Austin.

My Dear Mr. Dickinson:

I am very, very grateful to you for what you did at the Trustee meeting. I must write and thank you myself, although I think Mr. Todd is also writing to you today.

I am so glad you take so hopeful a view of that comet— indeed I did myself after the day or two of rather sombre reflections which followed my first view of it; and it was during that day or two that I wrote to Mrs. Dickinson.

My extreme buoyancy of spirits would, I think, carry me safely over the final day itself, and I could not help being happy if I knew absolutely that the end of all things approached. Nevertheless, I am very glad the comet is receding so rapidly from the Inn. I love to live.

A more beautiful day than the present one never gladdened even the favored Amherst, only, instead of its glorious northern hills, so strong and tender too, I can see now only the distant and sparkling Potomac with the low, level banks, which are very lovely today, under a brilliant northwest wind and genial sunshine.

I positively long for the magnificent colors which I know must glow all about Amherst now. Our oaks are beginning to get rusty, and an occasional maple shows a red bough, but the tones of our crickets are growing fainter, and I feel more than ever before that Massachusetts is emphatically the land to see the autumn in its perfection. But as the actual chirp of the unappreciative Washington crickets becomes dim, I hear only more vividly in my mind their well-beloved Amherst song.

Most sincerely your friend
Mabel Loomis Todd

Washington
Sunday morning, 15 October 1882

The Mutual Discovery

David was appointed Assistant Professor of Astronomy at Amherst College, and his salary raised to $1,000 at the October 12 trustee meeting. Austin probably persuaded the trustees that Professor Todd's work at the Nautical Almanac was equivalent to the five-year instructorship that qualified an Amherst faculty member for his promotion.

Washington
30 October 1882

My dear Mr. Dickinson:

I dont think I like second thoughts any more, nor the girl you gave them to. I had not the happiness of viewing a bunch of superb gentians. No, I am sure I could not endure that girl.

As far as our plans now seem to extend, I have a very certain prospect of arriving in Amherst on Saturday of this week, probably by the eight o'clock train. The California trip has almost hopelessly collapsed, by a manoeuvre which I shall be happy to characterize verbally, when I see you. The President of the Trustees of the Lick Observatory feels more than disappointed that there is to be no astronomer sent there for the Transit of Venus, because, I believe, several instruments were bought for its proper observation, and all were set up and made ready for Mr. Todd's arrival. I have a great many adjectives stored up for use in connection with this expedition. But, in reality, the loss of a journey to California was not such a great disappointment to me as I might have imagined, & I confess I start from Washington on Wednesday having Amherst as the objective point, with as great happiness and expectation as if I were actually departing for a western trip. This time Millicent is to stay with mother here, until Christmas at least. I regret every day that I lose the glory of the northern woods in October, but I am not at all sure that I do not love November equally well, with its delicious grey skies & rustling brown leaves, and the intoxicating autumn winds. The most perfect day I ever saw

[1 3 1]

in my life was that Sunday which contained the drive [with Austin, Sue, and Gib] to Belchertown, and once last week there was a day so much like it that I almost wrote you a note, to merely express my joy in it, which you would have understood.

Well, Mabel Loomis Todd is soon to be on the wing again, and has in the mean time the great pleasure of subscribing herself your friend.

Returning to Amherst the evening of November 4, the Todds took a room at Mrs. Robison's boardinghouse on Prospect Street, several blocks from the Evergreens. Sue and Mattie were away visiting Martha Gilbert Smith in Geneva, New York, for a few weeks, leaving the Dickinson males in the care of their servant, Mary Moynihan.

Dear Todds   *[5 November 1882]*

Come down home and let us see if you are really here—and the same.

Come to dinner quarter before one and drive after—Or if you prefer to meet Mrs. Robison first, come right after, and come just as much earlier as you or either of you will.

The day is too fine for a single room, and here is a whole house and all outdoors.

Ned, Gib, Mary
and Wm. A.

Sunday morning

While the date of the next letter can only be approximated, it seems to fit November 7, for which Mabel's diary contains: "A rare November day, grey & cold. Ned came in, and just after dinner I went to drive with dear Mr. Dickinson senior. We did not come back until six o'clock. Among other lovely places we went to a little red house which stands high on the Pelham hills, & stopped beside it ten or fifteen minutes for the wonderful view—the kingdoms of the earth & their glory lay spread out below. When I returned David met me with the news that he had been sent for to come immediately to the Lick Observatory on Mt. Hamilton in California to observe the Transit of Venus. We went to tell the Dickinsons immediately."

AUSTIN TO MABEL   [*ca. early November 1882*]

Miss Humphrey has a previous engagement. Will you go now! And shall I take you at your door, or where?

As you say. Be definite both as to place and time.

I am ready any minute.

My horse is here.

Austin called the following Mabel's first love letter; it was the first he copied and placed in the envelope later entrusted to Vinnie. Sue had returned from Geneva at the very hour David left for California (on November 10, Mabel's twenty-sixth birthday), and Mrs. Edward Dickinson had died at the Homestead. Mabel attended her funeral on November 16 by request of Vinnie and Emily. The evening before this note was written, Mabel played whist at the Evergreens with Mattie and Ned, while Sue, Austin, and the visiting Rev. Jenkins talked before the fire. Then Austin walked Mabel home. (Austin later told her that when Jenkins teased him about going out into the cold on his gallant mission, Sue's response was, "For pity's sake don't laugh at him. If there is any one person he actually likes, I am too rejoiced.")

MABEL TO AUSTIN   [*18 November 1882*]ᵛ

Is not this a royal morning! I recognise you in the beautiful day somehow. "With a thrill too solemn & deep for joy. Too perfect & pure for pain." Do tell me if everything was serene upon your return. I am very happy today.

ᵛ Letters so marked were among those entrusted to Vinnie (p. 128–9).

The following passage and other letters of Austin's (marked with an X) survive in a group of sixteen fragments Mabel explains "were copied in the days when I feared to keep the originals, and not all of any one is here. They were inspired & are holy to me." Some may be parts of "fifteen very precious notes" she mentions on December 11, 1882, which she is finding hard to consign to the flames.

AUSTIN TO MABEL   [*ca. November 1882*]^x

I love you. I love you! Why should I! and why shouldn't I! Who made & who rules the human heart! Where is the wrong in preferring sunshine to shadow! Does not the unconscious plant lean toward light?

MABEL TO AUSTIN   [*23 November 1882*]^v

I am glad beyond expression to see you. I have an accumulation of things in my mind for you. The letter was and is a very great joy and comfort.

AUSTIN TO MABEL   [*ca. November 1882*]^x

Just a word my beloved before I harness to work, to tell you that my love is only stronger & richer this morning than ever—that I have had never half as much to say to you.

[*ca. late 1882*]^x

But I remember too what I have found, what has come to me, what you are and what you have given me, and am filled with the deepest most solemn gratitude & joy. I am feeling this morning that you indeed are drawn to me by the same mysterious

X Passages so marked were among the sixteen fragments, as described above.

unbidden influence that draws me irresistibly to you. I wish I could have just one look down into your eyes before I take up the day—and yet I feel quite sure what I should see there.

Yours and ever.

MABEL TO AUSTIN   [*27 November 1882*][v]

The note was very comforting. Yes, I know something is impelling me—I think it is the same. Whatever it is, I know the effect, which is immeasurable—and like the whirlwind in its invisibility. I am not sorry—for otherwise—but it is all very strange. You too may be sure of me, of just what & how I am thinking of you and how infinitely I am trusting you. Through and above every other feeling, is this wonderful restfulness, expressed by nothing so nearly as complete trust. And I love you— I cannot say how much.

AUSTIN TO MABEL   [*ca. late 1882*][x]

It nearly broke my heart to go through the day yesterday with only that passing sight of you.

During the first four weeks of David's California absence Mabel was in and out of the Dickinson home daily, practically an adopted member of the family. She enjoyed constant opportunity to walk, talk, and drive with Austin, and wrote David that the Dickinsons had "thrown open to me their home, their horses, & their hearts with a truly touching and magnificent generosity." Not to be outdone, David wrote back of the congeniality he found among his Lick associates, which led Sue to wonder aloud why Mabel had not accompanied her husband to California. As the following letter suggests, Sue's suspicions of Mabel were now aroused, and within a day or two were confirmed by Ned's revelations.

Mabel to Austin   [*4 December 1882*][v]
                                             Monday evening, 9 o'clock

I have been all alone since supper—but not in the least
lonely. I thought it possible that you might look in for a moment—at least I knew you would if you could. But I am unaccountably tired. So I am going to sleep now, with the last
word you said to me this morning in my heart. I love you more
tonight than I have ever done before. It grows and grows into
a wonderfully rare and beautiful something, every day richer
and stronger and more all pervading. I hope everything was in
a lovely and serene state upon your return. *I* was rested and
made happy for all day, and more, by the far too short hour we
had. When shall we have another? As soon as I have you I immediately think of a dozen things I want to have said to you,
but which I forgot in even more interesting ones which *were* said.
    Good night—I love you. I *love* you.

Tuesday morning. Well I have started on one more day which
may hold happiness for me in its kind hand.
    My last thought and my first thought were of you. And
all the intermediate ones. I shall be very busy this morning, but
I may be out about eleven or soon after. How is the Home
atmosphere? I am anxious to know that. I have not said one of
the things I meant to in this brief time, but you cannot imagine
far wrong, for you know my feeling.

Austin to Mabel   [*ca. late 1882*][x]

    My darling, my darling—and my darling. An angel from
heaven wouldn't have been as welcome as your note just from
the mail.

Mabel to Austin   [*6 December 1882*][v]

    [Sue's coldness last night] was dreadful, but I should not
have cared so much if I could have thought it accidental, or
natural. Of that I am not in the least certain.

I find on becoming thoroughly awake that I am very much troubled and worried and even more than yesterday. But that has not the slightest effect on my love for you, which is apparently deeper and stronger—almost in proportion, as outer things disturb me. You are sure of me. I do not expect to come out at all this morning except perhaps just before [midday] dinner for the mail. May I find a word from you! Things look to me of much the same color as the leaden sky, but I love you.

Wednesday. 9 a.m.

December 6 was the day of the Transit of Venus. During the afternoon Mabel took four ladies, including Mrs. Dickinson, to the college observatory to look through the telescope, but the event was obscured in the northeast by clouds. At dusk, Mabel and Austin took a walk southward toward Mill Valley, and Mabel gave him the preceding letter, which she had written in the morning. This second letter was prompted by an evening telegram from David announcing "Splendid day. Splendid success."

MABEL TO AUSTIN   [*6 December 1882*]ᵛ
Wednesday, 9:30 p.m.

Several things have occurred which have made me very happy since I left you—I will not write of them—but I will tell you at the first opportunity. Only I thought you would be glad to know *my* sky has changed from leaden clouds to sunshine, as the day did. Even if the happy things had not occurred, I think our walk would have made me peaceful & joyous, alone. It is almost more to me than any of our previous experiences. I told you there were episodes in it which would last for hours, and it is so. They do not pass away from me a particle. I have had several visitors, but I should not have felt alone if there had been none. You *know* I love you. I must see you in some way tomorrow. I shall be out on various errands in the street soon after eleven. I am so happy and proud tonight when I think &

know what you have given me—what I am to you—that everything is radiant. I do not think I have entirely and fully appreciated its magnitude before, but I do now—*thoroughly*—and what I give back to you is now great in proportion. That I could very easily prove to you if you were but here at this moment, as I most devoutly wish you were, but you asked me to imagine your presence—always—and I do. In fact I could not help so doing if I would. Oh I love you *thrillingly*. Do you know it? *Dont* you know it! You brought me very close to you in that walk—so that I know I can never leave you again, in reality. I am going to seal this letter tonight and so not put in anything more in the morning, but you will know that I shall love you more when I awake than I do now, and that I give you a kiss such as we know at this moment.

AUSTIN TO MABEL   [*ca. late 1882*]x

Dearer nearer, sweeter every time—those forty minutes last night, the happiest fullest most joyous yet. It seemed to me we touched bottom in that walk and talk so far as words can do it. I have been happier in the hours since than ever before. I do believe you, my darling, and believe you love me as I love you. It was no fault of yours or of mine that I could not take this in at first. My experience of life was too firm & encrusted to permit it. It contradicts everything, revolutionizes everything, overturns everything with me—astonishes & overwhelms me as much as overjoys & intoxicates me. I love you, I admire you, I idolize you. I am exalted by your love for me. I am strong as not for a long time before—elastic, well. I walk the street airily & with high pride, for I am loved—loved as I love, loved where I love. You fill my heart & my mind & my life & my world x x x x Your note has just come. Great Heavens, my darling, I am transported by it, almost overpowered. We love.

When posed against Mabel's diary entries, this note suggests the exciting double life she was leading with the Dickinsons. She wrote it after playing whist at the Evergreens and spending the night (Sue now kept a bed made up for her), then practicing the piano and returning to Mrs. Robison's next morning. She gave the note to Austin at his office, where she stopped midday on the pretext of borrowing catalogues, and later enjoyed the hoped-for walk before tea. That evening (December 9) Mattie spent the night with Mabel at Mrs. Robison's, then Mabel returned to the Evergreens for all day Sunday, the tenth, and overnight.

MABEL TO AUSTIN   [*9 December 1882*]ᵛ

I am as much famished as you are. It was very hard to keep up, wasn't it? I think I had best not appear this noon, but I do exactly what we did on the last walk—if it is a possible thing—the same in time and place. If I should be late a few moments you will know that I am detained, & you will wait for me a little while, won't you?

It seems ages ago since I talked last with you.

I love you. I *love* you.

I hope you get this in time to come.

MABEL TO AUSTIN   [*11 December 1882*]ᵛ

I have just been reading over fifteen very precious notes. You know who wrote them to me. And I have been struggling with myself to get to that point where I could put them in the fire. But I could not do it tonight. So I read every one so carefully, & oh! so tenderly, and put them all back in their resting place. Tomorrow, or the next day I will try again to destroy them.

The town is empty and desolate & cold & dreary to me, & why? I walk the streets apparently as usual, but the spirit & joy of my life are gone. I know you are [in Boston], and I have no further vital interest in anything. But I have the infinite joy of knowing that wherever you are—& whatever you may be doing—you are loving me through it all & thinking of me with a tenderness & devotion which are almost divine. I know you— I trust you—I rest in you—I *love* you! . . .

It seems as if I cannot possibly bear it until you come. You have waked into an overbounding life things which will not let me rest away from you. It is wicked, as I said, *said* to you by word of mouth, how far away such bliss looks! To speak face to face with you at this moment. Heaven could hardly offer more. You would know me as you never knew me before if you could suddenly step in now. I am all alone. It is about eight o'clock. An occasional student passes whistling. My work lies idly on my lap. A dangerous visitor called imagination holds sole sway. What do you suppose I am dreaming! I want you—I long for you—I need you in every way, at this moment. Good night, my own. I must bring this rhapsody to a close. The moment you get it and read it I want you to write me something in return that I may know just how it strikes you. I am a little tremulous about sending it.

Good night.

Monday, 8 p.m.

AUSTIN TO MABEL   [*ca. late 1882*]ˣ

The loneliness & lonesomeness & longing for you last evening were beyond anything yet. The thought began to dawn upon and overshadow me that these strange, marvelous weeks are drawing to a close. The fulness of the present had hardly left room for this before—that you are going to leave me [to go to Washington for Christmas]. The cruelty of life never seemed half so cruel. Why are we endowed with all this wild love & longing & the person to gratify them never laid hand upon! Such blankness & dreariness & darkness & chill!

And yet, my darling, my darling you have given me in these weeks more than all life before—incomparably more. I would have lived for these alone—lived exultingly. I would die for them—they are memorable forevermore. They cannot perish —they are mine, mine. Nothing has ever been like them. I am grateful for them beyond all expressions. And they shall never end! Why should they? Why shall they? I know I cannot change and you will not, & who shall stand between us?

The word "Powers," used in the next letter for the first time (at the end of the second paragraph), was a code word by which Mabel and Austin referred to other members of the Dickinson and Todd families, in this instance Sue.

MABEL TO AUSTIN   [*15 December 1882*]ᵛ

Friday, 9:30 p.m.   I have been at home for half an hour. I saw a light in your office as I came by, and did *so* wish I could let you know in some way! But I thought of everything—and it all seemed impracticable. So I am sitting here alone—in a state far from quietness. I thought you might think of the possibility and pass this way, and I have put the strongest power of my will on you to make you know I am here. Everything is highly propitious, dont you see! It all could not be better. Again I have an occasion to tell you how bare everything is without you. I felt an inward glow every time your name was mentioned [at tea at the Mathers']. I cannot tell you how it comforted me. But why dont you *know* I am waiting for you, and come! The occasion is too rare to lose. When I see you I will tell you how nearly I did something rash tonight, since my return. I must see you in some way tomorrow. I think the noontime will do, if you can arrange it—or what perhaps is less noticeable, could you not come here for a few minutes at quarter of one? That is better than for me to come out because I am never interrupted here at that hour, and I have one or two practical things to tell you x x x x x x

Do forgive so much vacillation. I have been thinking of it very carefully—and I will come. We will meet as heretofore at noon. I will run the risk once more. If you think of anything against can you not write a note as soon as you read this? Then

I can get it about noon or after as I come out. It is too dreadful that I should be here an hour in entire solitude and that you do not know it. This day has been in some respects the most trying one I ever passed. And to have it crowned by such a missed opportunity! Did you have a sleigh ride today? The "Powers" did not give us one together. And is there any chance of that tomorrow?

Do you know, I have come to look for your daily note as for the bread of life. I do not know what I should do if it failed me. You had two today—one of them reached you very clearly, did it not? I saw the appreciative pleased look in your eyes.

If anything should occur by which I should be prevented from seeing you at noon would it do for you to take me up at the same place where you did once, at the same hour as last week? You will understand that. Why wouldn't that be a rather good plan? But we will have the noontime too, as we have had all the noontimes, at the same hour and place, and you will tell me in the same way if the coast is not clear.

I am too sorry about a splendid chance being lost, this evening, to think of anything else. If I should begin to write all I want to say, I should not dare put the note in the [post] office—again—so I must reluctantly stop, for I could write all night. I feel preternaturally bright & far from well. I know you are thinking of me every minute and I hope you are writing me a long letter. I love you, and again, and again, with all adjectives—and a very near approach to the last you asked for three. What does that mean? When the last seal is broken, as you so daintily put it in your note of this morning. Will the full sunshine of the regions beyond be any lovelier than this borderline of delicate mists and golden possibilities?

You thought you were all alone in the "by-paths." You loved the grass and the blue sky and the birds and crickets. And you said you wanted the crickets to chirp about you when you were finally sleeping. You did not know then to whom you were saying that exquisite thing. But she loved these lonely walks too, only now they are not lonely—and she is thrilled with every little bit of lichen on an old stone wall and the scent of dead leaves, and the passive little buds that know so wondrously when to awake and breathe the rapture of spring.

And we walked toward the sunset—and leaning on an old fence, began to reach [each] other a very, very little. It was very peaceful, and very bright—but it was the beginning, unmistakably.

Do you remember how calmly all those cows came up and examined us? It was dewy when we came back and I meant to have gathered a handful of wild roses. But I somehow forgot them—the stillness of that evening I shall never forget. It quiets me in tonight's intense restlessness, like a gentle hand on my forehead.

Sometime you will take me there again—and we will go to the same place. It may be still and bright again. It may be sunset—but how differently shall you and I see it! You reached out your hand without knowing, almost—in the darkness—and you met another, warm and tender—you clasped it, knowing it was your fate, and it staid with you. It will never be withdrawn. It is months ago now that you heard some one say she had come to stay. She knew then what she said and what she meant, and what she had given—and every day has increased the certainty, and the largeness of the gift. And now this is all at this moment. Good night beloved. In writing to you the nervous tension under which I began is soothed—and I think I can go to sleep. Love me. Love me every minute, and think of me. The stars are shining brilliantly. I see many bright things for us in the future. Good night.

Austin to Mabel   [ca. late 1882]ˣ

I remember all the rest too, said & done & looked. It was all very delightful—almost staggers—does stagger my belief that so much should come to me! to me! who had * * * * dreamed of no brightness, to whom the heavens were as brass. But now I am another man—in another world magnified, clarified, glorified. The earth & the past drop from me, into the innermost remoteness. With you I tread upon the stars. I love you my darling, & again I love you with all my soul—you are my all in all. No gift could be offered me like your love. All the victories in the world are dross to it. I *love* you.

Austin and Mabel anticipated that her Christmas journey to Washington would give Sue, who was watching them constantly now, a chance to relax her vigilance. On December 19 Mabel received word from David that he was delaying his return from California to coincide with her next "auspicious occasion" in early January. Anticipating that her husband might arrive back in Amherst before she did, Mabel informed him of the "nonsense" that had arisen with Sue, and asked him to be sweet and cordial to all the Dickinsons when he saw them. She left town next day, December 20. The pair of letter fragments that follow probably are excerpts from two notes Austin sent Mabel in Newark, New Jersey, where she stopped en route to visit her sister-in-law, Naomi Compton.

AUSTIN TO MABEL   [*ca. late 1882*][x]

But then I recall all the unspeakable proof you have given me that you are mine as I am yours—that I am light and gladness to you, as you to me, and find I am possessed of a great joy which nothing can take from me. You and I in the same house, alone, only us, day & night, week days & Sundays, through Spring & Summer, & Autumn & Winter. Going in & out together, free to look down each other's eyes by the hour. At the fireside, over the fields & hills, driving, walking, talking; going over the past, drinking in the present, looking forward endlessly. I have said nothing, & yet I have said everything. It is the same every time, & yet ever different—ever fresh, ever new. I love you *love* you, LOVE you. I think of you every minute—am yours ever & forever.

The Mutual Discovery

[ca. late 1882]ˣ

Do you know that I would like, after seeing you once more, to go to sleep, & sleep through the months or years that must be—and, while its minutes are rolling by, I shall hear the divine whisper that eternity has begun—perpetual spring. For I have seen you and you are henceforth my world. The sun cannot shine without you, the birds can make no melody. The flowers have no other beauty nor perfume—all is a meaningless waste. I love you darling, *with my love*, & my love is timeless & sleepless—cannot be divided—insatiable. You are in every thought, dream, hope, desire. You are the key, the significant figure; all others cyphers, of no, or of boundless import, as you take your place to the right or the left. I cannot begin to tell you what you are to me x x x x You reach easily & lithely every height I touch, of your own choice seek the paths where I have walked entirely alone before. Know every shade of every passing thought and feeling almost before they have taken shape to myself.

The two weeks in Washington were anxious ones for Mabel. She did not hear further from Austin, and only enough from David to suggest he was infatuated with one of the wives at the Lick Observatory. She wrote a long, episodic letter to Austin, composed over eight days, but dared not mail it without knowing the "climate" in Amherst.

MABEL TO AUSTIN　　[*Washington, D.C., 24 December 1882*]ᵛ
9 p.m.

It is Sunday—and I do not know whether or not I shall dare to send these words to you. One moment I think I will, and the next it seems impossible. You will understand why, I am sure. Yet when I think how you are waiting for it and wishing for it, it seems to me I would brave anything rather than to disappoint you. You have not been one moment out of my mind. And the much longed for letter—with the two previous notes—

both of which *did* reach me safely—have been more comfort and consolation and joy to me than I can tell you.

You said "I trust you, my darling, I trust you" and later on you said "I trust you as much as I love you," which means infinitely. So I have rejoiced every day since I read those words, and everything seems worth while. I want you to read a poem in the January *Century* by Mrs. Burnett, called *A Woman's Reason*. When you read it you will know why I asked you.

If you could know how I love you at this moment. Good night.

Christmas Day

I have had no mail today, but I have hoped all the day that something from you was on its way to me, and I shall be most grievously disappointed if a letter should not arrive for me tomorrow. I cannot tell you how much I have thought of you today. As I read that short note of yours again, which begins "This is our first Christmas" the wonderful delicacy and daintiness which are your strong characteristics impressed me more forcibly than even the first time I read it. And on that subject of which that note consists principally I shall not attempt to say a word on paper. I told you it had overwhelmed me, entirely— and it did. . . .

Tuesday night. Another fatiguing but interesting day has just passed, and no word from you! It has troubled me very much, and yet I have felt very sure that you have written, and that Christmas has in some way delayed the letter. As soon as you read this I want you to write and tell me if you did receive the letter which you expected and watched for last Friday. Because it was written and sent and I have wondered so much since if it came safely to your own hand. I have thought a great deal within the past few days of your and my complications, and several things worry me exceedingly. But that does not affect the real life and spirit of it all, in the least. They are renewedly wonderful and rare and satisfying.

Wednesday night. And nothing yet from you! Why can it be so! I have watched and expected and hoped all day. . . .

The Mutual Discovery

Thursday morning. This morning too has brought me silence. I cannot understand it. If you could know how troubled I am I know you would send me at least a word. . . .

Friday evening, December 29. The outside circumstances and incidents of my life are very pleasant. The thought of you is joy always. And yet I am very much troubled to think what can be the possible reason why you do not write to me. And I am wondering too how the "Powers" are talking and acting and feeling. I hope it is not they—in any way—who keep you from writing. I feel very badly to think that you are probably wondering why you get nothing from me. But dont you see? It may be some idea of danger to us that keeps you from writing to me—and so it may not be safe for me to write to you even in the manner you suggested. I have "braced" myself to the idea now that I am not to hear from you and I am struggling in a truly pitiful manner to bear it, bravely. I am just as lonesome as I can be tonight. . . .

Saturday morning

Your queer note [following] has just come. I think I see now why you have not written, but as you will see when you have read these previous pages it would have been entirely safe. It seems so odd to read a note from you in a conventional style, and pretty dreadful, except that I see beneath it. Letters have been sent to two of your "Powers" since New York. They were not mentioned, I suppose. I know nothing of the movements of my "Powers" beyond what you know. If you should come as far as N.Y. or beyond, why could not you come still farther for a day!?

I don't know of anything exactly, but I expect to start Thursday afternoon next, to go through without change. Whether you can be likely to meet the *Power* in N.Y. I have no idea. I suppose I shall hear from him soon.

I only know I love you & that any kind of note in your writing is joy.

I love you. I *love* you.

[147]

Amherst, 28 Dec. '82
Thursday evening, 5½ p.m.

My dear Mrs. Todd

I presume you reached Washington all right on Saturday, though I have not heard of you beyond New York.

Ned went to Boston Monday—from there to Pittsfield today—Mattie joining him at Palmer, to stay there till next Tuesday. Of course our house as well as the Village is quiet without them and you. I am liable to be sent to New York— possibly to Philadelphia—next Tuesday and Wednesday and in this vein it occurs to me to wonder if Mr. Todd may not be along in New York about that time. If he is to be I will try to meet him. I suppose you will not return so soon.

If you have heard again from him and know what he plans please let me know.

I may not go—but am urged to and think quite likely I should.

Hope you are having the most delightful time and that your health is better, and to be better.

Most sincerely
Wm. A. Dickinson

I think you asked me before you left for my sister's ad- dress—

Miss Lavinia Dickinson
P.O. Box 207*

Mabel returned to Amherst on January 6, 1883, traveling north by train. To surprise her, David timed his return East to pick up the same train, coming aboard and greeting her at Palmer, the last connection before Amherst. After a night and

---

* Since Austin had free access to his sisters' mailbox at the Amherst post office, and usually delivered their mail to the Homestead himself, he was signaling Mabel to use Vinnie's address to reach him safely. In this and other small ways, Vinnie was engaged in the affair from the beginning.

a day's joyful reunion, the Todds called at the Dickinsons' the evening of January 7.

MABEL TO AUSTIN   [*8 January 1883*]^v
                              [*mailed to the Parker House, Boston*]
                                              Monday, 10 a.m.

The evening was too horribly chilling.

The whole atmosphere was cruel. I felt as if all the surroundings were pitiless. What new thing has occurred to make everything so dreadful? I must see you. It is necessary for me to see you soon. When I left—after the evening's unhappiness, and strain and reached home—I buried my face in a pillow and wept the bitterest tears I have shed for years. But they are the last. In fact the last two or three weeks have been very dreary and sad. I am the same to you as ever. Please do not ever lose sight of that—you know what it means, and I trust you infinitely, as I know you trust me. If I could have one hour with you, I should be far happier. But things look very cold and bleak to me this morning—in spite of out door brilliancy. I am trying my best to be brave and strong, and keep on my usual cheerful course, but I truly think that my light-hearted and careless expectation in life has gone for always. I am going through a most bitter experience, and it has suddenly changed me from what was almost a child's irresponsible joyousness into a woman's somewhat sad and sombre outlook on life. I have grown years in the past few weeks and it does seem to me now that I never can look at anything just the same as I used to do.

I shall undoubtedly come out of it, and be bright and cheerful again—but today my cheery philosophy has almost deserted me. My sunshine is sure to come out again—it always does, I cling to that—but I suffer not less now.

Forgive my writing in so melancholy a strain, but I cannot dissemble with you. If I am sad I have to tell you—for it comforts me. I am afraid I have not time to write more. There is an ocean of things to say to you, but I will wait. Only be sure that I am entirely unchanged to you, except for an additional strength of feeling! Good bye. I hope these days will be happier to you than they seem to me, but I know you feel with me, so I fear you are not cheerful either. But sunny days are coming—I am sure. In the meantime I will try to be brave and wait for my happiness, knowing that it is certainly coming to me again.

AUSTIN TO MABEL   [*ca. early 1883*][x]

It is inexpressible pain to me that you suffer, & suffer partly for me. If I could be with you I could drive it all away. In spirit I always am. Will you not let this comfort you a little?

A few evenings later the Todds endured a very unpleasant tea at the Evergreens. As Austin wrote the following note, Mabel was holding a "frank" talk with Sue, which temporarily cleared the air. The next months were not easy ones, however. David had no teaching assignments until the next term, Sue kept a constant vigil, and the lovers had little opportunity to be alone together.

[*13 January 1883*]
Saturday morning, 10 o'c.

My dear Mrs. Todd,

I expect to leave for Pittsfield on the 12:00 train. To return Tuesday afternoon. I greatly regret that it seems impracticable for me to see you before I go.

I send you and Mr. Todd my love, for whatever it may be worth, to keep while I am away, and shall hope to find you stronger when I come back than you looked last night!

Very sincerely, *W. A. Dickinson*

This note was handed to Austin, probably concealed in a book or newspaper, when David and Mabel stopped at his

[150]

office before tea on January 17. The same day Mabel wrote in her diary: "David & I are very happy together. We love each other freshly every day, and our life with each other is inexpressively joyous." That day she also began writing "Footprints," a romantic story of two lovers' discovery of each other, which she hoped *The Atlantic Monthly* would accept.

MABEL TO AUSTIN   [*17 January 1883*]ᵛ

I love you infinitely. Better than ever this moment. I feel sure that somehow we shall have a talk together very soon. Let us hope for it. In the meantime you *know* I have come to stay.

I trust you every second—through everything. Cannot you trust me? I "love you while I wait" more than tenderly. The thought of you is joy. Oh, for one hour with you!

AUSTIN TO MABEL   [*ca. early 1883*]ˣ

I love you, my darling. I love you, I want you, I need you. It takes all my nerve to hold myself away from you.

Saturday, January 20, was a pleasant day with the Dickinsons. Sue and Mattie made a lively call on Mabel in the morning, Mabel and Sue went for a sleigh ride together in the afternoon, and in the evening after choir rehearsal Mabel and David stopped at the Dickinsons' and Mabel sang for them. Her diary reports an "exceedingly satisfactory time."

MABEL TO AUSTIN   [*21 January 1883*]ᵛ

It was so very sad to me to be so near you and yet give no sign. I felt as if you must know and understand. *Did* you know that the room was brightest light when you were in it to me? I want you more than ever before. But I seem to feel newly that

I can wait—with a patience like that of the hills for something (I know not what) which will surely come. And you can wait. And we both know. And the ecstasy of being sure that you love me as you do is swallowing up everything else. I think of it and feel it thrillingly all the time. I LOVE you.

MABEL TO AUSTIN   [*28 January 1883*]ᵛ

I think of you all the time and the little glimpses I get of you are almost more than not any arent they? The atmosphere of your home is far more serene to me than a week or two ago, but still the constant air of watchfulness is very uncomfortable. When I think of the one person to whom it was all due in the first place [Ned] I confess that I experience a perhaps immeasurable feeling of wrath. And yet it is all not unnatural—I wonder if I shall ever again feel thoroughly careless and lighthearted. I think I shall, somehow—and all this time my presentiment (of which I told you) gets stronger and stronger. Are you glad of that? But above everything, *do* be careful of this note. It frightens me when I think of your having it with you when you come home. Will you not destroy it before you get home? *Do.* And I should feel infinitely happier if you would burn all of the others too. They, you know, are the only tangible things there are, and I find myself thinking of them constantly. Please destroy them, yours and mine too. No, I am sure that you and I never can deceive ourselves, however much we have to *act*, on the surface. It seems to me that with both the *real* thing has penetrated so deeply that it must stay. I am sure of it. How I should enjoy going about Boston with you! Can you not imagine one or two things as changed somewhat by which we could have a happy day there? And in the meantime I will love you every minute—as I know you are loving me. . . .

You must hand me a note, somehow, before very long—if it is possible. Indeed I do not see very much use in my staying here any longer. Do you? By saying the word (as on one previous occasion) I could start off any day. I am not very happy here, and those chances for which we wait seem to be so very short and few and far between. What do you think of my going away quite soon? . . .

I hope in some way that we may get something this week. A drive—or an hour in some way. But do not get it at the expense of any home wrath—for that is disastrous. I feel, notwithstanding a sadness at the changed circumstances since the fall, an entirely intrusive and apparently causeless hopefulness which I wish I might impart to you. My presentiment is coming to pass—I *know*—sometime. And I love you, and I will wait.

AUSTIN TO MABEL   [*ca. early 1883*]ˣ

When will that tomorrow be today? Days & weeks go by when it would be wine to me to see even the hem of your dress, not so much as that permitted me.

MABEL TO AUSTIN   [*17 February 1883*]ᵛ

It was to me a very painful evening. Never was the difference toward me more manifest by the leading "Power." The utter coldness (combined with unimpeachable courtesy) was well nigh unbearable. Several times I thought I must leave the room, it was so suffocating in its mental atmosphere. Then when you came, a bright light shone for an instant for me. There is something radically wrong somewhere when two people who have looked each other squarely in the face and have spoken most intimate truths, and have so entire an understanding of each other as we have, are obliged to meet in public in this distressing way. Every thought of you is joy—but last night I felt as if I would not bear the feeling exhibited toward me any longer & much as you *know* I love you I shall be glad to go away. Do you think it would be wise for me ever to ask her what is the reason of this last change—within a week or two—or had I best let it go, trusting that it may get better without interference?

About the sleigh ride next week I think perhaps the best way will be to go, and tell of it when you come back, as if it had been quite unpremeditated. Do not you? . . . I do not dare to come out at noon any more, because I ran upon the Chief Power shopping the last time I ventured out. They all seem to have taken to irregular times of being around lately. You said "I am famished for you." That was worth all the rest of the note. I read it a dozen times over, just that one sentence, before it was burned. It seems unfair that she should be cold and dreadful to me, and overpoweringly sweet to you, because of this thing, does it not? Whatever happens, you are petted & cajoled, and I am hated. I suppose it is always so. But I wish she wouldn't. Suppose you say on Sunday evening that you are coming here to call and invite her to come too. I am curious to see how she will act here. I think that will be a good idea. Will you do it? . . . I feel perfectly discouraged this morning. It does not seem to me as if things would ever get any better with her. *Had* I best have any conversation with her? But all the time grows and strengthens a certain presentiment which you know about. At this moment it is tremendously strong. Can you see how I can still love her very much? But I do—she stimulates me intellectually more than any other woman I ever knew. She is fascinating to me. I would do *any thing* to make her like me again. She has such pretty feminine hands and wrists, and she had some very pretty little quaint bracelets last night. I could have gone to her and kissed them at any moment. I do care a great deal for her— and I am inexpressibly sorry for her—when I think of the great, rare, wonderful true love which she has not and which you have so superbly given to me. Oh I appreciate and rejoice in it. I do, I do—goodbye. I love you as ever—wait patiently.

MABEL TO AUSTIN   [*26 February 1883*]
                                            Monday morning

And you did not come in last night. You do not know how I miss you when so long a time goes by without my seeing you. Here with this scrap is the "bit" I wrote to you on Saturday. I am quite ashamed to send it—with its pin holes and general crumpled appearance. But when I have to wear a note around in all sorts of queer ways to get the chance of getting it to you, mere daintiness cannot be considered. It hurts me to give you any such disreputable looking documents. Well [Sue's tea for Professor Tyler's fiancée] went by with less awkwardness than I feared it might. I am anxious to know what was said about it— if anything. I have not had a note from you for a long time. I need one very much. Your written words are strong and tender, next to your voice in helpfulness. When shall I see you again?

AUSTIN TO MABEL   [*ca. early 1883*]ˣ

I fell to wondering *why* I loved you—why, after having gone so far stirred only in the most general way by fair & fine women on every side, I should suddenly have seen something in you different from any other, that waked me into new life, inspired me with new thoughts & feelings, filled my imagination with possibilities undreamed before, transformed the world— made everything exuberant, wild, thrilling, satisfying. I had always thought I liked _____ and yet you are the one. I would leave the whole race for you. I have already done so. The wonder will never cease, of course, for the secret is too deep for discovery—it eludes all search, is fixed in the original constitution of all things—like life, & light, it is, and it is—that must suffice.

I trust you, believe you, rest in you, abidingly, most lovingly, and with this good night, dear heart. I say it regretfully for it implies I leave you, but that I never do. You are with me & of me every instant. Once more I love you, I *love* you.

On February 14 Mabel and Austin had trysted in the dining room at the Homestead for the first time. It proved to be a good meeting place, although Sue was not fooled. When Austin visited with Mabel and David there the evening of February 27, his diary records he was "sent for by Sue to escort her to Coll. Hall to look at the dancing there. After which a night of it." By mid-March Mabel was being made so uncomfortable by Sue she decided to leave Amherst for a time—without David, who was resuming his teaching responsibilities.

[*16 March 1883*]

I trust you as I trust God. I love you unutterably. I hardly know how this coming long separation has come about, but it may not be so long after all. I do not know where I shall be—or what I shall do this summer, except this possibility of a long journey, and that is indefinite as yet. I have a great many things to tell you, and the presentiment is overwhelmingly strong. Something will come very soon for us. I cannot be deceived in a feeling which is as certain of its fulfillment as my tender presentiment is. I have thought of you during the past week [while away in Cambridge] more lovingly than ever before—and constantly. Oh! I love you. I *love* you. Imagine it as written again and again. If I could only say it to you, and I must within a day or two. Read the first sentence of this note again. Can you *feel* all that means to me? Oh! I want you so! I love you so. Darling, darling!

[*Washington, 25 March 1883*][v]
Sunday morning

Your two letters have been perfectly delightful, and welcome beyond anything you can imagine. I could not resist the temptation of sending you a line or two in reply. I shall be alone (you know in what sense) until Friday next [when David came for her "auspicious" time of the month]. Not after that, for a week; and I am very sure that not before that will there be any new arrivals. So if you write me as soon as you receive this, your reply will come before Friday—as it must.

The pictures which you have drawn in these letters are bewilderingly lovely—every word is read and re-read. Sometime they will be realities. And the joyous trust expressed in them is almost the tenderest and most satisfying thing of all.

Yes, you have not only looked within the wall—you have come in and taken up permanent abode there. And it is joy to know it and feel it. I should like to write all sorts of details. They would interest you, but I think I will reserve those until later. Do you think the Powers were very angry with *me* because of that final drive?

It is so beautiful to me, to think of you, sitting by your open fire alone, and knowing so well what you are dreaming about. Do you remember all I said to you on that drive? Well, I repeat it all now, only more of it, deeper and stronger. . . .

I think it will be well for you to enclose with [your next letter] a pleasant, conventional note, which if necessary I can show—and perhaps address the outside yourself. Yes, I am sure that will be very advisable.

Someone is coming—goodbye. I *love* you. The realization of my presentiment is nearer today than it was yesterday. — Later. This seems such a poor return for the glorious letters you have written me, that I am almost resolved not to send it. But here it goes. And I am seized with a great tremor, as I send it. Do let me know, just as soon as you get it. Do, *do*.

Amherst, 28 Mar. '83
Wednesday afternoon

My dear Mrs. Todd,

All Amherst has cleared out [for spring vacation], Mr. Todd included. All but Mr. Chickering [English professor at Amherst College] and he goes tonight. Even [your friends] Mrs. Tuckerman and Miss Glezen. Seelye and I alone are left to look after the wreck. It is sunny here, and muddy, and windy, and generally springy. Not warm enough to walk with pleasure, and too rough to ride. The best time in the world to go to Washington, or Florida—or Mexico. I wish I were in either for the long transition from Winter to Spring in this latitude. Sue and Mattie, you know, are in New York, and report a brilliant season. So much so I have advised them not to return. From the gaiety of the metropolis to the desolation of Amherst I fear will be too much for them, and I am sure it will for me. Ned, Gib & I are having fine bachelor times, enjoying rare freedom. Would put up with an occasional break however, if of the right sort.

Mr. Todd told me before he left he had directed Mr. Lovell to bring your photographs when finished to me to select one for myself, and send the rest to you. This I shall be very glad to do especially selecting one for myself, but if Lovell isn't more rapid in this work than in others where I have had experience with him, I shall see the original first and deliver the package in person.

I hope you are having a lovely visit—and will be ready to come back *some* time. Should be glad to hear how you are filling your days. All of which is respectfully submitted—not quite as necessary, but done for the dash.

With much love
Your friend as ever
Wm. A. Dickinson

Washington, 9 April 1883

My dear Mr. Dickinson:

I have so many things to thank you for, that I hardly know which one to begin with. Your note came during my sickness, and did me a wonderful amount of good. And the substantial "greeting" [of Maple Sugar] from Sunderland Park was the most welcome remembrance I could have had. It is an especial weakness of mine—and I saw beyond it the great trees in the little glade of last summer's picnic ground, and the wonderful cloudy sky above. . . . The photographs [see jacket] arrived in the best of order on Saturday. I am curious to know which one you preferred. They are certainly not in the least flattering, not as much as I wish they were, I am obliged to confess.

Yes, I had what is for me a very severe illness, but I escaped a much greater one by the kind and constant attention of our good Doctor. I fear it was not a very cheerful welcome for Mr. Todd, to arrive in the midst of it. But I am very much better now, indeed almost well again, although a little tremulous occasionally. This genial physician has announced to me that I am tired out, and must take an almost entire rest this spring.

He told me a number of unwelcome truths. So I have abandoned my long-desired piano study and I am devoting myself to sleeping—and other occupations too mundane for expression. I think I shall not return to Amherst before the latter part of May, and I may stay here until June, then going directly to Hampton with Millicent and Grandma. There is still a possibility of a California trip, I believe. But my coming days are all rather misty.

Will you give my love to your sisters? I hope I may hear from you again soon. I shall be very forlorn after Mr. Todd's departure, and a word from you is always most welcome. . . .

Mabel Loomis Todd

While attending Mabel, the Loomis family's young physician, Dr. Eaton ("our good Doctor"), fell under her spell. The following fall he confessed that he thought of her all the time, and "prayed heaven [she] might have some little illness that he might have the joy of curing [her]." But Mabel wouldn't let this flirtation progress very much, having had "all the experience I ever want with jealous wives" (Journal, September 16, 1883).

MABEL TO AUSTIN   [*Washington, 25 April 1883*]
                        [*mailed to the Parker House, Boston*]

Your letter came this afternoon—Wednesday. I thank you so very *very* much for relieving my mind so soon. I found a four-leafed clover on my way home this afternoon, and although it was a little thing, it cheered me so that I made up my mind that my sunshine is coming out again. I take it as a sort of hopeful omen. I do not know what is going to happen, but I feel sure of coming brightness. Am I foolish to be cheered by a superstition? It is more than that. Yes, I want you to write me as you did in March, and just as freely and naturally. I am sorry you have only two more of the covers, but you will put these two between the others—first one kind and then the other. Either is always unmolested. Has your sister had a note from me within a few days? I wrote her last Sunday.* It troubles me very much that you are enduring so much nervous tension. I am fearing that you will be injured by it. *Please* be careful. You wrote, "Time will prove that omission a costly one." It is not an omission anymore. I have heard; and I will tell you all about it sometime.† It is true that I have suffered terribly, and I can hardly bear to think of again placing myself where I may have renewed cause for pain. Still I am undecided. I do not know what to do. I am peaceful now, at least, if not particularly happy. Will it be advisable for me to appear there? Do write me, "how things seem to be going," and everything else you think of. I do understand your longing—I appreciate it all. If I could talk with you an hour even, but this week will not last forever, nor this month, nor this year. I came to stay; and sometime you will look back upon all these days of pain with exultant, triumphant happiness in their entire banishment from your life. In the perfect and joyful satisfaction and contentment of some sunny day in the future, you will think of them as only a dreary and dark, but transient portal, through which you came to light and peace. I know this. Good night. . . .

[*Washington, 12 May 1883*]
Saturday evening

The two letters did come safely—and the one this afternoon; I should have written you of it before, but I was really

---

* She had. Vinnie replied on April 30, "I think if the real reason of your absence was known, there would be great indignation."

† Mabel's reference is to a box of arbutus she sent Sue in mid-April, for which she received no thanks. Instead Sue insulted her by sending money to pay for the piano lessons Mabel had given Mattie during the fall and winter. In a letter to David, Mabel reported her response to Mrs. Dickinson: "I am sorry that you have given money for what was only a pleasure to me. You have done for me that which no number of lessons could repay, & I hoped you would allow me the satisfaction of this slight return."

cowardly about the mental distraction and anxiety which always overwhelm me between the time of sending you anything and the hearing of its arrival in your hands. I am coming at the time you know of. I am having unusually happy times here,* and I would give *anything* if I were coming back to an entirely serene environment. I should like, at least, to have outer courtesies sustained. I should like to have [the members of your family] call, at least with an appearance of cordiality. I *think* they will do this. But I am very anxious to have nothing occur to cause an open ceasing of all civility. That I could not bear. I think you had better not ask them to do anything, or express a hope about anything. If sometime next week you mention that I am coming, they may say something. I leave here the morning of the twenty-first. I *wish* they were cordial and sweet to me, but I am getting not to care as much as I did. I feel much happier about it all. For you I am always unchanged, as you know. I am very hopeful, and brightness seems coming nearer and nearer in the immediate future. I shall not stay very long even when I do come—for many reasons which I will tell you. But shall I see you, to have even a quiet half hour's talk? Can it be arranged? It will I am sure, and yet I cannot do anything to excite any new displeasure. But happiness is coming—it travels very fast, and is very near. Don't you know this? I feel it constantly. . . .

Mabel returned to Amherst on May 12, bringing her daughter, Millicent, and Grandma Wilder, for a month that began well but gradually soured as far as relations with Sue were concerned. At the same time, Mabel's friendship with Vinnie and Emily Dickinson flourished in an exchange of notes and flowers, and she met Austin several times at their home.

* Recovered from her early depression of spirits, Mabel wrote David in late April that she was "almost reproducing my girlish experiences of sixteen engagements in four days." She also assured her husband she felt "bereft, and I love you unutterably. My David, my David Darling!" Mabel was planning to return to him in Amherst for her "auspicious" time.

Only one letter survives the period. It was copied by Austin and later misfiled with his 1884 correspondence.

Mabel to Austin   [*ca. early June 1883*]

I have thought all day about you and I want to see you more than I can express. I love you most deeply every moment, and a drive alone with you seems radiant joy even in anticipation. I have looked with great tenderness upon two or three places lately—where we were once together—the Mill Valley walk, and another—just beyond Mrs. Heaton's. Do you remember them?

Oh! My darling, *sometime* we shall go *together* over all the drives, and walks, and places of happy memory. Did you know that the crickets have come! In every little chirp I seem to hear one expression of your wonderful love for me. It is a love which cannot fail to move circumstances and conditions, and bring its reward.

It is of God—true and marvelously tender and rare. And I love you! How can I help it. You understand me. You appreciate every little fineness. You bring out every truest part of my nature.

I feel very hopeful and happy today. As I have told you before—*something* is coming to bring us nearer together—and that soon. I have no idea what, but that does not matter—I love you.

Will you *please* burn this today! I know you will, because I ask you. I have *so* many things to say to you, but I hope this one note will say a little to you.

Mabel left for Winchester, Massachusetts, near Boston, to visit Wilder cousins the last week in June, then went on with Millicent and Grandma Wilder to spend three months at Hampton, New Hampshire. She wrote to Austin very little during this long summer, out of fear Sue would intercept her letters, and instead devoted herself to painting, singing, surf bathing, and enjoying three loving visits from David. The following two letters from Austin, the first a "cover" letter, were written and sent to Hampton on the same day, probably in the same envelope, soon after Mabel arrived there.

Amherst, 12 July '83

My dear Mrs. Todd,

Yours of 7th received Monday, and that of 11th this morning.

I have been out of sorts the last two or three days, and quitting my office Tuesday afternoon—I have only returned this afternoon.

That's the reason you haven't heard from me. The chairs have not yet announced themselves at this end. I will make special inquiry in the morning—and soon as possible—see what about more. Just now Seelye is in the White Mountains, back Saturday.

Things progress slowly at Walker Hall, but Boston promises to make up for any and all delays in the home stretch.*

No movement of the gymnasium. About Town the French School is the feature—over 250 they tell me.†

Nothing here suggests Amherst College. All is friendly and gay. On the whole rather a pleasant change for a while. The little there is of more special & peculiar interest.

I have just written to Mr. Todd. You are to see him so soon

---

* Austin was supervising reconstruction of Walker Hall, the college's science building, which had burned to the ground in April 1882. David lost his astronomical library and all his calculations in the fire. The reference here is to the architects, Peabody and Stearns of Boston.

† Plans for the Pratt Gymnasium were underway. The French School was a six-week language institute that took place in the village each summer for many years.

I wont repeat. I am very much complimented by your invitation to join you in Boston and go on to Hampton—and wouldn't I like it! but just at this time I hardly think I shall be able. Shall be interested to know when you choose to give it to me, Mr. Loomis' view of the Librarian question. It seems to be understood generally that the place is being held open for Goodell. At the same time Mrs. Scanton told Vin that she didn't think he would take it, that he thought first the Agricultural College needed him, and second that he was more free there than he would be in the Library. . . .*

Hope you will come out all right from whatever you are in at New York. The stock market is to me perfectly sickening.†

yrs vy ty as ever
W. A. Dickinson

Amherst, 12 July '83
Thursday afternoon

My dear Mrs. Todd

Your note to Vin was information to me too of your safe arrival at Hampton, and first impressions there after five years. Now I should be glad to have some of your second—and how you are using the time as the days go by. If you wont write me directly, or dont dare, write Vin, and I'll keep a little track of

---

* Mabel had inquired about the library opening on her father's behalf. The trustees voted at their July 26, 1883, meeting to appoint H. H. Goodell, later president of the Agricultural College, and when he refused they appointed William I. Fletcher at their autumn meeting. Mabel mentioned to her parents in early September that the position was still open, but did not urge her father to take it. She was curiously unsympathetic all summer toward financial woes that filled her mother's letters as Molly and Eben struggled to meet the debt on their home.

† During the short financial panic of 1883 David ran back and forth to New York City, where he was engaged in railroad speculation.

you through her.* I intended to have made report of myself—
and matters here before this—but between the oppressive
weather—duties I could not omit, postpone or delegate, and
people I could not escape, I have been put to close quarters lately
—and pretty well fagged. To begin at the beginning—and with
the most interesting—after I left you at the station I finished my
errands and was back in Amherst at eight o'clock.† [John] Sanford called almost as soon as I was fairly in the house and sat with
me on the piazza till after 11, which precluded examination that
night. At breakfast next morning the question came square—
after leading up properly—"Did you see Mrs. Todd." I had
anticipated it and said at once, "Certainly, that was what I went
to Boston for." This unhesitating frankness was somewhat stun-
ning and the rally wasn't prompt. When it came, it was, "She
told me she was to spend a few days in Boston before going to
Hampton and I concluded you would see her." I replied yes I
said I did. This ended it. There has been no allusion to it, or
you, since. I dont know whether on the whole I am supposed to
have lied about it or not, but *you* know I spoke the truth. Nothing exciting of any kind since. The usual eating and sleeping,
riding and sitting about. Sue and Ned have been to Lock's Pond
and Leverett, and to Shutesbury, among other places, and have
definitely arranged to leave for a fortnight of Shutesbury 1st
August, with more or less of a party not yet organized. They
say I am to come up every evening and return in the morning
in season for business and that this will be for my health.

I dont know but it will and I dont know but I shall do all
this driving. We shall see.

Mr. Todd writes me he is to be in H. next Saturday morning—and asks me to join him in Boston and go with him. Isnt
that an idea! And wouldn't I like to. I wonder if such a trip
would benefit my health.

---

* Vinnie wrote Mabel this same day, "I hope the sea will wash away
all bitterness."

† On June 29 Mabel and Austin had met in Boston during the morning
and walked about the Common together for several hours.

The Town is full of the French School, and the streets are quite gay with their strolling about at evening.

Will write you again before long—and hope you will let me hear from you.

I send you herewith half a dozen Village views, which you may like occasionally to take up—my love, my best wishes—and my goodbye.

I hope the summer may be most pleasant to you. That the brightness of the passing days at Hampton may crowd down all memory of the unpleasantness of the days here. And that circumstances may so change as to make your return home in September easy and agreeable. I cannot but believe they will.

I suffer for every wound you have received from my family, but for the time have seemed powerless to prevent them.

What strength I have however will be pitted against any more of them.

I will straighten the matter out before the summer is over, or smash the machine—

I had rather be under the wreck than under what I am. There would be several other broken heads, certainly, and I would take the chance of coming out on top.

Amherst, 7 August [*1883*]
Tuesday evening

My dear Mrs. Todd

I think you ought by this time to expect some further report from me, even if it has not occurred to you before. At any rate I have had it in mind to write for several days, but business has precluded pleasure.

To begin, the family are at Shutesbury—as I wrote you they would be, on and after August 1, and have had an accident, Gib and [cousin] Issie Cutler having been pitched out of a wagon backwards in Montague, where they had gone to attend an evening entertainment the night after they had reached their Mecca.

It turns out they are not seriously injured however, though

Issie Cutler didn't understand where she was for about fourteen hours. Gib was a little dazed, and had some headache the next day, is all right now.

They sent a messenger for me next morning, and I went up, and again Sunday afternoon, returning Monday morning. So they are fairly started. "Brad" Hitchcock and Will Bliss their only company at present. Everybody seemed to give out when the time arrived.

I suppose I ought to be jealous or something of that sort over Mrs. D living up there with those fellows, but I dont seem to be.

I am at Northampton day times this week, driving over in the morning after an early breakfast, and back between 5 & 6. Had an early adjournment today and I was with Fred Law Olmsted from 3 to 6 on the everlasting gymnasium location. Haven't nearly had time to enjoy my loneliness. . . .

They'll be back before I know it, and not so very long before *you* will be back too.

Mr. Todd writes me he is to meet you in Boston Friday, and invites me to join and sail up to Hampton next day. I certainly would make some business for Boston if I were not absolutely tied here. Am very sorry it happens so. I think Vin wrote you of Henry Hills' failure—and the way it shattered him. He seems to improve very little.*

Are you going to New Jersey to keep house? And is there anything new in your life? The French people keep the town looking gay—and just now the Dickinsons are pouring in.† The regular residents here make very little show.

---

* Henry Hills, neighbor of the Dickinsons, owned a straw hat factory, the largest local industry. Austin helped Hills recover financially, and was a good friend to Henry and Adelaide Hills through this trying time.
† The large, widespread Dickinson family traced its American origins to Nathaniel Dickinson, who landed at Plymouth, Massachusetts, in 1630 and moved to Hadley in 1659. A family reunion, which Austin usually attended briefly, was held each summer in the town, and still is. The 1880 census listed more Dickinsons than Smiths living in Amherst.

Perhaps sometime or other you will venture a short epistle to me again.

This is nothing, but must go for tonight. Goodbye.

Wm. A.

[enclosed note]

Can you endure this silence longer?

I cannot

I said too much when I said you needn't write

'Tis too dreadful!

Do speak

MABEL TO AUSTIN   [*Hampton, 25 September 1883*]
Friday afternoon

Your brief note was like a gleam of sunshine on a cloudy day. I could not imagine why you had not written before. Yes, it "covered all," but I should have liked to hear it reiterated. You knew why I did not write. I sent a verbal message of appreciation for the most welcome gift you sent me from Boston. I will add to it when I see you. Am I ever to have an opportunity of saying anything to you? And are you *sure* things are going smoothly, and will go in a serene and pleasant way? I feel much happier about it than before for a long time. And I remember every incident of a portion of a day which I spent in Boston last June, with more and more delight. It is as clear as if it had been yesterday. Yes, "I am the same." And never to be otherwise. I am sorry "just to miss you," but perhaps it is as well, since everything has to be so prudent. And other days are coming. I have had a very restful, and advantageous summer. I feel well and strong, and mentally peaceful. . . . You must send me one of your wonderful letters when you have received this. And *will* you destroy this before you leave Boston? A smallest slip now would destroy all the approaching peace, and with it many happy days. . . . This is my last writing to you for this season. Please let me know right away that you have received it. Have you *anything* in my handwriting now?

Saturday evening, 9:30. I must come again tonight. I have been thinking all day about one of the very first anniversaries— already past—the going by the gate. It rained and I could not see even a step ahead. But I did not want to see. There was a rare delight in not knowing what was coming—either on the glistening sidewalk, or on that other mental path which was to lead me—even now can I say where? Yes. I entered it boldly and happily, led by something thoroughly outside of myself and my will. And now there are anniversaries all the time. I have thought them all over today—*so* gladly—every one, from the very beginning. I believe it to be an experience wholly exceptional. An opening so strange, so unexpected, and so ineffably beautiful, could not lead to anything commonplace or trivial. . . . And that same rainy evening, after I had come into the light and talk, I remember so well what suddenly came in and filled the room with a strange and delicious warmth and fragrance, and a far more shining brightness than fire or candles could have made. With the entrance of that, a whole new future opened—possibilities quivered before me—although even then I scarcely comprehended its significance. That evening made one of my whitest days. What has followed was inevitable. . . . I can forget all the pain, bitter as it has been, and rejoice strongly; for it has not really injured *me*—only my happiness for a time—and I can see by the way it affects me how wonderfully tenacious and vigorous that wonderful something in my life is. . . . It came to stay—not a day only or even a year, but for always. And this you know; and can walk about with that consciousness in your heart, during all those days which you call "simply waiting." . . .

Monday afternoon

How the crickets are chirping today, and how the asters shine from the roadside! . . . I have made up my mind to do everything possible for peaceful and courteous relations. If only they might be cordial! But perhaps that will come in time. At all event I cannot have such coldness and more than that as last spring showed. It nearly killed me. When you write, will you tell me how everything looks, and what I had better do and say under all conditions. Will any questions be put to me? And am I ever to see you yourself? . . .

Tuesday morning, later

Your sweet, sweet little note has just come. "Do I want to see you!" If only you knew how much I want to see you! And "do I think you are talked out." That is not possible—nor will it ever be. If you only might be "incog." What delight . . . *be careful* of this. . . .

Mabel returned to Amherst with Millicent and Grandma Wilder on September 29, browned, high-spirited, and ten pounds heavier, to find herself acclaimed for the recent appearance of her story "Footprints," in the *New York Independent*. But the Dickinsons were preoccupied with the illness of Gib, who had contracted typhoid fever. When he died on October 5 (the Todds attended his funeral on the ninth) Austin was in despair. Mabel told her parents, "It is terrible even to think of his grief." She saw little of him for about six weeks, meanwhile becoming the toast of the village by acting the lead in an amateur production of Frances Hodgson Burnett's *A Fair Barbarian*, which was performed on November 23. "Footprints" was reprinted in the *Amherst Record*, and David had copies privately printed. Toward the end of November, regular meetings, walks, and drives with Austin began again, but Sue seemed too wrapped in her grief to know or care. Perhaps Sue realized that with Gib's death her last hold on Austin was gone. Walker Hall was finished, the science faculty moved back in, and David created space in his office rooms for Mabel to have a painting studio and receive friends.

The Mutual Discovery

Can you guess so long before whether you will be in mood
for a walk at 5—or short drive—and which? and where shall I
find you? at your house, the post office or on the street—

The advantage of the house is that we might promise ourselves a sight of our mutual friend [David].

Or if you dont care for either, I will come in for a little call
not far from 8.

W.A.D.

Nov. 22, early afternoon

It is so warm & pleasant, why not the drive?

Mabel to Austin   [29 *November 1883*]

Thursday

I must say a few words to you on this Thanksgiving Day.
You know how I would joyfully brighten it to you if I might—
and how I could. But I probably cannot see you all the day. You
know that my thoughts are with you every moment, and my
tender love; and please let this thought be with you if you ever
feel sad and lonely today. I know the day must be in some respects a very sad one, but do you remember what our mutual
friend [David] said to you Tuesday afternoon—that you have
some things to be thought of thankfully this year which you
never had before? And I knew as you heard this, what you
would remember—and I was glad. . . . I thank God that my part
in your life has been a joyous and a helpful one. I rejoice more
every day in the immensity of the love which you have given so
magnificently. You have made me grander and nobler every
day—you have yourself made me more worthy of the splendid
gift in which I so rejoice. . . . I trust you as I trust God. The
way in which you love me is a consecration—it is the holy of
holies, and a thought, even commonplace, would desecrate it. I
approach it even in my mind as a shrine, where the purest and

noblest there is in me worships. Ah! I appreciate your love for me—I know I do. And in return I give you my own true, unwavering, intense love, as well. It has never known a fluctuation since the beginning. . . . My darling, I love you infinitely.

The following letter was scissored into five paragraphs, which originally may have occurred in a different order.

AUSTIN TO MABEL   [*29 November 1883*]

Love, Love, dear love. This is our second Thanksgiving. I loved you a year ago, and I know it. I love you a great deal more now though. My love and your love have expanded and exceeded one. All I am—and all I can be—I give to you. I want to write now—I have.

Yes, darling I *have* something to be thankful for, and grateful for, this sad day, with my boy gone, and except for you, alone. I have *you*. Would to God I had you closer—in my house, at my hearth, in my arms! Would not this be too much? *Would it!*

Darling, I love you in all the ways I have ever told you, and in all the ways love has, but my love for you today is a more solemn and sacred thing than ever before.

I realize that it is you and your love that stand behind it—and are revealed by it. We have indeed come to the holy of holies.

I know you will not change either. You are beyond your years—vastly, in knowledge and experience of the human heart, and in subtle distinction and realization of the deepest secrets of human life. If anything is true—and real, our love is. We were made to give joy to each other. I love you—I love you.

AUSTIN TO MABEL   [*ca. early December 1883*][x]

Written words alone are too insufficient now. We have come too near together. We want the true quick speech of the eye—the personal presence which allows the wild life current to throb back and forth from one to the other, with its subtle messages of information and response in no other wise to be imparted or conveyed, as we stand just before the veil of closest intimacy. We must wait for these—we will get them as soon as we can. Meanwhile, my beloved & my own, soul of my soul, & life of my life, rest assured of everything—everything that I am, can say, or think, or do, or be—all are yours. And my business must be to keep the white heat which engulfs my being from flaming in the surface.

Between this letter and the next occurred the consummation of their love, in the dining room at the Homestead on December 13, 1883. It took place with David's concurrence, for he and Mabel had talked things through three nights earlier. Mabel's justification of the step is found in her journal three months later: "[Austin] has expressly told me over and over again that I kept him alive through the dreadful period of Gilbert's sickness and death. He could not bear the atmosphere of his own house, & used to go to his sisters', & then he or Lavinia would send for me—& it was on those oases from the prevailing gloom in his life that he caught breath & gathered strength to go on. . . . He recovered from the blow enough to wish to live *for me*. . . . My life has a sort of consecration now, & all outward things seem changed. His love for me is something sacred; it dignifies me & elevates me. I thank God daily for it.

"And all the time my dear David & I are very happy & tender & devoted companions. My married life is certainly exceptionally sweet & peaceful & satisfying, & [David's] nature is just the one to soothe & rest me. I love him better all the time, and appreciate him more."

Late on December 20 Mabel, David, Millicent, and Grandma Wilder left Amherst for Washington, to be gone seven weeks. By then Austin and Mabel had met twice more at the Homestead.

AUSTIN TO MABEL

[20 December 1883]
Thursday eve
By Lamp light

What words are adequate now! Wonderful and beautiful and inspiring as they have been in these months and days of the last year and a half, we are beyond them now. We can hardly more than repeat with them. There is more now in the deep silent look down each other's eyes—in the consciousness of nearness, even to absolute unison of being. What language is to measure our last experiences! We know them—they are a part of us forever more—they are ourselves—and they are ours.

I understand them, darling, I appreciate them, even to the finest shade—all their greatness, all their solemnity, all their sublimity. *I do*—and for what you have given me I give you the whole devotion of my soul for time and for eternity. Can I say more!

As the darkness of the evening deepens I find I am to miss you terribly, more than I had thought before. But I shall have a great stay in my near memory—and I shall try to bear it bravely. I shall know that at 5 every evening, the time we have had for walking and smiling, and at nine again, and at ten in the morning, you are thinking wholly of me and that you know I am thinking wholly of you. We shall probably think of each other at several other times in the day.

Now I must leave to find you at the station.

I love you—how! *As I can love.*

One more goodbye dear, dear heart—

Sweet goodbye—

[24 December 1883]
Monday morning, 10 o'clock

A cold, snowy morning—

A lonesome Sunday gone, and tomorrow Christmas. What of it! The day I was brought up to believe was a joint device of the Devil and the Romish Church for the overthrow of the true religion, and accordingly to be frowned upon by all good people. I wasn't very good and didn't frown much, but seeing none of the brilliancy and joyousness of it in Amherst, thought little about it any way.

True religion has changed, and it is almost as bad now not to smile upon it. So I send you this my word greeting, reserving the right to add something to it a little later from Boston just to keep you from entirely forgetting me, perhaps this week—perhaps not till next, depending upon my getting some papers I want from the West.

You went through all right of course—reached Washington on time, were warmly welcomed, and all together, must form a happy circle. I should like to look in upon it.

Up here it is mid-winter. Everything is buried in snow, cold as Greenland and a trifle dreary to me. The fact is I have been seeing so much more of you lately than anybody else outside of our devoted household, I am quite bereft by your absence, and dont adjust myself at once to the allied condition, hesitate whether I will go to walk at 5 or not, my health for the time being not seeming to make special demand upon me.

I have been up to Walker Hall once—sent for—but haven't walked since our family meeting on the moon that bleak Thursday noon.* That was good enough for a story. . . .

Well no allusion has ever been made to that meeting in any way, and no act has suggested it. All is Tranquil, perhaps a little more attention is paid to my comfort, and wishes, and perhaps there is a little air of having discovered that it has all been of no use, that I have not really been brought under, but have maintained a supreme independence beneath the surface. I think on the whole the fact was impressive, and the lesson perhaps salutary.

---

* On December 20, the day Mabel left town, she and Austin had a farewell walk together north from the village at noontime. To accommodate it, Austin told Sue he hadn't time for a drive with her, so it was a tense moment when Sue and Ned in the Dickinson sleigh came up alongside the strolling couple.

This is a pretty abrupt ending, and I haven't said all I would—but it is this or nothing for the mail that reaches you tomorrow morning—best wishes for you all.

Tell Mr. Todd we had an alarm of fire about 11½ yesterday forenoon. The Methodist church, which broke up all the services, and made a general riot, but didn't burn much.*

MABEL TO AUSTIN　　　　[*Washington, D.C.*] 26th Dec. [*1883*]
Wednesday, 10 a.m.

Ten o'clock, and five o'clock, and nine o'clock! How glad I am for all those times—and how *near* they come! Have you noticed? "So that I may not entirely forget you!" That was a touch beyond what I could have given. Even our mutual friend remarked "as if you could ever do that?" Of course I understood, but it almost frightened me. I was thankful beyond words to see your handwriting again. I had watched for the letter for two days. It has just come, this morning. I am very glad that Christmas is over. I knew it would be hard, and desolate for you, and I thought of you all the time—as always, to be sure. It is a long interval between ten o'clock and five. I do not limit myself to them; but I always have a special memory about one, when I know you are alone. I am very fond of that time—you are alone at your desk, and in the room I come unseen, but I come as emphatically as when I made you that entirely unexpected little call one morning last week, and far more. I have, in these few days of absence from you, such a bewildering accumulation of things to say to you, that a month will not suffice to convey them all to you. I miss you terribly, but I think of you every moment. Permeating everything I do and think, is this wonderful memory of you. I am glad and grateful for it; and everything. Twilights are eloquent of you—sunny mornings mean you—

---

* The tone of this letter suggests it was intended to be read by both Mabel and David. It is more revealing than former "cover" letters, but lacks the intimacy of a love letter, indicating that David, while cognizant of his wife's relationship with Austin, was not privy to its passion.

everything bears some relation to you, and my memories glow like bright and present realities—all.

This is all for this morning. You know the rest, you know everything—you appreciate; you know.

MABEL TO AUSTIN   [*ca. 1883*]

P.S. FIRST*

You are all that I have to live for—
    All that I want to love,
All that the whole world holds for me
    Of faith in a world above.
You came—and it seemed too mighty
    For my human heart to hold;
It seemed, in its sacred glory
    Like a glimpse through the gates of gold.
Like life in the perennial Eden,
    Created, formed anew,
This dream of a perfect manhood
    That I realize in you.

Perhaps not out of place here is a letter from Sue to her son, which suggests her state of mind as 1883 came to a close.

SUE TO NED†   [*29 December*] 1883

My dearest Ned,

It were idle to tell you this morning that I do not miss you. It were cruel to tell you *how* I miss you. Neither of us could

* A poem, apparently composed by Mabel and assigned by her to 1883. References to "P.S. 1st" proliferate later on. With the poem was a note, perhaps originally enclosed:
    Always P.S. I
    Will this do?
    P.S. II?

† Ned was away at Pittsfield, visiting the Jenkins family.

bear it. I rejoice that you are away—just the change of different objects is worth something to you. . . . You must not be anxious about us. We are well and need only what no one can give us. Papa will not go to Boston until Tuesday night so you need not come till then unless you want to. I know how congenial and lovely the family all will be to you, and I am sure it will heal your wounded spirit. Give my tender love to them all. It is a handsome winter morning so we shall all drive and enjoy the sunshine. Matty will write you and Papa also. Mrs. Scarritt comes down to play [the piano] with Matty this morning and that you know I shall enjoy.* Keep well and God bless you and then all will be well.

Ever lovingly
Your Mother

* Mrs. Elizabeth Scarritt was Mabel's friend, a fellow boarder at Mrs. Robison's, whom Sue had engaged in place of Mabel to give Mattie lessons.

2

AMUASBTEILN

1 8 8 4

MORE of Austin's letters to Mabel survive from the next year and a half than do hers to him, probably because Mabel no longer dissembled with David but remained terrified lest anything fall into Sue Dickinson's hands, so that she regularly reminded Austin to destroy anything she wrote him. But Sue was surprisingly benign throughout 1884, sustaining a curious hiatus of hostility toward Mabel while she mourned for Gib. She held aloof from Austin's activities, projecting by example her disdain of his uncurtailed business and social pursuits, instead staying indoors, or riding out discreetly in black garb with her children. She may have hoped public sympathy would accrue to her as Austin and Mabel patently took advantage of her grief, but her melancholy, holier-than-thou air only succeeded in driving Austin farther off and in giving her rival a clear field. Well inured to martyrdom, Mabel felt no sympathy for the bereaved mother, nor had she compunctions about capitalizing on happiness, given the opportunity.

The nine months following Mabel's return to Amherst in early February 1884 stretched like a long honeymoon during which a special relationship evolved among Mabel, David, and Austin. Mabel enjoyed the undivided attention of both men, one her earthly mate, the other possessing lofty, spiritual qualities, "a divine sympathy," that lifted her to religious awe. Exercising great discretion, she and Austin took long drives through the beautiful countryside surrounding Amherst, and met frequently at Mabel's Walker Hall studio or at "the other house," as Austin's diary always termed the Homestead. Mabel's intimate involvement with two men was noted in her diary, where she had always recorded her sexual relations with her husband, but now began to indicate lovemaking with Austin as well, though not to the same degree of specificity. Austin's diary also contains the record of his intimacy with Mabel (he had ceased relations with Sue entirely), and although not all his symbols are clearly interpretable, those of full intercourse can be read. (Austin's symbol was ===; Mabel's was —.) When the diaries are matched, it appears that during 1884 Mabel was making love with David an average of eight times a month, and with Austin twelve, about half of all these occasions involving full intercourse and most of those clustered during the last ten days of Mabel's menstrual cycle, which she considered her safe period. Although this first year of physical involvement with Austin probably marked the zenith of her sexual activity, it is clear that energetic physical commitment underlay Mabel's strong utterances of love for both men. At the end of 1884, Mabel dropped for good her record of relations with David, only continuing to note, but never so explicitly as he, her most intimate moments with Austin. Thereafter, his extant diaries are a more dependable and specific record of the sexual aspect of their relationship.

The prolonged period of bliss came to an abrupt end in

October 1884, when Mabel's parents made a visit to Amherst and caught wind of what was going on. Afterward Mabel blamed herself for having said too much about her "rare friendship" with Mr. Dickinson during a trip home in May, naïvely assuming her mother would appreciate its "unconventional" nature. But Molly Loomis's expositions on the standards of goodness to which she was raising her granddaughter, little Millicent, who was left for long stretches in her care, should have served as warning to Mabel that her parents were not prepared to understand. Their attitude was a painful thorn for Mabel during the ensuing years of the love affair.

AUSTIN TO MABEL   [*11 January 1884*]
                                   11th, 10 o'c. a.m.

     Just a word, before I set to work—then I shall be sure of the noon mail—that you may know before Sunday—you make so much a point of it—that your brief note of Wednesday reached me yesterday afternoon. I took it from the office myself before 4 o'c., was read appreciatively, and is not, for the flames took it.
     This is all you asked of me, I believe, for this time—but it seems a little short, and although I am conscious that my handwriting is appearing on College Hill Terrace oftener than the Law requires, it can make it no worse if I elongate a very little—and I will say, first, that I have learned that letters to our evening mail do not reach you the second day. Second, that I think you need feel no anxiety that what you direct to Vin Box 207 will go into any other hands than hers, unless mine. No one in my family knows where her box is, or would think of calling for its contents, or that it could in any way interest them. Third, that Mr. Todd makes no sound, nor any one for him. What is he doing all the while? Fourth, that Mrs. Scarritt tells Mattie that [newlyweds] Mr. & Mrs. Elwell come to [Mrs. Robison's] table "hold of hands," and hold hands *under* the table, which Mrs. Scarritt thinks very improper, not to say low. The Vaca-

[1 8 1]

tion is at last at an end, and the days and the Village are beginning to seem more natural. There's nothing new here that would interest you except that young Dr. Hitchcock has, through his father, secured the appointment of—*Professor*—I think they call it of the Crowell Gymnasium, and will leave here in about six weeks,* and that Mrs. John Tyler is getting up a chorus to be trained by Leichtmann.† The mantels are up in Walker Hall, the Treasurer's men finished—and your [studio] room is to be reddoned tomorrow. The radiator has been fixed so that the shutters swing over it.

The sleighing is fine—the weather mostly bad—I drove Tom from 4 to 5 last night—he went like a bird. I wished you were with me.

No change at my house. Sue spends her time reading old letters, and assorting them. I asked her yesterday if she were preparing to edit them or at work on her memoirs.‡ She rides occasionally, goes out no other way, and the doorbell rarely rings. Your name is never spoken. Mr. Todd's has been once, in connection with something at College. On the whole I like it—think it is much the best way. All complications—in the ordinary way of speaking—are thus avoided. I didn't begin it—and so am the more braced.

You have been gone now three weeks, and in three more, I suppose will be about returned. I shall find no fault if they go quickly. At the same time—delightfully circumstanced as you must be, at home—with nothing specially requiring Mr. Todd

---

* "Young" Dr. Hitchcock was Austin's old friend and contemporary Ned Hitchcock, who since 1861 had taught hygiene and physical education at Amherst College. A pioneer in the advancement of physical education programs, he had inspired the gift that paid for half of the slow-building Pratt Gymnasium and was setting out to raise the rest of it.

† Mrs. Todd became accompanist for this choral society, directed by a conductor from Worcester, when she returned to Amherst.

‡ In preparation for his biography, *The Life and Times of Samuel Bowles* (Century, 1885), George S. Merriam had asked Susan Dickinson for access to the Bowles letters in her possession, and it is probably this task she was engaged in.

in Amherst, I wouldn't advise you to hurry back, for it is unusually dull here, and to my feeling, it is to be.

I guess I had better stop. Drop in when you come down at one—Cooper goes off by half past 12—and say whether you will walk or drive at 5.*

Shant write you again for a week at least, unless something very particular occurs. Do you know you have^nt written a word about yourself, and what you are doing—hardly, since you left, and I have seemed to be writing all the while.

My love to Mr. Todd, and by the way, tell him it strikes me that with all the rest of the furniture in the building ash, it would be quite as well to make the bookcase of ash. Though the difference in cash need^nt weigh, and he may have his choice. Marsh is ready to begin on it at once.

Goodbye___

[*21 January 1884*]
Office, Monday morning, 9 o'c.

I wonder if you want a whiff of New England air, and a passing glance at me as you go to your easel,† and I go to my desk, this bright Winter morning. It is^nt so very long since you heard from me, to be sure, and I from you, by the calendar, but theres been a Sunday between—and one of these, nowadays, seems any where from three weeks to a three months passage, a suggestion of Eternity here below, with the heaven part left out. It used to be to me the day of all the week the best—not in the missionary or hymn sense exactly—but to my own inner nature.

Well, it is a bright, clear still, fairly cold morning. It snowed gently all day yesterday—and as the wind has^nt waked yet, the town and bushes are softly covered, a perfect Winter

* See Mabel's letter of December 26, 1883, in which in fantasy she calls at Austin's office at 1 p.m. each day. James Cooper was Austin's young law partner.

† Mabel was painting on commission six panels of a scenic frieze of wildflowers, birds, and grasses at the home of Mrs. Bigelow, Sue Dickinson's Washington cousin and former owner of the Loomis home.

Landscape. Just the morning to be driving through the pines with those you like.

On the square people are flying about, on foot, and in sleighs, as if life still had meaning for them.

The cars are just in and with them the papers, filled—of course—with all the rumors and sermons they have been able to glean the world over in the last twenty-four hours. Cooper this moment appears clean brushed and ready for any light, never soiling exercise that may offer to the profession. I am going at a problem involved in the division and rearrangement of some College funds.

I was in Walker Hall Saturday and took a look at your room. The color gives it quite a rich, studio air. The bookcase starts this morning. Old Mr. Magill died yesterday morning. Miss S [*undecipherable*] slipped, going from Church at noon, was stunned, and borne to the Convent,* by two or three students, creating great excitement, not of the most serious nature, among the rest. She had nearly recovered by the time they got to the house.

Seelye preached—so they say. I wasn't there. On improving one's opportunities.

This is all the news that has reached me. And all a simple good morning ought to hold. I have no particular plan for the week, except as each day brings it, regular duties. No plan for being away anywhere at present, unless, possibly, I go to Norwich for a day and a night, and after a while to Boston, for a day. Probably not for some weeks however.

If the Gods blessed me—and gave me free run—I would start for Florida tonight, and the South, via Washington, and come back—when!

I am not in their favor at present, and shall stay, accordingly, and do my roaming in my imagination, which does^{nt} give out yet.

* "The Convent" was the local nickname for Mrs. William Stearns's school for girls, kept by the widowed daughter-in-law of former President Stearns in the Amherst College president's house (President Seelye preferring to reside in his own house on College Street). Millicent Todd later attended the Convent for many years.

I miss you, and want to see you immensely, and yet, I advise you not to shorten a good time down there for an uncertainty here.*

It just occurs to me that I haven't given you all the Village news. Mr. Scarritt has preached the last two Sundays in Hadley—not as a candidate of course, nobody does that—but still! Gough is to perform here February 1st, and Cable is probable for 7th and 8th. Then Mrs. Tylers chorus is growing—they assemble tomorrow night, I believe.

Now I'll cover this in one of Vin's grasshopper tracked envelopes, mail it, and by ten be ready for a steady pull till one.

Good morning, good morning. Thats all this you know.

Mabel and David returned to Amherst on February 8, 1884, leaving Millicent in Washington. Mabel had asked Austin to enumerate his reasons for forsaking Sue, but as the next letter attests, he could not do it.

AUSTIN TO MABEL   *[early 1884]*

Yes, my darling, I did promise you that sometime I would put into your hands the story of my life, to use as a shield, if ever—when I am not here to answer for myself—any attack shall be made upon my love for you, or yours for me, or our relations to each other.

And yet is it not better and nobler that I say nothing which involves any other, reflects upon any other! may offend or wound. Is it not better to begin with my meeting you, and for the first time feeling clear sunshine! What is the past in the face of the present and the future, as we now see it!

Is it not better, and enough, for me to say, simply, what I have said so many times before, that I love you, love you, love

---

* Mabel was enjoying a succession of "brilliant" social events, including a reception at the White House given by President Arthur's sister, and a tea for four hundred at which she received, wearing a silk dress remarkable for a sash on which she had hand-painted rosebuds.

you with all my mind, and heart, and strength! and that I know what I mean when I say this, that with you my real life began! That with you I have found what life may mean! That in you I have found the sweetest, richest dreams of my boyhood, youth, and early manhood more than realized! That I have found in you what a woman may be to a man, hope, courage, joy, inspiration, rest, peace, religion! That in you I have found my perfect soul-mate, for time and eternity. . . .

Conventionalism is for those not strong enough to be laws for themselves, or to conform themselves to the great higher law where all the harmonies meet. I love you, love you, now and forever, and it is my great joy that my love is as much to you as yours to me. The fullness and sweetness and brightness—and excellent happiness—and hope, and thrill, and ecstasy of the days since in that sudden flash of light when we stood revealed to each other, through and through, and saw that each was, in the divine order, the other's world—are part of our existence forevermore.

How much we have to be grateful for, even though we have been obliged to defer some of our hopes—everything will come in good time.

Once more I love you—and again I love you, my dearest, dearest Mabel, and without my will, and with my will am your

own Austin.

[early 1884]

And still the marvel grows. Every day I love you more, more sweetly, more thrillingly, with larger power. Every day I am filled with profounder gratitude and joy for you, and your love for me. No other heaven could ever compare with you.

Brilliant, Brilliant, beautiful star, what can I say, what can I do! how can I act to even shadow to you my appreciation of the immensity of richest life and hope you have given me! But you know it all, without a word. You read me through and through and mark the daintiest lights and shades that play among my innermost thoughts, and so you know just what I am thinking and remembering today.

Sweetest, sweetest love, all I am, and can be—I am yours, and yours only, and with gladdest joy.

[*1 March 1884*]

If we had been boy and girl together, darling—the luscious bud within us swelling at the same time and with even pace— we should have turned to each other as naturally as we breathed —hardly knowing, or caring why. We should have gone berry- ing in the same fields—one basket would have held the nuts we had gathered. Together we should have roamed the woods and hill sides for wild flowers. You would have been by my side in all the sleigh rides. It would have been always Mabel and Austin—and we should have loved each other as dearly and tenderly and wholly and forever—as we do now. We should not have known much outside. Our own world would have been too full—and too blissful.

The rare and romantic experience of the last year and a half—so wild and wonderful—so fascinating, outrunning the imagination, and which seems sometimes to have imparted a richness and an aroma to our double life it must otherwise have lacked, would not have been, to be sure. But we should have been the same. This experience will by and by seem a mere brilliant episode, a bright sparkle on the surface of the great strong cur- rent of our ever growing love.

It is beautiful to meet as children, perhaps most beautiful— and yet there is a dazzling charm in the meeting of two mature, richly furnished souls, destined for each other from the first—at the fullness of their power. All the stages, from the suddenly arrested attention to the final and complete discovery and over- whelming consciousness that each has met his and her perfect counterpart, wherein every longing is satisfied, every ideal rounded—a present full to overflowing with the sweetest sweet- ness of existence—and an infinite vista of bliss beyond. This has

[187]

been our way—and we could hardly wish a line of it to have been other or different. Every day and every hour of our nearing—and deepening, surer recognition, has been all we could for the time bear, and to carry the joy of today taxes my utmost strength.

After so much wandering, then—under sunshine and cloud, with others—and alone, we have found each other. A new voice, like none other, strangely soft, struck my ear—a new face, beautiful beyond compare met my eye. I took a hand I could not let go, and that did not let go mine. I walked along—was I in dreamland—or in the world of the real! I thought it must be dreamland—I feared to wake—and I could not believe, even when I *knew* I was awake. It was too much, too great, but I doubt no longer. I accept all. I believe all. We are under some outside limitations but our spirits are free and brave. We have the best—and we *will* have it—the time approaches, when we will have all. This is my little say for this time, darling. Do I love you? Do I love you!

MABEL TO AUSTIN   [*2 March 1884*]
                                                   Sunday afternoon

. . . Your "new idea" is another dainty touch of poetry— it is exquisite. But I feel with you that our present experience is richer and greater than the childish idyl could have been. There is a strength now of which that other phase could not have dreamed. And the end will be infinitely larger and more satisfying—*dear*. Instead of wandering hand in hand through actual woodland ways, in the freshness of morning, we—you and I— had watched the sweet unfolding of nature's heart to us, alone. You, as you said to me, had walked on through clouds and sunshine—all alone, and oh! grateful am I beyond words, that the lonesomeness and the grey skies have not dimmed your clear eyes to any of nature's sweet, half-told stories. That uncurling ferns and open-eyed daisies, and far blue hills speak with just as much response and tenderness to your dear heart now, as when you first felt their wonderful charm—and it has spoken volumes to me of your rare nature that all these lovable things meant so much to you in the well-nigh fatal absence of other things which should have sweetened your life. I loved you for it—I revered you for it before I saw all those other phases for which I also—now—love and revere you. And in those dewy "by-paths," you either stopped and waited for me, or I ran, with a strength divinely inspired, and overtook you—because here we are, together. The hand you took does not seek to go away— rather it clasps yours tightly, and with an infinite love and trust goes whither soever you shall lead. . . . You have deepened my life, and broadened it, and exalted it. Your marvelous love for me would have done that to some extent, even if I had not responded to it. But now all the best in my soul stretches forth its hands to you. And what has always seemed to me like the dear God's love, is embodied to me in yours—magnificent, all-embracing; true and noble and divinely tender. Oh! my love, my dear love, God will forgive me if I see Him in you and through you principally, now, for it is surely a revelation to me of Himself. And *I know* He did it. This wonderful companionship and sweet, sweet knowing of each other never emanated from this world solely. Dear, it was heaven-born, heaven-guided and sent. And it is sacred forever. You have come into my life and changed it all. I look upon the outer and the inner world with clearer vision because of you. . . .

AUSTIN TO MABEL   [*3 March 1884*]

Dear, dear, great heart, to have even that letter is enough for a life. With that trophy alone on my breast I could face death undaunted. Where in story, in all the ages, has portrayal of love reckoned the most superlative and exceptional, reached the heights where we habitually move! Equalled in passion probably, but unapproached in subtle delicacy and sympathy— mental, moral & physical. Enveloped in an atmosphere all its own, of its own creation. I read it before I went down—came up again in the evening to read it again—and had hard struggle not to fly straight to you before I should sleep.

The full hour I had with you seemed but an instant, time hastens so in your presence, lags so out of it. I dread to go off even for over one night, but I shall think of you constantly.

I love you—I love you, as you know I can love. I admire you—and am yours, wholly yours, forever and forever.

Austin had moderated the annual town meeting most of Monday, March 3, before visiting Mabel at her Walker Hall studio late in the afternoon. He was going to Boston the next day on a court matter, and planned to return to Amherst on Wednesday, but in fact got out of court so late that he stayed a second night, thus missing (perhaps on purpose) a surprise wedding anniversary party Amherst friends gave the Todds on Wednesday evening. Mabel's diary for that date says, "Our fifth anniversary—David & his happy little wife!" The relationship among the three was delicate, as Mabel noted on March 30: "We [David and I] see him [Austin] in some way every day." When the Todds visited Boston for a week in April, Austin came to the city two days and enjoyed several dinners, concerts, and excursions with Mabel, and with Mabel and David together. During this same Boston trip Mabel renewed a friendship with her cousin-once-removed, Caro Lovejoy Andrews, who lived in a stylish apartment on Beacon Street, where she invited the Todds to dine. Plump, well-dressed, extroverted and bored with her marriage, Caro Andrews took David's fancy at once.

AUSTIN TO MABEL   [*Spring 1884*]

With favorable weather I shall probably drive this afternoon.

Possibly I may get off alone.

If I should, what would you think of going [with] me?

If I am accompanied, I will drive past your windows, down Amity St. at 2:20 as announcement.

If I do not then drive by, you may know that ten minutes later, at 2:30 I shall reach Hutchinsons Hedge, just beyond the entrance to the Cemetery, on North Street—and if you think well of it, and will be walking there, I will pick you up.

Use your judgment—and act on it.

Not seeing you before, will come around about 7:30 this evening.

Notes similar to the one above, arranging meetings and carriage rides, are scattered through the Mabel-Austin correspondence. The awkwardness of public comings and goings undoubtedly spurred Mabel's longing for her own home, where she could conduct arrangements in private. Two other things may have abetted this urge: the influence of Caro Andrews and hesitancy about meeting at the Homestead, where Emily was grieving at the recent loss of her friend Judge Otis Phillips Lord. In late April Mabel and David decided to rent the Lessey house, a large, handsome, white-columned structure with two acres of grounds planted in huge oaks. It stood only two houses northwest of the Dickinson properties, and would be available as soon as Mrs. Lessey, who lay on her deathbed at Mrs. Robison's, departed life. To be ready for this anticipated move to housekeeping, Mabel made a swift trip to Washington in early May to arrange for removing her own and David's possessions from her parents' home. She brought Millicent and Grandma Wilder back to Amherst with her.

AUSTIN TO MABEL   [7 *May 1884*]

Wednesday. I am for the first moment this morning alone. I hope I may stay so for a little. You leave [Washington] Friday. That's day after tomorrow. I dont know at which hour, or whether a word later than this noons mail will reach you before then, so I wont risk it—say it now.

[191]

The lonesomest moment I have had yet was yesterday noon, when I saw Mr. Todd hastening toward Mrs. Robison's, reading a letter which I fancied might be from you, and the wrong, cruelty, injustice which should take your letter to any one but me filled me with sadness. I shall not let you go away again with the understanding and agreement that you are not to write me a single line. *Even one* would go a great way, and I would go a great way for. I had determined to give myself pretty thoroughly to the demands of my business and outside affairs with which I am connected, during your absence, as the shortest cut to your return—and I have done so—thought but little, except straight ahead—dreamed but little, hardly entered my mental flower garden.

But I have looked back occasionally over the enchanting path we have been walking together through these twenty moons, with all its sweet asides, shady nooks, lovely views. You and I—drawing ever closer and closer to each other to perfect knowledge—perfect sympathy, most absorbing love. What a marvelous experience! Where was ever its like? So unexpected, so sudden in its opening, yet so promptly and unhesitatingly entered upon, followed so daringly, defiantly, brilliantly, its very boldness protecting us from all common eyes, and yet most heartbreakingly sweet and tender, and satisfying.

Whatever is—or is not—this is ours. Ours forever. Eternity cannot efface or change it. We went not out for it—we had not looked for it. It came to us, went with us, became a part of us, made us inseparable, made us one. I wish you could look into my heart this minute, my sweet, my Mabel. I am not quite sure that you have read every feature and phase of its devotion to you even yet. My love for you is so very great, and your love for me is so very sacred to me. It sometimes almost frightens me, often. It seems too pure—too much—for Earth. But Heaven preserve it to us, and preserve us! I would rather die a thousand times over than that the least speck should touch its outermost edge. And this may be my last word to you till I see you. You know that I am thinking of you constantly. I want to write more —I hardly see how I have written as much, broken in upon as I have been.

My love, and my love, come back to me just as you went away.

When Mrs. Lessey died in late May, the Todds moved into Oaklawn, a process that took a month. Mabel's plan to bring her possessions North was causing her mother consternation. Mrs. Loomis wept over losing the piano and other objects she loved, and finally decided to buy $600 worth of the Todds' furniture so her home would not be denuded. She hoped to borrow the money from Grandma Wilder, who was owed a sum by a Boston nephew. After considerable delay through the spring the nephew defaulted, but by then Mabel, frantic to begin decorating her new house, had borrowed $400 from Austin and gone to Boston in early June to purchase Wedgwood, furniture, and curtains. For additional rugs and hangings she borrowed again, probably from the bank. Slowly and painfully her parents paid her the $600 over the next year.

Then by an unexpected stroke of fortune the Todds' friends the Scarritts departed Amherst for Kansas in late June, loaning Mabel and David their possessions (including another piano) for the year until they should be settled. The result was that the Lessey house looked very elegant on June 21 when Mabel officially began keeping house with a servant, Phebe, whose talents turned out to be superior, as Mabel lost no time telling her servantless, sorely vexed mother: "I tell her after supper what we will have for breakfast, & she is up, & everything done when I get down at half-past seven. I am charmed with housekeeping."

The three months that followed—July, August, and September 1884—were perhaps the most idyllic of the thirteen years. Austin could call more regularly and easily now, Sue stayed indoors, and David was away twice for a week or more. Throughout the summer Mabel and Austin took long carriage rides. One, across the bridge to Northampton, north on country roads to Hatfield, back over the Connecticut River by ferry to North Hadley, and home, stimulated the exchange that follows.

MABEL TO AUSTIN   15 July 1884
                                                                  Tuesday morning

My darling, I am in a state of intense mental exaltation this inspiring day. Our yesterday's experience has been an elixir to everything which is noblest in me. A great and grand purpose—which has before been merely an occasional impulse—has been born to me. To live for character, and richness and depth of feeling and life—to strive every day for a loftiness which shall fitly match, even equal, yours—has come to me as my aim and object. It is not only that through you everything outward is changed—that the hills are bluer, the sky serener, the bird-songs more ecstatic—but my whole mental constitution is undergoing a transformation. I watch my actions and my words. I scrutinize even my innermost thoughts, to be sure that there is nothing which is unworthy of you. To be noble and true to you and my best self have come to be the springs of my being and life. . . . Through you I am finding my spiritual way back to God's hand, which in the darkness I had almost lost. But I think it is still waiting for me; and with what I have already had of your wonderful love & nobleness, I could happily go to the stake, if it were necessary.

AUSTIN TO MABEL   [*15 July 1884*]

I found yesterday that I had not learned all of my love for you—even yet.

That there are depths and heights still in our natures, unrevealed, undreamed, depths profound, and higher, sublimer, beyond any past strength—I was drawn to you—and stirred by you as by no previous experience.

It seemed to me I could not be separated from you for a

single instant ever—my whole being craved you, so I could hardly control the action of my mind. The mighty power of this immutable passion, so gentle at first, holding us now in bands of steel, never stood before me in such tremendous proportion.

What—what can a human soul contain!

I dont dare give way for the now. Darling, Darling, hold tight to me. Love me. Love me.

I love you so ten thousand times more than my own life! Why, why can we not be together?

In late summer Mabel began urging her mother to visit Amherst (Grandma Wilder would pay the fare one way and loan it the other), for she wanted to hold her first party in the new house in October. Molly Loomis arrived October 1 and was overwhelmed by Amherst and the Todds' home. Two days later she was even more overwhelmed as Mabel decorated the Lessey house with bright October leaves, artichokes, yellow daisies, and partridge vines to receive seventy-five Amherst residents at an evening supper featuring chicken salad and cake.

Shortly after the "brilliant party," Mrs. Loomis learned from Grandma Wilder something of Mabel's comings and goings with Mr. Dickinson. She sent at once for her husband, urgently insisting that "on the 15th of this month if possible you must get here. You are to spend all the rest of the month here with me." Though unenlightened, Eben obeyed the summons. From then until her parents left on November 5, Mabel endured a series of "terrible talks" with her mother, in and around a succession of social events and constant calls and callers. Her father seems not to have participated in these discussions, but had at least two private conversations with Austin. It is not clear whether the Loomises understood the full nature of the affair. The argument apparently focused on appearances and seemliness, on Mabel's risk of her name and reputation. Mabel's parents were not reassured, nor did they effect any change. "David," Mabel wrote in her journal, "is superb through it all. He is a truly remarkable person."

Mabel to Austin [*9 October 1884*]
Thursday

If people only realized that the more they try to keep lovers apart, the more they brood upon and think of each other—that their thoughts are flames for the general conflagration even more than being together, I think there would possibly be less effort at this absurd separation. People in general are fools—there is no denying that. However, there is, of course, no "treatment" of any kind which could be effectual in the case of which we know. Everything adds to its intensity—nothing even approaches, or dares to think of coming near to tarnish its glory. Nothing can. When I waked this glorious morning and saw the sun shining so brilliantly and realized my sacrifice for the day, it seemed almost more than I could bear, and just now, after I had finished my first duty for the morning, I put my head down in the sweet warm sunshine on the rug, and a sense of almost overwhelming loneliness seemed to turn all the brightness to black. But nevertheless I *can* live for an ideal. Your faith in me is, & shall be, completely justified. I should not be great enough for you, my beloved, if I could not live, even go away from you, with a lofty peace which passes the understanding of all those who are not capable of so very great a love—and they are very many. I dare not write to you all which throbs within me for you this brilliant morning. I am suffering intensely, and yet all outward things are exceedingly serene, moving smoothly. How is it possible for persons to carry within an intense & lonely suffering —a longing beyond words—and still smile and talk brilliantly & be apparently happy. I cannot understand, but I can do it. I tested it last night [during tea at Mrs. Cooper's], & it externally succeeded.

Later. I am most weak-mindedly near to tears all the time. The eyes of my day are put out. I see now what it was that gave light & hope to each day—what it was that gave the eye through which I could look out on the plains of eternity—the great level stretches full of hope, & which lead out to infinity. But I can remember—and I know what is coming, and so I can bear. And only you can know the sorrow; my own!

AUSTIN TO MABEL   [*ca. 10 October 1884*]

Reflections upon what you told me had been said to you last night.

————————————

We are not to be frightened—we are not of that cheap stuff.

We are not afraid of the truth. This is what has given us to each other.

We love each other. How can we help it? Who brought it to pass? Did we ourselves? And is love anything to be ashamed of?

Our life together is as white and unspotted as the fresh driven snow.

This we know—whatever vulgar minded people, who see nothing beyond the body—may think—or suspect.

All our thoughts, tastes, likes, dislikes, aspirations, imaginings are alike—just alike. We were born for each other—and we will stay with each other. No one shall—or can—separate us. We would rather lie side by side in death than share dominion over all the world—and perpetual youth—with any other.

We love one another. God forgive us if there is in that any wrong—but we love one another, and we will give up life for our love, any day if necessary. There can be no life for us, without it. Death would be a relief, and again—we will not let go. No.

But my darling and my own—my sweet, and very blessed child. While we breathe the heavenly air, and see the beauty

[1 9 7]

beyond the gates, and are buoyed by an invisible power, and our highest hopes cannot but soon blossom into matchless realities, we move on a lower plane, in the world, but not of it, among men and women who do not understand us—cannot comprehend us—hold to the letter which killeth and not to the Spirit which giveth life—and we must, if we would not be followed and tormented, conform—in a measure—outwardly to the elements of the great throng.

We will be more careful—we will—for the time—be more abstemious of each other. I do not believe we are watched—unless by my own household, who subsist upon my industry. Still we will not presume upon that—we will proceed with caution—we will not let a spy have anything for his pains—we will see each other less often for a while—as often as we can, of course, safely—we will carry ourselves ostensibly in individual channels—we shall not be deceived—we have tested ourselves, and found of what we are made. We can trust each other to the end—and against all odds.

Stand straight up in your house, and say if they will make any distinct charges, you will explain—disprove or confess—but you will not listen to vague insinuations from a source that does not come to the light.

I love you—I love you—and I love you—

[*ca. 25 October 1884*]

Strictly business

The charges, I believe, are that we drive in by-roads—that I am at your house constantly, five or six times in seven days. That I get there through back ways and hedges—that you meet me in the grounds—that I stay late at night, after Mr. Todd has retired—that you neglect your house and family, and are devoted to me.

To the very last I agree—but about this will say nothing.

As to the by-roads—I have driven with you over the same I drive with my family, my friends generally, and alone, when driving for pleasure. Leverett roads, and not the turnpike to Northampton.

As to getting in by back ways and hedges—I have been in through all three of the gates that open upon paths that lead to the front door.

I have never approached by any other way except to drive my carriage occasionally to the north end of your piazza for convenience in getting out or in.

What meeting me in the grounds means I dont know. If sitting on the open front piazza in a summer evening till 10 o'c. not infrequently—sometimes with you alone, sometimes you & Mr. Todd, and sometimes you & your grandmother, is bad, then there is bad to that extent.

As for your neglect of your home and family, the universal testimony is that your housekeeping is poetry, that no child goes through the street that shows so much home taste and care.

And I can say that your loyalty and affection for Mr. Todd make the most constant and remarkable feature in your character.

There is nothing to the whole of it, beyond the fact that we are earnestly interested in each other. I see you frequently because I like to, and you like to have me.

More so perhaps than [word unclear] and busybodies approve, unless they can hear what we say.

Wouldn't it be well for your father—if he talks with you —to understand that these are the facts, and that if he has heard differently, he has heard wrongly, and is suffering unnecessarily, and causing you great pain?

Ought he not to have something pretty well attested before setting me down as a sneak, and an improper person, given to mischief, and treachery?

Is he as kind to you and as considerate of you as he is of the friend who is ready to poison his ear with evil of you, and then skulk into darkness—till he will tell you who he is—and give you the opportunity of relieving his anxiety about you as well as your father. . . .

[2 November 1884]

Unless you say no, I propose to drive around shortly after two, to ask your mother to taste this mountain air with me.

Austin to Mabel's mother   [4 November 1884]

My dear Mrs. Loomis:

If it may afford you the least satisfaction to supplement our Sunday afternoon talk by any word unspoken, any question un-asked, or unanswered, then, any new thought—you may com-mand me for such time as you will, after 5 o'clock, this or to-morrow evening.*

Very sincerely
Wm. A. Dickinson

Tuesday

After the Loomises left Amherst on November 5, Mrs. Loomis resumed writing her daughter excessive, sentimental letters, but Mabel was angry and answered with short, bright, breezy notes, starving her parents for the full, self-absorbed descriptions of her doings she had always supplied. In early January she received "a terrible letter from my father," evi-dently inspired by new observations from the saintly Grandma Wilder. Always particularly unnerved by disapproval from her father, Mabel was cast into gloom for many weeks. The letter itself does not survive.

* Eben Loomis, rather than his wife, took advantage of this invitation, and drove with Austin that afternoon for the second time of his visit.

3

A New Epoch

1 8 8 5 – 1 8 8 6

By the new year Sue Dickinson was abroad in the village again, her appearance in mourning giving rise to Austin's appellation, "the Great Black Mogul," which Mabel cherished and privately used. With Ned as escort, Sue began crossing paths with Mrs. Todd in the little town she had always dominated socially, but where Mabel now played an active role. In February, when the Chi Psi students at Amherst College asked Mrs. Todd to "matronize" their dance, Sue informed Mattie's Chi Psi swain that Mattie would not be allowed home from Farmington, Connecticut, where she was at boarding school for the year, to attend the event. When Mabel began singing in the quartette of the First Congregational Church choir, Sue was prevented from attending the weekly service. Instead, she mounted a missionary effort to establish a Sunday school at a small impoverished settlement east of Amherst called Logtown. She was faithful to this project for six years, though criticized by some for ostentatious slumming.

Sue's tensions dominated the Evergreens. In January 1885 occurred the wallpaper incident described by Ned. And even though Mattie was away, Sue managed her daughter's social affairs, editing Mattie's letters to and from Amherst College students and instructing her minutely what to do and say in given situations. Through the late winter and spring of 1885, Sue was bedridden with a mysterious illness for which she took small doses of arsenic prescribed by the doctor. She was tended by Ned, no longer in college, yet restrained by his mother from going off to earn his living. Ned's devotion to Sue at this period, and her role in the household, are aptly portrayed in a message he added to one of her letters to Mattie in March 1885:

My dear little Mopsy. Mother has read me her note to you, and the amusement part has cut me to the quick—for her, who has given her whole life to me, to feel that she ought to entertain me is too much. As if I wanted anything else than to be near her —and try in my humble way to make her life a little less hard and solitary than it is. That woman is a daily wonder to me— and example—my only prayer is that Almighty God may leave her with [us] for many years to come—that *we* may in *some way* recompense her for what she has endured here for us. If there is any beautiful, peaceful, restful place hereafter, and she dont have a seat among the saints and martyrs, I dont care to go there. Such superhuman efforts to keep up & cheerful, for those around her, mortal eye never witnessed. And she thinks she must *entertain* me. I would willingly lay down my life for her, if for one day I could see [her] happy—treated as well as the servants. I fear mother thinks from my talk that I am anxious to *get* away from her—my only ambition in life Dear Mopsy, is to have a quiet, pleasant little house somewhere—with you and mother in it where things can be *pleasant*—no fame, no brains, no family, no scholarship, no *anything* amounts to anything beside that. "But the greatest of these is charity" and pleasantness. . . .

A New Epoch

As for Mabel and Austin, few letters survive from the seven months between November 1884 and early June 1885, but Mabel's diary indicates she was teaching two painting classes, one to pupils at Mrs. Stearns's school and another for ladies at her Walker Hall studio. She also took on a piano student or two, and in March 1885 bought with her earnings an elegant sealskin cape, like one of Mrs. Dickinson's she had long admired. To avoid Grandma Wilder's surveillance, Mabel and Austin again met more regularly at the Homestead, where Emily was slowly recovering from a "bad turn" suffered the previous October.

A new era began for the Todds in mid-April 1885, when their friend Caro Andrews paid a week-long visit. Her presence led to an enlargement of the friendship among David, Mabel, and Austin—a squaring of the triangle. Mabel thought Caro the "noblest woman, & the largest minded, I ever knew." She inspired a new and "strange relation," Mabel confided in her journal, "a wonderfully beautiful one, & truly ideal. I cannot write it out, but if I could, it would be more remarkable, & almost unbelievable, than any novel I ever read or dreamed of." David enjoyed the new relationship most of all, and escorted Caro on many drives into the countryside during her stay. Then Caro invited Mabel to accompany her and her husband on a three-month tour of Europe. After determining she could afford it if she was economical, Mabel sailed from Boston with Mr. and Mrs. Andrews aboard the *Pavonia* for Queenstown, Ireland, on June 6, 1885, leaving David and Austin to comfort each other through a long summer. The latter's intense suffering throughout Mabel's absence provoked some of his finest letters.

MABEL TO AUSTIN   [*16 April 1885*]

I am going to the observatory right after dinner, or lunch. I expect to start about quarter of two from the house. I am so glad you are going. I shall take Millicent. Won't you join us somewhere in the street about ten minutes of two, & walk up there with us?

I am very happy, & full of hope & peace, & enthusiasm.

I remember [Austin's fifty-sixth birthday].

AUSTIN TO MABEL   [ca. Spring 1885]

You were never so beautiful, my darling, never so pure and tender, and soulful—so exalted and exalting as last night. I saw you before I reached the gate, sitting on the edge of the piazza, robed in white, like an angel, and waiting, I knew, for me.

I was not thrilled, nor was it ecstasy—but pervaded—and overborne by the great, solemn, sacred joy which can freight only such souls as ours, made for each other from the beginning, and by rare experience at last led to each other—once met— never again to be separated.

I cannot write this morning—you have just passed my window and I must find you—this one word to take back with you for the day. That yesterday consecrated me to you anew— that I am yours—for time and for Eternity, that I live for you— will live for you, that I love you with all the strength of my being, with a love perfect and holy—that I love you and admire you and reverence you, and that I pray God to keep us, and guide us, and protect us—and bless us.

Before Mabel's departure for Europe on the *Pavonia*, they handed each other the following farewell letters, each written in Boston. Austin wrote on Parker House stationery. Mabel began her letter while he was still in Amherst, and finished it on his arrival.

MABEL TO AUSTIN   [4 June 1885]

I love you, and I love you. And in all the rush & whirl of cars & carriages and worldly tumult, my heart & soul are away

& off in the sweet green fields, with you my beloved, & my own, and my God-given mate. . . . I find there is much happiness in my memory of that last little walk we took together in that sweet, sunny afternoon. There was a domestic & peaceful feeling about it which stays by me very happily. And every one of those last drives is a picture in my heart. Our sweet little flower-covered valley—the entrance to Paradise—our lovely morning on the knob, seeing the kingdoms of the earth, & caring not one whit about them & their riches if we can only have each other—and our *park* drive that divinely sunny & shady morning. Not one incident, not one picture, escapes me. And that Sunday, with the rare scarlet maples, & the little house close to the waterfall— and that dear, dear morning when we found the little town half burned up. Oh! beloved! Are not our lives inextricably inter- woven? And is it not bliss unutterable? I *love* you, dear. And there is not a brick nor a stone in these pavements which does not echo to me with you. And I love them so! Oh! darling, my soul is yours—forever and forever. Keep me in your innermost heart, which you told me is your home for me, and never let me get out. My joy is to be there, and my peace and my great need. By you I reach to God. He would not have given me so wonder- ful a gift if he had not loved me some, & so, through you, showed me my highest. Sweet heart, dear heart—a kiss, until I see you, very soon now.
Thursday.

Now, dear love, it is Friday, and you are here, & have left me for a half hour. So I just come back to my little note to tell you again how tenderly and how devotedly I love you; and that you may know renewedly how every thought is of and for you, how you are ever present in my heart, how permanently and inextricably you are woven in with my every fibre, so that to try and remove you from my life would be to pluck out that life by its roots & leave it dead indeed; like the little pink hand on the sweet cheek of the fair maiden in Hawthorne's story, which defied every effort to remove it until the supreme & last one was made, when it disappeared—with the life of the fair maiden simul- taneously. Your love and my life are one and indivisible. Your love & my soul are synonymous— & oh! how glad am I! Ah! dear, we did not know that it was God who led us by that gate, that rainy night! But it was—and you and I stand hand in hand and let Him search our hearts without faltering. He never made a purer love nor a rarer, and through it I feel *His* love warming my soul as I have not known it for years. I know He led us, and I know He keeps us; and I go in perfect faith that He will put us together sometime, somewhere to stay—forever. What else could make heaven to us, but each other? Oh! darling. I am proud of our love—it is so great & strong & pure, so satisfying & so holy!

Again I give you my soul—again I promise to stay with you forever, again I write my recognition of you as my mate for all eternity— & I kiss you, again & still again. I love you and I love you!

AUSTIN TO MABEL   [*5 June 1885*]

What in this hurry and excitement can I say for my last word my darling, but the old I love you and I love you. We have learned what these mean, how much they hold for us, and that they hold more with each new day. Our separation is for comparatively short, and no separation in the future will be but temporary. For the great main we shall be together—and we are not to be lonesome, for you leave your heart behind, enshrined in mine, and take along mine in yours. You will in no moment be out of my thought, nor I out of yours. We are at rest with each other. Whatever may come or go, we abide—and change not, each the others hope, and joy, inspiration and strength.

AUSTIN TO MABEL   7th June [*1885*]
                                                   Sunday evening

Well, one day has gone—and that, Sunday, one of the twelve. I am glad of that. It has been harder than I expected, much—a bright sun, but a depressing south wind. A south wind is always depressing, more than ever today. And what to do. I had no one to meet in the morning on the way to church. The afternoon was a dreary expanse, without a green speck or fleck of light. I did^{nt} drive—I could$^{nt.}$ I sauntered around, trimmed some shrubbery, righted some of my things in the house, read a little, sat with one or both my sisters—right after tea I went up to the deserted house, my heart beating faster, as always, as I mounted the Sweetser terrace, and walked hastily through the lower rooms.* The stillness and gloom were as if all life had departed forever. If it had been the evening after your funeral the blankness could hardly have been more appalling. I hurried out—and walked across to the cemetery, to look down upon the grave of my little boy, the next most natural thing to do. Came back—started to call at the Hills'—before I reached their gate, decided I could^{nt,} turned and went into the other house [the Homestead] for a minute—and from there home. Am at the dining room table. In the Library are [Mattie's friends] Issie Cutler, Fred Bliss, Tucker, and someone else has just rung the bell. I found Fred Bliss at the tea table—without knowing he had been invited. He is playing the piano in there. My door is shut. Sue and Ned did^{nt} come last night†—sent word they should be along Monday. So had I known, I need^{nt} have left at 11. It was as well, though, better, that I did. It would have been harder for me to part from you in the common rush and crowd. It would have hurt me. I was at the station in time, and some minutes to spare, and had a rather pleasant ride up, with nothing to divert or distract my thought from you. I followed you by my watch every instant, to the time of your leaving the wharf at 3, when we were stopping at Dwight's, down the harbor, among the islands, to Sunset, dark—9 o'clock, wondered if you had gone to your state room, to 10, when I felt sure you were there, thinking of me, and of our ten minutes there that morning.

* The Sweetser house, next door to the Lessey house, stood vacant at this time.

† Sue and Ned were in Grand Rapids for the funeral of Frank Gilbert, who died on May 25. Mattie was on vacation from Miss Porter's School, and, together with her cousin Issie Cutler, was "keeping house" for Austin.

And today I have tried to imagine the new, inspiring, expanding sensations you were having as your monster of a boat stormed on toward the unyielding horizon of sky and water. The bells rang for church tonight as usual—it seemed strange that they should—and I saw the same people entering—perhaps they did^{nt} know that you were not there—and perhaps it was not as much to them that you were not, as it was to me. Last Sunday night *I* was there, waited for you to come out of the choir box, took your arm in mine, and headed for the Sweetser piazza, and a few minutes by ourselves. Tonight how different! I rode up yesterday in the smoking car, had two seats to myself. After we were well by the suburbs of Boston, approaching Framingham, I drew out the letter you had handed me the night before, and as I read, never in my life felt weaker, or grander. It so far surpassed, darling, anything that had ever passed between us before, on either side, that it seemed as if you were getting away from me, out of my reach, had taken new wings, that I could^{nt} follow you.

And then it seemed enough alone to have lived for. A brighter crown than is worn by the kings of the visible world. It was a marvelous note, my darling—beyond anything and everything. I think I shall let Emily read it sometime, when it comes right, that she may know of what stuff you are. I feel a holy and consecrated man to be the possessor of such magnificent love, and my highest aspiration is to be not unworthy of it. God help me. Oh, my darling, my darling, I love you, I love you, I *love* you. *How* I love you, and now I kiss you good night, this night after the first day alone. There is nothing in all the wide world but you, for me.

Tuesday, 9$^{th.}$ David returned last night—and so did the others. I made a short call on D. between 9 & 10, and heard a little about your getting off—all I wanted to. It made me feel worse than ever, and I was so glad I did not stay. I went back to my room, with a new sense of your being borne further and further from me every minute, and it was long before I found sleep. The others [Sue and Ned] had plenty to tell of their fortnight's experience—it was all sad and depressing. They are off driving this afternoon, with Issie Cutler, as she leaves tomorrow. I am filling myself with all the work I can, the more the better. Thats the only thing. O, darling—Love me, Love me—and stay by me. If I could only touch you now, for an instant, and hear you say again, yes, I love you! And yet I know you do. . . .

Saturday 13th. Seven days out and away. If you would only come back for five minutes and let me look once more into your eyes, and hear the sound of your voice, to help me through another seven—was there ever a week so long! It seems an age— it tires my memory to follow it back—and you are not yet in sight of other land. O my darling, what are you, and what are you not to me! To have brought you into existence—and me, and brought us together, even to be separated but temporarily would be the bitterest device of the bitterest malignity. It does not go with the external beauty and harmony—it cannot be. You are for me—and I for you, and nothing—not height nor depth—nor principalities nor powers—nor any living creature can part us. I love you my sweet. I love you, and I love you. More, every day and every hour. You fill and bound everything. You *are* everything. Dearest, dearest. How lovely you were to me in Boston! How lovely! Nothing of those days and night escapes me, but the beauty of it all bewilders me sometimes, and challenges my belief in my personal identity. I dont know whether I could have said go, if I had realized in advance what it meant. You should have waited for me, or I should have hurried for you.

So much new grandeur and glory should have come to us together. The first impressions of the ocean should have been ours together, and of all that is beyond.

I shall never forgive myself quite—that I didn't say this must be—but it didn't seem quite practicable, and we must now make the best of it. As it is you are in a new atmosphere and life. I am in the old quiet nook. You can summon me to you almost any hour, but while I am hunting Dublin through for you, you are as likely to be in the highlands of Scotland. We will see—the weeks will go by. I have known lots of people go over there and come back so near the same I recognized them at the first glance, but you will take a new and richer bloom. I want you to be the same girl though that I have walked with, driven with—and all the rest.

I am expecting to see the announcement of your arrival at Queenstown in the Monday morning papers. I shall think of you tomorrow afternoon as landing, and in a little more than another week I shall expect to know what you have been thinking in all these last days. I am going down to tea now. I love you, and I kiss you good night, my sweet.

Monday 15. Not reported yet, but you must be in today I am sure. I spent most of yesterday with David, sorting, shaking out, packing, in the rooms whence the spirit had fled. Else— who created them, breathed in them the breath of life? Have you any conception of how sadly pathetic it was to me, and yet solaced a little by the thoughts that you had touched them all, cared for them. We took nearly all the pictures, the best chairs, the little sofa over to Vin's, and all your good dresses I carried over in my arms. I wanted them near me.*

Tuesday, p.m. June 16

At Queenstown, June 15. *Pavonia* from Boston for Liverpool. On time. Thats all. On time—and the *Pavonia* had braved

---

* The year's rental of the Lessey house was up. Its new owners, the Amherst College DKE fraternity, planned to enlarge the dwelling, so David was moving his possessions to the old Amherst College gymnasium and himself to a room at the Amherst House until new living arrangements could be made in the fall. The Todds' personal and most valuable effects were stored at the Homestead all summer. Austin's role in the move was crucial. When a letter from David caught up with Mabel in London a month later, she wrote in her journal: "Poor little David has been very sick. . . . He writes very tenderly & enthusiastically about our dear Mr. Dickinson, who has been the truest of friends to him, doing all our packing & moving, when he was too sick to stir, besides sitting by him & holding his hand when he was sickest. Oh! he is a rare soul—I never saw another like him, although he & my sweet, rare father have many points alike." The reason nothing about David's illness surfaced in Austin's letters probably relates to its very private nature. In later years David decided he had had a urinary tract inflammation.

the trackless Sea, alone, for eight days and nights—and had on board the woman who carries my heart in her bosom. How wide the World is! . . .

MABEL TO AUSTIN [*At sea*]
7th June 1885

My darling, my darling, and my dearest,

This is Sunday—*our* day. And ever since I took your hand in parting that last brief moment, my soul has been full of you. When I looked in your dear eyes that moment, and then you went your way and I mine, your face and your personality were again indelibly impressed upon me, so that it was no parting, for we were, and are, one only. There can be no more partings for us, dear. It is only that I do not see you, for a few weeks, in body. But I am truly with you every moment—as you are with me. Well, there were many to see us off. . . . After we were entirely free from the shore & all backward looks, I went down to my little stateroom, and curled up for a few minutes in the little corner of the sofa where you and I had sat, & which was therefore infinitely dear and sweet to me—and read the few little words you, my dearly-beloved, had written for me. You said they were nothing—and of course they are a mere nothing compared with all that fills your soul for me, dear, but if you could have known how tender & comforting & cheering they were to me, and how very much they seemed, when I was out on the sea all alone, you would have been as glad as I was that you wrote them. And, oh! how I loved you as I read your words! And how wonderfully these last happy few days came back to me! I lived again through every tender detail, until you seemed positively present with me. . . . After dinner I sat on deck again a long time watching the gathering darkness. There is something deeply solemn to me about the coming on of twilight and night over the ocean—something never felt else-where. So I sat & watched & thought, & saw one star come out after another, until Caro asked where I had been—she had spoken to me many

[2 1 1]

times. I told her I was then in Amherst. Finally I walked with her; and finding that the delicious sea-wind was making me sleepy, I went down to my stateroom about half-past eight, and went to bed, thereby losing supper at nine which I forgot all about. I slept solidly until half-past six this morning, and got up-stairs on deck about half-past seven. Brisk walking for an hour made me very ready for breakfast, and it was a remarkably fine meal—as all are, apparently. . . . Well, my darling, I have just come back from the bow, which is my favorite spot in any-thing that floats, where I went with a Miss Drowne & her brother, who are friends of Caro, & went very unexpectedly to her, on this steamer. I am writing in a sheltered corner of the deck, next a huge mast, looking at the rail, which is sometimes elevated far above the horizon line, and next, as unduly de-pressed. And every few moments a wandering breeze seeks me out, & blows my paper most ungenteelly—as is witnessed by numerous small blots. I write of every little detail, my sweet darling, because I want our lives to follow along together still, just as they do when we are together. And I want, if possible, every new feeling & sensation to be shared by you. It is half-past three now, sweetheart, but we have already gained more than half an hour, & I have had to put my watch forward, to keep pace with the meal-times. So you are just through dinner—or more than that. And I know you are thinking of me—oh! darling—and remembering last Sunday afternoon, or better still the per-fect days since. So here counts one Sunday off, & I should not be surprised if we come back on the *Pavonia* as well, starting September 2nd. It is very cold now. I am wrapped in my old green flannel sack, my fur cloak & my plaid shawl, & a knitted hood. The sun is over-clouded, & the sea is cold grey. Most of the passengers have given in, & are below, or else lying out flat in their steamer-chairs, on pillows & wrapped in blankets. I feel superbly; and oh! oh! how I wish you were here! And how I love you—darling! To be out of sight of land, with you by my side! It would be next to going into Heaven together, I think. But we are together, dear, every-where & always. I kiss you, my darling.

A New Epoch

Darling, I think so very much of you all these thrilling days. There has been an immense wind all the time since I stopped writing. And the sea is perfectly magnificent. The steamer rolls and pitches in what, to most of the passengers, is a very disquieting and dreadful manner. But it is not necessary for me to tell you how exhilarating it is to me. It rained all day yesterday, but I spent my time on the extreme stern watching the huge waves chasing us, & sometimes, as we dipped down, breaking entirely across the deck. I was thoroughly drenched, but it was all like wine to me. I feel better with every hour of this high sea, with its thrilling whitecaps and tremendous power— which tips this great steamer, and plays with it at will, like a toy. But in reality, it is pretty rough, and the number of those who come to the dining-room is pathetically small. The Captain, the doctor, the purser and I, have not missed a meal, & there are, possibly, five or six who keep us company—out of the eighty-two cabin passengers. The steward says I am "the best sailor among 'em."* I sleep, as if every breath of sea-wind were an anodyne. Only, last night I was shifted about in my berth rather suddenly every minute, from one side to the other, which almost bruised me. But the sea did it, so I could not complain, & I feel like a new creature. Oh! darling, we did decide wisely, and I did need the change. I love you enormously—you are present with me every moment, and I know the joy you would feel if you were here, & could see the brightening of my face from day to day, & the appetite which I have not had before for years. As for my mind it is quiescent. I have grieved a good deal over the fact that I left my mother unhappy†—but the sweet peace of our parting, dear, and the serene beauty of our "rest in each other," are with me all the time. You are my gate to God—

---

* Mabel took great pride, always, in her immunity to seasickness, a trait that deserted her after a stroke in 1913.

† Mabel had had only an unsatisfactory "flying glimpse" of her mother on June 4, when she handed Millicent and Grandma Wilder into her keeping at the Boston depot. Mrs. Loomis traveled north from Washington to Hampton, New Hampshire, for the summer.

the high-priest of my best self. I can never swerve a hair's breadth from you, but only grow closer, inevitably, with every day & hour—even if they should bring physical separation. Oh! darling, darling, how I love you. . . .

Saturday night, 11:30 o'clock. The electric light in my stateroom went out at that moment the other night, my beloved, so I stopped perforce. But I was going to tell you this one thing —that I miss your absolute congeniality & sympathy terribly. I have lived so upon it that I feel bereft without it, & what I find in all other people, no matter how brilliantly we may talk, is only a very occasional flash of understanding. My inner self is a blank to them, as I suppose theirs is to me. Sometimes a flash gleams in conversation, as of a suggestion of fine sympathy— the next sentence shows me as a closed door to them by what they say. I am more astonished at your and my absolute union of thought & feeling. It is rare, rare* . . . Sunday . . . Darling, darling I belong to you—never forget that. And my life is only waiting until I am with you. Tomorrow (Monday) morning, we expect to see land at ten o'clock, & reach Queenstown about two p.m. So this is goodbye for this letter. P.S., P.S., and P.S. Also P.S. 2nd, dear.

I dearly, dearly love you. From the other side of the sea I am yours.

Austin to Mabel   [*17 June 1885*]

Gracious, the idea of your being over in Great Britain all alone, wasting your fragrance on strangers, this bright, clear, clean breezy 17th June afternoon—when we should be in Pelham or Shutesbury or some other of the outlyings of Amherst, Mass., U.S.A.—you and I. I grow more and more impatient at my lack of forethought in letting you go. It is all wrong, and

---

* Nevertheless, Mabel's diary indicates she was having very happy, exciting times aboard the ship, playing and singing evenings in the music room and enjoying "jolly long talks" and a "jolly tour" of the boat with the captain. To David she wrote: "Do you know, dear, I am called 'the life of the steamer.' "

can never be made right. Nothing but a long way into Eternity will mitigate it, and not a word from you either—and not one to be expected for another week at least. Meanwhile our days are all numbered, and each night another is counted off forever. All New England could go—and I should^{nt} notice it, except in the added serenity—but you! *My* Mabel. Gift of my God—how could I have said go—to you!

18th. Another of these most perfect of fine days—and you not here. What are days for, now! I dont want any of them— they are a burden—there's no life or meaning in them. They are as blank as this paper untouched by pen, ready to be filled— may hold everything, or nothing. Theres nothing *for* them to hold but you, my darling, my beloved. I would rather they were all blotted out till you are back. I think of you sometimes, recalling all our past, especially the last weeks—especially the last days—with the sweetest pleasure, but a great deal of the time I almost wish I need^{nt} think of you at all, it is such pain that I cannot have you. Hereafter, if we live to meet again, you must never leave me. I cannot even work with any zest. It is all the most barren drudgery.

Thanks to my stars a good deal presses upon me to be done, and I am kept pretty closely at it—the closer the better. I see David as it happens in the day time, and go over every evening for a while, as regularly as before you walked off, that morning of the fourth. We talk some—each, I think, feels nearer to you through the other than in any other way. We pack some, and when I say good night I take a picture or some other choice thing along to put into Vin's keeping. The Town is beginning to fill up with Commencement people—and the seniors are making up their books for the dance, just as usual. *The Rivals* is to be given Saturday afternoon, 3½ p.m. 27th—and a concert by the glee club in the evening, the rest according to the programme you have. Monday after Commencement I think I shall go to Boston for a couple of days. You can pretty surely think of me as there the afternoon and evening of the 6th and through the day of the 7th—and I will think of you as so thinking.

At my house everything is unruffled. I have invitations to a variety of pleasures which tax all my diplomacy, but I shall rise to whatever strain may be put upon me. They did^{nt} attend church Sunday forenoon, but went in the evening—from which I infer that your absence has been brought to their knowledge. There has been no allusion, or suggestion, in the remotest way. I see Vin and Em more than I did—and you are the constant theme. Emily has had great pleasure in looking over your pictures [Mabel's oil paintings of flowers and grasses stored at the Homestead]. I have^{nt} made a call outside, am going the first I can to Morses' to acknowledge the politeness of their invitation to their party—and I must go to the Seelyes' too. Have^{nt} seen Mrs. Emerson, indeed hardly any one but Mrs. Brill, whom I meet every day—and who seems by her bow to express disapproval in some way, as if I had spoken disparagingly of her. Perhaps I have. I dont remember—and it is of no consequence. Nelly [Mrs. Mather] returns next Wednesday or Thursday.

But how must all this domestic prattle strike you—in the capital of Ireland or the metropolis of the world! And yet I know you love me—and I trust *you* implicitly.

Friday. 19th just after 4 o'c. As beautiful as yesterday, and wasted. I have been at my desk all day.

The mate of the *Pavonia* sails tomorrow from Boston, and this is going along for you to read while I am at the Alumni dinner Commencement day. You dont know how I long to get my first letter from you. Others will then follow, there will be no other such space of time. Seelye came in when I was in this last line—and now I have only time to get the mail. I love you—and I love you. I keep your letter handed to me the evening before you sailed in our room at the Parker Ho. with my Bible—and as part of my Bible. I read it, and reread it. Love me. Love me, darling darling darling, and God keep us.

MABEL TO AUSTIN   The Shelbourne Hotel, Dublin
                                            Sunday, 21 June 1885

Dearest, *dearest*—my whole soul is with you today. I have thought of you constantly, and it sometimes seems as if I were really nearer to you now than when we were together. For you are my luxury. I go to bed early, so as to lie still in perfect peace and think of you. I steal off by myself continually to be with the richness of my memory of you—and with my anticipations as well. Everything brings me closer to you—nothing takes me one moment from your side. I have been very busy ever since we came here with writing an article on some of the queer things I have seen in this past week, and now the first part is done, & I shall begin this afternoon on the last part. It has been a great pleasure to do it, & I hope you will like it. I shall copy it & send it as soon as I can. I never saw anything like the showers in this island—my umbrella is my inevitable accompaniment, & used every half hour or so all day. It is now quarter past one—you are just finishing your breakfast, and are thinking of me—and oh! if you could only know the infinite tenderness of my love & thoughts of you! We went to St. Patrick's church—no cathedral, this morning, which had a fine high-church service, but the music was not as good as in the Church of the Advent in Boston. I only came for this little minute, sweet love, to tell you how dearly, *dearly* I love you; and now I am going to try & finish my article to send tomorrow, before we leave here. . . .

7:30, Sunday. I suppose, dear heart, that it is now three o'clock with you, & your Sunday dinner is over—& oh! don't I wish I were with you for the rest of the day! After I stopped writing the first part of this brief note, I finished & copied the first half of my article, & it goes in the envelope with this.* I love you, & I love you. I try not to be homesick for you, & to enjoy everything I can, but, darling, this is a very half-hearted way to see Europe—to leave all the soul of one's life behind, & try to enjoy with what is left. . . .

---

* Mabel wrote David this same day asking him to forward her essay, "Five Days in Ireland," to the *Christian Union* with a covering letter. That publication did not accept it, nor did the *New York Independent*, which David also tried. "Five Days" finally appeared in the *Amherst Record* in two installments on April 7 and 14, 1886.

THE LETTERS

[Edinburgh]
Sunday, 28 June, 2:30 p.m.

I was going to write you a long letter yesterday when I began, my beloved, but most unexpectedly "John" [Caro's husband] invited me to accompany them on a drive to Dalkeith & Hawthornden & Roslin Castle, so I stopped to go. And all through the sweet, sunny country I thought of you, & whenever a particularly lovely lane or road branched off through fields & trees, I knew how we should go through it, and how deeply we should love it all. I have lived in such an atmosphere of perfect sympathy & understanding with you, that I find myself (though constantly less frequently) wondering why nobody says anything about views or flowers or sky—only in general admiring, but with absolutely no intimacy with nature. I am, in many senses, more alone than as if I had no acquaintance on this side of the Atlantic. It is so very rare to see a truly congenial soul! And about one, in five hundred who look at things, genuinely loves and appreciates nature. Not more. If I could see all these beauties with you, *joy* would not begin to express my emotions. As it is, I take it all in, & put it away to talk over with you, but as for seeing whole-heartedly, & absorbingly, away from you, it is not possible.* Edinburgh is the most beautiful city I ever saw. Immediately opposite my window as I write is a deep ravine, laid out in gardens, with lawns & paths, away up to the top of it on the opposite side—& it is crossed by a handsome, massive bridge, which connects the old & new cities. And crowning the height, just over there, is the immense Edinburgh Castle, its origin lost in twilight ages, three hundred feet above the people who walk

---

* Ten days earlier, in Ireland, Mabel had expounded in her journal her woes at being caught up traveling with members of "the wealthy mercantile class—a class any member of which I recognize at the first sentence, and from whom I feel ages removed, in everything. . . . I often think of the delight of going about on this side with my own—our refinement, education, position and cultivation patent to all—instead of being shocked every little while by some loud-mouthed speech, of questionable grammar & worse taste, & having all about think I am of that party—as indeed I am. After a little conversation, however, everyone sees that I am not of them."

below. You cannot imagine anything more deliciously picturesque. And tomorrow we start again on our way to London, stopping at Melrose & Abbotsford, & Dryburgh, & York, & other
places on the way; but it will not be later than Wednesday night
or Thursday that we reach London. And I am *so* glad! And I so
long to hear from you that these three days still to wait seem
interminable. Oh! to read even a word from your dear hand
again. . . . I remember all about Commencement beginning
today & in general what you will be doing through the week—
& oh! & oh! how many things I wish, darling! *darling*! Love me
every minute as I love you—and count the days off, & hope—
oh! so earnestly for the kind future. Never be lonesome, sweet;
of course, we cannot—and remember everything—& hope for
all. Dear heart, I have not said half, but you know it all, and you
are with me. And so for this letter goodbye—for a little while,
darling. I love you and I love you. P S. 2nd?

AUSTIN TO MABEL   [*3 July 1885*]

I am just back from Northampton, darling, where I have
been since morning, till it is now after three o'clock—it is Friday
afternoon—and a steamer leaves East Boston tomorrow afternoon, which will take a mail your side. Dont I wish it might take
me! It must take something from me, however brief, and insufficient. No time would suffice—I have a thousand things to
say. What first! Perhaps that at last, and at last, after years and
years, two weeks after their parting, the letters from Queenstown
arrived. Monday July 1st—but David was away in Pittsburgh,
had directed me to open them for anything there might be for
me—and then forward to him. Two little innocent harmless
notes, seemingly of the least possible consequence, lay there as
I unlocked Box B. that morning, but the superscription of one
put every nerve in me in a quiver. I got into my office, broke the
seal for what I knew was there for me, read it and the first
chance reread it, and knew that you had gone through the tremendous experience of an ocean voyage in rough weather—my
idea is that nothing but death can exceed it—and were unchanged
to me, that you held to me just the same, that I was no less to
you. Vin's letter came all right by the same mail, same morning.

The next day two more came—one in your hand, one in another, I did^{nt} know whether Caro's or not, to David. Nothing for me, and I forwarded them at once. Since then Commencement has come and gone—by much as usual—over three hundred of the Alumni here, parents, lots of girls, new and old, speeches, parties, concerts, dinner, dancing. I scanned the gathering at dinner for a face my eyes could rest upon with pleasure for a moment, but could^{nt} find one. They were all to me as manikins, or wax figures. Last year you were there. How different! What a fearful thing for one human soul to live so wholly upon another. What should I be without you! The drive from Northampton alone this sweet afternoon brought you so vividly to my side. The clouds were the lightest and airiest, the shadows slanted down the side of Holyoke. The smell of clover was in the air, and of new-made hay. The road sides were lined with big purple eyed orange daisies, wild roses, buttercups—the elder just in bloom, now and then a mullein. The haze was billowing in the fields, the bobolinks flying about like mad with delight. We have looked at all these together so many times, and they mean more every time. O love! my love! love me. What else! darling, darling, now this must go. So little said, but you can supply the lack from your own heart. I have been crowded one way or another every minute till I am too tired to stand or move. There will be a let up of social demands now, which drains me the worst of anything, and I can keep straight on my work, and take a little care of myself. Mr. Seelye has just come in and is by my side. I shall write again first or middle of next week. Expecting it will find you in London still. Eleven days ought to be enough to carry a letter from here there.

I love you—and I love you, and I kiss you all over. I remember everything, everything, and everywhere. Do you? You do, I know. Sunderland Park. The Knob. Shutesbury. Parker's. Good night my sweet. Hope you can read this.
[*across top p. 6*] Write to me often if only a word.
[*across top p. 1*] So busy I cant fill up these blank spaces, but I have been interrupted too much.

Do you love me, sweet?

A New Epoch

MABEL TO AUSTIN   London, England
                                    Saturday evening, 4 July

We reached here last evening—or afternoon, rather, and I was *so* glad to settle down for a week or two & rest—& get my letters. So I alighted as happily as could be at the door of the pleasant boarding place where we are to stay until toward the 20th, and very soon after, "John" went for the letters & brought me your two wonderful ones. Oh! how I love you; & oh! how *terribly* I need you! For after I had read them I was filled with various emotions—exultation at the grandeur of your love for me, sadness at our separation, but a happy hopefulness for the sweet day when we meet again. Then I took up the third letter. It was from my mother. And it was twelve pages—and ever since I read it, every breath has been an agony. I have wished repeatedly that I could die, and I almost thought I should last night. I cried for hours, until from very exhaustion I stopped. Caro sat by me, and said what she could to comfort me, but she cannot see it all just as it is, of course. The letter was absolutely terrible—perfectly scathing, & it has struck me dumb. I suppose it is quite what I might have expected, considering the unfortunate few minutes I had with her just as I started, with her probable subsequent conversations. But I could not have anticipated anything quite so direful as what she has actually written, & it has almost killed me. For through it all I see the most agonizing suffering on her part—and that hurts me almost more than anything else in it all. What *can* I do? I am melancholy beyond words, & right in the midst of lovely things to see and do—& no one within three thousand miles who really loves me, or would think a second time if I were to perish utterly from the earth. . . . A pall, as of black darkness, has settled over everything. I cannot feel, I am benumbed—& still I keep crying out as in protest, "Why *couldn't* she let me have my pitiful little three months of absence in peace?" "Oh! why need she have followed me across the sea with words too terrible to think of!" . . . Caro says suffering never kills. Perhaps not. At all events, I feel, physically, somewhat better tonight. I shall be well (in health) by tomorrow. I can only pray that God will straighten it all in His own way. He knows how pure my love for you is, & how lofty is yours for me. He did it, and I can only lie passive in His hands, knowing that if I were to be gradually killed by inches, & torn in shreds, it could not stir to the breadth of a hair the intensity & overwhelmingness of my love for you. *That* is as fixed as the everlasting hills. . . . God must, & will, interfere for us *soon*, in some way. And I will hope, forever; and I will love you through time and eternity. Good night, dear heart. I am so glad to know how & where to think of you next Monday. Do not tell [David] of my mother's letter. I have not fully decided what to do about it, but I think I shall continue to write as if it had not come.* Good night, dear. God help us!

Sunday, 3:30 p.m.

. . . I am trying to forget some of the terrible words in that letter. I read it once only—I truly think I should perish to read it again, and if a dimness would only come over my memory of it, possibly I could smile again sometime. But I cannot smile, even superficially, today. My whole soul cries out for you. Well, if I had staid, it would have been verbal words, & now it is written ones—that is all. She had things to say, & she has said them on paper. I have decided not to answer it, & write in general, as I have done before. There, my darling, I will not say any more

---

* Mabel wrote much more sketchily to David about her mother's letter and its effect upon her, but he was upset enough to send Mrs. Loomis an angry response on his wife's behalf. Mabel's decision not to respond at all was the wiser course, for having expressed herself, Mrs. Loomis evidently felt calmer—until David's letter arrived. In her journal, Mabel disclosed that her mother attacked not only her but all the Dickinsons: "Every phase of my life comes into her general scourge. Millicent has no clothes—her boots were of the cheapest, while when I was a child no money was spared on me. I am inordinately vain, abominably selfish, as weak as water & only stubborn. This after pages of abuse of my dear Austin, & not only his own family but his sisters—cynical, carping, irreligious people. One thing which my mother lacks utterly is the faintest sense of humor, & Vinnie's funny way of putting things, which she seemed to enjoy at the time, has made her unreasonably wrathy."

about it in this letter, not a word; and you must forgive me for adding my burden to what you were already bearing—but you must know everything. . . .

Monday morning, 9:30 o'clock

Good morning, darling. I feel better today, even a little cheerful; and I have gained the victory over my own feelings about my mother. Nothing but pity for her remains. I shall take no notice of her letter, but write as kindly as I know how, and when I get back shall go & stay a day or two—or two or three with her, so that she may go home perhaps happier. I will be as kind as I can, & as sweet, & so try once more to help her to be happy. . . .

AUSTIN TO MABEL   [*6 July 1885*]

Amherst. Our Amherst—bounded on the north by Sunderland, Leverett, Shutesbury. East by Pelham, south by Belchertown and So' Hadley, and west by Hadley—July 6th. Monday afternoon—at my desk—my office, the window wide open. The air warm, dreamy, enticing, and sweetest thoughts and reflections of you filling and perfuming every chamber of my soul. This is my where and how, my darling. I expected to be in Boston, but couldn[nt] get ready, and besides one of the men I was to meet is sick. Will another note reach you before you leave London? That is the present question—and if not, will it ever— if sent. Your plans, as in the most indefinite way I have it in mind—for I was thinking more of what was—in those last hours, than what was to be—the to be hanging over me as something to be borne—crude, uncertain, oppressive, almost ominous, was to make London about 1st July, that was last Wednesday —on Commencement day, and remain there about three weeks. If I am right in this, the next mail from New York ought to hit you, and I'll try. Your second note—from Dublin, 21st June, your second Sunday over—came with the "Five fine days in Ireland," both parts together. Saturday morning, 4th—David had not returned from Pittsburgh, and it was my pleasure to break the envelopes as he had directed, for what they were sure to hold for me. I read the "Five Days" too with great interest. He arrived in the evening by the late stage, and I gave him what was left yesterday morning. The note was a great comfort and delight to me, assuring me that the ordeal is being passed safely, that you are in no whit changed by all the great changes that encompass you. I knew of course that you would not be. For what are the Kingdoms of the Earth to the Kingdom in which we dwell! and which is ours alone! What has the ocean—the British Empire, another civilization, another continent, all the triumphs of travel to compare with a quiet afternoon in the heavenly valley at the base of Toby, threaded by two lovers, hand in hand! What, with the same two at Parkers! Still there is a rest and satisfaction in having it from your own lips, or pen.

I am getting on better than at first, bearing the separation more philosophically, but it is not easy, and I chafe under it. I ought to have gone too, and if I had—and had had it in mind long enough to put all my matters clearly before my sisters— I doubt if we should have returned. You are all, darling. You hold my soul in your keeping. What I am in the future I am through you. You—I speak it most reverently—are my Christ. God reveals Himself to me through you, and in you. You lift me to the highest reach of my being, and in that extreme tension I thrill to your exquisite influence to the very verge of heart breaking. Do I love you—do I *not* love you, terribly! Do you like to think of me, working steadily on here, waiting for you? Caring for nothing else, waiting—pure and clean, and earnest, for you. O my darling. You are unlike any other to me. Unapproached, unapproachable—and you alone have found me out. I never revealed myself to another—you know it—there was but one key, that you had. You have turned it, and entered in. You have conquered me, by such sweet winning ways, made it all so delightful, been so deliciously fascinating. You sweet dear, dear creature. You seem to me the very incarnation of the spirit of nature —nature just as God left it. I am afraid sometimes you will go back to it, disembody yourself, and exist only as a spell in the air, that I may feel but cannot touch or see. Dont—keep a woman just as you are, just as you have been, with the old green dress.

Keep for me, or I shall die—and die not to live again. O Mabel, my Mabel, I love you—and I kiss you. Love me, and kiss me. Who are they who say our love is a base thing!

Tuesday forenoon

Just here—about 5 yesterday afternoon—David walked in for a little sit before going to the Neills' to tea, and I suspended. Later, about half past eight, I went up to his college rooms for a call on him. 'Tis very funny—and interesting the sort o' unspoken sympathy that has seemed to grow up between us, since his Caro and my Mabel left us to see what they could see. I shall have something to tell you about it when you are back. He has seemed to lean upon me—and confide in me beyond anything I have known among men, and I make a point of looking after him. This is my fourth—or fifth, I am not certain which this instant—note to you. Where will the next find you! We have no address after London, till you answer in Paris, four, five, or six weeks hence. Next Sunday makes the sixth. Six out of the twelve, the way we were to count. The last six will go with accelerated motion from the gathered momentum. I have engaged Miss Seelye to sing till these are gone. It is understood that you will resume your place then. I talked all over with the [Parish] Committee yesterday—that is the first actual practical preparation. But the French School opened yesterday—a hundred the first day. Many more expected. Strawberries have disappeared. Blueberries have come. My haying is done—the rowen is growing. The summer is deepening, and the meaning of it all is that you are nearer. O, Love me darling—how I love you! We were made for each other—we are each others—and we thank God. This must go in this forenoon's mail, and Mr. Mather has just come in with Mr. Frink, the newly appointed Professor in Chickerings place. I make them wait a minute. Write me often. Ever so short. Tell me every time you are mine, all mine, forever. I kiss you again. I love you. Tell me where to write you next. I want to say more. I must^{nt.}

Vin is going to write you. She says she misses you more than she thought possible.

[225]

I dont believe you had better write for the papers, it is too much drain upon your time and strength. Make your news, and write when you are back.

How can you read this! I dont want to stop.

12 July [*1885*]
Sunday forenoon, 11 o'clock

A bright perfect day, warm in the sun, not too warm in the shade. Just enough motion of the leaves and awnings to point a little life in the air. Not a human sound, no passing, perfectly quiet, and I alone on my east piazza, my every thought of you. Can you not see me, even from London! Sue went to Farmington yesterday afternoon to spend the Sunday with Mattie, help her pack, and bring her back on Tuesday. Ned is off somewhere. The [servant] girls are at church. What luxuries! The yellow butterflies are flitting through the light before me. A squirrel is chattering from the ridge of the barn. Now and then the note of a catbird in the trees. Now and then a robin. Now and then a cock crow from a neighboring yard. All is peace and sunshine. Only one lack. You are not here, but it is the sixth Sunday, darling, half of them, a full half. Your dear note from Edinburgh, written two weeks ago, came yesterday morning. David was off for the day at Holyoke, so it was my pleasure again to open the envelope and take out mine. Even then you had not heard from me in all the long time since I parted from you. . . .

I have two or three visits with my sisters every day and we talk you over always, and I look after David as a part of my charge. He seems to like me, to rely upon me, and to confide in me to a remarkable degree. I think we three would have no trouble in a house together in living as you and I should wish. He admires you more than Caro but with you away and Caro present he would be filled while I should die and so should you without me!* O I love you and I love you and I love you. My

* Austin, Mabel, and David were planning to build a house for the Todds in the Dickinson meadow, a house that Austin would frequent.

heart, my own. Love you with all my mind and heart and strength, love you dearly and sweetly and tenderly, overpoweringly. This for now. The organ is driving the devout from the church. Miss Tyler will have another opportunity. She sings in your stead, as she puts it, and for you, not for the parish. Does it seem as if you were ever in that choir chamber and would you be again you dear child. Or as Lucius Williams says, She likes everybody and everybody likes her.

I haven't cautioned you about taking care of yourself. I want to. Dont try to do too much. Get your rest. Be regular in other things. Careful that you use no inferior water. Skirt fruit. Remember that you are not living for yourself, and remember dear that if anything should happen to you—there will not, you have a charmed existence—you are to wait close by for me. It would not be long. I could not stay here with you and my boy there. . . .

MABEL TO AUSTIN   London
Saturday, 18 July, 3½ p.m.

Dear darling, your letter of yesterday (written & sent on July 7th) was like wine to me. I have been a new creature ever since. I feel very badly when I remember that today you will probably receive my first London letter, written when I was so sad that it could not help overflowing to you. I think I had no right to burden you with my woes. But you have been my strength so long that I could not help it. The sharpness of that wretchedness has gone, of course, and I try not to think of it at all—in which I succeed tolerably. At all events I am much interested in outside things—which I was not for days after that letter came. I have not heard since from her, at all. . . .

The other day at Hampton Court Palace the sunshine and the sky and the sweet scents seemed so like home that I was in a sort of enchantment all day. From "Queen Anne's bower" I looked across a soft and luxuriant green field, where a mowing-machine—the first one I have seen on this side—sent its lazy, dreamy thrill out into the summer air, and the faintest possible odor of new-mown hay was wafted over to me. I seemed to be in a spell. I stood & watched it, until the rest of the party had wandered far away; but I saw Hatfield and the blessed Sunderland meadows, and the Hadley farms—and the day was sweet to pathos. Blended into one beloved picture before me I saw everything—and I remembered—absolutely. What did I care for the smooth lawns, and the trim gravel walks, and the elaborate flower-beds, and the orange-blossoms opening in the sunshine for the Princess Beatrice's wedding, and the largest grapevine in the world! With you, all that would have been poetry— away from you it meant only waiting; one more day counted off, until I get to my home again.

This morning I went alone to the Royal Academy, and I enjoyed the pictures more than any other collection I have seen. As for the old masters, I don't care a straw about those I have thus far seen. I infinitely prefer these beautiful modern paintings, so exactly like nature that it is almost like looking through a casement at the scene itself. I am tired of the unnatural bluegreens, & conventional landscapes which surround the everlasting "Holy Families." And as for crucifixions, and poor be-stoned St. Stephens and arrow-struck St. Sebastians, they are so familiarly ghastly that I have almost ceased to shiver at their horror. But I was very happy in the Royal Academy today, with the beautiful ocean views, and level meadows, & love-scenes and Scottish mountains. Remind me to tell you something (about pictures in general) when I come home.

Last night I went to see Madame Tussaud's Wax work. It is a wonderful place. I will tell you about it when I come. I have so much to tell you, dear, but the burden of it all is—I love you, and I lean upon you, and I miss you, & long uncontrollably for you, and you are absolutely necessary to the life of my soul— to my happiness of course. Yes, dear, I will love you—forever. I cannot help it, nor would I. And I have seen your necessity to me in this separation more than I ever dreamed of before. I will write you more tomorrow. I have never failed you one Sunday, have I? I will not write any more for the papers until I come back, as it really did take time. But I enjoyed it, and I am glad you did. Dear, forgive me, but have you put that little wee note in my box yet?* I think about it and wonder—once in a while. You will, will you not? Now I must stop until tomorrow. It is a little after eleven in the morning where you are. I can see it all, & you—sunny little town, with its long, dreamy summer afternoons stretching themselves out under big, white cumulus clouds, odorous, songful, bright. Home of my soul, to which I am coming most joyfully back. I shall not want to travel alone, very soon again. I love you. . . .

AUSTIN TO MABEL   23^{d} July. At my desk
                                        Thursday forenoon

How, where, shall I begin. What, of all, shall I say! My own precious darling. I am pressed with work, I am interrupted constantly, I will take it just as it happens and say what I can.

I was out till 2 o'clock this morning—David with me, looking after a bad break at our reservoir dam, which has baffled all our local skill to stop—since Sunday morning. Still at it. Since middle of yesterday afternoon we have been without water in the Village and you can imagine the way I am beset, but no matter for that any further—only you will understand. Now to begin back. I came from Boston Friday evening last. Went down on the six a.m. train Wednesday morning—Saturday was a busy day, of course. I told David we would drive in the evening and we did. A little way out he told me he had just got a letter from you—and something about it. After a little more he took it out and read some passages from it to me. Then said he guessed there was something there for me—there was a little envelope unaddressed, and unsealed—he didn't know whether you meant him to read it or not, he did^{nt} stop to do it however. I waited quietly for him to hand it to me—& put it into my breast pocket. It was clear to me. And went on reading more of his own. Our ride was spent in discussing the special contents, and what to do about it. Considered seriously telegraphing you to return at

---

* Mabel had again asked Austin to write out for her protection his case against Sue. See his response of 13 September 1885.

once, finally agreed to think of it over night—he read his letter more carefully—and I read mine, and meet at my office next morning at 9 to decide. This we did. I gave my opinion, with the grounds—against sending for you. He coincided. By the time this was settled men were after me about the trouble at the Dam, and the Sunday was not restful. Well, dearie, if there had been a possible way to get at you, I should have risked everything to do it. Crawled on my knees, my arms tight around you. You would have felt better—safe—and it would have been infinite sweetness to me. I cannot and will not attempt to express my feelings over that letter—and its effect upon you. David said it would do no good to write to your London address again, that you would get nothing more till Paris. By the way I mailed quite a long letter to you from the Parker House 15th· I hope it will not be lost. So there was nothing but sit still. What you wrote Monday morning though—was a good deal of relief—and I trust the victory you achieved lasted. Vin's letter too—written a day later, Tuesday—encouraged the hope. The practical thing I should have said—seeing you—is this—not only dont reply to that letter, but dont write another at all to your mother, not another word, till this is atoned for—and the firmest assurance given you that henceforth you shall be treated like a woman—grown up, independent, free—of your own convictions, affections, responsibilities, conscience, and these not to be meddled with— tried by her standards, or another's. That you are what you are before God—and you will answer to Him and to Him alone for your manner of caring for the talents He has entrusted to your keeping. I think this is the true way, and the self-respecting way, and the politic way too. The pursuit of you is intolerable—and it is time to turn at bay, and face it down, and drive it back upon itself. Write to Millicent—as ever—but let the authors of such outrageous cruel stuff have no notice. Knowing your power to rise to any requirement, or determination, I cannot but think you struck the Continent in fair condition to see what there is to see there with profit, and some pleasure. You know I am thinking of you, lovingly and longingly every minute, and O, wanting you so much, beyond words, and it is so cruel I cannot be with you. It is only to be borne on the ground of its being a choice of evils. Wednesday afternoon I went by boat—down to Pilgrim Cove, Cape Ann—and stayed there till half past four the next afternoon. There—instead of Nantasket—as I wrote to you I might. To be nearer to you, to look out upon the water where you had been and trace the track of your steamer, over the horizon line, and imagine it returning, pushing into Boston, you on board, hurrying to me. It was a very dear day, for it was so wholly with you. I picked a wild rose in the neglected field on the coast and wore it all day—and back to my room at Parker's for you, and I walked down the hall and looked at the door of no. 182, and thought of the great volume it had shut out from the common world.

MABEL TO AUSTIN   Friday, 31 July [*1885*]

My darling, my darling! We are stranded at a little station in Germany—Offenburg—having missed connections and trains, for the first time in our journeyings—and several hours of waiting, with occasional car-rides of a few minutes between, are the result. It is all in consequence of going to Strasbourg, to see the celebrated clock at noon. I was disappointed in it. The apostles hitched along like a slightly better class of Punch & Judys—the whole thing was disenchanting. But we sleep somewhere in the Black Forest tonight, & I do not mind the waiting, for I am not well today. But if we should fail to reach Lucerne for Sunday, I should be most sorry, for there I expect letters. And I love you dearly, and do hope you have sent a letter to me at London at such time that it could be forwarded for me to get at Lucerne tomorrow. It seems ages since I have heard from you. You know the day I sail. Are you glad it is coming so near? And do you love me? Some of your last letters are so wonderfully expressed that you must have been inspired when you wrote them. I never conceived of such heights to be reached in words. "John" & Caro are at a sort of supper-lunch, but I cannot eat today, so I took the time for these few words to my own.

The Letters

Lucerne, Switzerland

3 August 1885

Dear heart, sweet-heart— I need you sadly. I think about you all the time, and I shall have to talk for at least a week, right along, to you, when I come back. Oh! I do so hope things will be pleasantly arranged for me when I get back. I am really thinking a good deal about a house—one or two requirements being so necessary, and I suppose nothing especial has been done about it yet. I still hope a good many things for the autumn, the joyous autumn! I have seen a few trees turning bronze, two or three leaves fluttering down, yellow—and I have heard one cricket— and I love you overwhelmingly. I think of you, *literally*, every minute. I wish I could lay my whole mental state entirely bare to you, all the time. I want to write more—I can't now, but I will send another letter very soon. In the meantime, darling, I love you—& I love you—in Switzerland as in Ireland & Scotland, England, Holland, Belgium & Germany. I meant to write yesterday, Sunday, but we went up the Rigi, & I couldn't. *I love you*— I LOVE you.

The following letter, which Austin sent to Mabel in Switzerland, was preceded by one dated July 31, enclosing a letter to Mabel from Emily. It appears as #1004 in Johnson's *Letters of Emily Dickinson*, and in it Emily greets Mabel as "Brother's and Sister's Friend," signing herself "America." She expresses her appreciation of a picture of hollyhocks Mabel had painted the previous summer, her pleasure in Mabel's friendship, and asks Mabel to "Touch Shakespeare for me."

AUSTIN TO MABEL   [*4 August 1885*]

Here is a note from Vin, dearie—and I hide a practical word in its envelope. Your letter of Saturday Sunday 18th–19th came Saturday, 1st Aug. I was waiting for it, and you can imagine what it was to me. David also allowed me to read part of yours to him, about the next two or three weeks' plans. Time seems to be culminating—and we must not lose sight of the way things are to be—and to be managed when you have stepped from the *Pavonia* at Boston. . . .

You say you sail 2ᵈ Sep. I appreciate all that is covered by that date*— At the same time—how? if you come alone. Do you see the way? *Perhaps* (never allude to my having alluded to it) the uncertainty of restoration being entirely complete yet from an illness you mentioned may of itself settle it. It seems rather that way to me now, but perhaps *not*, too. Some considerable time must elapse to make sure there is nothing vicious left.

I have not the facts sufficiently before me to advise. Still the question arises, whether if Mr. A—— and Caro are to come within a week or two of the 2ᵈ it may not be better, regarding future relations with Caro, to wait and come with them. This is not to dissuade you from any plan, purpose or desire. You know how much I want to see you. Every hour is too long till you are here. But the future is to be protected—and we must see how present action will bear upon that. You know too that much as I delight in the incidentals, with all their deep, solemn, meaning, *you* are beyond all and everything, and that I am perfectly, perfectly happy to be even near you, just within kissing distance. You had example of this just before you left. Look it all over and decide, and be sure I shall welcome any decision you reach.

So you have read the July chapter of *Silas Lapham*. I thought you would come across it. I was so disgusted with it I would like to have thrown it at [William Dean] Howells' head. But will see what the end is. Haven't yet seen the present months number. . . .

I have been reading lately of some of the famous loves of history—but find no parallel to yours & mine. Antony and Cleopatra. Abelard and Héloise. Chateaubriand and Madame Récamièr. And others. Héloise loved as well as you. What other!— and what man, as I love you! What a fool Abelard was! and Antony. Madly in love with Cleopatra—but with the opportu-

---

* Mabel was planning her return to coincide with her "safe" time. The Andrewses booked passage on the *Catalonia*, departing September 9.

nity before him marrying Octavia instead, for political policy. I love you darling—all I am I am yours—for time—and for Eternity. Are you not equally mine!

The note which you ask about has not been written, dear heart, but I will not go to meet you till it is. I have^{nt} wanted to write it, but I will do something and try to satisfy you it is right. . . .

MABEL TO AUSTIN   Interlaken, Switzerland
                                                        5 August 1885

Dear heart, I want you so today that I am almost suffocated with loneliness. Cities and plains and people I can see alone, but these solemn, heavenly mountains are too much for my soul to bear—all alone. . . . When I first saw the Matterhorn, its snow-covered sides gleaming in sunlight, against the blue sky, something rose in my throat so I could not speak, and it was hardest work to keep back the tears. Then in the midst of our ride came a wild mountain thunder-storm. The top [of the diligence] was put up immediately, so we had no rain upon us. But as it cleared away, clouds in glorious, white fleecy masses clung about the great peaks; & as we descended through the Brünig Pass, & saw the bright green valley below, with near mountain-sides enclosing it, with waterfalls rushing hundreds of feet down at one leap—& turning back, saw the great snow-covered mountain at the head of the valley, its top surrounded by sun-infiltrated white clouds, connecting it with heaven, I could bear it no longer, & tears rolled down my cheeks; while the voluble little Irish gentleman who has the same route as ourselves for a while, chattered away glibly with all sorts of adjectives—entirely unheeded. Oh! I am so tired of people—fancying they are seeing Switzerland in lounging on hotel piazzas, & sauntering along well-gravelled walks, & eating elaborate dinners at seven o'clock. I hunger & thirst for *one* natural soul to walk on foot close up to the beauty, & know it. It is not a panorama to be languidly looked at in the intervals of a veranda flirtation! And in all this summer I have scarcely met one person who thinks as I do—not one with whom

I could start off & walk, & see a single natural sight, naturally. I cannot express, even to you, my intensifying hatred of conventionality. There is the everlasting tourist—& there is the habitual, fashionable hotel frequenter. Each is vile in his way. How the mountains stand, & bear it, I cannot see. Well—forgive this little fury of mine—I had to let out a little of it, or suffocate. But my longing for you has been almost unbearable. How I have loved you! How I do love you! And you know when I sail for home! Every day I count one off. And you know I want to see you when I land—then and there. I have written a good deal about it [to David], & I hope you will get it arranged, college or no college. And oh! "love me, love me, or I shall die!" In the midst of all this grandeur, I am all alone. But I have sweet memory, & sweeter anticipation; the days are sliding by, & this terrible separation will be at an end. oh! how I love you! . . .

AUSTIN TO MABEL   [*6 August 1885*]

　　Amherst—Our Amherst—
　　*Thursday afternoon, August 6*th. A year ago today, my sweet wife, was Wednesday—it was the afternoon we drove across the River, through Hatfield meadows, and Whately, and back by Sunderland. When you told me—I remember just where —of your first visit to East Boston—at fourteen—and a delicate personal something had before we knew it, scintillated from you to me that brought us still closer together—and seemed to connect us more completely with all our past, from early boyhood and girlhood. When we saw foreign looks. What a bright, fragrant afternoon that was! What wealth or luxury could the world give us that was not ours for the time! We were together —and out of the reach of molestation. How far was it then from our thoughts that the anniversary would find us three thousand miles and three months apart! Where will another year find us, and how! The afternoon following—7th—we met at the other house just after two, and had two sweet hours there ==== Do you recall? Has Switzerland anything to match them. Or Paris, when you get there! How simple the great things of life are!

and with the right conditions, how easy to be had. two congenial souls—close to nature, seeking God everywhere—true, honest, open, aspiring, what more! You and I. What beside! What can mortal add!

Your little note of 24th came Tuesday afternoon (4th). David handed it to me, saying he didn't know whether it was for me or not, that it was not sealed, or enveloped, and nothing on it indicating that it was for any other than himself and he began to read it before he concluded it might be for me. I thought perhaps you meant just that, and thought better to send once to me that way. All but one line would be read by even your mother without a shudder.* You said but little of your plans in that, but David says to him you are firm that you shall sail 2^d prox. You will consider beforehand, of course, and have it clear just how it all is to be managed, and whether it is best for me to come down till you have been in a day. You understand.

I shall have to husband my time, in good policy—and I shall be unable to divide you with any one, very much. Think it over, and have the plan as definite as may be. I can hardly write about it quietly. The thought of seeing you again soon, touching you, folding my arms about you, having you say you will never, never leave me more, thrills me through and through. I am not philosophical about it, cannot take it stoically—you are all. It is you and no other. Take good care of yourself every way. Remember that you are only partly your own, that you are carrying my life and hope with yours—and that I am waiting, waiting for you, my gift of Heaven. . . .

I shall write you again between now and then at Paris, but when am I to tell you all I have to say to you—and hear all you have to say to me! Everybody will want you, and no one will

---

* David evidently sent unsealed notes to Caro inside his letters to Mabel, at least one of which Mabel read and refused to pass on—perhaps, as she explained, because something David wrote suggested Mabel had been complaining about Caro (which was true). Perhaps, too, Mabel was bothered by David's lustful language directed to another woman. In such small ways as these unsealed notes to others did David and Mabel stir jealousy, and try trust in one another, within the context of "large-mindedness."

help me, for I am branded—*married*—with no right to reach for the tiniest flower beyond the length of my short chain. This will demand our best wit—and it will have it. We have out run all probabilities in the past—and we wont despair.

The Crickets are here, dearie, those weird creatures from the border land—half spirit, chanting as the evening sets in, their crisp purring lullaby, soothing to rest, luring on to the shadows, requiem for the dead—and the living as well. It was these that first touched a chord of sympathy between us—and started a vibration which will never cease—and is melody for the angels. We will listen to them together soon now. My arms shall be tightly around you. We shall not speak, we shall be too full—we shall be each others and we shall know that we are beyond all possible power to separate. Forever and forever. . . .

MABEL TO AUSTIN   Paris, 16 August 1885
                                   Sunday, 2:15 p.m.

My darling, and my darling!

Perhaps you can imagine how I love you! I have read and re-read the five magnificent letters which I found waiting for me here—until I feel as if you were beside me in body, as well as spirit. Indeed, a peace as of an eternal calm has overflowed me all day—a certainty that we are protected and cared for from above. All my little worry & restlessness have stilled, and you and I stand together, hand in hand, in God's light & sunshine. I feel it, and its eternal certainty, as I *never* have before. Oh! I needed all those beautiful words you have written me. I was getting lonely & tired away from you, but the sweet personality which has come to me through them has put new life and new patience into my soul—even the ability to wait quietly the few days now between us. I never think of the ocean as rolling between—only of the fewer & fewer days which separate us—time is a worse divider than distance. These five letters of yours are dated July 15, 23, 28, 30, and August 4th. Some came directly to Paris—others were forwarded from London. All were heaven-sent. There were seven others awaiting me also—a most loving & sweet one from my mother, notes from grandma & my sweet child, & my father. Some of them I opened tremblingly, almost fearing to repeat my London experience, but I need not have dreaded anything more. That one dreadful one was more than nine-tenths the result of that ridiculous mistake in Boston, and the hurt & disappointment which she suffered there. Of course I must go to see her when I get back, although one of my letters says I shall not—please talk [to David], & see that I go, for I *must*—I have thought it all over, & I see it all. It is necessary that I should go to her for a day or two, or be forever tormented with an unrest, of duty unfulfilled. Please make it clear that I must go—for my own happiness, as well as hers. And I want to keep house & not board—*cannot* that be arranged? It must. Oh! this lovely Sunday afternoon! Clear & sunny & cool & fresh—the leaves of the trees just moving in the west wind— & Paris so white & clean & broad & beautiful! You would like to see my initials as I cut them on a tree in the Heidelberg castle grounds. I put them on a tree on a secluded, shady walk to which I could go directly years hence, with you. I have so many little incidents to tell you, so much to talk of—oh! it seems actual heaven in anticipation, just to think of our being together again. I shall try to go to the Cunard office tomorrow, & find out as near as possible the day & hour at which I may be expected to arrive; but I thought the Sunday would probably come in awkwardly for you—and upon thinking it all over, I decided that, considering everything, the plan I wrote yesterday [to David] was perhaps best. Could you get there by 9 or ten o'clock on Monday? Of course it ought all to be different, but I fear it would not be best to do anything *just* as we planned when I left. I can explain it all to you & I will write more fully when I have more dates to go on, hours as well. Bless you for the buggy-drives! And you *will* have the little note for me, I know.

At this pleasant boarding-place, we dine & lunch in the garden, in the most foreign & delightful way. I spent this morning at the Louvre—oh! that you were here to see it all! Caro is at a hotel—they enjoy *throwing* their money away needlessly. Much of mine they have sent with it, but I nearly turned grey over it for weeks, & now I am trying to slide along peacefully & not worry any more. Oh! the blue of the sky, & the green of the trees, & the golden sunshine! It is enchanting. If you were here, how radiant & buoyant I! Dear, we *will* go to our sweet valley again; I would rather see it with you than all Switzerland alone. You know how I enjoyed the Alps—I have written bits of it from time to time—but I have more than oceans to tell you of it all. My pleasant hostess has just invited me to go to drive, so I will not now write more. I shall stay with her until Monday, 24th August. The next week in London. Oh! my love & my darling! How unutterably my soul is yours. How unchangeably we are together for all eternity!

Tuesday, 18 August. I am sure, my darling, from what I hear of the probable time of my arrival (Saturday at noon if winds & everything have been favorable, at night, or Sunday morning if not), that we cannot, policy considered, have everything just as we tried to anticipate in June. Of course it is dreadful, but you & I can bear that too, & you can come as early as possible on Monday morning—did you not write of getting there at nine or ten o'clock? I have had meetings from much shorter absences when anything interfering with a long talk & time at once was cordially detested. I have thought & thought, & I cannot see any way to arrange it. There will be some little delay in the custom-house, & a general *mêlée* at the wharf—as when I sailed—and I would almost rather see you peacefully & happily a little later. Considering everything, it is best, dear. And Sunday you can bear, knowing I am probably landing, & getting my things straightened out, & myself rested to meet you. Dear, as a personal favor, I ask you to destroy this half-sheet. Will you? I shall write you twice more—& then—oh! then! I love you—and I love you. I am glad you belong to me. P.S. 2nd? P.S. 1st a hundred times. Dear heart!*

---

* Mabel's quandary about meeting both men was well-founded. On August 9 she had written her husband: "David dear—*dear*, DEAR, how I will kiss you & caress you when I once more get you within reach! How you shall *feel* all that I think now about you from afar."

Mabel's last two European letters were cries of relief that her journey was ending, while Austin's last three to her were principally devoted to the uncertainties of her arrival and whether he or David, or both together, should greet her. Mabel docked at the Cunard wharf in Boston early on Sunday, September 13, where David met her. They stayed a day and night at the Parker House, and the next morning, as David returned to classes, Austin arrived on the 9:40 train. Late that afternoon he accompanied Mabel partway to Hampton by train. After a day of peacemaking with her mother, Mabel brought Millicent home to Amherst to make plans about where the Todds should live. As promised, on the day of Mabel's return from Europe, Austin tried once more to sum up his unhappy relationship with Sue.

AUSTIN TO MABEL

With my trust all yours, dearie, irrevocably. Willingly, gladly yours. With my soul in your keeping—holding my happiness in your hands—with only you and my boy to redeem my existence from utter failure, having learned through you what life means, and may be. Sure of the present. Trustful of the future. Why should you care for me to say one word about what is behind—at any rate so far as it may involve any other unpleasantly—why do you care to have me put on paper what, involuntarily, I have from time to time in ranging moods dropped from my lips? You know it all, believe it all, and it is all True. Let the Tragedy of a wicked, almost ruined life go. Let it suffice that I saw you and lived.

My earlier experience is the experience of thousands—my later of how few!

Is it not enough, my darling, in the line of what you have wished of me—this that I have called freshly to your mind? It is so much better to suffer any amount of wrong than to take the chances of doing the slightest injustice. Believe me. Believe me. Always your own Austin, as you are my own Mabel.*

13 Sept. 1885

During the summer in Europe, Mabel had written David of her disillusion with Caro Andrews, for the "strange poetry of our relation last spring" had evaporated. Mabel found her friend "jolly enough if she is never crossed, & if a question of money never comes up," but Caro made no effort to supply the "wealth of devotion" Mabel was accustomed to, nor was she considerate of Mabel's financial limitations. The two women found their closest bond in a common dislike of John Andrews, who drank too much and was frequently bad-tempered. After her return in the autumn of 1885, Mabel began painting an elaborate three-panel screen which she hoped Caro and John would accept as repayment of money she had been forced to borrow from them during the trip. Caro thought Mabel had been naïve in her estimate of what the trip would cost. The Andrewses refused the screen so ungraciously that David promptly borrowed money and repaid them without letting Mabel read their letter. This and the pecuniary demands of housekeeping inspired Mabel to take up her painting classes, piano pupils, and church singing in earnest, even though David's salary was augmented by teaching two weekly astronomy classes at Smith College.

The few letters remaining from the next eight-month period are almost all Mabel's. Their anguished tone, and the tone of her diary entries, suggest how discouraged she was by the major block to her happiness—Sue. The longer the circum-

---

* Three months later, apparently in need of recording the facts somewhere, Mabel entered in her journal the startling things Austin had told her about his marriage.

stances of Austin's marriage remained unchanged, the unhappier Mabel got, and the more bitter about Sue's rights and privileges with her husband. Sue's existence seemed to Mabel unjust when the relationship among herself, David, and Austin was so perfect. "[David's] depth of affection for Austin is beyond anything I ever knew of between men," she penned in her journal the autumn of 1885, as the Todds rented and moved into the Lincoln house, near the foot of Lessey Street, just west of the Evergreens. In Austin's diary their home became "the third house," or "3ᵈh." There Mabel, David, and Austin spent many hours companionably, even intimately, together, according to corroborative evidence in the diaries of all three, which are available for the single year 1886. In Austin's diary his symbol ═══ is ten times accompanied by the notation "with a witness," all but one of the occasions being Sunday evenings that he, David, and Mabel spent together at the "3ᵈh." Whatever else can be speculated about the "witness" entries, they testify that David was fully cooperative about Mabel and Austin's liaison. At least some of their time together was devoted to planning the Todds' new Queen Anne cottage, to be built on a road Austin had recently cut through the back of his meadow. Judging by inclusion of a back staircase providing access from outside to the second floor, some kind of *ménage à trois* arrangement was contemplated. As plans progressed, Austin took responsibility for siting and landscaping the new house, David for building it (he was simultaneously building the Smith College observatory during 1886), while Mabel took over from David the family bookkeeping, demonstrating skill at keeping the Todd financial affairs more orderly.

A major event of the spring of 1886 does not surface in the letters—Emily Dickinson's death on May 15 of Bright's disease, from which she had suffered periodically for over two years. "It was a very great sorrow to Austin," Mabel recorded in her journal, "but I have lived through a greater one with him—when poor little Gilbert died." Her own sadness was measured in the uncontrollable tears she wept for the unseen friend who now "went back into a little deeper mystery than she had always lived in." But it was Vinnie who grieved most, for now she was intensely lonely and no longer had her sister as buffer between herself and her sister-in-law. Henceforth she felt prey to and fearful of Sue's arbitrary behavior.

Emily's funeral, May 19, was by several accounts an extraordinarily beautiful event. On a glorious spring afternoon a few invited friends gathered in the Homestead parlor to hear Colonel Thomas Wentworth Higginson read Emily Brontë's poem "Last Lines," and Rev. Jonathan Jenkins lead a simple service. Sue had arranged violets and a pink cypripedium at Emily's throat, and covered her white casket with violets and ground pine. The coffin was carried by Irish laborers who cared for the Homestead premises out the back door of the house, across a sunny, sparkling meadow strewn with wildflowers, to the cemetery, where Sue had lined the grave with boughs. Sue also wrote a moving, perceptive obituary for the *Springfield Republican*, but it is not certain whether she attended the funeral. Neither her presence nor her absence was noted in accounts by others, but Mrs. Todd was there, "dressed in black —looking haggard as if she had lost a dear friend," according to neighbor Mrs. Jameson. It is unlikely that both she and Sue stood at Emily's bier in the Homestead.

AUSTIN TO MABEL   [*In the 1885 file*]

Remember—Remember my dearie darling that I love you, love you, and that I am going to fly through all eternity with you tacked close under my wing. Thanking God for you with every breath, and dont be too rebellious about what in the clear air beyond will seem to us but trifles.

Will you?
Wont you?

MABEL TO AUSTIN   [*2 November 1885*]

Oh! I love you so tenderly! And so longingly, and so appropriately! And in spite of everything, I feel such a peace and contentment in this howling storm this morning, at the knowledge that we have each other forevermore—as long as there is a vestige of either of us left—in this or the other life. And I think the beyond grows more attractive to me all the time. It would seem to be wrong not to round out one's life here to its fullest capacity, to get all of it we can, before starting into the other. But if deprivations grow insupportable what can we do? This sweet world is so beautiful, & could—*will*—be such a heaven in itself. There may be dim blue hills & tender sunshine in the other; I hope so. But I would so dearly like to see all of this, and get its whole charm first. I want to stay, and wait and hope— and I want to rush away into liberty with you. Of course it will end in my taking up the endurance again, and going on still hoping, led by that little star of a presentiment which never wholly leaves me. But the time looks so long, and we cannot measure its slow length of months—God forbid it should be years—until the fulfillment comes. . . .

[*15 December 1885*]

It is Tuesday evening, my dearest heart, and I am all alone. I miss you *so* much! And I am wondering what you are doing [in Boston]. I did not hear the whistle of the train this noon, but I knew you were in it, and at half-past twelve I knew you were speeding away from me in the distance, but never in spirit. And I wished so much I had spoken about your *farewells*—after ours, you know, just as you were leaving the house. You know what I mean. But you didn't have that, did you? . . . I miss you, and I love you—*so* much. We must not be separated a great deal— time is too precious. Yet with one turn of God's hand—I wonder if He does hear prayers! . . .

Wednesday morning . . . A part of your encumbrances have just gone by, in sight. I am glad you are at least at peace, for a few days. There is negative happiness, & there is a very positive kind. Perhaps you have the first, now, away as you are from annoyances. But when—oh! when is the second coming! We know it is on its way, which is something. . . .

[*29 March 1886*]

. . . You will not think it necessary to write [from Boston] to anyone but me in this town? Will you? I meant to have spoken of my hope that you would not. . . .

[*30 March 1886*]

. . . And before I forget it, my request to you about a certain kind of farewell, at your house, holds just as intensely strong about the kind of greeting you get on your return [from Boston]. *Please don't* have it. . . .

A nine-day visit from her mother and grandmother in June 1886 was just what Mabel needed to feel bluer than ever, even though when they left on June 17 Mrs. Loomis and Mrs. Wilder took Millicent with them to Hampton for the summer.

Austin to Mabel   [*June 1886*]

This beautiful, beautiful day, and you and I held apart, by a prejudice as light as air, as irresistible as granite. But know, my darling, that I love you every second—and that in any and every event I will guard you and protect you, with all that I am, and all that I have. That you shall suffer nothing without me— and I will enjoy nothing without you. These dreadful days will be gone soon—and there can be no more so bad, I am sure. This week and the next cover them. Hold up as well as you can. Think of me, and love me. You—my light and my life.

MABEL TO AUSTIN   [*14 June 1886*]

Oh! my dear, my dear, this drizzling, sad, gloomy day is
going by somehow. It is a comfort that it is passing, at least, and
I do hope that my mental horizon will brighten, at least when
the outer sky does. For I am having a very hard day. In the first
place, the contractors [for the new house] have discovered that
they have made a mistake of three hundred dollars in their estimate, and are not beginning anything today, in consequence.
Then I have had a very trying conversation here, about my
deficiencies in general—and the sky weeps in sympathy, and it
is hard to remember that there ever was bright sunshine & hazy
hills, and two lovers hand in hand in the happy valley. But these
things *are* true and real, darling, and I live in my joyous memories, and more radiant hope. Today is dreary beyond expression. I am plunged in blues of the deepest dye. I miss the thought
of you in town, but still I am glad you are away [in Boston], for
I am nearer you there than here, today. Remember how I love
you; remember that you are my salvation & my conscience, and
that I thank God for you, in spite of everything. I am sorry
people suffer over me, but how easily we could make them rejoice! I think of the maple tree sometimes, & pray. Oh! I love
you, & I need you beyond my power to tell you.

AUSTIN TO MABEL   14 June 1886
                                                Monday evening
                                        My room [*in Parker House*]
                                    next door to the Ladies Parlor

I couldn't have gotten off more to your mind than this morning. No one being disturbed but Agnes, not even Mary. Had to
talk with Villagers most of the way to Palmer. There fell in with
my friend and classmate Gould,* bound for Worcester, and
talked with him to there. Read the papers most of the rest of the

---

* Rev. George Henry Gould had been Emily's good friend also during
his student days at Amherst College. Undoubtedly he and Austin talked
of Emily's death a month earlier.

way. Carrying along an undercurrent of thought all through— did your errands first thing, then two or three of my own. Then to the Vault, where I was, cutting of coupons till near 3. Lunched, looked after two or three matters of business, and it was 6 o'c and dinner time. I am not going out tonight, for there is nothing to go to!

If you had^{nt} written Mrs. Andrews, should think of calling her, but I don't think it advisable to mix the things. This is my day—barring memories, reflections, dreams, wonderings, philosophizing, hopes, fears, gladness and sorrow. These another time. I think I never was so strangely lonesome in Boston as this time, and never so yearningly wanted my own with me. So easy a garden of roses for a desert—and yet the desert, but I know where I am and what makes life to me. I never waver here, have no doubts.

I have thought a little of your mother's remarks to you. What do you say—if she resumes the talk, to—after hearing her through, saying to her that you acknowledge her and your father's responsibility—under God, for your being—whether of purpose or without, that you appreciate their care of, and for, you, all through. That you would give your life for their happiness, but that you will not belie it. That you are answerable to God alone for your conscience. That before that you are pure white—and that you will hold to that as the martyrs to their faith. Even to the same consequences. That she had better try to accustom herself to the fact that if she is a hen, her chicken is a duck, and water wont drown it.

That it is your chiefest sorrow that they find no delight in you, but that you are as you are, making the most of yourself under such circumstances as surround you. Seeking the best— thinking no evil—and confidently trusting the result.

It is possible I may not be able to get off on the 3 train and have to go around by Northampton later, in which case I should hardly see you tomorrow night. I shall be ready—myself—and shall have no trouble if those with whom I have to do are on time.

This must hold you till I see you. You know all, and it is all as you know it. Unqualifiedly. The Heavens do not fall. The

Hills do not give way. The Law of Gravitation is never relaxed, and we are builded into the foundation of each other, and cannot be separated.

Early in July 1886 David decided to go on a hastily planned four-week trip west to participate in some Library Association meetings in Milwaukee and to visit observatories and other sites of interest in several cities. He and Mabel left on July 5, Austin going north as far as the Millers Falls depot with Mabel, before she joined David at Greenfield for the journey west by railroad.

MABEL TO AUSTIN   Chicago, 10 a.m. Wed., 7 July 1886

We got in about ten o'clock last night. I should have written then, only the heat & cinders of all day had made me unable to think, even. . . . The heat of all day yesterday was appalling, & even in the parlor car, cinders sifted through the double windows & covered me in a melancholy manner. Part of the way through Canada was pleasant scenery—a good deal very monotonous. But the flowers were beautiful. How I did want some of the gorgeous scarlet lilies hanging over like bells, & various other new things. It is cooler here this morning. We did not go on to Milwaukee with the others at 8, but I suppose we go this evening. A little sail on the ferry across the St. Clair River to Detroit yesterday was lovely, the only comfortable incident all day, except a good dinner—at which (remembering) I tried to do my duty. I have not fully got into the spirit of the trip enough yet to say how I like it. On some accounts I am glad to have come, but you know what would be to me the happiest of all. . . . Everything was all right at Greenfield—the enclosed note [from David] was written you there & handed to me to send. If we go to Washington, I am coming back to N.Y. by boat from Baltimore—two days I think it takes—& then we shall, in coming back to A probably take a Sound boat to Bridgeport, so that will arrange it all perfectly for our plan [to meet in New York], in the getting back. You see that is the end & aim & anticipation of all the journey to me—what we talked of. . . . I am happy in thinking what teaming & so on is progressing in Amherst to-day.* Do save the pear tree. And I think you had better open all letters which come to me, at least—& I should be glad if you would the others too.

I distinctly remember whose and what. Do get all the work out of the way in these two weeks, won't you? Because then we must take our vacation, you know, & I have a great many plans for then. . . .

AUSTIN TO MABEL   12 July 1886
                                              Monday afternoon, 5 o'c.

The second dove back safe and sound this morning after a fly of about forty-three hours, and a dear refreshing delight to me beyond words. There is so much to say I dont know where to begin—and it would take the whole time. Everything suggests you. Everything is for you. You are the soul of all this beautiful world—and it is nothing without you. With you away there is only to work—and to wait. I miss you more than I had thought, and know even more surely than before how absolutely *essential* you are to me. Last week I worked myself, aided by the heat of Tuesday, almost to a wreck, so that yesterday I had to send for a doctor. Am better today—pretty well—at my desk, but am to be more moderate. Everybody else has gone to the seashore—or is going tomorrow morning. I alone am left behind. Mrs. Emerson thought I forgot her.† Whom I shouldn't, for she has called upon me three times at my office, and offered to treat me to beer or lemonade any time I will come down. The Prof. is

* Work was beginning on the new house. Somehow Sue had been in-duced to sign the deed, dated June 8, 1886, which purportedly sold the 86-square-rod lot to the Todds for $1,200, although in fact it was a gift.

† Mrs. Benjamin Kendall Emerson, wife of the Amherst College pro-fessor of geology, was very fond of Austin. Before the advent of Mrs. Todd, the affection was mutual.

worn out again and off for repairs. I am not making calls, however. One is enough for me—*The* one. The weather has come fine—it is perfect summer, in all its fullness, and if you were here I would not care to be nearer Eden. Those hay fields in Hatfield and Sunderland meadows which we were to see together this year are just in their glory. Where will you be *another* year at this time? Perhaps we may get in the second cleaning of the fields, when the great cricket choir has possession of the earth to chant the season's lullaby, if nothing new turns up.

You get back to Milwaukee, it seems, by your programme, Tuesday the 20th. Leaving only four days before Sunday—for Chicago, Cleveland, Pittsburgh and Washington. You will not reach New York at the earliest before Monday. Shall you by that time? 26th Our last Leverett ride was June 27th Sunday afternoon. Do you still think I had better come?* and will the others be satisfied to clear the track for two days or nights? By the way, if you have occasion to telegraph me sign yourself George Davis. I shall understand.

We fixed the level of your house this morning—and it looked so high as we had planned it, I ordered it a foot down —I think this is all right. . . .

This for tonight. I love you my darling, darling—take every care of yourself, and remember, remember, for us both. God bless you. I thank Him for you more and more with every added hour and power. . . .

AUSTIN TO MABEL   15 July 1886

You are to be at Ashland according to the itinerary, over Sunday. Yes, but what Ashland! Every state has one—East and West.

---

* This is an oblique reference to Mabel's menstrual cycle, though just what Austin meant by it is not clear. He and Mabel had had intercourse during the ride to Leverett on June 27, the fifth day of her cycle, and he may have been reminding her that July 26 would fall on the eighth day, or during a risky time, of her new cycle. Austin's 1886 diary indicates he and Mabel were making love five to six times a month. Their pattern shows no consistent regard for a "safe" period.

My guess is for Wisconsin, foot of the Lake. If then I am right—and this hits you—know that so late as four of the clock this Thursday afternoon, July 15, 1886, I was still at my post of duty, and thinking of you, believing you then just in Minneapolis, and reflecting generally on the spend you were making over the marvels of nature and of Man out West, and its probable effect on you.

Reflecting also on our own need of more geographical information, and the enlargement, and illumination which comes from it. It certainly must be my turn next. I must go—and go— till I have brought myself up to your level in outsidedness. It wont do for us to cultivate so onesidedly.

Perhaps I will take Mexico. I always had a romantic fancy that way. Or Peru. Something with a Spanish Tang.

But I will see you about it—and we will talk it over.

Shall send your draft to Chicago tomorrow, and shall write again for Saturday evenings mail there.

The same—the same. It ought not to be. I should be more traveled. I will be. I know nothing of the world or its people. Am altogether too unsophisticated. The same—and thats the pity of it. But what of Ashland!

[*Note enclosed on Amherst College Treasurer's Office stationery*]

> Sent as per request
> Draft on N.Y. for $100.
> Where will you have the next?

MABEL TO AUSTIN   [*Ashland, Wisconsin*]
                                  Friday morning, 9 o'clock, 16th.
                                        [*July 1886*]

Of course the very first thing was to ask for letters, & I found yours written last Friday afternoon—just after you had received my first one. There have been three since that—this is 5. Yesterday we spent in St. Paul & Minneapolis, according to program, being received in each city by the citizens with carriages for us all, & taken to see everyone of interest which they could in three or fours hours. Truly I am amazed at the beauty

& extent & possibility, in those two cities, particularly the latter. Some of the dwellings are most elegant. Well, I rode in the engine coming back from Minneapolis to St. Paul in the evening, which was highly exciting. Being a special train we do what we like. At St. Paul we got into the sleeper for Ashland. I slept perfectly as I always do on the cars, waking about six—just before we arrived. And here I am, on the shores of Lake Superior, with a hundred miles of solid forest to the south, between me & civilization—yet with electric bells & gas & every modern convenience in this great hotel. . . .

Externally the trip has been brilliantly successful, & being with these people we have seen more than could have been possible in the same length of time alone. You know it all, all that I wish to say. And that is my joy. I will write again from here on Sunday, & twice during the week after, but not after Pittsburgh unless something in your Washington letter calls for an answer. . . .

Cleveland, O.
Thurs., 22 July 1886

We got in at 8:25 this morning, & I have just read your letter. I was *so* happy to get it. And what you have said in it has delighted me more than anything else you have written. I am *so glad* you want me—and gladder still that you *must have me.* And I forgot to say before that I was especially glad you ordered the house a foot lower (it has haunted me all the way that it would look perched up like a chimney) and I am also charmed that you have had it set back. We might just as well have some of the land in front for beauty. Now this morning, here in Cleveland, comes another aspect of affairs. I have had two exasperating days in Chicago . . . where I washed my hands on an average every fifteen minutes all day—& then looked & felt like a grimy servant-girl who never heard of finger-nails. And spots of soot on my nose, & on my cheeks—& I wiped them off & then gradually turned black-lead color. Well, as I say, being so sooty, & hot and I not brilliantly well, I did not feel like doing anything in the [extra] day I was forced to spend there. So I read nearly all day in the public Library, seeing many acquaintances in & out, stragglers from the excursion; & was most delightfully looked out for by Mr. Poole, the librarian. But I was thankful to feel myself moving out of that great, & prosperous & splendidly built & impressive, & dirty & irreclaimably exasperating city. Now I am here. We just went, upon arriving, to an office to buy tickets, to leave for Miller's Falls at 2:45 this afternoon, then getting home in the noon train Friday. Giving up (as I wrote you from Chicago) Pittsburgh & Washington. But what *do* you suppose we found as to prices! "Cut-rates" at the lowest possible notch— ten dollars from here to Washington—about $4.50 from there to N.Y., & then the regular four or five from N.Y. home, making it all only $19.00 from here home, stopping in Pittsburgh, Washington & N.Y. . . . Having written to Washington that I was not coming, & to you that I should probably come home tomorrow— & being in my heart tired to death of traveling, & longing frantically to get home, I persisted that we had better go home straight, for I feel like an utter fool to change my plans so often —or should if I could help it. How I do wish you could advise me for one moment! I am alarmed at the amount of money I have spent. . . . I have an exact account of it, & still I cannot understand it. Well, I cannot do much shopping in New York if I do go there, but I can look at wallpaper & mantels—by the way, I don't know the width of any of the chimneys inside—and I shall get a dress. And best of all. Yes, it can be most smoothly arranged. . . .

Pittsburgh, Friday, 23 July 1886

Well, we came after all. I am homesick this morning to think I am not in Massachusetts, where I could have been. But perhaps I shall be glad in the end. I am thinking a great deal about next week. . . . I have been again solemnly promised that the business there shall only last Monday and Tuesday. We will start for New York Wednesday morning. . . . If you think this comes too late for the answer to catch me by mail, then telegraph, addressing it to "our friend" Nautical Almanac Office. . . . We shall reach the Metropolitan sometime Wednesday afternoon or evening. If you will be there to meet us perhaps you need not telegraph, & I will know by your silence that you will be there then. . . .

AUSTIN TO MABEL   [*26 July 1886*]
                                                  Monday forenoon
                                                  11 o'c. and after

Your letter from Cleveland and Pittsburgh received this morning—my interruptions have been so incessant I have just had time to glance it hastily through.

I will leave here Wednesday noon for New York as proposed if you think it best—and I will presume you think best if I hear from you nothing to the contrary.

Sue and Mattie leave home Thursday for a week or ten days at Martha's Vineyard.

Ned will be about here. They will all go off Monday of week after next for a fortnight or more in Ashfield.* Mary is to be off the month of August.

So my house will be practically closed two weeks, though Agnes will be about there some, for want of any place to go.

You may think in view of everything New York is not advisable for me.

But just as you do think. I am ready and can go Wednesday or Thursday as you prefer.

I think you had better telegraph me as soon as you can balance things in your mind after receipt of this—same name

---

* What Austin didn't say was that a week earlier he had succumbed to his family's "oratory" and accompanied Sue, Mattie, and Ned on an overnight expedition to Ashfield, Massachusetts, in the Berkshires, while they made arrangements for their fortnight vacation. To his great surprise Austin enjoyed himself, finding the carriage drive through the lovely hill towns very restful. On June 21 he joined the same trio for a "very pleasant" picnic at Mt. Sugarloaf, in Sunderland, and on the twenty-fourth he took Sue, Ned, and Vinnie on a long evening drive to Leverett. None of this would have made Mabel happy, and none of it did he mention in the several letters he wrote during the period.

as before—saying "come" and what day, or "just as well later in the season'" so that I may get it at any rate tomorrow night, and know then for myself what I am to do.

You can understand all. I need not explain. "George Davis" or "Pratt," as you prefer.*

Through the weeks Austin's family was at Ashfield, he and Mabel enjoyed daylight and moonlight drives, and evenings on the Evergreens piazza and in its parlor, sometimes with David accompanying. But Austin did, at Sue's insistence, join his family twice for short visits. When he planned to return a third time to help them home, Mabel evidently put her foot down. It was the first disagreement she and Austin had had in four years. Austin did not go, but he told Mabel she had "made a mistake," and she, as the following letter indicates, felt "wretched."

MABEL TO AUSTIN   [*26 August 1886*]

The thought that I could have conflicted even remotely with an idea—& a conscientious idea—of yours has been torture to me. My intense joy in our love has always been, I see now, my unalterable certainty that it was divinely right, that having it I was able to live out the very highest in me. It was this harmony between my best, & my love for you, which has enabled me to go serenely, even joyfully through a great many sad things—which has enabled me to bear with a certain degree of fortitude things which seemed to come upon me in consequence of it. I could not go happily on in a line which I knew to be wrong. I have faith enough in myself to be sure of that, & I know that my love for you is the *realest*, & truest thing in my

* Austin and the Todds met in New York on Wednesday, July 28, for two intensely hot days, staying first at the Metropolitan, then at the Everett House in Union Square, which was cooler and less noisy.

nature. But here you rose to a height of nobility & generosity where I did not follow you—and that thought is maddening. I always did before, albeit sometimes by means of a hard tug upon myself—and I feel sure I should have risen to you in a little longer time—*this* time. But the terrible fact remains that I didn't, that you expected something of me which at that moment I had not moral grandeur enough to give, and the woe of my soul over that, this morning, is pitiful. I have always told you that you ennoble me—that through you I see God, and find my religion through your unutterable tenderness . . . that after years of the most divine sympathy & congeniality, I could fall short of both my own best & what you expected of me—and worse than all that I could have hurt you—*you* my king, my heart's idol, my everything—has brought me suffering to which the worst that ever came to me before is a mere nothing. With you to understand & sympathize, & love me, I can bear anything. With the faintest shadow, even of gossamer thinness, between us, I should die instantly. . . . That one human soul can so live in another & for it only, is the most beautiful, & most terrible fact in human nature. I do not think many do or can. But when one does, the dependence is absolute; & if that other ever has to go from it, nothing but broken & bleeding nerves remain. . . . I would make ten thousand sacrifices rather than hurt you. Oh! dearest I never failed you before, I never will again. Trust me, & love me, & know that I have suffered the tortures of death since last evening. . . . I love you, *love* you, LOVE you, with an intensity which is agony, today.

Mabel was away ten days in early September visiting first her mother at Hampton, N.H., then an acquaintance at Newport, R.I. Mid-trip she stopped in Boston, where she had planned to meet Austin at Leonard's Auction Rooms on Tremont Street so they could select together mantels, wallpapers, and stained glass for the new house. There this letter was handed to her by Mr. Marsh.

A New Epoch

Sunday afternoon

It is uncertain—at this writing—if I am able to go to Boston tomorrow. In stepping carelessly from the plank walk to the stone at my back door this forenoon, I turned and wrenched some of the muscles near my left ankle so severely that I nearly fainted—and until within an hour have been able to bear not the slightest weight upon it.

I have just now hobbled a little about my room—and shall only give up my plan at the last moment. But if tomorrow morning I cannot wear a shoe—and cannot stand tolerably firmly—that will have to settle it—and in that case I suggest your going to Newport tomorrow, one day earlier than your plan, and return via Boston Friday, giving you some time there—and I will meet you at any place and hour you may say.

This is for explanation if I do not appear as arranged—and will be taken by Mr. Marsh, who was going down with me.

4

Ménage à Trois

1 8 8 7 – 1 8 8 9

ALTHOUGH by 1887 David had been a college professor for five years, he was no closer to directing a good observatory, or becoming a renowned astronomer, than when he left Washington in 1881. During the next several years his struggle to make a reputation for himself outside Amherst, and attract a donor for a new observatory at the college, involved the mounting of two solar-eclipse expeditions—one to Japan in the summer of 1887 under the auspices of the National Academy of Science and the U.S. Navy Department, and a second to West Africa in 1889–90 sponsored by the U.S. Navy. David's vigorous efforts to draw attention and publicity to his professional undertakings led Mabel to resume her early aspirations to write. Resisting the oppression she now felt so keenly in Amherst, which she was convinced emanated from Sue Dickinson, she turned her energies to numerous literary endeavors, including a project Vinnie urged upon her—putting Emily's poetry into print. Through 1888 and 1889, transcribing and arranging the hundreds of poems became an increasingly absorbing task.

Meanwhile, the Queen Anne cottage, or the Dell, as the Todds came to call it, became the setting for a more complex harmony than its three planners may have envisioned. Mabel now considered herself married to Austin in all but name, an attitude that inevitably took some of the vitality away from her marriage to David. By the spring of 1887 David was signing his letters to his wife "Husband/David," instead of "Lover/Husband/David," as he had since their wedding, and several remarks exchanged by Mabel and Austin suggest that her sexual relations with her husband nearly ceased during 1887. Meanwhile, David's interest in other women, some of whom visited the Todd home, became subtly apparent in Mabel's diary. Austin and Mabel had begun employing the terms "policy" and "concessions," which suggest that negotiated agreements governed the relationship among the three of them. They all apparently remained affectionate, warm, and accommodating toward one another, with David often at the observatory long stretches of the night and Mabel willing to play friendly hostess to visitors of her husband's choice. As time went on, the Todds found camaraderie in working together professionally, supporting and assisting each other's achievements, a satisfaction which possibly eased for Mabel the relentless unfulfillment attending her devotion to Austin.

The year 1887 began with Mabel and David suddenly learning that they would have to vacate the rented Lincoln house. Their new home wasn't ready—its plumbing and heating were installed, but only the basement, where the kitchen was located, and the third floor, site of Mabel's studio and another attic room, were habitable. They moved anyway in late January, "camping out" through a bitterly cold winter, amid continuing commotion and clutter from carpenters, painters, and other workmen. In and around painting classes and many local singing engagements, Mabel worked steadily, painting oil friezes around the upper walls of her unfinished parlors and entrance hall. She and Millicent suffered throat and ear infections as winter progressed, but it was David's violent attack of kidney stones in March (diagnosed at the time as "introsusception" caused by a misstep on some stairs) that nearly exhausted Mabel. Few letters were written during this difficult winter and spring, but diary entries of March and April portray Mabel running up and down in her vertical new house, anxiously nursing her husband while drawing emotional strength from Austin.

The invalid recovered barely in time to organize his June eclipse expedition. Mabel wrote her mother on May 11 "from the midst of a whirl of every kind of thing such as you cannot imagine. I write, doing things which David does when well, directing the grading & setting out of trees, the floors, & carpenter work, & the painters' finish, trying to complete my friezes before the paper is on, & being assailed on every side for society purposes—singing everywhere & asked to join everything. I can hardly see for the tumult." Ten days later, when David went to Washington for final preparations for the Japan trip, Mabel's conflict—whether to accompany him to the Orient or to stay in Amherst—made her frantic. The Loomises wrote long, strong letters of persuasion, as did David, who even hinted that his sister Naomi might accompany him if Mabel didn't. After two final weeks of unusual freedom to be with Austin, Mabel departed with her husband on the extraordinary voyage. Her letters of the journey display her developing narrative style.

MABEL TO AUSTIN   [*17 April 1887*]

I would far rather drive this sweet day. David was out in the sunshine at noon, & he felt so much better in the air, that he says he will go to his class at Smith tomorrow if it is pleasant,

& if he could try the motion of driving for ten or fifteen minutes with you this afternoon. . . . I am so anxious to have him begin his work again regularly, that I am willing to sacrifice a few minutes at the beginning of our drive, as he says he should not try to go tomorrow on so long a drive without seeing the effect on him today. So, *will* you? And there will be no reason why you should not come here for him, & bring him back. Then I will be ready & get right in here. I will say more when I see you, but I know it is best to take him awhile. He will probably cease being an invalid from the time he gets started.

AUSTIN TO MABEL   [*6 May 1887*]
                                          Friday afternoon, 3 p.m.
                                                        Office

I went down from here Wednesday night—sick all through —went to the dinner table, but gave it up almost at once, and retired to my room and to bed. Have not been up till now to get your mail and write you a line. Am not going to stay, but it wont hurt me, and I will be pretty well by your return [from Boston]. It was the result, and part of, the savage cold which got hold of me—and to which I did not pay sufficient heed.

Yesterday was beautiful—and so today, with a shower or two. I have thought of you every minute, and am anticipating tomorrow night, and next day.

Your letter came all right, this morning. Hope the visit [to Caro] will be a success all around. . . .

MABEL TO AUSTIN   [*The Parker House, Boston, 9 June 1887*]
                                          Thursday, 1:15 p.m.

And my darling and my dearest beloved—& my king & master—my sweet husband, it is almost the little goodbye. Don't think of it, dear, as anything permanent, or very dreadful, because four months—in the eternity of our love—are so very short. . . . You said last night, some of the most satisfyingly lovely things to me which with all your wonderful words, you have ever yet said. And they sank *deep*, deep into my heart. You seem sometimes to take for granted my entire knowledge of the depth of your great love for me. And sometimes for two or three days you *say* little about it. Of course, I know it—every minute—but when you open the doors of your soul to me in speech, then it is the heavens descended upon me, & overwhelming & engulfing me. And that radiant, noble, permeating joy fills every crevice of my being today. And I love you so grandly that I am even lifted into a serene & sunny atmosphere by it, where the pain of parting is made far less. . . .

[*Boston, 9 June 1887*]
Thursday, 5:30 p.m.

We found your boots, my darling, and we send them herewith by express. When I came up to my room after seeing you go down, I found Caro's card. I went to the parlor immediately and there she was. We talked awhile, & then she made me go out & finish my errands, while she waited for the traveler from Cambridge [David]. (I think in our writing we will speak of him always as Josiah.) He came in presently, & I got in from my shopping, and I started them smoothly, & they have a very pleasant memory of today. . . .

[*Montreal, 10 June 1887*]

. . . Friday morning, later. So far, all well, dearest. I have seen nothing of the city yet, except in the drive from the station, for the baggage is not yet on board the through train, and I am left here, while it is being transferred. Then I am going out, for I have never been here before.

Do go all over the house as soon as you have time. And when the rugs are to be whipped, please dont let any man stay in that red attic alone—at all. The desk is not locked, & the cupboard is full of things—some in bottles—& very desirable to quench thirst on hot days, though somewhat strong. The little front chamber over the hall is full of painters' things, & oiled rags. I suppose it is safe, but I would like you to look in there. If you do not easily find, in the big closet with a window (in my room) those three keys tied with a string, it is just possible that I may have put them away myself, though I do not remember it. The front door key which I left with you . . . is for the latch only—upper keyhole. In the desk (of which you have the key) is the bank book, upper left hand pigeonholes, & the check book, & various other things, & somewhere in the desk is a letter, sealed, to Burditt & Williams, which contains a check which I wrote them weeks ago. If you find it, do send it. Forgive details, my darling, these things come to me, although I would far rather write of how tenderly I love you, and how near I feel to you. Distance is annihilated in the face of such love as ours.

But to go on—how I hate the practical—I have all the salary up to July, out of what will be due between July & October, must be paid the Life Ins., interest at the Bank, and I believe Accident Insurance: I gave you a memorandum of those three things in pencil—also fifty dollars to Mr. Putnam, about seven to Mr. Rawson, about eight to Mr. Russell, and I promised fifty to Mr. Paige at the stable, sometime during the summer. I shall be perfectly satisfied to come back & find nearly nothing remaining of the quarter's salary from July to October, because I would far rather have these bills paid. I can accomplish it all, I know, in time, and I expect to use the first quarter of "next year," as you called it, in that way. There is also a small bill at William Kellogg's. That pair of big iron hinges in the front hall on the floor are to go back to him. Mr. Gates will take them any time, I suppose. There is also a bill at Deuel's, but I have already paid Dr. Hall for most of those things, & there is a bill at Mr. Holland's. All of these I was unable to settle until the next quarter. But I would rather come back to find nothing due me until Oct. 15, than have the bills go unpaid. I imagine there will be a kindergarten bill, too. But the last four, or more, weeks of that term are to be deducted.* Perhaps she is not in a hurry. If not, that can go until I come back. As for Steeves, I do not owe him anything, & if Mr. Graves wants anything, I have

* Millicent went to her grandparents' in Washington on May 20.

written out an exact record of his time & his men, since May first, & I thought I brought it to give you, but took another similar paper by mistake. You will find it in one of the three left-hand pigeon holes of the desk. I am afraid the P.O. box is not paid after July 1st. That must be done. . . . That will be, I should judge, in the neighborhood of $325.00. I shall be surprised & delighted if I find fifty dollars to my credit out of that quarter's salary. Kellogg's and Holland's can be left if you think best—since you would not know if the items were right—but Mr. Putnam *must* have fifty dollars, & the insurance & interest *must* be paid, & Mr. Rawson & Russell. The others, I suppose, could wait.

Forgive me for these hateful details, darling.

Goodbye to them for now. . . .

If you should feel like it, & have time sometime, my journal which I wrote in Europe might interest you—because there is much personal writing in it, aside from description.

11 June 1887
[*En route to Vancouver by Canadian
Pacific Railroad*]
Saturday, 11th, about 7:30 p.m.
No. 4

I do not know just where we are, my darling, but we have passed Lake Nipissing, early this morning, & it was very blue & lovely, with wooded islands—& we have passed Sturgeon Falls, & Woman River, & I don't know how many more places which look very large on the map in print, but which have so far seemed to consist wholly of two or three log houses chinked with plaster, & surrounded by an acre of black stumps instead of trees. But the whole country is full of lovely little lakes, sometimes four & five in ten minutes, and they make the scenery home-like & pleasant. The saddest thing to see is the great extent of the fires —miles of charred & dead trees—sometimes seeming to have been burned a good while ago, for ferns & flowers have covered the ground, & once in a while we have passed through fierce fires still burning, when the stinging heat came into the car, & we could see cords of cut & piled wood in flames, as well as standing trees. But much of the country has been very beautiful. There happen to be very few through passengers on this train . . . so we practically have a private car, with a whole section apiece, which is refreshing, & much care and attention from stewards & porters. . . . If you could know how I lie in my berth & feel the soothing motion, & think, & *remember*, & anticipate! And how you are as closely with me really, as when I looked into your sweet eyes, & you bade me remember whose & what! And I do—darling, I do! Good night my own, my dearest.

Sunday morning

Ever since I woke up we have been skirting Lake Superior, & the scenery has been thoroughly magnificent. Splendid rocks, and more deciduous trees than before, very few traces of fires, & this grand expanse of water. Just this minute we are stopping at some little station which is full of silence—all but the sound of waves on a pebbly beach. And I love you with all my heart. . . . One thing occurs to me—when paper is put up inside some of the windows, please have the west one in the study done *first of all*, for the hot afternoon sun on the ebonized end of the piano will inevitably blister it. And nearly all the paintings of my own which I chiefly value are in the attic—front attic, a few in a box in the south attic, & some under the roof, leading off from studio. I suppose I ought to have brought them out, but I didn't. However, I suppose the house is not going to burn up.

Now darling, I love you again & again, with a sweet nearness which I hardly ever knew before. I belong to you for always, and it is my joy and my crown. The porter has brought me in a little wild rose, all wet & fresh—the sun is coming out, & the sky is blue. Oh! darling, darling, *I love you so!* Say our prayer every day, dearie, and I will—I do.* My king & my master & my mate!

---

* The prayer, to which they often referred, was said in unison when they were together: "For my beloved is mine, and I am his. What can we want beside? Nothing!"

The Letters

AUSTIN TO MABEL [*13 June 1887*]
Monday 13th, 4 p.m.
No. 3

I step right out from my surroundings for a moment, my beloved, in the hope to get one more word to you at Vancouver. Especially to tell you before you launch out upon the Pacific that your wonderful, lovely, sweet notes from Montreal, and along route came to me this morning. Mine written yesterday and earlier this morning had already been posted. I am overwhelmed with work, and by people, but the nights are quiet, and there are breathing spells here and there in the day. You are not out of my mind an instant, and you never seemed so great, and so grand, and so beautiful as now. All the homage of my being goes out to you.

I will attend to all the business errands. Have seen Thomas about the House insurance, McEland about the accident, Steeves about his paint, and Graves about his.

The check came for Altman. The shoes came. Dennis [Scannell, a Dickinson hired hand] is packing up the rubbish. I love you—I love you and God keep us.

Remember, when you get upon the water, that there is no moment I am not thinking of you, and loving you.

I go to Boston again Wednesday, for over one night.

MABEL TO AUSTIN Maple Creek, Alberta Province
14 June 1887
No. 5

All day yesterday over plains, all day today too. And yet not uninteresting, or monotonous. Great herds of cattle & horses—cow-boys galloping madly—prairie-dogs sitting straight up like surveyor's sticks, or running along like squirrels—Indians, tents, feathers—bleaching skeletons of hundreds of buffaloes, & today many ponds or lakes which are thick with gulls, cranes, pelicans. But not a tree, and the level horizon *so* far away. Watches already put back two hours. I have read *Elsie Venner* with pleasure —I have spent hours in thinking of you—and I come to you today, my own beloved, with a sense of absolute nearness and *belongingness* which seems to grow stronger with every mile. Distance is nothing, sweet. I nestle in your heart every second. Do you not feel me there? The entomologist, H., joined us at Winnipeg.* In some respects it is pleasanter to have him than not. He knows all the birds & flowers we pass, & shrubs, & he gets out at every station & picks things for his collection, which is pleasant for me. We tried to make the engineer let us ride on the cowcatcher, but he wouldn't. . . .

Canmore, Alberta, or
North West Territory, 15 June [*1887*]
No. 6

Well, my darling, "this one" is stranded—for a while, at least. This morning I awoke in the midst of scenery of Alpine grandeur. The train ran along by a rushing stream through a narrow valley, and on both sides, & in front and behind, rose mountains covered with snow on their summits, with every ravine & gully filled with snow down into the green below—& there it melted & became rushing torrents. It was superb to look at, but we speedily found that the increased melting of the snows within a day or two had swollen the rivers ahead of us so that the bridges were endangered. We went along slowly & cautiously over the first of the threatened bridges against which tons of floating logs were pressing, but found later that we could not get over the second one. So we backed off & returned to this little station, where we have been all day. The men are hard at work on the bridges, but we cannot get off before tomorrow morning at the earliest. The engine ran over there again, an hour or two ago, & Josiah on it. A telegram has been sent to Mr. Tuttle [Montreal agent for the Canadian Pacific] to telegraph the Steamer-Captain in case we are delayed too long. So there is probably no danger of losing the Steamer. But it is an-

---

* This was a Mr. Holland, described by Mabel as a naturalist and wealthy clergyman from Pittsburgh. He was paying his own way on the expedition.

noying. However, I have walked about, & feasted my eyes on the glorious scenery; I have written some, & read some, & talked to the numerous Indians who fill the place. But the dining-car left us some time in the night—and the next one is on the other side of all these bridges. So we are sorely put to it for decencies to eat. We bought some sardines & crackers at the store, & I got out some figs which you remember about—they were bought for a ride, but not used. Well, they are a great comfort here— in all senses, my sweet. What a lovely day we would have together dear, if you were out here with me in these trackless wilds! With the sound of rushing waters filling the stillness, & these solemn heights looking down on something just as grand & noble & sacred as they. I love you so dearly, & so tenderly, & so splendidly! Darling, *darling*, I belong to you.

Beyond Kamloops, Friday, 17 June '87

Good morning, my darling! The detention was more than we thought, & made us 33 hours late. We did get off yesterday morning, but the bridges were not safe for trains, & so we waited until the east-bound train came up on the other side of them, & then yesterday morning all the passengers & baggage from our train, & also the train just a day behind us, which overtook us as we waited, were transferred by handcars six or seven miles, over the bad bridges to the train on the other side—& all the east-bound passengers & luggage were transferred to our train, & reversing the engines, we continued on our way. The bridge— one of them—seemed very dangerous, even for a handcar, for it was bent down almost to the boiling stream below, & swayed uneasily. So—remembering you—I waited until the last hand-car went over, & then I walked with no weight but my own on the bridge, and Lieutenant Storey & his wife, of the Navy, following. The workmen laughed at the idea of its being too weak for handcars, but I remembered you, & some things you said to me. I am not cautious of myself, you know. Well that took time —we did not get off until eleven o'clock, Thursday morning. But the scenery from that point on, until night covered it, sur-passes any power of words which I possess. Some parts of it are grander than anything in Switzerland. . . . The grandeur was almost more than I could bear—ah! if I could have touched your hand! There was enthusiasm about it among the passengers— but not *my* kind, or yours.

Vancouver, B.C., 18 June 1887
Saturday morning

Good morning, my darling. We got in last evening without accident or further detention, & we slept on board the *Abyssinia* —finding the officers and railroad men expecting us so that everything was easily managed—baggage, instruments & all. . . .

AUSTIN TO MABEL   Saturday morning, 18ᵗʰ June [*1887*]

I posted a letter to you by the half past four mail yesterday afternoon—for the *Belgic*—but hope to get a later word on to the same steamer, to tell you that when I went to the office at six I found yours of Saturday's and Sunday's dates—and as far as off Lake Superior. How ever since I have wished I were with you! and except for the riot that would be made by those who are too barren to find any interest in themselves, I certainly would be at Vancouver in season to go out on the *Abyssinia's* next trip, stay with you through, and return, unless we should decide—not to return. I can think of no other trip that I need, till you start on some other—to Borneo! Tierra del Fuego, or perhaps, the promised land.

I saw by the papers last night too that the *Abyssinia* had arrived at V. in thirteen days and fourteen hours. So now I know all is right so far and promises well for the entire trip, and that you will be received by the Japs about 4ᵗʰ July.

I am having matters attended to at the house gradually— fast as I can. Shall have the corridor all finished Monday. Shall take the pictures I find in the attic closets out tomorrow, take some of the choicest over to Vin's, and put the rest in as good shape as I know. Have had the rubbish sorted and piled, that under the porch removed, have washed and housed, am looking up stuff for flooring—the Springfield man had only North

Carolina pine etc. The sweet fern you shall have another time, dearie. I shall be up there again before that. . . . Another kiss my dearest, my darling—my angel wife. Waking or sleeping you are with me.

MABEL TO AUSTIN   Monday morning, 20 June [1887]
                                                          No. 7

Still at Nanaimo [a coaling station on Vancouver Island]. About 1,000 tons of coal on board, but I believe they want 1,500. We shall not leave here until about noon. When we get to Vancouver I shall get the mail which came yesterday—Sunday—and also the mail on today's train, as we shall not start permanently until that is in. . . . I have written notes of the journey all the way, & yesterday I copied down a few items which Josiah sent to the *Nation* editor, telling him if there was not anything among them which he cared to make use of would he kindly send them to you. So when they come—as nearly everything does come back that I write—will you re-mail them to the *Independent*? There have been so few descriptions of any of this region that it seems as if it must be interesting to people, but you never can tell. Ask the *Independent* man to send it back if he doesn't want it.* Now two more details. In the closet of the "guest room" are three or four woolen dresses—& one in the big closet of my room, which I know will be entirely spoiled by moths if they are not done up in paper. You can find Phebe & she will do them up. And Mr. Graves wanted to know just what I wanted him to do in my absence. I want him to put wax on the floors when they are down, no varnish; and also on the stair treads & landings. And I want him to put the first coat of hard-oil finish on the two parlors. They are already stained. Of course

* Although *The Nation* didn't take this first article, three others she wrote during the voyage, including her account of climbing Mt. Fuji, were published in that periodical on September 1, September 22, and October 13, earning her $78. The articles were reprinted by the *New York Post*, the *Springfield Republican*, and the *Amherst Record*.

there is no reason why the *last* coat of finish & the *final* rubbing should not be done on all the ash, & the two parlors, if you think best, in my absence. It will be a relief to have it done, but perhaps there would need to be some watching—as to time, etc. You know best.

Now my darling, I cannot send another letter for two weeks, you know. You ought to get it by a month from the time you get this one, but I shall write continually to you on the voyage, & send it all at once by the first steamer. . . . I take you with me every step. . . .

AUSTIN TO MABEL   19th June [*1887*]
Sunday afternoon, 4 p.m.
No. 6

In my room. Have just come back from your house. Went over as usual at 2, have been airing, getting your pictures out from under the roof, on the further corner of the low attic shut away (what on earth ever led you to put them there!), picking up, straightening out, taking your ardent spirits down cellar, and looking around. It was pleasure, and it was pain—how much pain I am not going to tell you now. I find, dearie, that I am not as strong as I thought, not as strong as when you were here. I didn't realize what it was to be without you—-and to know that the summer, just begun, the summer of one year must all pass, and the deep rich foliage of today all fade before I shall look into your eyes again. It seems so long, and there are so many chances, and liabilities between now and then, it is to be a terrible test of my endurance. I have grown so away from everything else, I have grown so entirely to you. I dont know what to do—nothing else interests me—nothing else is of the slightest moment. You are absolutely all. I am absolutely dependent on you. You are my life, and soul—without you, all is an empty shell. . . . I am imagining you in Victoria today, and I remember that your steamer was advertised to leave Vancouver tomorrow, so that the next two weeks I shall think of you as on the water, forty-two hundred and thirty-two miles from shore to shore, and the good God keep you safe on it all. . . .

Sunday afternoon, 26th June

Here in my room—Sue gone to Logtown. . . . [Your] No. 6, which I had been looking for a day or two, came yesterday morning, addressed to the Lawrence Observatory, but it didn't deceive me. I am familiar with "this one's" kinks. Told of your trials and perils by the way and arrived you at Vancouver and on board the *Abyssinia*—so far, well. Told of other things too —which sustain and support me back here, alone. Hardly anything you say, and say so often, presses upon me more sweetly than "I belong to you"—no matter what else I want that every time—too. . . .

Sunday forenoon, July 3ᵈ, 11 o'c. Over at Vin's. To E chamber—to be out of the way—as they are all around at my house.

. . . Where am I to begin after all this crowded week! Perhaps as well with telling you that your No. 7, written on the *Abyssinia's* coaling trip, Sunday and Monday, 18th and 19th, and mailed 20th, reached me by the 3 p.m. train Tuesday, 28th. A[lpha] D[elta] P[hi] day, and that from Victoria, No. 8, 21st June, on Commencement morning. I got it about 10:30, read it in my room, just before going up to the Hall with the diplomas.*

Next perhaps, your business inquiries. Altman sent his check, Burditt & Williams sent their receipt. Cowles at the Bank tells me you have overdrawn your account there $60 to $70. I dont remember exactly, and I have told him I would deposit enough to make it up at once. Shall do so Tuesday—tomorrow is a holiday—and shall attend to the Savings Bank int. same time. Life and accident insurance premiums and other things as they come along. Phebe left for Springfield Thursday noon. I shall bring all the woolen dresses from your closets up here this

---

* Austin and Mabel usually made specific mention of letters sent and received, so that none would go unaccounted for. They also paid close attention to how long mails took, to take advantage of the swiftest.

week—for Vin to look over and do up. Will have the rugs beaten the first good day. I keep some of the windows in the upper part of the house open all the time for ventilation. The attic is very warm. Have had the grass mowed all around, and the yard now looks like quite a settled lawn. Have had my own grass cut the last week too. The lot is clear, and shorn—and the [indecipherable] is full. Nothing has come yet for the floors—the Springfield people make no replies to letters. In course of a few days I shall make it my special business to get the stuff, somewhere, and have it sawn and finished. The trees are all looking well, except the outside chestnut, which I always suspected.

This covers the business—I believe—and now the week, since Sunday afternoon last. . . . [Omitted is a seven-page detailed description of 1887 Amherst College commencement events.]

I must tell you sometime, and might as well now, that on the way down from Walker Hall Wednesday night Seelye said to me that he didn't quite know what he was going to do about the Analytic Geometry (I think that was it) next term, that Josiah [David] was not to be back, that he had brought it before the trustees, and they had voted that he should employ some tutor—without expense to the college—which means to be deducted from Josiah's salary. I told him you were to be back early in the term, but he said J. told him he should not leave there till last of September, which would not bring him here till sometime in November, and he thought of employing Mr. Willcox, who I know had been wanting awfully to get in here, in almost any capacity. I said that I would write you at once about it—the mere matter of money didn't trouble me, but there was something unspoken in Seelye that left in me an uncomfortable feeling. The Summer term was practically broken up you know, and with the Fall term counting for nothing, a year is counted off, there being no duties in the Winter. I hate to write this, for I know it will trouble you, but it seems to me I ought, for our safety, all around. Seelye doesn't feel toward J. just as he used to, or just as we want to have him. He evidently thinks the college is not the first thing with J. In this vein it will be well to bear in mind, and balance what is to be gained by a longer stay in Japan than is necessary for thorough completion of the work in hand with what may be gained or lost in his regularly appointed place. The eclipse is the 18th I think—and you will get this about the 3ᵈ or 4ᵗʰ before—that is all there is about that. . . .*

In fact up here, in this to me strange room in the heat, and south wind, and in writing what I have last, I have grown too sad for another word. Why, why am I here, alone, and you off the other side of the globe! How hollow, and empty, and meaningless all but you to me! And you, what limitless delight and joy! If I could only have you an hour tonight, what help, and strength to bear another—the next—of these terrible months! I am nothing, dearie, without you—that is settled. You hold my life in your keeping—you know that—and you have known it long. I am glad you do, and that you are glad it is so, and I feel perfectly safe in that keeping. But I do so long to be with you again, for one hour of our last fortnight.

MABEL TO AUSTIN   Thursday, 23 June 1887
                    S.S. *Abyssinia*, 433 miles from Vancouver
                                                     No. 9

. . . Awoke (yesterday morning) a good many miles out from Cape Flattery, in the midst of a *gale*, blowing straight from the west. I went on deck at once—after dressing with difficulty— and saw a superb tumult of waves, & a blue sky above, and a wind against which I could not keep my feet a moment. I sat down, however, in a sheltered place & had my usual ante-breakfast cup of coffee & toast, on deck. The ship was pitching

* This gloomy report from Austin reached David about the same time he learned of another professional problem. Simon Newcomb wrote him that he was embarrassed to discover that none of David's observations from the Lick expedition of 1882 had been turned in to the Transit of Venus Commission in Washington. The photographic record had been forwarded by Lick Observatory, but David never had written up the time observations, measures of focal length, or chronometer comparisons of the Transit, so that reductions could be made.

about in the wildest way, and I am ashamed to tell you that I afterwards lost that cup of coffee overboard. Well, the nineteen passengers were all prostrate in their berths. . . . I had my lunch on deck, but came down to dinner as well as ever, & was highly applauded there by the Captain. He & I dined alone, except [for one] missionary. The purser was dreadfully ill, & the chief engineer rather "knocked over," while the Captain's wife, who has sailed around the world with him, & has been constantly afloat since the *Abyssinia* left Liverpool last January, was flat on her back, & utterly wretched all day. They called it the "nastiest" day since they left Liverpool. Well, I can't describe that tremendous gale. When I first went out, I and my chair rolled over together, down to the lee scuppers. The Captain ran & picked me up, & called a sailor to tie the chair firmly down. . . . Josiah was very badly off below, but he had a nice little Japanese waiter who took far better care of him than I could, for it was impossible to stand for a moment. Every wave broke completely over the deck, which often ran four or five inches deep with water—but I was in a partly covered place, beside the stairs which go down to the cabin, & I only got showered once or twice with spray. It was wildly exhilarating, and I had the deck to myself. . . .

Sunday afternoon, 3 July, about 3 o'clock

. . . It is a funny collection of passengers, certainly. Every one is a missionary of some sort—minister or doctor, or wife of one—except *this one*—& the other. They can't & won't play whist, they drink no ale, only ginger pop, and they have prayers in the saloon every evening, & sing hymns for recreation. There is a young Chinese girl, Miss King, who has just graduated as a doctor, in New York, & she is going back to practice. She is very bright & interesting. She & old Dr. McCartee, who has charge of her, want to join the eclipse party—but we have not decided about that.* The Captain's wife is very pleasant, & I stay with her a good deal, but I am ready to have this voyage finished, much as I love the sea, because it is so cold, & it rains half the

* They did. Both assisted with photographing the eclipse.

time, & is foggy most of the remainder.* I love you so___and I think about you all the time, and dream about you at night, & think again straightway of you as soon as I wake in the morning. . . . How I long for you! But I shall not allow myself to begin to get impatient yet. In looking over the whole thing calmly from this distance, and seeing everything as it is, I cannot but feel that we did wisely in deciding as we did. The reasons for & against, stand as they did when we made up our minds to it, and I am very sure it is best. Yet God forbid that we should ever have another such trial. How many we have borne! Surely He has tested us enough . . . if I should let go my hold of myself one instant, I should cry out for you in bitter longing unquenchable. . . .

Wednesday afternoon, 6th July

. . . I think of the sweet familiar hills all about you, and the roadsides full of bloom & sweetness, and the smell of hay, & the sound of mowing. And then I think of the meadow, & the little house which I love so well, and the grass, which must be green & thick around it now, and the little trees which we watched so lovingly. And then I think of the cool evenings by the fire, and how the shadows danced on the wall & ceiling—and I remember your voice and your tender words, until I can picture you close beside me. Then suddenly I become conscious of my material surroundings—the grey, white-capped sea, the steamer rolling back & forth, the dull sky, the great brown albatross flying astern—and Japan only about a day ahead, somewhere down below the horizon. . . .

The Grand Hotel, Yokohama
Saturday morning, 9 July 1887

Oh! my darling, we landed yesterday afternoon as I expected, & I have had three rides in *jinrikishas*, & it is all too funny & queer to be described. It is all like a Japanese fan, or a screen, set down before one, & living, & moving. What would

* This was the return leg of the Canadian Pacific's pioneer run between Vancouver and Yokohama. The usual route, out of San Francisco, was warmer but longer.

I give to see it with you! . . . The high dignitaries have all called, & we are told there are extensive preparations to "receive" us in Tokyo. . . . The *Belgic* is not due here until the 18th. Just think how long I must wait before I can hear from you. . . .*

AUSTIN TO MABEL   Amherst, Mass., U.S.A.
                              Friday morning, 15 July [*1887*]
My office.   No. 9

Darling, *Darling*, *Darling*. Here's my week since last Sunday. Went to Boston first train Monday morning, as I said. Returned by 4:30 train Tuesday evening. Every moment was filled with business errands and engagements. It was awfully hot, and Monday rained all day. With it all—and a man in the next room to me snoring all night, and so keeping me without sleep—I returned pretty well used up. Came to my office Wednesday forenoon, straightened out my letters, went down towards one, and did^{nt} leave my room again till I was brought up here for an hour yesterday afternoon to direct about some matters that had to be attended to. Wednesday night was very sick, and did^{nt} I want you! Am better and shall be all right in a day or two. Am up here to stay, but am weak. The weather since Commencement has been almost intolerable, till yesterday when it was cool and delightful as one could wish, and today is the same. I went over to the house before I came up, and through it. It is still all there, ready for use. I have decided (with Steeves) to put an oak border around the Lower Hall and parlors—and all oak in So' W room, and have ordered this to be here early next week. I thought this would be to your taste. Steeves will then do it all up, and Graves will finish. Next week too the first time I could arrange to personally superintend it.

* A full month into her voyage now, Mabel had received only one of Austin's letters, his second, which reached her at Vancouver. Her intense and constant longing for him, exacerbated by the tedious slowness of the mails, filled many more passages than have been included here. Also eliminated are sections Mabel devoted to discussion of mail routes, steamer sailings, and sending and receiving letters.

I am going to have the rest of the ground on the south graded and seeded. When Steeves and Graves are out of the inside I shall have the porch floor, and steps, painted, and latter part of August, a week or two after you read this, the brick walk laid. I have paid the July interest, and made up your overdraw at the Bank, $76.72. Vin has your jelly glasses filled with currant, and the tomatoes are faring to go into your cans. It is settled now that I dont go west till fall.* Sanford's family decidedly object to his going now, and he shrinks from it himself. Besides, the gentleman whom we expect to see most of there in our business arrived in Boston while I was there, and he advises us not to go till after next month—says the heat is severe there, even for those who are acclimated. I shall therefore in the main be here, working and waiting. I think Sue & Ned and Mattie will go to Mt. Desert, or the Adirondacks for two to four weeks very soon, and that I shall be here—with the house shut up. They insist on my going, but you know I shall not. I think you would approve of me could you look on & see. . . .

MABEL TO AUSTIN   Sei-Yō-Ken Hotel, Tokyo
                                          Sat., 16 July [1887]
                                          No. 10

Oh! my dear, my dear! I want you so today I can hardly bear it! I am bitterly homesick, although I have had a very good & interesting time this week. At Yokohama I saw a great many delightful people, & enjoyed it. Wednesday we came up to Tokyo. . . . I have been to temples & gardens & bazaars, & everything. The heat is excessive. I feel thoroughly well, but the great heat & moisture are intensely disagreeable to me. Josiah went away a day or two ago on business—necessary, I know— with some of the officials of the Japanese government. . . . We go to the eclipse station probably Monday. But I am dolefully blue. Josiah has felt pretty sick a good deal of the time, & the heat is

* True to his pledge of the summer before, Austin had determined to travel. He was going West and South by train on a combined business and pleasure trip with his old friend John Sanford, Taunton lawyer and trustee of Amherst College.

telling on him a great deal—so that one night I was really afraid he would be ill. As a consequence he felt homesick, but he has no time to indulge it. He *rushes*, from one day's end to another; & indeed the time is short. . . .

17 July 1887
Sunday, 10 a.m.

The heat is terrible—but today there is a strong breeze, so it is bearable. I sleep under mosquito netting, so I have not been bitten very much. So far I have only eaten European food. . . . When I go out, I always carry a button-hook, because we are not allowed to go in any of the beautiful temples without taking off our boots. The floors are of polished lacquer, often, & I feel as if I were walking on a piece of fine furniture. One old priest took a great interest in the way I put on my boots, & jabbered away like mad in Japanese, at the rapidity with which I buttoned them. . . . The naturalist, H., is about as antipathetic to me as a man ever gets. He is good in his specialty, & a good man for his work. I am just enough to acknowledge that. But he is a tower of conceit, & loud-mouthed pretension. It is impossible for a fine-grained person to say a word, without constant correction. . . .

Tokyo still
Monday, 18 July

Darling, *darling*, DARLING!

You lovely dear, to send me TWO letters on the *Belgic*! Josiah is not yet back, but they were brought to me from the Legation this morning, together with one from my mother, & Millicent & Caro. Your two have cheered me up so I feel like a different creature. . . . I wrote to the lady who has the tin boxes [Vinnie], sending it from Yokohama July 10th. Did she get it? . . . . I am finding out all about amateur cameras & photographing from Mr. Hitchcock, who takes charge of the photographing department of the eclipse.* Perhaps I may learn how to do it, a little.

---

* Mr. and Mrs. Romyn Hitchcock of Washington, D.C., had called on the Todds in Yokohama and asked to join the eclipse party. Formerly with the Smithsonian, Mr. Hitchcock was now teaching in Osaka. The party also included Lieutenant Southerland and Chief Engineer Pemberton of the U.S. Navy.

He says people *can* be done with the same lens as landscapes. But he says a *good* outfit cannot be prepared much under fifty dollars. He takes views everywhere he goes. It is very interesting. The perspiration is positively rolling down in streams, so I will finish tomorrow, & say for now good night, my dearest love.

Tuesday, a.m. 19 July

Josiah is back. He was quite sick while he was away, & had two doctors. They made him stay to rest after the pain—which detained him until late last night—after I was asleep. The eclipse station is to be at Shirakawa, on the railroad, & toward Nikko, the wonderful place of temples and so on. So I shall see that—which, it is said, is worth going around the world to see. If Josiah keeps up until the necessary work is done, I shall be almost surprised, for he is as white as paper, & he hurries about in the heat, seeing one man & another, with this pain haunting him almost continually. But I am very well. . . .

AUSTIN TO MABEL   Saturday morning, 16ᵗʰ July [*1887*]
[No. 10]

My last word for you by the *City of Sydney*, Dearie—must be sad to be true—and nothing but the truest true ever went between us, or could. For it is that I love you to downright pain. And long for you to bitter suffering. I had not even yet, before, realized the power of its overwhelming, overmastering strength in and over me. To have had you, and to be without you, it racks me through and through, to my lowest foundations. I can turn nowhere for relief or alleviation. There *is* nothing else. You transform, transmute, translate everything. The lilacs flower for naught without you to look at them with me. I have no heart to drive—every bit of sweet road, every beautiful glimpse of landscape, every breath from the fresh hay fields, every bird note only deepens the sense of your absence. I have no disposition to go off to any place of pleasure resort, for I dont even want to enjoy anything, apart from you, if I could—and I couldⁿᵗ. And the days are so numerous, and so slow. I count them off, and count them off, and they are here still, just the same. O, will you ever come back, and claim your own again! Yours—because you have made me yours—yours in the divine order, and by original ordainment, in the constitution of human nature, of necessity, yours from the beginning, yours always—devotedly, reverently, worshipfully, and through you, religion and God, and the brilliant beckoning future—rest, and hope, and trust—and belief—and joy beyond power to express. A soul, all glistening, and aglow. Yours—and you are mine!!!! You need not say. I know—know by every strongest word—and fullest, by every sweetest act, by every dearest look, by the constancy of years, by the supremest woman's gift, and seal—herself—of her own free will, and gladly, madly, given, given, over and over.

Yes, I know.

Well this must be on its way. It is hardly more than a word and a sigh—but it tells you all. A kiss and another, and another. Good morning. Good night. Come back.

Greetings and best wishes for Jacob—Josiah—or whatever his name is. I trust everything is all right in his plans.

MABEL TO AUSTIN   Shirakawa, Japan
                          Sunday morning, 24 July 1887
                                           No. 11

I am in a Japanese hotel—flat on the floor—nothing to sit on, nothing to eat on, nothing to write on, nothing to lean against. The room wide open to the street on two sides, wide open into other rooms on the third side. Heat, mosquitoes, fleas *ad libitum*. So much for the disagreeables. There are many pleasant things to offset them. First there is a cool breeze this morning. Next, the eclipse station has been pitched upon the ruins of an old castle about ten minutes' walk from here, which is a marvel of picturesque beauty. It is about 75 feet above the town & large enough to contain an army. It was burned in 1868, when there was a war between the Emperor & the powerful Shoguns, & this castle was one of the hardest to be subdued & taken—but it was at last, & the Emperor triumphed. There is a great moat—planted now with rice—& two sets of ramparts & stone walls, the whole overgrown with wild flowers & great pine trees. From the top an indefinite distance of beautiful fresh fields & distant blue mountains can be seen, with a river winding below, not unlike the view from Sugarloaf, only the castle is not so high. . . . Three tents are put up—army tents, stout & dry, & tomorrow I am also going up there to stay. We have ordered a stock of American food which is here in boxes, & the real camping out begins tomorrow. Anything but a Japanese hotel—& that is all there is, here. The whole population gathers in the street, & watches us most of the day. This town brought me my first experience of a Japanese hotel—those at Yokohama & Tokyo are European hotels, with elaborate bills of fare & foreign furniture. Here, we sit, eat, write, sleep & live on the floor. It is somewhat cooler than Tokyo, & I expect to paint & write a great deal up in that old castle for the next three weeks. There are beautiful wild roses up there, pure white—and many lovely things to paint. . . . The naturalist is off, by the grace of heaven, bug-hunting, so we are spared him. Nobody likes him. My health is perfect, in spite of the great heat, but the bites are very dreadful. My mind is full of *you*, all the time. Whenever I am in some particularly queer place, I always wish so that you could see me; & yet what I want is for you to *be* there too. . . .

Tuesday, 26 July. The tents were not finished as soon as they expected, so we are still in the Japanese hotel. It is cool here, and clean, both of which are desirable features, so I do not mind the delay. When bed-time comes, a little maid, looking exactly as if she had stepped out of *The Mikado*, comes in with a boy in a *kimono* (one of which I shall bring home), and they spread down something like thick comforters on the floor, two or three deep with one folded up for a pillow, since I cannot sleep on their wooden pillows, & then they string up a kind of house of mosquito netting, fastened from four corners of the room, & then I crawl under & lie down. . . . Last night four of the feudal knights of the old *régime* called to pay their respects. They were barons under the father of the Count Somebody whom we met in Tokyo, who was the lord of this castle where the station is fixed. They came in one after the other, bowing their heads to touch the floor. Their present preceded them. This time, two ducks tied tail to tail in bamboo cloth, & two well-grown chickens similarly fettered, laid in a big red lacquer tray. As they were solemnly bowing the ducks quacked loudly, which made "this one" smile most inopportunely. Then each one bowed low again to each of us, & we all seated ourselves on the floor in a circle, while the young Japanese student from the University interpreted their compliments to us, & ours to them. Then we each drank a cup of tea, brought in by our "boy" on his knees, & then they bowed themselves out. They are to visit the castle & view the instruments next week. . . .

Thursday morning, 28 July. . . . We are to move up to the castle today—everything will be ready for us there after lunch. Mrs. H. is a great invalid, & it remains to be seen how she will enjoy tent life. . . . I see almost nothing of Josiah. He is busy all day & all the evening. I see him only at meals, for he comes in after I am asleep, & we breakfast at 6:30, & they are all back at the castle at 7. He has said once or twice that I must send his love to you—but he is more than filled with business, & hardly knows when the American mail does leave. . . . About the floors—I am sorry you were troubled to re-order them— and if some other kind is used I think it decidedly best to get enough also for the study—the oak idea must be abandoned. . . . Nothing, I think, had better be done to the ceilings, for I may bring back some queer Japanese paper for some of them—I am not sure. I was much troubled that you had another bad cold. God preserve you, my darling, in safety, for the joyous autumn. I will say to you as you said to me—guard yourself every moment, knowing that you are not your own.

AUSTIN TO MABEL   Monday evening, 1 Aug. [*1887*]

I was greatly surprised—and no less delighted, as you may imagine, my darling, to find in Lock Box 13 this morning a letter from Prof. D. P. Todd from Yokohama—mail marked July 10. By the schedule they gave me at the office of the Union

Pacific in Boston the first steamer to leave San Francisco this way, after your arrival there, is the *Gaelic*, July 20th, due at S.F. Aug. 5. I had not even *hoped* for a word from you before the 12th. So I have the story of the voyage at once. And shall have to wait hardly the other fortnight to hear of the figure you are cutting in the Empire of Japan. But of that I care little—comparatively. The one thing important is that you love me and with your whole soul, and that the grandeur of the mountains, and the vastness of the sea, and the strangeness of a strange race do not impair or obscure it. I suppose Josiah is along, though you hardly mention him. I am full of thoughts, and wonders, and hopes which I shall pour upon you when I see you—but not write. What a relief when this needless, trying experience is at an end! and I have heard all, and we are once more locked close in each other's embrace. Death itself could hardly be more cruel. Lovers should not be parted. . . .

For the picture of myself, I am in my room—the yellow room.* It is between 9 & 10. After supper at Vin's I came over here, lighted a cigar, and went out upon my piazza, where I had the sweetest hour alone with you and the crickets—almost the first quiet hour I have had. My moods moved from glad to sad, you were the substance of them all, you are the substance of everything for me. I love you with all the strength and depth and passion and power of my being. You are my world, and my Christ. I say it most reverently, and if there is a Heaven for me, you are that—God pity such love! Of one man for one woman. The mystery and the might of it! Yes, and the shining glory. The consummate flower—and final triumph of Divine achievement. Love, which is creation itself.

Then Dr. Irish came to report programs at our reservoir, for you must know that after four or five days of most un-

---

* Austin's yellow study was the result of recent redecorating at the Evergreens. In early May, Mabel had pleaded with Austin, "Please, you *won't* do over six rooms in your house, will you? I mean with painting and so on," and her diary reveals that on June 5 she and David called on Austin at the Evergreens "& saw his decorations," presumably in Sue's absence. These are the only clues suggesting Sue's reaction to her husband's helping the Todds build the Dell.

precedented rain, a tremendous shower early last Friday evening, almost a cloudburst, carried away the dam of the pond above us, and the accumulated water, tearing down the narrow valley, burst through our dam, leaving it a wreck. I gave directions all night for gathering men and materials for beginning at light in the morning to do what might be possible, to get water into the village again at the earliest moment, and have been occupied with it largely since. Hope to get it in by tomorrow night. The permanent structure will use every day till frost in its construction. . . .

MABEL TO AUSTIN   Shirakawa, Japan
                                      31 July 1887
                                          No. 12

The American mail reached the castle yesterday—with your two beautiful letters. . . . Of course what you told me of J. and J. H. [Seelye] troubled me, but I told him about it, & I trust he will take it to heart. Also it annoyed me that I had overdrawn at the Bank. But I do not believe it is 60 or 70 dollars. I kept my check-book too accurately to have made any such blunder. . . . But it was not for either of those items that I cried, after reading your letter, as I have but seldom cried in all my life. It was in connection with your brilliant time that last week in June, and the clearness with which the hopelessness of my own life came over me. Of course I am bitterly homesick without you here (yet I cannot help feeling just as near you in soul as if my hand were actually in yours, as it is spiritually)—but that homesickness for you is as nothing compared with what would have been if I had been near yet not with you during those sparkling days. Far better for me to be on the other side of the world. I cannot tell you of the horror of it all to me. But I feel today as if I would far rather die, with you holding me, than come back into the sharp misery of it all. As I review my life, here in these foreign surroundings, and see clearly what it is, what makes its happiness, & how well-nigh infinite must be its pains, I wish most strongly to die. For five years I have borne a strain which every day was a little more than I had strength for, and I feel as if a little more would snap me in two. . . . As for God, I feel utterly deserted by Him. I have tried so hard during all these years to trust Him, & to wait patiently. Yet He gives no sign. I am pitifully helpless in His hands, & dare not even reproach Him. The heavens are dumb. He has shown us the possibility of a life as happy and as pure & noble as heaven itself—and then He lets us go. He sits silently up in the great spaces and watches us suffer—if indeed He cares enough even to notice the pain—and we pray & entreat in vain. Only I shall always be glad that He did show us each other, even if I die for it, which I think not at all unlikely. A sensitive nature can not hold on forever against such odds. We have each other—but we have each other against the bigoted spite of the rest of the world. And we can not make it otherwise. There seems no real help but in death. After we are together again, and have talked it all over, we may decide that this is all that remains for us— to go together to some possibly kinder sphere. You have, as far as the outward circumstances go, the great advantage of me. You can rule & compel some things which I cannot, and although I know you count all such things as nothing when weighed with me, still they make your outward life much more bearable than mine. I do not want my life to end so soon. I have capabilities which will grow in time into larger accomplishment, sometime. I mean to do something worth while. But rather than to suffer all the pain & even horror of the last five years in the next five, I would die twice over, & be glad of the choice. . . . I am rather alarmed about another thing too, which I cannot write you, but which I hope to be able to write (before this letter is sent off) has been happily adjusted.* Now I shall get up & go out—pick some white roses to paint, perhaps. Now & always I love you to agony—& I belong to you.†

---

* Mabel's menstrual period was about four days late.

† The unconscious message of this entire passage, in which Mabel rails against God, becomes clearer on remembering that she has set Austin up as her God, and their love as her religion, so that it was he whom she was begging to intervene in their fate.

Ménage à Trois

Wednesday afternoon, 3 August. First, my darling, I am better than I was when I wrote to you the foregoing. I have been very much depressed & discouraged the last few days, but I am trying to be more cheerful, though I have not as yet reached hilarity. . . . That tangible trouble of which I wrote in the last sentence of the Sunday installment has passed me by—for which I am deeply grateful. But enough remains to sadden. Still, I am convinced that I have been less unhappy away here than I should have been had my summer been passed nearer to you in miles, but even more separated, actually. And I am getting morbid about that terrible hatred of my three enemies. I can feel it pursuing me here on the other side of the world—the positive hatred & persecution, as well as the negative disgust. I feel it every moment, & it is killing me. Perhaps I am nervous, but I certainly do feel as if it would ultimately be my death. I do not know but that something is being done by them now, for my destruction— at all events, I have been most horribly conscious of their malignity for more than a week, so that some days I have hardly been able to speak for the crushing power of it. But today I feel a little stronger and I am trying my best to throw it all off— my love for you is so very great that I live in it, in spite of these perhaps foolish alarms. . . .

Shirakawa, Japan
No. 13

. . . *Tuesday evening, 16 August* [*1887*]. It has been a hot and oppressive day—thunder all about in the afternoon, & cooler now. Two nights ago there was a strong earthquake shock. Fifteen or twenty times the bed went to & fro, & the boards creaked, & the effect, waking from a deep sleep, was to say the least startling. But the old castle has stood for three hundred years, & I do not fear its crumbling now. Another night about thirty houses in the city below burned, & I was out watching the fire about an hour. . . .

Wednesday morning, 17 August. The heat is all but intolerable. I can scarcely breathe, & yet the night was cold, so cold that I awoke to put on more cover. The expectation & anticipation are very strong in the party—the sky today is blue, but a light, whitish film of cloud is scattered over. It has been oppressively hot ever since the earthquake. Mrs. H. is sick in bed with one of her numerous diseases. Tomorrow people from Tokyo will begin to arrive for the eclipse, & the eclipse day will be one rush. I am going to draw the corona, & I am trying to get the paper & disk ready today, but the heat is almost too much for me & besides I am expected to stay with the invalid so much that I am in a whirl.* The inhabitants of Shirakawa have all set upon me to paint pictures for them. I began by saying yes to one, & now seven or eight ask, I have stopped. I am surrounded by Japanese now, watching me as I write, & this with the terrible heat is making me nervous. . . .

6 a.m. of the great day, 19 August. The air is clearer than it is apt to be so early, & the sky has light, fair-weather clouds over it. I do *so* hope it will be clear this afternoon! . . . . The more I see of life & the world the more I appreciate you—and, I may add in a whisper—myself! To be a lady through to the core is a rare thing. Once in a while I have met it. I must not write any more—it is nearly breakfast time—but I slept in the tent up among the instruments, so felt the first early freshness & woke & came out. I love you—oh! I love you so!

Saturday, 20 August. Oh! my dear, my dear! How can I find words to tell you of yesterday's disappointment! The sky was as clear as I ever saw it—blue & beautiful until after one o'clock. The heat had been stifling all day, & when I went up by the instruments about one o'clock, I saw the least speck of a white cloud near the western mountains. It rose with immense rapidity, & covered most of the western sky within an hour, but

---

* To aid in drawing the corona, Newcomb had proposed an occulting disk be set up sixty feet from the viewer's eye to block the eclipsed sun and brighter rays of the inner corona, thus permitting the eye to interpret an extension of the corona several solar diameters in every direction. Mabel was not the only one participating. David had given everyone in the eclipse party an assignment, even providing Mrs. Hitchcock with a camera to take one or two pictures.

that has happened before—when it has all been dissipated in less time. But unfortunately it grew cooler, then a thundercloud sprang up in the east, & they joined forces, & some more from the south, & the sky grew black, & thunder muttered. . . . . Well, I can't write much about it, for I am too heart-sore, but they took a few photographs through rifts in the clouds of the crescent sun—but totality was utterly lost. No rain fell, but the black clouds accumulated all the afternoon. At nine in the evening a few stars began to come out. Well, the chief of the party stood it like a hero & philosopher. I knew that he was losing what up to this point is the chance of his life, for his method of observing this had never been used at an eclipse before, & all astronomers were watching*—he had worked day & night, oblivious to sickening heat, or working all night long, & everything was in perfectly brilliant condition for a world-wide success. The castle was filled all day with the dignitaries of the land, & most of the distinguished foreigners—& admiration unstinted was poured out upon him for his really magnificent way of taking so disastrous an afternoon. I never respected him so much, for I know that all his enthusiasm & all his energy & power are put into his work—it is his life—& I would have given anything (but *our* one joy), out of my own life, to have cleared away those clouds for only three minutes—just the totality. As it grew darker & darker, the landscape became almost lurid, & when totality was called, I felt that I must be in some other planet. A few lanterns down in the town flickered feebly, & I could just see the outlines of where the rice-fields & mountains lay. In the east was a streak of sulphurous yellow— the only light in the world. While the whole body of spectators was trembling with the weirdness & disappointment, he was perfectly calm & clear, watching for some half a rift to catch one gleam of the corona—but none came. I held my breath until I

---

* As Mabel explained in her September 22 *Nation* article, David was experimenting with recording the eclipse by photoheliograph. He anticipated that the device he had rigged to photograph the sightings of the heliostat would produce larger-scale impressions of the corona than had ever before been possible.

saw the little crescent shine out again—which it did for a second or two after totality—& then I realized the bitter, bitter disappointment. He says far worse astronomical disappointments have happened to others, & that this work—the preliminary observations & photographs, & the few taken during the eclipse—make it far from valueless, but he feels terribly. Last night some noise disturbed him, & he partly awoke & said, in the most sad & hopeless tone I ever heard him use, "Oh! I did so hope I might never have waked again!" And that is all he has said about it. Well; the Castle was full all day of lovely people, & I had presents poured in from various officials, five or six chickens, half a dozen quail, a bushel-basket of apples, one of pears, & one of peaches, pounds of beef, an immense tray of Japanese sweetmeats—I cannot remember all the things. And today is cool, & sparkling clear—I cannot express my pain at the terrible afternoon yesterday. I feel, with deep sadness, but a pretty strong conviction, that God is against me, & that he would have had a clear day if I had not been here. . . . Mr. Greathouse [the American Consul-General] has invited us to stay with him at the Consulate when we go back to Yokohama—& there will be dinners & social things of all sorts. But I long for you, & cannot be satisfied without you. . . .

Sunday afternoon, 21 August

. . . If any divine visitation occurs to the big black Mogul, you will come to Vancouver & meet us, won't you? In spite of my half-feeling that God has deserted me, I seem to be waiting for an answer to my prayers on that subject all the time. Oh! I do so long for just one gleam of pure unalloyed happiness! I was made so intensely to enjoy, & yet I have been made to suffer so deeply! . . . The Hitchcocks are going [to Nikko], & wish me to accompany them, meeting Josiah after his packing up is done, on his way to Fuji. I do not like them much—she has been very unladylike to me, but I think I should be sorry afterward not to have seen Nikko. . . . The Hitchcocks have to go to Fuji so as to make Josiah some scientific photographs. I am sorry—but he says it is best, so I am willing. I am so sorry for him that I would give up any small personal feeling to gain him some good observations & results. Of that which you dreaded the most for me, I can almost say literally there is none—you know I told you I expected it to be so. . . .

At the top of Fujiyama, Japan
Sunday afternoon, 4 September 1887
No. 15

This is the queerest place I ever yet wrote to you from, dear love. Twelve thousand three hundred & something of feet right up into the air, on the edge of the crater of an extinct volcano, where there is nothing but lava & ashes, very great cold, & air so thin that I breathe with some difficulty. The climb was terrific. Twelve coolies went along carrying instruments, provisions & a little personal luggage.* The first day we rode from the end of the railroad in jinrikishas, & through a lovely country, sleeping at night in a fine European hotel. The second day there were about twenty miles to walk, to get to the foot of the great mountain, through beautiful bridle paths too narrow & rough for jinrikishas. We had among the party of six, one swinging sort of car, carried by two men & called a kago, so that I could ride occasionally if I got tired, or Josiah could if his pain came on. I rode a few times for perhaps ten minutes each time, but I far preferred walking. That night we slept in a Japanese hotel—quite a good one, but where I had a very silly though severe accident. I thought a hot Japanese bath would refresh me, so I got ready & stepped into the little bathing room, where the floor was slippery & wet & slanting. I fell flat & struck the back of my head hard on the step, & cut myself severely. Well the next morning, yesterday, I woke with a bad headache of course, but started on with the rest to walk the twenty-two miles to the summit. Two or three hours led us through woods— a beautiful walk. Then the steep ascent began, growing rougher & harder & straighter up with every step. Great blocks of lava

---

* David was climbing Fuji to make observations for E. C. Pickering, director of the Harvard College Observatory, who was seeking the best location for an observatory to be built with Boyden Fund monies.

& soft small pieces—up, up, dizzily, until I hardly dared look down. To make it harder there was a strong wind blowing down into our faces from the summit, & I often had to sit down flat so as not to be blown over some edge. At three o'clock yesterday afternoon we reached the eighth station—little huts built of lava where tea & rest can be had. This one is 2,000 feet below the top, but Mr. Holland gave out, & declared he should stay & sleep there—so we finally decided to wait. This morning it was misting heavily, but we started up & reached the top in an hour.* My head still aches a little, & my lump feels somewhat oppressed by the lack of air—but I have snuggled down into a pile of fourteen comforters to write to you, hoping for some chance to send it down for the 8 September. We shall stay here four days, or possibly five if we can stand the high elevation so long. Then down.

Shubashiri
Monday night, 5 September

Well, I am down again. I felt well enough during the daytime up there, but last night, all night, I had the most excruciating pain in my head—it was truly agony. But it was a clear night & there was much good work done, for which I was glad even in the midst of the pain. This morning the naturalist appeared on the summit, pretty sick & disgusted, & said that having seen the top he should now go down & try to get well. Whereupon everybody in the party said I ought to go down with him, "mountain sickness" when it really comes on in force being very painful. So I got ready & came down—in safety, & with little fatigue—reaching the little hotel here at the foot about five this afternoon. The workers of the party did intend to stay until Wednesday, but I have just received a note from Dr. Knipping, the meteorologist [of the Imperial Japan Weather Service], that the chief of the party has been taken sick, & is being brought down. That worries me of course, though I know it can only be mountain sickness, which sometimes seems very

---

* Until the revolution of 1868, no foreigners could ascend Fuji, or women go higher than the sixth station. Mabel was the first foreign woman to reach the top.

terrible. They will reach here at eleven o'clock tonight. He told me this morning that enough had been accomplished already to pay for going up, & carrying the instruments. Very few people can stay up there more than one night without feeling it terribly. At about six thousand feet down this afternoon, I felt my unnatural feeling all go away—the headache departed like magic, & I feel absolutely well again.

The above letter was never mailed. Mabel carried it home with her on the next steamer, the *Port Victor*, which left Yokohama September 14. Although she had written Austin of this plan, he did not receive the news until the day the Todds arrived in Boston, October 6. He had been expecting them about the seventeenth.

AUSTIN TO MABEL [*Addressed to Prof. David P. Todd at the Parker House, Boston*]
Thursday, 6th October '87
11 o'c. a.m. and after

I am perfectly nonplussed and confounded by a letter just received from you announcing that you would leave Yokohama 14th Sep. and arrive at Vancouver 28th. Here it is, 6th Octo., and you ought to be in Boston now.

Are you? If so, telegraph me at once.

Say—"*Would like to see you on Wood's case tomorrow—*
Gray"

and if so, I will come down first train tomorrow morning.

If you have not arrived in Boston, telegraph me as soon as you do,

thus—"*Would like to see you about Wood's case as soon as practicable*," and I will come by next train—after I receive it.

Gray

This is all I can say for this noon's mail.

If in any way I hear that you are in Boston before the train goes tonight, I will go down on that.

Sent three letters to Vancouver for you.*

Mabel was occupied throughout the autumn of 1887 putting finishing touches on the Dell—wallpaper, curtains, floor mattings. She saw less of Austin than usual, for a visit from her parents and Grandma Wilder during the last ten days of October was followed by Austin's excursion West with John Sanford. He was gone the entire month of November, and was sick for a week on his return. During these weeks Mabel indulged a "fierce impulse to write" by composing a long romance entitled *Stars and Gardens.* Although she invested considerable time and emotion in its writing and rewriting, the story was never accepted for publication.

At the same time, she also began to copy out for Vinnie some of Emily's poems. Her earliest diary mention of this activity had occurred before the trip to Japan, in February 1877, when, having acquired use of a Hammond typewriter to copy out her little book on flower painting written in 1879, Mabel also "copied a few of Emily's poems on the typewriter." But it wasn't until her entry of November 30, 1887 ("copied two or three more of Emily's poems, & took them over to Vinnie's"), that editorial work became a regular activity. Mabel's first full account of editing the poems came three years later, in her journal, just after publication of the first volume:

Now that Emily's *Poems* are actually out, and my name on the title-page, [Sue and her progeny] rage more than ever. *Why*

* The Todds had found no messages from Austin at Vancouver, and were in Montreal too early and too briefly on October 6 to telegraph. They arrived in Boston about nine that evening, where Austin, having somehow had word of them in time to take the evening train, met them at the Parker House for a joyous reunion.

is a mystery to me for they had the entire box of Emily's mss. over there for nearly two years after she died, and Vinnie urging them all the time, even with fierce insistence, to do something about getting them published.

But Susan is afflicted with an unconquerable laziness, and she kept saying she would, & she would perhaps until Vinnie was wild. At last she announced that she thought nothing had better be done about it, they would never sell—there was not enough money to get them out—the public would not care for them, & so on—in short she gave it up. Then Vinnie came to me. She knew I always had faith in the poems, and she begged me to copy and edit them.

Vinnie had first consulted Emily's friend, editor Thomas Wentworth Higginson, who thought the verses gifted but eccentric and uneven. He was also so busy that he would promise to look them through only if someone else undertook sorting, copying, and organizing first. Vinnie then turned to Sue, but grew frustrated when Sue did nothing but keep the box of precious hand-sewn fascicles or "volumes" at the Evergreens to read to passing visitors. Vinnie herself wanted physical control of them and the privilege of deciding who might hear them. She knew Mabel had had some experience with publishing, and also knew she would tolerate working on small batches of poems at a time. And while Sue had envisioned private printing, Mabel at once looked on the venture as a commercial one, which squared with Vinnie's desire for a wide audience. It is certain, too, that relations between Vinnie and Sue were not smooth (Frank Jameson's mother, for instance, describes Vinnie's distress when Sue gave "quite a party" on the first anniversary of Emily's death), while those between Mabel and Vinnie were cordial and strongly interdependent. But perhaps most significant of all, in November 1887 Austin had informed Vinnie of his wish to leave his patrimony to Mrs. Todd. Under these circumstances, sharing with Mabel her own cherished inheritance from Emily may have seemed to Vinnie—at least at that time—like turning to a member of the family.

Mabel's portrait of Vinnie as the insistent force behind her taking on the project rings true. Full of her own ambitions, Mabel possibly even resisted this tangential literary task, much as she believed in its worth and in the likelihood of public acceptance, for it presented several major problems. Emily's obscure handwriting was very difficult to read; many poems were unfinished, with alternate words scrawled in the margins; and there was an enormous number, nearly seven hundred, in the box retrieved from Sue. On top of this there was Vinnie's constant nagging. As Mabel worked along, however, she discovered "the poems were having a wonderful effect on me, mentally and spiritually. They seemed to open the door into a wider universe than the little sphere surrounding me which so often hurt and compressed me—and they helped me nobly through a very trying time. Their sadness and hopelessness, somehow, was so much bitterer than mine that

> I was helped
> As if a kingdom cared.

Most of them I came to know lovingly by heart, and I was strengthened and uplifted. I felt their genius, and I knew the book would succeed."

Mabel's words from the perspective of 1890 do obscure what her diaries and general state of mind suggest was probably true in late 1887, namely, that she undertook the copying of Emily's poems principally as a favor—an enormous favor as it evolved—to Vinnie. Mabel did not envision any vital role or glory for herself in their publication. It was Vinnie's project, *her* heart's desire, and Mabel took it on chiefly out of obligation to and affection for Vinnie and the late Emily. During 1888, Mabel's diary rarely refers to work on the poems, or to the late-evening visits from Vinnie, which now became a regular feature of the Todds' life. Her letters to and from Austin didn't touch on the poems until two years later. But then, Mabel and Austin were absorbed during 1888 by quite a different occupation—the attempt to have a child. They called their effort "the experiment."

AUSTIN TO MABEL   [*ca. 21 October 1887*]

I was glad to get your note this morning—which I did promptly. I do not change, and you do not, but it seems strange to be shut away from you, and I chafe under it not only, but find it hard to feel good natured toward the elements that intervene—or more accurately, not to feel quite ill natured toward them, one and all, and if it were not that it would add still more to the burden which you cannot escape, I should take pleasure in letting the shadow of my wrath fall distinctly before them.*
The cheap pettiness of the attitude I cannot but scorn, and only wish I could show it.

I shall try however, for your sake, to curb upon the surface—and wait. I did not dream when I left you Thursday afternoon that I should not see you again at 5, and that makes it harder.

I am as Wednesday evening. Does that satisfy! And I know that you are the same—always and invincibly. Nothing can shake me, in my confidence in you.

No one can move you, not even yourself.

We stand, firm as the everlasting rocks.

[*ca. early November 1887*]

I have made the will, not quite as I wanted it but best for now.

I have left all my share of my father's estate to Vin with

---

* Eben Loomis came on Thursday, October 20, and Mabel's mother and grandmother two days later.

the request that she shall turn it over to you. She has promised to do this, so you are protected in any case.*

I will see you tomorrow.

W. A. Dickinson

MABEL TO AUSTIN   Sunday forenoon, 6 Nov. [*1887*]
                                          12 o'clock

In a sunny south room, thinking of you, and wondering very strongly why I have had no letter. . . . I did not go to church today. I could not stand the strain of it. Last Sunday was too much,† & I have had several encounters lately which make me loth to risk any more pain. I am but poorly off in mental equilibrium without you—as well as in other regards. . . . I wish you would write constantly—but I think perhaps I had better write rather seldom, myself.

AUSTIN TO MABEL   St. Louis, 7 Nov. 1887
                                     Monday, 12:30

Came straight through from Cleveland, reaching here at 9 yesterday morning—have been seeing and doing to the limit of our strength since. Sanford has gone to his room to rest, and I am in mine, for same purpose, and to be more quietly with you. We lunch at one and then drive through the parks and about the city. Are undecided whether to go on to Kansas City

---

* Austin's will, dated November 3, 1887, left his share of his father's estate (the Homestead, the meadow, certain stocks and bonds) to Vinnie, a painting and an engraving to Mabel Todd, and all the rest of his property to Sue. This undated note confirms Mabel's later assertion that Austin intended his share of his father's estate to go to her.

† Mabel probably means two Sundays previous, when she took her parents to the college church and found communion being celebrated. "Wild horses would not have dragged me up there if I had realized that," she said in her diary.

tonight or not till tomorrow morning. Expect to be in Wichita Wednesday night or Thursday, and stop probably two days. Everything beyond is left till then. . . .

I am lost to be off in this way, without a connecting link with any usual experience, but I dont forget what I have left behind, and if she were here—should never care to turn around. We would keep on till we entered the flowery land. No, I remember all, and whose and what. I am not tempted, and I rely upon my own, with absolute confidence, and with absolute devotion. You know. The weather is warm & sunny, delightful, and there is much that is worth seeing. This hotel is the finest I was ever in. Report the substance of this to Vin, please. . . .

Wichita, Kansas, 13 Nov. 1887
Sunday afternoon
In the Bar room

Reached this place Friday evening. Found your two dear notes yesterday morning, on going to Mr. Davidson's office. I cannot go into my impressions and reflections. It would take volumes, and we shall have the Winter for them I hope.* We plan to start tomorrow, sometime, for New Orleans, stopping on the way down only for a day at Memphis. Stay in New Orleans over Sunday, and early next week begin our way back, without having yet determined upon any route. Though I hope to take in Nashville and Knoxville. No boy let out of school was ever more glad than I shall be to get the whole trip behind me.

---

* To Sue, Austin wrote the same day: "A Belchertown Cattle Show, Henry Nash, Lake Pleasant. Hadley meadows in the wildest tear of dust and dirt, all mixed—a storm of dry sand pouring over and through all, an electric light in the middle, and a band—no it dont begin [to compare] with the glare and blare & brag and tumult. In a word, though the land is rich, and much of the country impressive in its desolateness, it is all just a great nasty, horrid human hoggery. The Lord deliver me from a building city in the west. My whole nature recoils from it."

Time seems so everlastingly long, and I am losing what is so
much better. I think of you constantly, and my prayer is to get
back to you safely. There is my home. Shall write you at the
next stopping place—and shall rather look for a word from you
at the St. Charles, New Orleans. Hope you will see something
of Vin. I said some things to her before I came away beyond
anything I ever said before. Ever, ever the same. P.S.'s on & on.
You know all. Look within.

I dont forget one Monday night either.

There are no conveniences for writing here, or doing anything else.

Memphis, Tenn., 16 Nov. 1887
Wednesday afternoon, 3:30

. . . Everything is *about* here. Nothing on time but hotel
tables. I am so mixed up by all this night & day and strange
country business. I have lost all sense of days of the week or
month. I seem to be out in unmeasured space and time—the
experience is entirely novel, but will be profitable, bore as it is
to gain it.

I never before felt the beauty of those lines. He leadeth me
by the still waters. He maketh me to lie down in green pastures.
There is where I want to be—you with me.

Money, land, cattle, corn, railroads, sudden futures, are
all that is talked of in the west, or thought of. A man is a man
for the cunning or chance by which he has seized upon more
than his part of the heritage of this world. It is unnutritious to
me, and it is repulsive. I wouldnt give a volume of Emerson for
all the hogs west of the Mississippi. . . .

Tell Vin I think of you and her together.

Vicksburg, Miss., 18 Nov. 1887

On my window sill—just before going down to breakfast.
There is not a table of any kind—or stand in my room in "The
best Hotel in Vicksburg"—and the sill looks as if it had been
used for a chopping block.

Ménage à Trois

The strangest place yet—I must wait to describe it.*
Reached here at 6 last night—well tired—no parlor cars go
down the Mississippi, and we were huddled in with niggers,
poor whites, and other trash. Gentlemen and Ladies dont appear
to travel this way—we met but one, a real planter, and his
daughter, and got a little idea of what the word used to mean.

Leave at 8:45 for New Orleans—wanted to go from here
by boat, but the river is very low, and the boat time is any time
or no time as it happens.

Go straight through the heart of the Sugar & Rice country.

Yesterday it was through alternate forest, and cotton, the
hands in the fields, picking—reach N.O. at 6. Shall write from
there Sunday.

The other thing that this line carries you know. Look
within. Every bit of it.

[24 November 1887]
Birmingham, Alabama, Thanksgiving Day

At the breakfast table, waiting for my order to be filled.
Two days off from the Homeward bound—about seven more,
count one off every day. . . . My longing for the last day is beyond anything I have words for now. I shall be apt to think of
you as I ride along this Thanksgiving Day, in your sweet, cozy
rooms, and remember that we have not only to be thankful for
each other, but that our lives have been cast in pleasant places,
that we were born in New England and not in the South, among
mules, and niggers, and dirt, and alligators and slovenliness,
and ignorance, a people which one's respect for his creator for-
bids him to believe God ever made, but are the result of some
evolution, or the device of the Devil. . . .†

* To Sue he had written the evening before: "If there is anything beyond this I shall need new senses to take it in. I am dizzy and bewildered—all the strange variety of this variegated country is too much
for a single month—adjectives are unavailing. I hope New England
is not the dream and this the reality. If it is, then I am in Tophet already. The one redeeming feature, if there is one, is its ludicrousness."

† Austin returned to Amherst the night of November 30, so tired and
depressed from his journey that he required a week to recover.

THE LETTERS

MABEL TO AUSTIN

[Newark, N.J.]
Friday, 10 a.m.
23rd Dec. [*1887*]

The journey was tedious and long* . . . the train more than an hour late . . . trunk not at house, but afterward hunted up in express office. Not at the house until after six. Reception from six to nine, & guests arriving. Dressed in a jiffy—no time to eat anything for supper. 165 guests, & standing to be introduced until after ten. Then supper, and an appetite rarely excelled in my previous existence . . . then dancing—in which I took little part. Last guest out soon after twelve, then a little fruit, & a little coffee, & to bed. Slept hard till toward seven. Then a good opportunity for some effective conversation, which was improved—and taken well, and will be acted upon.† . . .

I am going to get a mental balance before long which shall be substantially unshakable—and you are going to help me. I have made up my mind that my life *shall not* be spoiled, and I *will* be strong and live out what is in me. And in the meantime and always, P.S. 1st with an intensity which was only faintly suggested on Tuesday evening. Remember that ___ and then think it was only an intimation of its depth & strength, beyond. And I have something as great to carry with me.

We know we can rely. And I remember whose and what, in all its forms. P.S. 1st through all a glorious eternity.

She

---

* The Todds spent Christmas 1887 with David's sister and brother-in-law, Naomi and Charles Compton, in Newark. Their visit began with a reception at the Comptons' home on December 22 and ended with a public lecture and slide show about Japan that David gave on December 29.

† Such a moment of conversation with David typically concerned "policy" or "concessions" relating to Austin. There is no clue as to the subject of this one, but it may have involved Austin's desire to give Mabel a desk for Christmas. The gift, "a very beautiful oak writing desk with some handsome carving and very effective brass handles and escutcheons," was probably selected during this trip, for Mabel made several purchases for the Dell while she was near New York.

Ménage à Trois

There was no conversation at all—or any suggestion of any future concessions. So I know no more than when you were here. But I think it may be safe enough to say Wednesday [to begin "the experiment"]. At any rate, considering the storm and the quiet evening probable, I should suggest your coming over about quarter of eight, & it might not be unlikely that something could transpire then. But I will not come out this afternoon, for I think I can easily keep things off until Wednesday at any rate, and if it seems all right perhaps this evening could be used.

Otherwise Wednesday as you suggested. But come over as early as you can conveniently, and we can see.

P.S. 1st __ __ __

12n. Ideas the same as at nine. I will expect you about 7:45. I am enjoying the snow so much! Shall write most of the afternoon.*

[*Washington, D.C.*]
27 March [*1888*]
Tuesday, 9 a.m.

The little Saturday note came yesterday morning, and was a great comfort. . . .

I am more and more disappointed with the failure of the experiment. It would not have failed, I think, if I had left *home* today. But I will try again—& yet again. And P.S. 1st oh! yes, almost too much. . . .

---

* In November Mabel had described in her journal "a little room upstairs fitted up for my little study—not the large studio in the attic, but a small north room opposite my own room, where I have my writing and papers. . . . For nearly the first time in my life I am collected together as to books & papers. And I mean to write a good deal." She probably had the Hammond typewriter on which she was copying Emily Dickinson's poems here.

Thursday morning

Still a steady downpour, & a restless east wind. Yesterday I went out & met ever so many interesting women. You know there is an International meeting here now, & I dined at the Riggs House & went to some of the receptions.*

AUSTIN TO MABEL   [28 *March 1888*]

Just a word for this noon's mail, for I am worked to the very limit.

I heard of the telegram announcing your safe arrival [in Washington] the latter part of Sunday afternoon, and yesterday morning I received your Sunday & Monday line.

I know so far, and I understand all the rest, and for the time you must—and will—understand me without words. You can be sure, you need have no fear, or shadow of fear that you have mistaken. It is all as you have supposed—there is no deviation, no tendency to deviation—pleasure lies only in the path followed so long.

I know what I like, and what I want, as you do.

Believe me, and be happy, for P.S. first over and over never more sweetly, never more strongly.

I am sorry to tell you that the manuscript [*Stars and Gardens*] is back in my hands, from N.Y. but you enjoined upon me to inform you the first minute—a short note with it [from *Harper's*]—very pleasant.

I am sorry too, frightened though I was, to some extent, over the failure of the last month. Hope, more time, and a different habit will be needed for success—such as would be easy for us—if only we had the world more at our command!

I work a while in the morning in my room, then am at the Savings Bank a while, where people have learned they can find

---

* Mabel may have timed her visit to coincide with the Celebrated Women Council being held in Washington. She was highly stimulated by this exposure to the burgeoning women's movement, and attended its receptions over a period of four days.

me.* Then at Walker Hall. The afternoon being not entirely different—except in proportions. Evenings I go over to cheer Vin. She is improving a little, but very slowly.† There has been not a pleasant hour since you left.

I *must* go—but you know, yes, unqualifiedly.

Hope the visit is going well with you.

Sue & Ned go to N.Y. next Monday for a day or two or three.

Never more.

MABEL TO AUSTIN [*Washington, D.C., 1 April 1888*]
Easter Sunday, 9 a.m.

My King! As ever, and always! . . .

Outwardly I am having a very pleasant time, and it is very refreshing to me, when I have been so much hurt & wounded in every way in a narrow & unappreciative town, to take a dip into the real world, wide and large, and see how warmly people come to me. I have met a great many old friends, and distinguished new ones. Nearly all have heard of me in some way, & come forward with so much real interest & friendliness toward me & my fortunes that I feel as if I had waked out of a night-

---

* Austin had lost his law office when the Palmer Block, a principal business building in town, caught fire and burned to the ground during the great March blizzard of '88. Caught in Boston, Austin didn't get to Amherst until a day later, and then after walking most of the seven miles from Northampton. So disheartened was he at the loss of his fine law library and many irreplaceable town records that he never rented another space, but instead used his home study as a business office. As a result, the Evergreens became something of a hub of village civic affairs. (It is amusing that during a subsequent snowfall David emulated Austin's heroic trek after missing his train from Northampton and determining to brave the storm to meet his afternoon class. Mabel wrote from Washington about the exploit: "You poor 'l David; I felt so sorry I almost cried, at your poor little trudging feet. . . . Goo'by dear. I love you, & I miss you. Maybill.")

† Vinnie had been ill since the middle of the month. David checked on her regularly, too, for he and Vinnie were very fond of each other.

mare, as I remember what I have been made to endure by people who are so far beneath me. The memory of it would sadden me for years, even if my prayer were to be answered now. . . . This visit is doing me good, in general, although I am conscious every moment that my life is a tragedy.

So the manuscript has come back! It was a very hard blow to me. I am only just beginning to realize it. I wish you had told me what the note said. . . .

Strangely, I have found something which I think will make the experiment a success next time. We have spoken of it— you know, & I have found out about it all.*

AUSTIN TO MABEL   [4 April 1888]
                                        Amherst, Wednesday, 11:15 a.m.

Not a word from you [from Washington] since your Tuesday, Wednesday, & Thursday note.

David has a note for me, but I didnt meet him yesterday though I was about all day, and when I saw him this morning, he had forgotten it, and left it at the house. He said he would get it and take [it] up to the College Church with him, and I was to get it there.

I have just been way up there—and waited for him to talk to workmen in the back side of the organ loft out of sight, telling me every time I spoke to him he would be right out without coming, as long as I could and be sure of ever getting my P.S. in to you. I am too provoked too to be interesting, even to you, but I am unchanged to you—and beyond change.

I read your letter to Vin before I came up this morning. I didnt see her yesterday. I judge you are enjoying Washington to the brim—that is all I know about you. I have no intimation of your plans for return, and dont know whether I am to write you again.

---

* Whatever Mabel learned about inducing pregnancy involved relaxing in a hot bath before intercourse, judging from changed habits noted in her diary.

Everything I have ever said or written to you which you have cared for, I say again, and add to it. I am quite mad to see you, but I dont want you to shorten your visit.

Always, always. I am writing at one end of the Savings Bank long table, interrupted by questions about this and that.

Always P.S.

Mabel returned to a servantless house, a variety of physical complaints relating to cold weather having driven Phebe off for six months. All through the spring Maggie came frequently from the Homestead, while Mabel coped feebly with an untrained girl and elected to entertain extensively in her now-finished home. She deliberately filled the house with visitors for commencement, which, because of Austin's college and family obligations, had become "a dreadfully trying time to me, especially if I am alone." She *was* alone; David went off to help celebrate the fiftieth anniversary of the Williams College observatory, thereby standing up (and quarreling with) Caro, who was visiting. But August was different: "After my visitors had all gone, and the Summer School was over, and the great, big, black Mogul had gone off with her two children for a month, then Austin and I had unlimited drives; nearly every day we went somewhere. The weather was ideal—cool and fresh and sunny. And the views we saw, and the sunsets, and the utter freedom, and the long breaths, and the foliage and flowers, and the delicious vacation to us both—it was all worth almost the eleven other months of discomfort and annoyance."

There are clues in her diary that Mabel may even have spent a night or two at the Evergreens. (Susan wrote to Austin mid-month from Maine: "I do not like to think of you as alone in the home even if you are not lonely. I am forevermore lonely —that goes without saying.") Other satisfactions during August included acceptance by *St. Nicholas Magazine* of her article "Ten Weeks in Japan," subsequently published in the

Christmas 1888 issue, and entomologist Samuel Scudder's request to use Mabel's painting of milkweed and a brown butterfly on the cover of his work on American butterflies, which appeared in November. *St. Nicholas* also took a piece Mabel had worked on through the spring about the swallows living in a nearby chimney, although "A Well-Filled Chimney" wasn't printed until January 1890. Despite these successes, when Sue, Mattie, and Ned returned to town on August 31, life seemed very grim. "Is there any mercy or justice, or pity, or sweet love of making pure happiness in Heaven?" she declaimed in her diary. "It would seem not." In a cloud of despair, she went off to Hampton until mid-September.

AUSTIN TO MABEL   [*10 September 1888*]
                                            Monday afternoon, 3

Your Saturday word came this morning—rather meagre, but that is all right. You are taking in the sea, and with your mother, and grand, and so on.

You say nothing of returning, so I suppose that is in the wind yet, and nothing of yourself, except that you are the same. I know what that is and am satisfied. So am I the same and I would like to rest my eyes upon you for a little just about now.

Saturday was rainy, yesterday—warm, damp, close, disagreeable—today bright, clear, brilliant. I have been at my desk, and up street, at 4 am to drive Miss Kellogg to Wildwood.*

* Anna M. Kellogg, an old friend of Austin and Vinnie's, was a handsome, intelligent, worldly woman who had run schools for young ladies in Paris and Washington. Sister of a former Amherst College trustee, Rufus Kellogg, to whom she was devoted, Miss Kellogg made occasional long visits to Amherst. David had begun to court her interest in funding a new observatory, while Austin encouraged her to consider a site in Wildwood Cemetery, whose seventy-four acres had just been purchased after eight years of village controversy. The gift never materialized, and after her brother was murdered in 1891, Miss Kellogg became melancholic. Rufus Kellogg's $33,000 bequest to the college, which established a fellowship and prizes in declamation, possibly was the source of Miss Kellogg's potential largess in 1888.

The stir of return for the term has hardly commenced. It must, right away.

Vin is still in a state very bad, about her paper.* She is afraid it will not be on in time for the wedding, funeral or whatever it may be, and feels very much alone. She always does if the world has^{nt} its hat off to her, and waiting her commands. Her ideals are very high. Nothing is to her mind but the impossible, and she wont compromise.

I unlock this [envelope] saved from [a] Nebraska [correspondent] to save my last envelope for tomorrow or next day, as I hear.

I hope you will stay long enough on your return in Boston to let D.P. accomplish all he can there [with Caro]. He will be the better man.

I am keeping, all right and full of P.S.3 1st, for you— same.

Keep in good heart, and believe.

[*26 October 1888*]

My cold settled so closely upon the top of my lungs during the night I did not dare go off today, and shall not leave my house.

It is better however this morning, and I think I shall pretty much clear it out by tomorrow. It need not trouble you.

Meanwhile remember what I have said to you. Keep cool, & own yourself. If you have done anything you are ashamed of, repent and begin anew, and better. If you have not, dont let gossip of weaklings upset you. Truth, and the right, come out top at last. The world is too large and interesting, and is not to be given up because gnats and gadflies, and carrion birds find a place in it—and must have their food.

Keep them off as well as you can—but have some other

---

* Mabel was trying to procure for Vinnie certain wallpaper she had used in the Dell, but it was no longer available in Boston, so Mabel had sent other samples. She frequently did city errands for Vinnie.

thought. I will see you tomorrow, very likely after you come down at noon [from painting class at Mrs. Stearns's].*

MABEL TO AUSTIN [*29 November 1888*]
Thanksgiving morning, 1888

The bells are ringing for church, my darling, but they awaken no devotional thoughts in me. Sometimes it seems as if I am made up on an entirely different plan from the rest of the world. That standing-aside-and-looking-on sort of feeling that I have always had used to hurt and make me very lonely. But I am used to it now. I cannot be one of a mass, and there is no use to try. Last night you did not come, and I missed you more than you know. But truly pain has come to be so constant a state with me that I take it rather as a matter of course. But I have been very loyal to you, so loyal that the bare thought of whether it is all worth while has never entered my mind. I loved you, and you loved me, and so there was only one thing to be done—just to recognize and abide by it. And that I did unhesitatingly, with never a mental reservation as to whether it might be more politic to put it down. I live absolutely by nature. There is no artificial hedge about me, and things look in my eyes merely undistorted. It has turned out that I, as well as you, have had to bear martyrdom for our love, but I think that makes it none the less precious. It is a martyrdom just as surely as that of old, when men gave up family and home and approval and even the daily necessities of life, and went out into the cold and bleak desert spaces to think and pray and clear their minds from mists— and finally came back laden with great messages, and were

* This letter turns upon an unidentified incident of late October, probably some local gossip about Mabel. Her diary entry for Monday, October 22, reads: "Mr. Dickinson went to Boston at 7:45. I arranged the parlors. . . . Began a little new story. Began to get ready for walk with David. He came in—thunderbolt had fallen, & I was crushed. . . . Cried all night." Amherst whispers and cold shoulders were scarcely new to Mabel, but she was always highly disturbed by them, and would have been especially concerned this time because Grandma Wilder was visiting, and her parents were arriving the twenty-sixth.

merely burned and tortured as their reward. Ours is a personal thing—theirs was for the world at large. That is all the difference. . . .

This sad and rainy Thanksgiving Day I suppose should bring me many thoughts of gratitude for many things. First for you, my dear, my king. But it almost seems to me as if there is a faint little shadow between us today—for the first time in six years. I am perfectly aware that I have brought it upon us myself, and that is a great pain. I do trust you—fully, firmly, even when your judgment seems to me over-cautious. I have hoped for changes to better us all these years. They have never come, but a steady pull, down in the other direction. Is it any wonder that I am eager for you to attack the fatal cause of it all?

I do ask you to forgive me for being impatient, intemperate in my eagerness, and too vehement in my expressions to you. For when I think it over quietly, I am so sure you are going to gloriously justify all my supreme faith in you that I am mortally ashamed of the intensity with which I urge you to save me. But I see the world slipping from me—I see it becoming daily more impossible for me to live in the little town which is yours. I see myself more and more alone, and I know that it is all merely the deliberately planned result of a hatred and a threat made and begun many years ago. I see power over all this lying idly in your hands, and you the only person able to cope with this terrible thing. . . . I see with eyes supernaturally clear that the day has come for you to use just a little of the strength which lies in you against the stronghold of all my hurts; and that has been the reason for an insistence which perhaps has passed the limits of your well-nigh infinite patience. Even when I have seen the most clearly, and waited the most breathlessly for what you should do, I have never had an impatient thought of *you*. You sit enthroned, always. But you have never seen the bitter necessity as I have. It would be cowardly for me to go away in the cloud I now live under, and leave it all behind. My spirit is very brave and I mean to live it out—and down, right here. But when you say that I do not control myself, you cannot know the almost iron hold which I keep on myself all the time to enable myself to get through the days at all. And the impatience which

I cruelly let you see so often, is only the superficial froth of a pain and struggle which are too deep for words, and which I cannot always hide from you. . . . I have continually put down the suggestion in my own mind that much of this pain was unnecessarily given me by your reluctance to step in and relieve it in the one place which caused it all. I have never admitted a thing into my consciousness which could seem like a disloyal thought toward you. But, oh! how gladly shall I see you do what you can in this line! It cannot make it worse, and I shall at least see that you have tried what could be done. . . .

Mabel's writing was progressing well. By year's end she published an essay on Hampton, N.H.'s, 250th anniversary, called "In September," in the *New York Evening Post* (also in the *Amherst Record*) and had had another romance, "The Sexton's Story," accepted by a publication that soon ceased publishing; the story didn't appear until the *Amherst Record* of August 1889. By this time she had copied over two hundred Dickinson poems on the Hammond typewriter, but had to give up the machine and was continuing on a less sophisticated, slower World typewriter.

Her literary activities were encouraged by David, who was beginning to place astronomy articles, and who actively promoted his own and Mabel's talents by calling on magazine and newspaper editors whenever he was in New York or Boston. David gave Mabel editorial assistance, while she did all his copying and made necessary drawings. On December 30, 1888, the New York *Herald* devoted a full page of the Sunday paper to David's description of the solar eclipse that would occur on New Year's Day. He was invited to New York to oversee publication of his page and to cover the subsequent news as dispatches came in from eclipse parties around the world. Always in his element when in charge of affairs, David grew heady from his experiences in the *Herald* newsroom ("David is a famous character in New York just now—and the whole *Herald* staff seems to be at his service," Mabel wrote her parents). He paid a call upon Mrs. Anna Draper, wealthy widow of astronomer Henry Draper, who lived in a "grandly magnificent" Madison Avenue house, and whom David had once met in Washington at the Newcombs'. He found her a very attractive woman, now in her late forties, and wrote Mabel on December 31 of losing his heart to Mrs. Draper's voluptuous charms. He insisted Mabel come to New York on Wednesday, January 2, to advance affairs, for he had strong hopes of wooing Mrs. Draper's money to Amherst for an observatory. Suddenly, before his letter reached Mabel, David decided things couldn't wait until Wednesday.

MABEL TO AUSTIN   [*1 January 1889*]
                                    on the train [to New York]—and
                                    likewise in something of a whirl

At five minutes of 12 Miss Russell rang the bell in a tearing hurry, with a telegram to me from David—"Come today without fail at twelve twenty-two." What to do I could not say . . . but an answer must be sent back at once— before 12. . . . *First* I sent for you—but Maggie was out & Vinnie in the attic, so Millicent could not get in at all. Meanwhile Phebe was packing me a bag—and I was flying. I wanted to find out from you whether I could not go later by the other road, but the telegram was so imperative I thought best to go today, because if in any way anything was lost by my not coming, it would be very uncomfortable in various ways later. I threw on some clothes, & rushed over to Vinnie's myself at quarter past twelve—& Maggie flew to your house. I could not find out anything about any other train—your servant said you had gone half an hour ago to the Bank.* So I flew over & started Phebe and Millicent

---

* Such commotion might have attracted Sue's notice had she been home, but she had gone to New York with Ned and Mattie the day before.

off to the train—while on my own way down the whistle blew. I bought my ticket on the jump & stepped on just as it started. Now that I am well off I wish I hadn't. For myself, I would give up or sacrifice anything or *everything* for a quiet hour with you, & to go off in this way without seeing you is already breaking my heart. Do write me a word for the five o'clock train this afternoon, that I may have it tomorrow morning. I am distressed beyond measure, if I could get off and go back now I would, but that sort of a telegram has something, some reason I know. If I could have seen you *two minutes* even! I am troubled beyond anything that ever happened before, chiefly not to have seen you, but I didn't want to go *at all. Do* you understand? And I left Millicent crying which added to my woes. I wish I had sent word that I couldn't come today but on various accounts which I will tell you I thought best to go if I could—& I just barely could. But P.S. 1st so that I am suffocating, oh! *do* you understand? . . .

[*New York, 2 January 1889*]
Wednesday, 1 p.m.
No. 3

I sent you a telegram this morning, after my second letter went, and I sent you a letter from Palmer—gave it to one of the railroad men who promised to put it on the 3 o'clock train back. But as I had nothing from you, this morning, I am afraid you did not get it. The distress of mind which this trip has caused me in various ways is something beyond anything I ever before experienced, & it has shown me one or two things in a new light which you will be glad to hear. . . .

Tonight I am going to dine with a lady [Mrs. Draper] whom you will like to hear about, & if nothing new comes which would make it seem best (for both you and me) for me to stay, I shall start home at 2 o'clock tomorrow, Thursday, alone. I shall send you a telegram tomorrow morning if I come, & will you go & tell my family. . . .

Ménage à Trois

So far not a word from you. I think if I had that I could go on—but it may come yet. When I said I was going back tomorrow Josiah was up in arms at once, and very especially asked me to stay until Friday at least. There is to be some pleasant pecuniary termination to all his days & nights of work, I believe, which is fortunate for I have just about enough to get back on, only. Please write to me at once, won't you? when you get this, either to the hotel (I will send this in one of the envelopes) or to the *Herald* office.* . . . And *will* you see that my little child is safe and happy? Tell her I am safe & coming back as soon as I possibly can. There is nothing to trouble you—as sometimes. Too much going on for anything else.

P.S. 1st forever.

AUSTIN TO MABEL   Amherst, 3ᵈ January 1889

I took your letter mailed at Palmer from the office as I drove down from Wildwood just at night Tuesday, and read it with my supper.

Received the telegram yesterday forenoon, the two New York letters this morning. One of these latter gives the first clue to where a word from me may find you.

I wrote quite a little note before breakfast this morning, which I thought to send you if I should learn your address, but I think I will let that go now. We will both get a little more settled before we talk.

Dont worry, or fail to get all you can of all you want to out of your visit, from any thought of me, or hurry back before you are entirely through. Having got there that would be poor policy. I shall probably be here for the present, and without great change. My love—you know—is not of the written bond, but of that subtle essence—past finding out—that charms two souls

* In her distraction Mabel had provided Austin no address until this letter arrived in an envelope of the Albemarle Hotel in Madison Square.

[3 1 5]

to increasing nearness, to perfect vision—one heart-beat for two, constraint only from within. Magnetism, not bands. One impulse leading both—but neither leading the other. We have thought we know ourselves, and we have tested each other. I cannot believe that we are not right, and right is absolute—and nothing can prevail against it.

I will go over now and see if Millicent is to be found, and tell you. . . .

3:30 p.m. Have just been over to see Millicent. She is all right but Phebe says is very lonesome.

Found the letter there which I enclose.

I opened it as I presumed you would wish—there being an immediate delivery stamp upon it. It was so late nothing could be done.

I am considering whether I will meet her at the cars and escort her up, to your house, or tell her the facts and let her go back if she wishes. Of course I dont know what to do about it.*

If Mabel said little to her parents about copying Emily's poems, the reason may have been that the Loomises had pressed her for nearly five years to help publish her father's poems. Now Mabel suggested Eben send his manuscript, which she had illustrated with watercolors, to Ticknor & Co., explaining that "we have a little inside track there," and referring to "one of their readers with whom I have fairly intimate relations."

* The special delivery letter was from Mrs. Lillie Oakie of Boston, announcing her arrival in Amherst on the evening train—as Mabel's diary put it: "a miscalculation of D.'s." David had met Mrs. Oakie, wife of Dr. Howard Oakie, through Caro Andrews in mid-December, and come home "full of a new experience." In his New York excitement, however, David forgot he had invited her to visit, until a telegram from Austin announcing she was at the Dell came the night of January 3, as he and Mabel came in from the theater. The Todds hurried home next morning. Mabel found Mrs. Oakie "very handsome & interesting." She was a reader for Ticknor & Co., so Mabel sought her advice on several manuscripts, and took her twice to the Homestead to have Vinnie talk about Emily and read some poems.

After the Loomis poems had been politely declined, Mabel wrote her parents, on February 23, of how her Dickinson work was progressing: "I am trying to finish the wilderness of Emily's poems for Vinnie. I copy two or three every day, but they are almost endless in number."

By now she had transcribed nearly a hundred more poems on the World machine, or about three hundred in all. In early March she hired a local young lady named Harriet Graves to help by hand copying. Mabel was busy with painting and piano students two full days a week, entertained frequently, and was writing book reviews for *The Nation*, whose editor she had met and charmed during the New York sojourn. She was also experiencing a "very trying winter," the result of "a new manifestation of an old cause," by which she probably meant Sue. During the first three weeks of April, the Todds went to Washington so David could promote his hopes of leading an upcoming eclipse expedition to Angola. En route to the capital they visited the Comptons at Newark, and there Mabel had a jeweler refashion a gold ring Austin had given her. "The little article in gold is very satisfactory," she reported to him. "I have wanted it for a long time, and it is very comforting to me." Whether Mabel wore, or simply kept, this wedding band is not clear. Millicent Todd Bingham's memory, remarked on twice, was that her mother put on the Dickinson ring when Austin died.

AUSTIN TO MABEL   [*6 April 1889*]
                                    Saturday afternoon, 5 o'clock

I feel quite sure you have written me since the scrap of Wednesday morning [from Washington], but I have just come from the office, and nothing has yet appeared. Unless something quite unexpected comes up to prevent I propose to be in Boston next Wednesday evening and Thursday morning at least. Very likely Friday too. Perhaps you will aim something at me there, which I can take in to the German Opera for company. I called on Mrs. Stearns last evening—as I said—and used an hour & a half talking in the main of India & its ways and people.* This morning I was a while at Wildwood directing about some work to begin there Monday, rest of the day on odds and ends, mostly at my table, a little in the street and at the Banks. Tonight meet the Parish Committee and two or three more at Thomas' office to survey the Parish field. It looks very ominous. The weather has got bright and fine again, and the roads pretty fairly settled. Only a few days more and the buds will begin to push and we shall hardly be able to look fast enough. It just occurs to me to wonder what I am to do tomorrow—what a leisure time it will be for me.† It will seem almost as if I were living a new life— or an old one. I might go to church and hear the new singing.‡ I guess I wont though, but prowl the ground, to see what wants righting and improving, stopping in at the red house for another look at the palm, and the rooms where I have spent several happy hours.

This for now. I shall still look for a word from you before Sunday.

MABEL TO AUSTIN   [*Washington*]
                                Sunday evening, 14 April [*1889*]

The Tuesday morning upon which you receive this, I shall keep as one of my best-beloved anniversaries—you will know why. You are apt to forget it yourself, but I remember [Austin's sixty-first birthday]. . . .

* Widow of a successful merchant, Mrs. William F. Stearns had spent fifteen years of married life in Bombay before her husband's sudden financial failure and early death in 1874. During the winter of 1889 in Amherst she rallied to Mabel's side in whatever fuss Sue was raising, establishing herself as Mabel's "unvarying, loyal, steadfast friend." She was a strong ally. Daughter-in-law of the previous college president, model teacher, and mother of seven children, she was well loved and respected in Amherst.

† Sue and Mattie were in New York.

‡ Mabel's paid quartette had been replaced by a general choir.

Except for the great need of you, it would be helpful to be here for a while, because it is such a relief to be somewhere where there are not any social shoals to look out for, nor any heart-breaking discourtesies. It is very comforting to hear one's old friends speak to each other in glowing terms of one's self, and say, "Ah! we have known of all these excellencies for years!" To my sore heart you cannot know *how* comforting. . . .*

Monday morning, 15 April

. . . From a scientific point of view, this is the leading week of the year here—when the leading geologists, astronomers, chemists, physicists & so on, do congregate for three days at the Academy meeting. Josiah's paper ["On Composite Coronagraphy"] comes tomorrow—its title has already excited attention, & Professor Langley, the head of the Smithsonian, has sent for him to confer about it today. The dinner at the Newcombs' went well. . . . West Africa is not finally settled yet. . . .

[*Washington, 17 April 1889*]
Wednesday, before breakfast

The plans for return are these. Josiah thinks of starting alone on Friday in order to see the "payrent" [his father]. He takes the trunks, which otherwise would lie over Sunday somewhere. Then I start at 7:20 Saturday morning, with the other two. He meets me at Jersey City, with a wheel-chair for Grandma to go from the train to the ferry-boat. There are then 40 minutes to get up to the Grand Central Station, which are enough, on the elevated road. What time that train leaves I don't remember, but we get home at 6:39. If Phebe is to be found, I shall want her to have supper, & also something for Sunday—but she *may*

---

* Mabel would return to just the sort of "shoal" she dreaded. On May 15 the DKE students at Amherst College mistakenly invited both Mrs. Todd and Mrs. Dickinson to the same reception. Mabel's diary records "a very enraging experience with vulgar Mrs. Dickinson & impudent Mattie." The students afterward apologized and pledged never to invite the Dickinson ladies to their fraternity again.

stay over Easter in Springfield. In that case, I shall be terribly helpless, with Grandma so startlingly feeble—she is only coming north to try & save her life a little longer—& nothing in the house to eat. If Phebe is there, please unlock the door that keeps her downstairs, & tell her Grandma is coming, & have her make, Saturday afternoon, a furnace fire. I am going to let her (g-ma) have Millicent's room, because I must keep the spare room free.

I expected an answer from you yesterday to Josiah's letter, where he asked you for a check. He expected one—to get home on—from the *Herald*, but it did not come, & so I need one from you. I hope you got his letter. Did Vinnie get one from me several days ago?

9 a.m. No letter from you this morning—the postman has just gone—and I have just two dollars left to get home on, tickets & all. I cannot come, therefore, till I get some money. He put his letter in, to you, on Friday last; I shall have to see about borrowing some tomorrow, if yours does not come. You cannot know how lonely and forlorn I feel, if I do not hear from you with about the same regularity always. I feel deserted of God & man. Tomorrow—Thursday—night, you may think of me as at Professor Langley's reception to the scientists, from 8:30 to 12. Today, the paper before the Academy, & an exhibition of paintings at the Cosmos Club.

Phebe asked me if I could get along over Sunday in case she should stay until Monday in Springfield, & I said *yes*. So I cannot tell what she will do. But there ought to be a furnace fire, & something to eat in the house. It troubles me some, because Grandma is so feeble [at eighty-seven] that she seems as if she might die any day, & yet her will keeps her about. If she took cold it would kill her. She will stay into June, when my mother comes north to take her to the seashore. I appreciate all its aspects—but I can manage it, I know. I never needed you so much. I never was more lonesome—except that I know you *are*, & so I have companionship. Oh! P.S. 1st ══ is there any necessity to say it? ══

Ménage à Trois

[*Boston*]
                                                8 July 1889
                        My room, half past eight, Monday evening

Just a word, for you asked it. The old word. Yes, always—
you gave it its meaning to me, and it must hold—or the foundations go out. I wish you were here. I would like to write, but I
dont want to indulge my mood, it is of inexpressible sadness.
Everything has gone smoothly of my business matters, but life
and humanity are too overpowering for me tonight. The loneliness that takes hold of me when I remember that I have had my
Gib here with me, that I have had you. What are men and
women for—what are they about! Why have I won a kingdom,
in you! and lost my father and my boy? Why are you kept from
me, when I need you! I am not going on—I should^{nt} sleep. I will
tell you what I am thinking when I see you. Since dinner I have
been wandering in the Public Garden—alone.*

I hope to return at 7:19 and to see you at 9 tomorrow
evening. Good night. And—you know.

Mrs. Loomis did not come North until August 1, so
Grandma Wilder stayed in Amherst through commencement,
and through a flurry of Mabel and David's writing projects
(they were coaching and helping each other steadily now) and
David's preparations for Angola. Because she expected to go
on the expedition, Mabel was pushing to finish up Emily's
poems, but was exasperated with copyist Harriet Graves, who
had no empathy for poetry and, after 180 poems, still misread
Emily's handwriting. Mabel transcribed the last couple of
hundred herself, mostly by hand, working particularly hard
through August and September. She was also writing two

---

* Austin's despondency may have been increased by Ned's epileptic
seizure the night of July 6–7. He noted in his diary on the seventh:
"Ned has bad attack in night & another less bad—spitting of blood &
nausea."

articles on Japan—the first, on Nikko, appeared in October in *Frank Leslie's Popular Monthly*, where David had placed a couple of astronomy articles, while a second about Fuji was written for *Century*, where David again had preceded her. In addition, Mabel prepared a piece about the coming eclipse (the *Christian Union*, October 31), and worked on one or two fiction pieces, although it was her non-fiction that was meeting success.

By mid-August 1889, Grandma Wilder and Millicent were at the seashore, David away, Sue and her children off on vacation, and Mabel and Austin could enjoy a few weeks of carriage rides and intimate hours alone at the Dell and the Evergreens. David was gone all month, until mid-September, back and forth between New York and Washington on expedition affairs. Mabel wrote to New York after him: "I truly hope you will not think it necessary to resume any old relations—it would trouble me a good deal." Her blueness through this period seemed to derive as much from his comings and goings and changes of plan as any troubles involving Dickinsons. The U.S. Navy was firmly opposed to a woman sailing aboard the man-of-war assigned the eclipse expedition, but David remained so optimistic that he could wangle an exception that he had a piano installed in the ship's saloon. Eben J. Loomis was going along in the official capacity of "instrument maker," and plans had to be made for the welfare of Millicent, Mrs. Loomis, and Mrs. Wilder during the long absence. As so often, Mabel felt frantically torn and pulled about by the uncertainties of her two lives, but even her best efforts to cooperate with David's erratic movements did not prevent a rare outburst of displeasure from him from New York on October 10:

> How in the name of heaven do you think I am going to get all my work done here without your assistance? When Grandma has gone, & I have got you free to come here & help me, then you wait & wait in Amherst, & get me covered in feet & feet deep w. papers, & letters that ought to be answered instantly. Now

I have got to leave all & go to Washington to finish up there. I am utterly disgusted—& doubt if I shall even ask the Secretary to let you go. All the work I planned in Washington, & the printing of the Bulletins & the prestige too that has been spoiled by Mugs keeping your father when I needed him,* & now you stay away when I needed you here, till it is too late. You & Millicent might have been here in the *Pensacola* as well as not for the last 3 or 4 days. I have been rushing about, & everything of mine here is in confusion, & not half the work done. . . . Nothing has been bought in New York—all of which you might have done & saved me the fear of failure. What have you been thinking of? I *should* like to know. Of course I can't send you any notes for articles or anything of the sort. And then you suggest my coming to Amherst to loaf away another Sunday with Lavinia's cats.

The bulletins have got to be given up—the dinner can't be given—& as for your reception I won't have that.

The boxes are here—I thank you for them.†

Goodbye—perhaps you can leave Amherst long enough to come & see the ship off Tuesday. . . .

Mabel packed her trunk and went to New York on October 14, prepared to be away eight months, but found she would not be permitted to go after all. The last hours before the *Pensacola* sailed at dawn on October 16 were so hectic that David worked through the night, and never came to the Albemarle Hotel, where Mabel waited to say goodbye. "I was blue to tears all day," Mabel recorded in her diary, although a hasty parting note caught up with her that evening. Fighting her wrath at the denied opportunity, she returned to Amherst and a week

---

* "Mugs" refers to Mrs. Loomis, whose family nickname, "Muggy," was bestowed by Millicent during babyhood. Mrs. Loomis was packing the Washington house in anticipation of renting it out, and required her husband's assistance.

† At David's instructions, Mabel and Austin had packed up and mailed several boxes of instruments and equipment from David's Amherst College office and the observatory.

later went to Boston to make arrangements for herself, her daughter, her mother, and her grandmother to spend the winter there. She intended to capitalize on David's absence.

MABEL TO AUSTIN   In Boston
                                          Sunday morning, 26 Oct. '89

Reached Cambridge after a while Friday—being taken into Boston because the train wouldn't stop—& back on a local train. Then leaving the two in the station, took the electric car over to Porter's, & found a stable, brought back a carriage, & took them to the visiting place.* Found it rather dispiriting— with one daughter ill. Staid to dinner, the afternoon & night also, however. Into Boston alone Saturday morning. Looked for boarding-places till toward one, finding nothing whatever, avail- able. All the houses back of the State House condemned to be torn down at once for new State House extension, so Mrs. Barrons no use. Finally came up to look at a place on Boylston St. & took the risk of running into Caro's to see when she would be back. Found she had just come—Friday. Staid to lunch, & started out after with new list. Nothing promising at all. Prices enormous, accommodations small & horrid. Spent night with Caro—today & tonight also. New list for tomorrow morning. Am almost discouraged. Everything decent up three flights at least, & $15 a week for one. What *can* I do? Please send me a letter here—The Kensington, 307 Boylston St. [Caro's address]. Shall be sure to get it then. . . .

AUSTIN TO MABEL   [*28 October 1889*]
                                                    Monday, 5 p.m.

Yes, I am with you, remember that—all the while, and I am fretted by your experience. Dont commit yourself to any place

---

* Grandma Wilder and Millicent took temporary lodging with Wilder friends in Cambridge. Mrs. Loomis was still in Washington trying to rent her home.

till you feel clear that it is all right. There must be those in numbers—the thing is to find them, and that is a matter partly of time, partly luck.

I will be down [to Boston] Wednesday if nothing very unusual occurs to prevent, in which case I will notify you, and will be at Doll & Richards at 3½ if I can— if not then at 4. I may then be of some service—meanwhile, keep calm, dont jump, keep at it quietly, and as a steady piece of business. Shall very likely add another word tomorrow, shall at any rate if I find some letter to remail, or if there is anything requiring it, and shall send to the Kensington unless you say differently beforehand. . . .*

MABEL TO AUSTIN   [*Boston*] 7 Nov. 1889
                                   Thursday night, 10 p.m.

Your little note came this morning while I was at breakfast—the usual time, and it gladdened me greatly. If I were entirely free to pursue the interesting things that come in my way, I should be *almost* contented, that is, for the time—under the circumstances. Of course I am hampered some, but I eased my mind by writing a very mean letter to my mother today. She writes that she is homesick to come, which I have no doubt is true. I am homesick to have her. I go to Melrose tomorrow again. It was not a mistake to come, dear, only some of the circumstances are not precisely as I anticipated. But they will be better, and soon I hope. I thought of you very much all day today, and

---

* Austin's letters for the next month are missing, probably the result of Mabel's hectic life during the next few weeks. Although she shortly took a $14 room at 124 Boylston Street and brought Millicent to it, moving Grandma Wilder to the home of other family friends in Melrose, she was constantly on the go, arranging her new life, Millicent's schooling, and visiting Grandma Wilder. Mabel also went to Amherst overnight every couple of weeks to give music and painting lessons at Miss Buffam's school. She usually stayed with Mr. and Mrs. Hills, saw Vinnie at the Homestead, and met Austin at the closed-up Dell.

hoped your part in it all went somewhat to your mind. I hope it was not a dreadful bore to you.*

I had a very interesting call from my co-laborer on the poems, yesterday.† I will tell you (and your relative) all about it when I come next week. I mean to arrive at 11:18 on Thursday next. I will come directly to the other house from the station.

And at the Trustee meeting—*please*—don't let anything interfere.‡ Will you carefully save the *Nations* that come? I miss them so much—I wish you would send them. It is the only paper I ever really read. And please keep a slight lookout for my two express packages. My trunk came all right, and thank you very much.§ I needed it. What ails this paper I have no idea, but I *cannot* write on it.

I am interested in a great many things here, as I said. I worked hard *all* this afternoon on the poems, and I am getting

---

* Mabel probably refers to an adverse court decision involving Austin. As trustee of funds for the Boltwood family, he had overinvested in Union Pacific stock, and when the money was lost, the Boltwoods sued Austin. In a precedent-setting case the State Supreme Court held that he had been injudicious in his investment distribution and he was ordered to repay the Boltwood trust $2,500. Personal relations between the Boltwoods and Dickinsons became less than cordial.

† Until this meeting on November 6, only Vinnie had communicated with Thomas Wentworth Higginson about publishing Emily's poems. Now, at her request, Mabel brought the "immense pile" of Dickinson transcripts to Boston to show him. At first he was not encouraging, but Mabel insisted upon reading a dozen or so of her favorites, and Higginson warmed to them sufficiently to agree that if Mabel ranked them into A, B, and C categories, according to merit, he would read through the best ones.

‡ The Amherst College trustees were about to vote on a proposal granting half salary to faculty members who took leaves of absence after a certain period of service to the college. Chairman of the leave-of-absence committee was newly elected trustee Rev. J. Winchester Donald of New York, with whom the Todds had become friendly. Although at the November 13 meeting three other teachers were granted leave at half salary, Professor Todd was not, which may explain why Austin subsequently helped Mabel take a second mortgage on the Dell.

§ Austin forwarded Mabel's trunk, filled with her winter clothes, when it arrived from New York.

[326]

them into good shape. You had better tell her [Vinnie] so. And in the meantime, how I live without you I do not see. Of course it is not living, but every moment of my life has been waiting ever since September eleventh, 1882. I had my vision then, and it has never wavered or faltered or grown dim since. I am so tired of *bearing*! If I could be once more happy—I have not quite forgotten how it feels—I could take breath for more pain. But I am simply so worn out standing things that I hardly feel as if I have any life left in me. You must not leave me so long again without coming. I must see you every week.

Well, dear, P.S. 1st eternally. And a sweet good night, on both your soft pink cheeks. I wish, I remember, I hope, I anticipate all. Some day it is coming. Good night.

[*Boston*] 17 November 1889
Sunday evening, 10 o'clock

I have just finished my final revision & classification of the poems. Tomorrow morning they go by express to my co-laborer. There are *634* of them—about 600 of which I have personally written—and with all I am now about as familiar as if I had written them originally.* My brain fairly reels. I am too tired to think. But not too tired to remember P.S. 1st. That always.

Thank you very much for the express bundle & all the trouble I know you must have had in getting it ready. Everything in it is a great comfort to me. I cannot think *you* were responsible for sending me all that dry pile of Josiah's mail, instead of my own selected pile. *My* things were on the large

---

* Mabel had worked hard for twelve days classifying the poems. Modern Dickinson scholars have criticized the "revision" she also undertook, for by her own admission, she "changed words here and there in the two hundred [of category A] to make them smoother." Detailed analysis of these changes occurs in Ralph W. Franklin's *The Editing of Emily Dickinson* (University of Wisconsin Press). In the month after he received the weighty manuscript, Higginson reported twice that he was working his way through the A and B poems. Then, like so many that winter, he fell victim to the influenza epidemic that raged in Boston, and the project languished.

table. *His* especially laid aside on the little table. But never mind. Perhaps I can do without all of my papers until Thursday [when I come to Amherst], only please take good care of them because my bank-book & several other important things are with them. The symphony concert on Saturday was exceedingly fine. I rejoice in being able to attend them.*

I said P.S. 1ˢᵗ over and over again, & I do not see how I am to get on so far from you—bodily. In soul you are close, always, to me. *P.S. 1ˢᵗ*.

[*Boston*] 30 November 1889
Saturday evening, 10 p.m.

I wonder if you have any idea of the utter sweetness of your Friday letter to me! And I truly wonder if you have a genuine realization of what it has been to me, and of how many times I have read it, and how it has filled and refreshed and helped and strengthened me! . . . I felt pretty sick in the evening of Thanksgiving Day, unusually wee and worn, and I went to bed at once after running across the street to post my letter to you. Yesterday I dragged downtown to my practice, but almost fainted. I had no idea I was not fairly strong again, but staid in all the afternoon, getting bluer and bluer toward night. It annoyed me so much, too, that the one person who has driven me away from my house and home, and made it impossible for me to live there in peace, should have followed me here where I may see face to face my particular horror—and visiting also the people where so much harm can be done.† Well, I went down to dinner, but about half-past seven C. came to see if I did not want to go to the theatre with John & herself & three others.

---

* Austin had bought her a season's seat at the Boston Symphony. She also took weekly voice lessons with Signor Rotoli at the New England Conservatory, sang with the Handel and Haydn Society, and practiced piano at the studio of her former conservatory teacher.

† Sue was visiting in Boston. In a later fragment of the letter Mabel wrote: "Will you be kind enough to me to *not* write to the absentee from your house at all?"

So I dressed & went. . . . This afternoon I went to the reception on the *Chicago* given by Admiral Walker (Josiah's great crony), and drank some red wine, with sandwiches and cake. Met a lot of interesting people whom I knew. . . . Tonight the Symphony concert was unusually splendid, and I did enjoy it immensely. Tomorrow I dine in Melrose,* and back for Handel & Haydn in the evening. Monday night occurs the very remarkable *Cecilia* concert. . . .

AUSTIN TO MABEL   [*20 December 1889*]

What a funny, sweet, dear little thing for you to have a fancy you would wait till you heard from me! The most little girly thing you ever did with me. It seems like putting us into new relations. Are you getting shy? and coy? and do you want to try me and see if I am going when your back is turned! You can, dearie—you will find the instrument in action every time— *all* the time—you will find it going right on, all by itself. You are sweeter to me every day, and more of a wonder.

As to Chicago, I dont remember hearing you speak of a cousin there, but from what you say I should think she must be nice. Is it a Todd, or Loomis?† If you feel inclined that way I would advise your going. Certainly theres nothing in the way of expense to deter. One can go from Boston to Duluth and back for forty dollars I am told. It may be a pleasant break and change, and if you think it will, say yes, making the time to your convenience.

The exchange of Savings Bank deposit for Debenture bond can be made at any time. I have sent to the office and find I can get a 7% one, and I will have the deposit here applied on the note too, 1st Jan. . . .

Will send you check first of the week. They all go to Log-

* Mabel's mother had come North and was in Melrose with Grandma Wilder.

† Mabel had had an invitation to visit her Chicago cousin, Lydia Coonley, whom she met for the first time at the Celebrated Women Conference in Washington in March 1888.

town tonight for a Santa Claus performance before the student teachers leave. I shall be here. I shall think of you. If we could only move back and forth like a telegram, would^{nt} we do it! . . .

MABEL TO AUSTIN   [*Boston*] 21 Dec. 1889
Saturday night, 9:30

Just back from a rehearsal of the *Messiah*—it is given in Music Hall tomorrow night, and it will be done superbly. Even the standing-room is taken, & enthusiasm is great. . . .

Your sweet, lovely letter came at breakfast-time today, and has been a thrill of comfort to me ever since. If you *could* know what all such words of yours are to me! I am going to write to the Chicago cousin tonight that I will come in March, perhaps for four weeks. She is a cousin of my father's—very wealthy, and interesting as well. I met her for the first time in Washington a year, or two years, ago, & she took a great fancy to me, as I to her. She is considerably older than I, perhaps forty or forty-five, & has grown sons & daughters. She keeps open house in a royal sort of way, & is said to entertain delightfully. On the whole, & with what you said, I think I'll go, if March is convenient to her. Now I want to say two practical things. Will you please put the rest of the quarter's salary ($175) in the bank for me? If you have not already done so. I have overdrawn startlingly. If possible I would like to have the interest on the mortgage ($112.50) paid from it on Jan. 1st, but if it is, I shall have to draw on the next quarter a little, right after. . . .

Sunday morning

They all went to church, and I here.* I am almost nervous today—so many things depend upon the success of this thing [the solar eclipse] that I find myself almost trembling. It is raining here—but as one lady innocently remarked, "I suppose we

---

* Mabel's mother and grandmother were now boarding with her, in rooms upstairs. Mrs. Loomis had been in Melrose only a week when she telegraphed Mabel: "Engage board for mother & myself in your house today come out & help us into Boston by the first train."

could not tell from our weather anything about the day in Africa!" So I am only waiting, but the morning's *Herald* may have it all. . . .

5:30 p.m., Sunday

I feel unaccountably dragged & worn out & depressed. Have just been to Trinity vespers, & had the felicity of hearing Cotton Smith stand up in that magnificent place & give us from his stores of wisdom & culture, while Mr. Brooks sat by & listened. Faugh! the absurdity! Tonight I sing, & I shall try & rest some tomorrow. I am used up. I want you, & I could cry at a touch. Good night, blessed P.S. 1st owner. P.S. 1st again.

AUSTIN TO MABEL   [*24 December 1889*]
Tuesday afternoon

I have waited in the street as long as I can for a copy of the *Herald*, and get a line into this 4:15 closing mail, but it doesn't yet come. From the *Republican* I judge that the African observations may have been fairly successful. When I go up with this I shall hope to find the *Herald*—and know more.* In this connection Prof. Tyler told me yesterday that D.P. [David] had sent on a request for an extension of his leave of absence till 1st June, practically the year, as he could not get back before that time. Had you heard of it? I am disturbed by your account of yourself. Is it not possible for you down there—free, one would suppose—to be as easy as you please, to avoid tiring yourself to death, and wearing yourself all out? If you wont take any care of yourself on your own account, will you not, on mine!

I am not up to par myself the last few days. Nothing serious. The weather is awful for one thing, and last Saturday and Sunday I missed you more than in many months. More than

---

* Alas, the afternoon of the eclipse was cloudy at the Angola station, and David had to report his expedition a partial failure: his ingenious experiment with a pneumatic photographic process worked fine, but the corona and its spectrum were not visible. David grew very depressed on the homeward voyage.

since your return from Japan. The world seemed very strange and blank and empty. I did^{nt} seem to find you. You seemed to be gone. I am over that a little. As to coming down next Monday, had you rather I would come then than half way between your next visits here. If you had, I think I will.

I send check and receipt for $175. Send the check back to the bank—endorsed in this way other side.

"Pay to the order of the First
National Bank of Amherst
David P Todd
by M.L.T."

Then draw against it as you have occasion.

I think it may be as well to let the interest due at the Savings Bank come out of the next quarter, dont you? That need not be decided now.

I must go up—will send a word tomorrow. Have more to say now, but can't think of anything—and have no more time.

We will find something for me to write my name and 25 Dec. on when I am down.

It is 5 o'c. I have lost the mail and the train. A succession of calls which I could^{nt} throw off. Still this *ought* to reach you in the morning. Sorry, my head aches [from malaria]—but P.S.

MABEL TO AUSTIN   [*Boston*]
                                Thursday morning, 26 Dec. [*1889*]
                                                        P.S. 1st

Your letter came at breakfast, which after so long awaiting it, was welcome, you may be sure. On Tuesday I was morally certain I should hear from you, & was sadly disappointed; but when Christmas Day passed, & no word, I felt deserted & utterly forlorn, for I have been very ill. I am using all my will-power to sit up now & write these few words to you. I suppose I have had—& am having—a form of the common distemper. Back-ache, blinding headache, constant dizziness & vertigo, with a constant cough on the lungs. Also a mental confusion which makes it impossible to do anything, or think clearly. I only know I am exceedingly unhappy, & should be all the time, except as I fill my days too full for any thought. Work is my only salvation, & the first leisure shows me (unpityingly) the horror of my life, which goes on without the slightest interest from the Almighty, a life absolutely deserted by Him and left to swing for itself in space, unhelped & uncared for. Prayers are no more than so much extra breath wasted, or as Emily says, no more than if a bird stamped its foot on the air. I am utterly alone.

I suppose your Christmas day was bright & pleasant; but remember, please, those who made it so have driven me from my home.

I had two or three little presents. I always make a great many and receive none. C. is just turning the corner from a dangerous attack of pneumonia. Sits up half an hour. Today there is an additional complication in my illness—so I cannot sing or even think. I do not understand just why I did not hear from you either on Tuesday or Wednesday. If I can live through this day, I shall never try to acquire any leisure again. It is fatal. Work to the last, breaking point, is all that is left for me.

5

The Publication of Emily Dickinson's Poems

1890–1893

D URING the winter and spring of 1890, Mabel indulged in a constant round of cultural activities among fashionable people in Boston and Chicago. Unusually peripatetic, if not particularly original, she enjoyed associating with the famous and near-famous, and like a pollinating bee spread from place to place some of the new ideas stirring women during the last decade of the nineteenth century. Her experiences in Chicago, particularly, inspired her to bring home to Amherst a dedication to women's causes that she encountered there. While her motives remained largely self-centered, Mabel's compelling social powers and skill at eliciting ardent interest in her enthusiasms promoted her own welfare, and soon proved of enormous importance in launching Emily Dickinson's fame. Her publication of two volumes of Dickinson poems, and the collecting and editing of the poet's extraordinary letters, were at the heart of the next three intensely productive years.

AUSTIN TO MABEL   [*3 January 1890*]

Dear sweet child, woman, my beloved—Spring-time, Summer, Autumn, Winter, Sun, Moon, all in one. Your tender Tuesday night's last word [from Boston], and yesterday afternoon's report of the two days since came this morning, and I wished I could hold you tight to my heart as I read them, and I would like to tell you all I have thought about you since—it would disperse the clouds that the conditions beyond present control favor and create, I am sure—not that they wouldn't return and have to be brushed away again in the same way—but for the time. My last sight of you as that car moved on almost broke my heart.* I know what you are, darling, and what you are to me, and I am a man to take that all into my very marrow— and be purified and ennobled by it. None of your richness and fineness is wasted with me. I appreciate you to the full and admire you accordingly. Remember this and keep up on it till you come up Thursday, and then I will press it into you more deeply with my lips and my voice and all over.

I have got to make this short. I took the hour I would have had with you to take Mr. Mather to drive.† It was so bright and pleasant I asked him and he said yes. That's religion you know. . . .

[Sue, Ned, and Mattie] left this noon for New York— how I wish you could be here and keep house with me. This must go. . . .

* Austin had been in Boston December 30 and 31, which lifted Mabel's spirits. She was still not well, and her mother and grandmother had contracted influenza.

† Friend and neighbor Professor Richard Mather, teacher of Greek and German at the college, was suffering from his final illness.

MABEL TO AUSTIN Sunday afternoon, 5 January [*1890*]

Your beautiful letter has been a Godsend to me. Do burst out in that same again sometime. It does me more than good. I am tired out. They had a nurse for three days who relieved me a great deal, but Friday night she went home, sick, and that was the first day I had even begun to feel a little rested. She has not been back since. It is not only their trays for every meal having to be carried up three flights (and horribly long ones) but a dozen little things beside; because although they try very hard not to make me any extra trouble, people can't be in bed for nearly two weeks without being obliged to have a great deal of running done. Although it is not their fault in the least, I am tired and cross with it all. I went to see [Shakespearean actor E. H.] Sothern Thursday evening, and liked him, though it seemed all a little overdone to me. Friday afternoon, leaving the invalids for an hour or so, I went to a tea at Count Zuboff's, a Russian novelist. Saturday I had a fearful day—which ought to have been a pleasant one. I hunted up blanket wraps for the invalids, then took a vocal lesson, & had to go to the dress maker's. Back just before one, and prepared and carried up their two lunches—arranged them comfortably, & found I had just ten minutes to get dressed for that lunch party on Beacon Street I told you of [at Annie Fields's, wife of late publisher James T. Fields of Ticknor & Fields]. Got over there just *barely* in time to be decent, as it was made for me, and I sat on the hostess' right. It was a very pleasant occasion, but I had to come back & fly upstairs again, & then get the two dinners, & carry up; & then I arranged them for the night, & went to the Symphony concert. My own things, & duties, are now so clear, & so well systematized, that I should be doing things quite to my mind if it were not for this sickness. It is too bad my winter has to be so spoiled, but perhaps they will be up next week sometime. They offered to get another nurse, but I hoped this one would be back today. She did not, however, come. The stairs nearly killed her. This morning, after working steadily for them for just three hours, I went with Mrs. Okie to see [the writer] Norah Perry, and spent a delightful hour or so there. But I am very tired. The Doctor gave me a tonic which made me feel better of that horrid languor—what I have now is mere fatigue. Perhaps this is all religion, too.

I cannot come up Thursday unless the nurse is back, or one of them, at least, is up for all day. However, I shall aim to come, & expect to. I will write to you once more before then. I shall take the early train as usual, & be at Vinnie's about 11:30. I think I will write to you on Wednesday, so you will have it Thursday morning, & then you will know if I am coming. I am asked to take the editorship of one department in the *Home Magazine*, published in Washington.* Shall like to do it if I ever have my time to myself again.

Now it is growing dark, and I must stop. I sent the $112.50 check today, to the Savings Bank. Shall attempt to go to the Handel & Haydn society, if I get the suppers finished in time. I have carried your last lovely letter in my pocket ever since it came, & I have taken snatches at it in the intervals, & read & re-read it, & I shall continue to carry it until you send me another as beautiful. You needn't waste your time in writing to New York. P.S. 1st.

Austin to Mabel   [6 January 1890]
                                    Monday afternoon

I have yours [from Boston] of yesterday. I should think you would be tired out, dearie, in doing all you do, if the sickness were left out. I never heard of such a round except with a belle, at the height of the season, for a few days—but the drain upon you by all the sickness I have no patience with, and positively, my darling, I shall be disagreeable if you dont stop it. If it were really necessary, that would be one thing, but it is not.

---

* In January Mabel had published a piece on the December eclipse expedition in the just-launched *Mrs. Logan's Home Magazine*, a compendium of fiction, biography, and articles on housekeeping, health, education, children, and personal beauty. Mabel's proposal to write book reviews resulted in her contributing a monthly column called "Bright Bits from Bright Books" for a year or more.

Your mother is in receipt of abundant income to take care of herself and her mother, and a surplus. In my opinion she is meanly sordid—and would work the life out of you without a twinge—and without the slightest appreciation either. Some quiet, helpful girl—she need not be a trained nurse—can be had any hour in Boston who will go there and wait on them, and that is all that's needed. Now I wont excuse your doing this any longer. If I have any right to say anything about you, I say this, and I mean every word of it. You are not to run up and down those stairs any more, and to do more of this waiting unless there is a prospect of speedy death of one or the other, and it wont be necessary even then.

Next dont chase so—do no more things than you can do easily and well, and with pleasure. Plan your time so as to get to your different engagements leisurely—there will be nothing left of you by the time you get done, and I might as well be looking elsewhere.

I have had your matter at the bank arranged as we talked and will explain when you are here. Have arranged for a 7% Bond too—$1,000, which I think is better than 3. . . .

MABEL TO AUSTIN   [*10 January 1890*]
                                On the train [to Boston] 2:30, Friday

I judge there was no mail for me, as I did not see, or hear from, you. Mr. Russell [the stationmaster] tells me there is a package for me, which I instructed him to leave at Vinnie's. You can tell if it is anything I ought to have sent to me. At least I shall know about it. Will you send me that check, please. I went to the Bank, & find my balance to be four dollars, & I already owe $60 for board. Probably I had better take $200. Most of it will go for board. It occurred to me to ask you, and then I forgot it (and excuse the childishness of my business questions, please), what is there to show that I have paid $345 on the second mortgage? Is it merely endorsed on the note? And will they give me the note when the 500 is paid?

[3 3 8]

Now, business being over, I have one personal request—
PLEASE don't go [to the depot] to meet the great big black
Mogul.* . . .

Saturday afternoon, 25 Jan. 1890

How dear and sweet your little note was—which reached
me this morning in spite of having been mailed later than usual.
It was the word for which I hungered and thirsted, and when
it came, it filled me. How I regard you only you know fully,
and even you cannot know it all—only God and I.

I have been greatly troubled that an engagement which
should have been fulfilled Tuesday evening was not, neither on
Wednesday, Thursday, nor Friday. But this morning it was
made right.

Our friend F. called on Thursday after I had written my
little word to you.† The call was rather long, and in some respects bright and entertaining, but I did not please myself entirely in it. I have a good deal to say to you; and I think it quite
possible that I may be in Amherst on Wednesday afternoon
next; for I have been invited to read a paper in Springfield
Wednesday morning before a club of ladies, and I may spend
Tuesday night there, attend the meeting, & come up in the

---

* Sue and Mattie were due home from New York next day; Ned had
returned already to resume his duties at the Amherst College Library,
where he had a position managing the checkout desk. Although Mabel
stayed with the Henry Hillses on these 1889–1890 visits to Amherst,
her diary and Austin's both record that they had made love at the
Evergreens during the morning of January 10, before Mabel returned
to Boston.

† General Francis Amasa Walker had become enamored of Mabel, who
dallied at dismissing his attentions too promptly or firmly. Her ap-
peals to womanhood's higher virtues, and Austin's indignation as he
coached her at the same, provide an amusing and ironic commentary
on their own circumstances. Walker, a noted economist, educator, and
public administrator, was president of M.I.T. from 1881 until his
death in 1897.

[3 3 9]

afternoon of Wednesday, using all day Thursday for teaching, and leaving at 8:30 Friday morning. This is a possibility, but I will send you a letter Monday night deciding it.

Sunday morning, 10 o'clock

I took my [china painting] lesson yesterday morning in spite of feeling quite ill, but gave up everything to have a quiet afternoon. It was not very quiet, however, for there were callers from 2:30 until six. . . . In the evening I went to a very fine Symphony concert. I feel better this morning. I want greatly to take the other five china lessons—I have so much to learn about the mechanical use of the various kinds of gold, and so on. This week is to be full to the brim, and if I come to Amherst and Springfield I must give up many things. . . .

AUSTIN TO MABEL   [*26 January 1890*]

Well, really—is Lucy Stone going around lecturing! and have I got involved with one of the strong-minded of the sex! Carrying on a desperate flirtation too at the same time with one of the Beacon lights of Boston! I dont wonder the moon stands still before you—and that you lengthen or shorten the month as you will.

The plot thickens—it is too dense now for writing—only the living voice is adequate.

We will wait for this. Meanwhile dont kill yourself with doing everything, or utterly demoralize your health with hurry and tear. Three hours of the forenoon of a sick day off taking lessons in china painting. Three hours in the afternoon of calls—and a concert in the evening. What ought to be left of you! Nothing.

I am simply steadily at work—and waiting—and hoping, sometimes buoyantly, sometimes feebly, but I am what I am—I can be no other. I love what I love. I can love no other—myself and my love are part of the universal and eternal, for better or worse, for joy or pain—there is the satisfaction of permanency at least. . . .

The Publication of Emily Dickinson's Poems

MABEL TO AUSTIN   [5 February 1890]
                                                   Wednesday, 12:45

Do you know, my dearest, that through every moment of that call [from Francis Walker] just past, your sweet face was visibly before me—your pure, heaven-lighted eyes seemed close by. I do not know as I conducted it all just to please myself. I think I did not, in fact; but I believe there is to be rather a long absence, very soon; and almost immediately after that I go myself, not to be just here again. So I think it is all well enough. . . .

AUSTIN TO MABEL   [7 February 1890]

. . . Mrs. Lawrence, Dwight Hills' friend, died yesterday afternoon.* Grip & pneumonia—took to her bed Monday or Tuesday. Came back from New York after six or seven weeks there with Dwight, last Wednesday week. The mythical Mr. L. is in Toledo—or was, and cannot reach here until late tonight. Mr. Dickerman [the Congregational church minister] is to be away over Sunday, and I am expecting the funeral will not be before Monday. I should not feel that I could run away [to Boston] from it. . . .

MABEL TO AUSTIN   Sunday noon, 9 February '90

. . . I was greatly shocked at Mrs. Lawrence's death. Any woman's dying who is so much to a man seems inexpressibly tragic and fearful. Such a man must be doubly alone after. Oh! it is cruel! It hurts me. . . .

Our friend F. was not at C[aro]'s reception—did I tell you? But he says his wife told him my atmosphere was immeasurably

---

* The Dickinsons' neighbor east of the Homestead was Dwight Hills, half brother of Henry Hills, who at age forty-five was still a bachelor living with his elderly mother. He and the family housekeeper, a Mrs. Lawrence, who was separated from her husband, were secretly in love, providing a situation so poignantly like Austin and Mabel's that there was much unspoken empathy between the two couples.

[341]

removed from all the other people there. She and his daughter were greatly impressed by it. He leaves on Monday, I believe, for Philadelphia. . . .

AUSTIN TO MABEL   [*14 February 1890*]
                              Friday morning, right after breakfast

I am going to make sure that you hear from me tomorrow morning, my darling and my dearie—and O my own, by writing at once—before the calls begin that I cannot escape, for I have very much to say to you. Never more—never so much. If there were not demands upon me which I cannot ignore and be a man, I think I should go back for another talk with you before Monday [when General Walker calls to say goodbye]. I want to help you to put and leave these new matters just right—and yet can I not trust your own intuitions, your own heart, your own pure and high soul? I think you should take the ground that in your womanhood you are anchored safely, securely, happily, permanently, of your own choosing and abiding choice. No matter how, no matter where, that nothing could move you, and an attempt in that direction you could but regard as dishonorable, and dishonoring you. That you understand yourself perfectly, that you cannot be questioned, that you are not at all a prude, but that you are most sensitive to the fine and chaste and sacred honor that resides in a true woman's heart. You might suppose for him a glittering bandit attempting in his absence by every art and wile born of passion and greed to come between him and his best beloved, taking advantage of her human loveliness to try and tempt her from her high devotions to his base embrace. With what brand would he brand the villain, a man conceived an honorable man in such a role! The more I think of it the deeper grows my indignation. This is a great moment for you. It is your opportunity to rise to your best, to stand way beyond reach of profane touch or thought, and you will do it. With all your gentleness—and sweetness and attractiveness and ready sympathy, you have in you the stuff that martyrs are made of. The attempt to further obtrude himself would be an outrage—

and should be repelled as such. A woman in her virtue—and her honor—and her integrity—based on her affection. What else! If she values herself she will protect herself. She can do it, no one else can—a most rare and delicate vase, but ruined by the touch of a careless or rude hand. None so exquisite, none so precious as you, you my own dearest wife, to whom I have given all my confidence, never to other, to whose keeping I have committed myself without reserve, whom I love with a love an angel might envy, with the utmost power of my being, with the noblest of all that is in me. And your love for me, darling, sweet, is my life, the light that shines out from heaven. God is God for what he has given me in you. I say that reverently and sincerely, he must love us. We must trust him. We are only safe so, and at rest.

My heart is brimming, brimming, my Mabel—do you know it, do you feel it? Why can we not join hands now, and walk on and on in that enchanting path we shall sometime reach, that never turns and has no end. Do I love you! Do you love me! What would the birds say!

Dwight Hills sent for me yesterday morning. He was going west at noon, and did^{nt} care where he said. He gave into my care Mrs. L.'s diamonds etc. I told him your message. I will report. Now I must let the world in, but you are in my thought and I am always your own Austin.

Austin evidently handed Mabel the curious, undated letter that follows during his visit to Boston February 11–12. A note at its top in Mabel's hand says, "For me to say in substance to Fr.," but the last part sounds more like a message to Mabel herself.

AUSTIN TO MABEL

The domain of a woman's heart should be entered only with her consent. It is private and sacred ground—the veil which hangs between that and every eye outside is never to be touched. Allowing even an approach to it is sacrilege and unworthy the highest womanhood. In this domain I am filled, satisfied, at rest. Completely. There is in me here no desire, no dream unrealized.

I could not be disturbed. I would not. I am conscious of having done or said nothing to cause or encourage a different thought in you.

I esteem your acquaintance, your friendship. I should be sorry to have it broken. Maintained on the plane of that with Mrs. Palmer, for instance, it would be to me a continuing pleasure.* Anything beyond would be to me but pain, and would endanger all. If you care for the former believe and respect what I say. I speak earnestly, from within myself. It is my own voice—it is not of conventionalism.

You must not question me. You must not write me.

A snake charmer gratifies her sense of power, and passion for admiration by winding a boa constrictor about her body and neck. She does it day after day. She wins money and brilliant applause from the indifferent crowd. But some day the snake, true to his instincts, folds himself more tightly about her, and her exhibition is over.

What is she then?

More than a poor fool who might have known better? Has anyone a good word for her? Has she anything left for herself. Gained the world. But her soul!

MABEL TO AUSTIN   [*Boston, 27 February 1890*]
                                   . . . Thursday, later, 7 p.m.

Well, the little talk is over, and if I may credit what everyone said, was a brilliant success. Not so much as a fan

---

* Mabel had become acquainted through General Walker with Alice Freeman Palmer, recently president and now a trustee of Wellesley College, and member of the state Board of Education. She had left Wellesley in 1887 to marry George Herbert Palmer, Harvard philosopher. Walker was also intimate with the Todds' friend Mrs. Anna Draper of New York.

moved through it all. The drawing-room was full, and every one asked me why I did not talk longer. One said "The wonderful flow of choice language!" Another said "What poetry and imagery!" Another said "The bright points were *so* delicately brought out." Mrs. Sedgwick, whose husband is Professor of Biology at the Technology, said I was the easiest speaker she had ever heard. Another lady said it was by far the most interesting talk she ever heard. Do you mind my telling you all these things? They made me happy. My mother was overjoyed—she is a tremendous critic, & she said I had at last found my genius—she never heard anything so cultivated and ladylike and bright & perfect.*

Tonight I am going to spend the evening with Lucy Larcom. My china has come out beautifully from the firing, and I am going to get off [for Chicago] without much tearing, next week. . . . Another letter from Cape Town tonight.† P.S. 1st.

AUSTIN TO MABEL   [*28 February 1890*]

Your very dear words of Wednesday evening and Thursday I have read, and reread and taken entirely in. I shall want to hear the paper that elicited such encomiums. I dont quite know. I like it, and I dont know as I do. A woman's natural

* This parlor talk on climbing Mt. Fuji, delivered before the pupils and invited guests of Miss Brown and Miss Owen's School on Marlborough Street, initiated Mabel's twenty-three-year vocation in lecturing. Surprised and pleased by an experience so suited to her personality, she wrote in her journal: "It was really the first elaborate one I ever gave, but I knew I could do it more than well. . . . Before [it] I was as quiet and happy as if someone else was to have done it. I had thought out quietly what I wished to say, but I found that dozens of bright things came to me spontaneously which I had not intended— and the flow of words and pictures was smooth and uninterrupted. . . . I am not sure but this sort of thing is to be my specialty."

† David was en route home, but the *Pensacola* was calling at a series of ports, making the return route more leisurely than the outgoing one. Mabel also had a letter from Vinnie this day inquiring what she heard from Colonel Higginson concerning Emily's poems.

place to flower is on the tempting hillside, under the mossy boulders, by a quiet brook, at her own fireside, with her lover-husband. If you were not so thoroughly a woman, of the most womanly type, I should fear much of this experience would make you less of one. Your mother's delight over it, and discovery that you have found your genius at last, is more against it than anything else, her ideas to me being so entirely superficial, and for what seems, rather than for what is. But you can lose a great deal dearie, and still be incomparable. And I dont believe you are going to lose *anything* either. Your mother simply dont know anything about you—any more than a hen does about a duck.

My writing now is simply to say that I need every moment from now till Monday night about Town matters.* They cannot be put off. It is now or never with them. If I get beaten I shall. If I dont I shall feel pretty light! You understand. I love you— you know how much and how well. . . .

Never having fully recovered from influenza, Grandma Wilder now developed pneumonia and delayed Mabel's departure to Chicago by hovering on the brink of death for many days. While detained, Mabel responded to Vinnie's frantic inquiries by calling on Colonel Higginson to discover what was holding up the poems. Higginson's long illness had prevented him from tackling the pile of manuscript, but before much longer he found time to select two hundred of those he thought best, and to classify them by four general themes, and supply some titles. After seeking without success to interest Houghton Mifflin, where he was a reader, he put the manuscript aside again until Mrs. Todd should return from Chicago. Mabel, meanwhile, set off with Millicent on March 12 for the lavish

---

* Monday, March 3, was the annual Town Meeting. Austin, as usual, moderated it, and had a hard fight against a group that wanted to lay out a prominent new road from Main Street north to the cemetery, cutting across the west side of the Evergreens' lawn. Austin lost temporarily, but arranged subsequent meetings that saved his property.

hospitality of her widowed cousin, Lydia Coonley's, household, there to be exposed to constant social activity.

AUSTIN TO MABEL   [*13 March 1890*]
                                                Thursday, 4:00 p.m.

Dearie Dearie—*Dearie*. Tired and driven, but I cannot let this mail go without a word to you. I was dizzy and faint when [your] train [to Chicago] fairly passed from my sight, and thought at first I could not go to the [alumni] dinner. It was too *too* bad, and too hard.

I never loved you so wildly, and so terribly as when I had kissed you goodbye—it was the beginning all over again. We ought to have come together again immediately, and exchanged our thoughts. Just alike of course, but richer by being doubled.

Did^{nt} I think of you all the way along, till long after you were sound asleep, and wish I were with you! And even wish I had made the last break then—and that we had given ourselves up to be whirled anywhere, even into eternity—so we were together. So I have followed you today, and now in the lower part of Michigan. Shall follow you through—and into 391 LaSalle Avenue, and rest easier for your being there. . . .

MABEL TO AUSTIN   [*Chicago*] 19 March [*1890*]
                                              Wednesday morning

I cannot express to you my disappointment when the postman came this morning with no letter for me from you. . . . My mother received hers Saturday afternoon or evening—answered it Sunday. I had it yesterday afternoon. Grandma is the same, weak, white, painless, but liable, the Doctor says, to stop breathing any moment. Last night at a literary society which meets here, Miss J. Ray was present. Her studious and successful avoidance of an introduction savored very strongly of the youngest member of your household—indeed, I am convinced it is to her I owe the singular demonstration. I thought of it at intervals through the night, and I think I should like to have you do something for me. How would it do for you to write a pleasant little note to Mrs. R. (who of course would be highly flattered by it) and say that a friend of yours, —— one of our brightest ladies (!), etc., is to be in the city for a few weeks, and it would be pleasant to you if she should call—at such an address. As if you had just thought of it. I have seen friends of M.'s do so for so many years that I know there is something most effective said to them which does not affect you at all; and I think such a note from you would counteract it, perhaps. . . . I am glad Vinnie will write to my mother. I hope she has already done so. I cannot help feeling as if it was in some degree selfish to come away & leave that sweet, white frail grandma gently breathing her life away. She sent a message to me in my mother's letter, that I was right to come, and she was glad I had the change and rest. But I am not at all times quite comfortable with myself. I only hope she will live until I get back. . . . What I have asked you to do with reference to that lady seems to me a very natural and proper thing, as I think of it more, and I wish you would do it. There are times when I wake suddenly, and feel that I *cannot* endure the injustice and cruelty which are upon me. The world would be so beautiful & so interesting without it. If it were not for you & my fast hold upon your splendid love, I think I should be frantic. I am not lighthearted here, as I have been, in the main, for five or six months, and yet the friends are never-ceasing in their kindness. . . .

AUSTIN TO MABEL   [22 *March 1890*]
                                   Saturday afternoon

. . . I dont quite account for your being so blue out there [in Chicago]—with almost everything pleasant about you. You cannot but be affected by your grandmother's condition—you wouldn^{nt} be human otherwise—and as for Miss J. Ray, she cannot be all Chicago, or any very considerable part, and one thing is certain if she offers you any—the slightest indignity—she shall never enter my house again. I am very sure that Mattie has^nt the remotest idea where you are or that you ever thought of going there. The *Amherst Record* the day you left announced the fact that you had been in town a day or two but left for Washington. I dont believe, on second thought, you would think it wise for me to write Mrs. Ray, whom I have never, so far as I can recollect, met but once—it would seem such a very strange and unnatural and forced proceeding, and be the opportunity for making the most unpleasant talk. I think it would result in annoyance to you and embarrassment—and that you will see it in this way on reflection. I have made up my mind, my darling, that if it is in my power you shall be treated well when you come back here, and that I will break absolutely with anyone doing otherwise. Am I not right in my view—do you not think so? It is not cowardice, dearie. A man who would die for another, or with another, is not a coward, and you know I would do either for you—and find sweet pleasure in it. I am afraid some of the things you suggest would react, and hurt you. . . .

[*24 March 1890*]
Monday afternoon, 24th

. . . It is a bright March day. There is Spring in the air— and that means you. [Yesterday] I read again your letter received Saturday and then started afoot and alone across the lots for Wildwood, roaming over the east side hill, surveying every rock—for the sweetest, daintiest spot for two wild lovers to sometime lie together, with one stone at their heads, which shall say to the careless and to the thoughtful passersby, They loved with a love stronger than death—and beyond the love of earth.

MABEL TO AUSTIN   [*Chicago*] 30 March [*1890*]
Sunday afternoon

I fear me greatly there will be no chance for me to run out with this myself, today—for there are four boys haunting all parts of the house, & all very eager to do for me. But I am going out alone tomorrow morning at nine o'clock, so I am going to take it then, and run the risk of disappointing you, my own love, by a few hours. . . .

We had a very attractive evening here on Friday. Mrs. Sara Hubbard was invited to give one of her talks on birds here in the drawing-room, and about sixty friends to listen were present. I sang after. It was a charming paper—one of the very best of the dozens I have heard since I came to this "centre of western civilization," as my dear heart puts it. . . .

The love of Abelard and Héloise is as nothing compared to ours, for while Héloise loved with a more than human devotion and loyalty, Abelard was a coldly selfish nature who received all and gave little back. I cannot read of him with patience. Héloise writes to him these wonderful words, "Should Augustus, master of the world, offer me his hand in marriage, and secure to me the uninterrupted command of the universe, I should deem it at once more eligible and more honorable to be called the mistress of Abelard than the wife of Caesar." Do you know any parallel to words like those?

I am somewhat better of the headaches which so beset my first two weeks here, but I have a touch of pain every day. It is a dull, sick ache, low down in the back of my head, and takes the edge off of everything. But I think it is getting less. Many things are planned in the future for me—an elaborate musical "to meet" me, German opera, Von Bülow's concerts, drives all over the city, a trip to Winnetka this week Thursday, a "paper" here by Professor Davidson, a reception here next Friday for Elsie Leslie*—by the way, she is coming here to tea tonight— and no end of other things. . . .

[*Chicago*] 1 April [*1890*]
Tuesday evening, 11 o'clock

. . . A letter from St. Helena yesterday puts the date of [David's] return about June 5—arrival to be immediately fol-

---

* A young actress appearing in *The Prince and the Pauper*, which Mabel saw when she first arrived.

lowed by a short trip to Washington for settlement of business. That does not seem to indicate any quiet settling down much before Commencement, does it? . . .

AUSTIN TO MABEL   [*5 April 1890*]
                                            Saturday afternoon

. . . Now about the expedition. That *does* seem to be an independent state of mind. Not till June—this gives rise to some suggestions. Certainly DP should be settled here, and to appearance adjusted in this latitude, before Commencement. There is much to be considered about the College then. [Professor] Mather is out, [Professor] Henshaw will be out. [President] Seelye undoubtedly, quite likely [Professor] Montague, and quite likely [Professor] Wood and [Professor] Tuttle. One or two more could go to advantage. Some important committee will be appointed to look over the ground and report. I want they should find those I am interested in on hand and in good working order.* . . .

MABEL TO AUSTIN   [*Chicago*] 9 April [*1890*]
                                            Wednesday morning

Your dear letter came this morning. It was pleasant to know that you had my two on Monday. I fear you will be looking for another today or tomorrow—and I am sure I do not know why I did not send one on Monday. I had a sort of vague idea that Wednesday was my day to send you one; so it goes. I shall take it to the office myself in a few moments, and you will have it Friday.

I am not in a serene state of mind, for I am absolutely rebellious, and the state of things which I am to come back to

---

* Austin was aware that President Julius Seelye's deteriorating health would probably prompt his resignation that commencement, as in fact happened. During the last months of Seelye's tenure, Austin had assumed many of Seelye's responsibilities, largely holding the reins of power in that institution, just as he did in the town government.

seems more impossible than ever. Never to go through the street except as shrinking from a blow! It is too hard, & too unjust & cruel.

But that same coming back means seeing you, too—the one reality in my mind and heart—the one central, absorbing allegiance. Oh! yes, I belong to you, that is for always, but I need you every moment. Oh! if I might never again see any one of the three who are my evil geniuses! The three only ones in the earth who hate me so blackly! I cannot live under it many years more. Think how patient I have been, how truly gentle, under it all! Everybody says a long road must turn, but eight long years out of the sweetest & freshest part of my life seem rather too many to waste in such an unequal contest. And if things ever do straighten out, I shall have lost all my first bloom and sparkle. I fear I must join the everlasting ranks of what I so abominate—the middle-aged woman.

I sent a letter to Josiah telling him to get back as soon as possible. He will get it, I suppose, in about a month. We returned the Rays' call Monday evening, & had a pleasant call. The oldest daughter is very agreeable. I shall tell you my impressions of it all when I come. I took her, the eldest, to the matinee, last Saturday, to see *Romeo and Juliet*. On Friday of this week, the evening of the day you will read this, my cousin gives a reception & musicale in my honor. I am going to wear the white flowing Greco-Japanese dress which I invented. You must think of me every moment. Of course you were alone on Sunday when you drove? Did you fill the seat beside you with me? . . .

I suppose two of my persecutors return [from New York] by today. I am sorry for you, but (I fear) even more for myself, since mine is the worst, & most successful mauling. P.S. 1st.

AUSTIN TO MABEL   11 April '90
                                                Friday evening

Your Wednesday's note came this morning, dearie. So glad it was no worse—that you only forgot me. So glad too that even "a vague idea" that you sometimes wrote me on Wednesday flitted long enough before your mental vision to determine you to do it then if never again. Perhaps it was the accident policy that suggested it to you. *Any*how, *some*thing did, and was the means of relieving me of real anxiety. I had conjured to myself all sorts of direful things that might have happened to interrupt what I had come to consider my regular mail, and I was just miserable over it. So I wrote you as I did yesterday afternoon— a very babyish letter, as it seems to me now. A sort that will not be repeated. I shall expect something hereafter when I get it— it will be a surprise every time—probably that is better. It will avoid the danger of our getting humdrum, and writing a bore, from the feeling that it must be done, whether or no. Write in the future, sweet, whenever you happen to think of it and feel like it. I would have had you do that always.*

I have sent check to Accident Ins. Co. and asked them to send me bill for keeping [David's] policy, including right to travel, two months more, in force, or to mid-June. That will cover the extremest absence unless what an Insurance Company never expects should happen.

I am greatly pained that you feel as you do about coming back here, and cannot understand, in your present surroundings, how you have wrought yourself, or overwrought, to such a pitch of apprehension and dread. I am not myself sanguine any more. It is my natural temperament, but I have been too much chastened, and yet I feel hopeful, and quite confident that you will find much less to trouble you in the next years than in the last year and a half. I propose to make the talk I have mentioned to you and to make it effective—if it is within any power I possess. I can promise you, further, that if ever you *should* enter "the ranks you so greatly abominate" "of middle-aged women"—I confess I am not clear what you mean by the term— or ever turn hag, you can be sure of one man who will go with

---

* Always wounded by Austin's wit, Mabel responded to these caustic remarks in her next letter: "Don't you think you were rather too bad, my dearest, to try to be sarcastic to this one? . . . I shall keep this letter of yours within instant reach to show you when I get home— and see if you can really believe you could have been so brilliantly & stingingly sarcastic as your words seem to imply."

you even to the uttermost part of the earth and find his chiefest delight in serving you—or in any way ministering to you—in the hope of sometime throwing a ray of pleasure across your path, to be near all that remains of all the heaven he ever knew. I do not myself think love or loveliness confined to the teens and the first decade after—I suppose I have passed long ago all the bounds known to that kind of reckoning—but I know my soul never burned with a larger, purer flame than now, and never did the possibilities, the opportunities impress me so much. You are not the kind to grow old, youth with you is immortal. You are a splendid woman—you dont half understand and appreciate your power and your qualities, as compared with other women. It is so native to you to be charming, fascinating, satisfying you think nothing of it, and do yourself the greatest injustice and harm by your underestimate. Try, try, to realize more that you are an absolute entity, all by yourself, and that you should not be thrown out of gear with all the universe by a few petty creatures whose horizon extends not beyond the end of the nose.

You seem to be going it in Chicago as in Boston, if anything more so, with perhaps the man element eliminated. The Ibsen readings I am interested in. I suppose these are what raised such a row in Washington society. I take it the means are not wholly conventional. As to the Rays the elder daughter is an intelligent and cultivated woman. The younger looks worlds, but I never heard her say anything beyond a little pertness.

I am thinking of you in the Greco-Japanese gown, while I write, and should like to take it off for you by & by. . . .

[*At the Parker House, Boston*]
16 April 1890
Afternoon—late

I only came in this noon, my darling. Was detained by a summons as witness in the Buntly will case at Northampton

Tuesday—greatly to my annoyance, and in Mr. Mather's condition. Should not have left today except to get hold of your letter which was handed to me as I registered—and with which I made straight for my room. I shall be ready to meet the one it was in part reply to whenever you throw down the gauntlet, as for theater. You caught the paint, but hardly scented the humor in the atmosphere surrounding—we have noticed a little lack in that particular sometimes you know. It is hard always to resist, and yet I am not free from a shadow of regret when I have said anything I did not quite mean to you, or have ever suggested to you that I had something in my mind which was not there. But you give me such a tempting opportunity. . . .

I must tell you—on this sixtieth [*sic*] anniversary of my appearance among the sons of man—that you are my love, that I love you with a wild, passionate love, with all the love there is in love—the finest, the tenderest, the sweetest, the highest, the greatest, the most dependent, with all my heart, and soul, and mind and strength. That I learned my love from you and through you—or rather perhaps that you discovered it—developed it, purified it. That except for you I should not have known that in all creation there was anything to answer to the vague but everlasting craving of my heart. That in you in our eight years of closest intimacy, in which we have penetrated the most veiled recesses, each of the other—always with delight—I have found you only fresher, more charming every day—ever new. . . .

Thursday afternoon, 2 o'clock. I have just come in from my morning rounds and find your supplementary birthday letter, sweet as you are, sweeter than anything else, and daintier. A letter from Amherst and a telegram announcing Mr. Mather's death—and Mrs. Mather's wish that I should return at 3. It is too late for that—and too bad. I cannot get there till 7:30. That tragedy then is over, or part of it.

I dined at the Sanfords' as I wrote I should, and John asked me some questions when we were by ourselves, about him you speak of as our Boston friend, and told me some things that had been said to him which will surprise and startle you. Nothing in connection with you—but enough of an established reputation to show that you were moving on dangerous ground. I will tell you, but will not write it. You will thank me when you see me for insisting on all I said in the line of hands off—and only wish I had resisted him as I should, with authority, if I had known what I now know. . . .

MABEL TO AUSTIN   [*Chicago*] 20 April '90
                                        Sunday afternoon

I have been chiefly engaged, since dinner, in writing congratulations for weddings, two of which take place on Wednesday next. . . . I feel my power to do and to be with a perfectly overwhelming rush at times. You are right—I do not quite estimate myself sufficiently. An absolute simplicity in my way of taking myself and life has always been my mistake. I regard myself as a matter of course, whereas I seldom meet anyone who fills my idea of anything strong or fine really, or who is fitted to overmaster me. But I lose sight of that a great deal. I do not believe *a great deal* of appreciation expressed, even flattery, would harm me. I think I need it.

I sent you a letter yesterday. I suppose Mr. Mather was buried either yesterday or today—and I am immensely sorry he died. I suppose nobody in the town could be born or married or buried, or make an investment, or buy a house-lot, or a cemetery-lot, or sell a newspaper, or build a house, or choose a profession, without you close at hand. You dear, helpful, strong friend! And *I* am in your heart—alone—*your* help and *your* comfort and *your* joy! . . .

I suppose my grandmother was either moved to Lynn yesterday, or will be this week. Probably my mother has answered Vinnie's letter by this time telling her of it.

On Tuesday Mrs. Ray is to have a luncheon party of about forty ladies *for me*, and I am asked to talk afterward, informally, about Japan.

I suppose moths are running riot in my house, in portieres,

blankets, & clothes. But I cannot help it. Is it time to make those strawberry and asparagus beds? And just as soon as I get back I must have the house painted. I should be glad if you would ask Mr. Thomas how much he will paint it for. Not the second story nor the roof, but the lower part, and wherever the dark green occurs.

Oh! I know so well just how the sunshine would lie over the Pelham hills this radiant afternoon! How I wish I were sitting with you, up in the little gable porch, hearing your beloved voice, and watching the oncoming of spring's glory! . . .

Mrs. Chant speaks in the parlor here, this evening.* . . . Besides all these daily outside things, I am keeping up my regular work in writing. Read a lot of proof this morning. . . .

Tell me dear, *were* you alone last Sunday, on your first spring drive? Of course you were, but I want to have you say so. Don't laugh. . . .

AUSTIN TO MABEL   [*25 April 1890*]
                                            Friday afternoon, 25th

Your Wednesday's letter came this morning—number 18—but numbered 19, and half takes my breath. So you are really coming back, and on a day certain—and water and gas are to go on, storm porches cleared away, girl brought in, and so on. Well, all right, I will see to the various things—only I shall let the storm porches alone till you are here—on the score of protection, privacy etc. You will agree to this on second thought. It is better that the hum & buzz should commence when notice can be no longer avoided. About your engagement for the 12th. I suppose you reckon on a previous one, just before, and do you know that I have thought a great deal about

---

* Perhaps the most impressive woman Mabel met in Chicago was Mrs. Laura Ormiston Chant, a missionary, who stayed at Mrs. Coonley's while preaching magnetically in church on behalf of the poor and ignorant, and who moved Mabel most by her sympathy toward the unwed mothers in the Chicago Erring Women's Home.

one just after the 12ᵗʰ, for the "experiment." Had you? And is any time to compare likely to offer this side Heaven—that is the day when intervention, between us, of any sort, is no longer possible, and we are together close forever. . . .

Yes, I want you, and yes I know what wonderful words I have been sending you in this absence, and I have meant them all, and if there [are] any stronger words or more intense combinations, then those are mine too. Nothing can reach the measure of my love for you. You absorb me completely, you are a most wonderful woman and my mate. Just.

I dont know what you mean about "the poems" and their possibly delaying you somewhere. That is of no consequence.*

Hasn't the Ray business come out to your satisfaction? And isn't it better to have run clear in its own way, than to have seemed to be forced by me? . . .

My ride into Leverett & Shutesbury last Sunday afternoon was by myself, of course, as well as my only other ride, a fortnight before. No one has your seat, or ever will have. I ride with but one—you, and I love you.

You ask if it is not time the asparagus bed was made. She is all made, the strawberry bed too, and the yellow lilies are in, and I have sent to Boston for some red peonies, failing to find any about here. I love you. . . .

MABEL TO AUSTIN   [*Chicago*] 5 May [*1890*]
                                            Monday afternoon

. . . I have heard nothing from the Expedition yet—and do not expect anything very much. They are undoubtedly now at Barbados; and after that I do not know.

My Saturday night talk on Japan was eminently success-

---

* Austin still did not attach much importance to the publication of his sister's poems. Here he dismissed Mabel's mention of her need to see Colonel Higginson about them as soon as she got home and settled.

ful.* One very cultivated lady, whom I have greatly admired, said it was the most artistic thing she had ever heard!

This one begins to feel herself more than she used to. I do not mean her consequence, but she feels her ground, & knows her power a little. I have much to say to you about that. . . .

[Chicago] 8 May *[1890]*
Thursday morning

I debated a long time after the letters from Ascension came yesterday morning, before I decided to defer the date of my coming for a few days. If it had not been for your sweet and generous letter in which you said I had better stay over this Sunday if for any reason it seemed best, I should not have done it. But most unexpectedly to me, the letters did come yesterday morning, after my packing was nearly all done, & after my berth was engaged for this morning. In the letters the date of arrival was put farther on in June. The first one said as they could get no coal in Ascension they would have to sail to Barbados and the winds were very light, but they hoped the tenth or fifteenth of June would find them at New York. Another letter written a few days later, but sent in the same mail, seemed to indicate that the Ascension work was getting on well, but still that the 5th of June was the earliest at which they could get back. So as I say I sat & thought.† . . .

I think you would call it even touching, the way I seem to

---

* This was the third of four drawing-room talks on Japan which Mabel gave during her Chicago visit.

† The letters from David, which marveled at Mabel's successes in his absence, reported his own depression of spirits after the failed eclipse: "I feel mentally just as I should physically if I had been slugged with a sandbag. . . . I realize my own insignificance in the play of your life, and think I could not do you a greater service than by going off again some time; though I don't think I shall ever again be unselfish enough to do that."

be loved and admired out here. There are many ladies into whose eyes tears came when they said goodbye to me because, they told me, I had been so much to them here, and they *couldn't* lose sight of me. My cousin, who I feel sure had been rather studying me all these weeks, & while phenomenally generous & lovely to me, was, in her own judicial way making up her mind about me, suddenly turned to me, about a week ago, in the carriage one morning, & took hold of my hand, and said something which made the crown of my visit—to the effect that while she had decided that I was the brightest & most versatile woman she ever knew, I was with it so strong & sweet & companionable that I was one of the only three or four she had ever known with whom she would love best to live always, & be with all her life. You could not know this unless I told you, so I know you will forgive me for repeating such a thing. For you must know everything both for and against this one. . . .

AUSTIN TO MABEL   [*10 May 1890*]
                                Saturday afternoon, 10ᵗʰ

Your long, sweet, very dear and just like you letter of Thursday was in my hands at 9 o'clock. . . .

Your staying was all right, from every point of view— clearly from the Chicago point, and as well from this, for I believe I was never called so many ways at once as the last few days. I am hoping and expecting to be less bothered after I get back from Boston Tuesday night. Shall go down Monday morning, and begin with reading what you are writing me this afternoon.

It seems then that I am not wholly peculiar in thinking you entirely exceptional among women. I am half sorry—I dont ever quite want to share my admiration for you with any other. It seems as if they had got a little bit of you which belongs to me, but that is selfish—and only means that I love you desperately, as you know. If a majority, a respectable minority, of women were of your style and make, this earth would be an enchanted land, and man would be a new creature.

I have told you always that one of the greatest things I ever said to you is that I appreciate you—perhaps you are beginning to think that means more than you have—and perhaps too you still think that no one else appreciates you so wholly, and so finely, as this strange lover. . . .*

Mabel and Millicent returned to Amherst May 15 to find Austin waiting at the Dell's fireside and Maggie Maher from the Homestead in the basement cooking supper. Eight days later, David and Eben Loomis arrived home, and all the order and control of her life that Mabel had experienced for six months turned topsy-turvy as she was once more caught up in her husband's whirl.

At the end of May, Mabel saw Thomas Wentworth Higginson in Boston, approved the two hundred poems he had selected, winced at most of his titles, but carried the manuscript herself to Roberts Brothers to see if Thomas Niles, who once had published Emily's poem "Success" in *A Masque of Poets*, and had corresponded with her thereafter, would publish it. Niles turned to the poet Arlo Bates, one of the readers for his publishing house, and on the basis of Bates's conclusion that, despite "colossal faults," about half the poems displayed sufficient genius to publish, Roberts Brothers offered in mid-June to publish a small edition of five hundred copies if Vinnie Dickinson would pay for the plates. Should the book go into a second printing, Vinnie would begin to receive a 15 percent

---

* Mabel's cup must have been brimming, for David, too, in his second letter from Barbados, had penned his appreciation of her: "I have yet to see one that I can compare with *you*, darling; and I am indeed prouder of you than I can write. And, if my life is the success I hope it may yet be, I shall not rest till my ambition is gratified by seeing you in the highest degree honored & appreciated for your full worth. . . . My advancements and the little successes of my life so far have all come of you. Eleven years more will, I venture, see us more thoroughly in love than now. . . ."

royalty. Both Higginson and Mabel were disappointed that Bates criticized Dickinson's "extraordinary crudity of workmanship" so severely as to eliminate many of their favorite poems, and Mabel promptly reinstated about fifteen she felt were too good to leave out. Vinnie, Mabel said, was "inarticulate with rage," both at the faintheartedness of Niles and the criticism of Emily by Mr. Bates.

David Todd later claimed that Niles at first proposed a hectograph edition of five hundred copies and that he, David, called on him in indignation to say the poems would be properly printed or not appear at all. Since Mabel's diary and David's correspondence clearly place him in New York or Washington most of June and July 1890, and he did not visit Boston until after publication of the poems in November, the veracity of his story is questionable. Vinnie agreed, finally, to pay for the plates, Higginson began writing a preface to the poems and also an article for *Century* to stir interest in the book, and the 116 poems went to the printer. Mabel had the first proof in her hands by the end of July, and not long after she gave Niles the little painting of Indian pipe she had painted for Emily in 1882, to be used for the cover design.

Two incidents in July involved Sue, who still had no inkling the poems were to be published. Consulting no one, she sent off to *Scribner's* Emily's poem "There came a Day at Summer's full," of which she had her own copy. When the poem appeared in the magazine's August issue it contained a mistake, for Sue had misread the line "As if no soul the solstice passed" to be "As if no *sail* the solstice passed." That error, and the unexpected need to get *Scribner's* permission to include the poem in the forthcoming volume, annoyed Mabel, but Vinnie was upset that Sue had ignored her (Vinnie's) ownership of the poems and, in addition, had kept the $15 fee *Scribner's* paid. Vinnie was too intimidated by Sue to complain directly, but her aroused fears concerning Sue led her to commit what Mabel labeled a "treachery." She wrote Higginson in mid-

July asking that Mabel's name be kept off the book and her role in editing remain *sub rosa*. Alas for Vinnie, Higginson was unable to decipher the handwriting in the key sentence, so he routed the letter to Mabel for interpretation. After learning what was afoot, Higginson dismissed Vinnie's request lightly, placed Mabel's name with his own on the title page, and began to shake his head over the difficulties of "steering safely among Dickinsons."

The second part of the summer and the leisurely autumn of 1890, which Mabel called "one of the pleasantest I have passed here in seven or eight years," went by with unusual harmony. David, Mabel, Austin, and even Vinnie spent many delightful hours together in August. Merrill E. Gates was elected the new president of Amherst College during the fall, and the Todds were caught up in the welcome extended him, Mabel throwing her energies into decorating Walker Hall for an inaugural reception at the end of October.

Higginson's article on Emily Dickinson, entitled "An Open Portfolio," appeared not in *Century* but in the *Christian Union* on September 25. He introduced the poet through his own correspondence and two meetings with her, attempted to justify the unconventionalities of her verses by emphasizing her startling originality of perception, and quoted selections from the book. Austin wrote Higginson: "I do not see how she could have been brought before the world, if she were to be brought at all, more aptly and more favorably. . . . Whether it was, on the whole, advisable to publish is yet with me, a question, but my sister Vin, whose knowledge of what is, or has been, outside her dooryard is bounded by the number of her callers, who had no comprehension of her sister, yet believed her a shining genius, was determined to have some of her writing where it could be read of all men, and she is expecting to become famous herself thereby, and now we shall see."

Having been thus assisted into the world, it is debatable whether the little boxed white 5" × 7" volume with its innocent gold and silver stamping would have survived without further help the chastisements that greeted its appearance on November 12. Most reviewers shared the reaction of Eben Loomis, who wrote Mabel on the sixteenth: "The book is dainty beyond description, but in reading the poems I am mad (in country vernacular) all of the time. Why didn't she pay some attention to rhythm & rhyme? The thoughts are too strong and beautiful to be wasted, and half of their beauty is concealed, and to the majority of readers will be forever, under the rough exterior."

New England and New York periodicals began to carry reports of the book, including a guardedly admiring one by Arlo Bates in the Boston *Courier*, in late November. The most positive and influential critique, however, was William Dean Howells's in the January 1891 issue of *Harper's*. He wrote: "If nothing else had come out of our life but this strange poetry we should feel that in the work of Emily Dickinson America, or New England, rather, had made a distinctive addition to the literature of the world, and could not be left out of any record of it." Unlike critics who complained that the poet had never learned her art, Howells suggested her roughness of style was both purposeful and masterly. His consistent, sympathetic praise was directly attributable to Mabel Todd, who had met Howells when her mother and grandmother moved into his boardinghouse in Lynn early in the summer of 1890. Specific mention of two evenings spent with Mr. and Mrs. Howells occurs in Mabel's diary, and they may have heard her talk on Japan in their parlor one August evening. The Howellses came to dote on Millicent, who spent that summer with her grandmother, for they had just lost a ten-year-old daughter. Mabel found Howells "a dear, genial, warm hearted, helpful man," and seized the chance to promote the Dickinson poems and other literary projects of her own. Howells submitted the proof of his Dickinson review to Mabel in October. In addition, she busied herself reviewing the new book for *Home Magazine*, helping David and her father write reviews, and encouraging various publications she was associated with to give the little volume serious attention.

Despite mixed critical reaction, Dickinson's poems struck sensitive readers, particularly women and clergymen, with great force. Interest was so strong and the admiration of individual readers so compelling that the first edition sold out very quickly. Roberts Brothers produced a second printing in mid-December, a third by the end of the month, and a fourth in January. Two more occurred before March 1891, by which time Colonel Higginson and Mabel, with Thomas Niles's approval, were already planning a second volume of poems. By then, too, Niles had generously repaid Vinnie the cost of the plates, and would assume the cost of plates for all future volumes. Sue Dickinson first learned Emily's poems were being published when she read Higginson's article in the *Christian Union* in September 1890, and had not spoken to Vinnie since. Sue wrote Higginson and told many in town that she had intended to publish the poems herself, privately, and insinuated that Vinnie had been devious in pursuing the project without her knowledge (Mabel's role she never spoke of). Sue also claimed, mistakenly, that the hundreds of copies of poems Emily had given her over the years were hers to publish if she liked. For once Vinnie was too elated to care what Sue said, for her dearest wish at last had been gratified, and in addition, she was reaping the attention and approbation of the world.

Austin to Mabel   [*21 November 1890*]

My very dearling

It is 5 o'clock—and past. I have been on the wing every minute. . . . I had a stroll this noon first with Madam Stearns and Miss Glezen, then with Madam Cooper, the latter rather disposed to talk of the *Poems* and I set forth your part in them with what seemed to me good judgement. Jim Cooper made a long call on Vin last night to tell her how great he thought they were and how much he admired them, said that his family had bought four copies of them. Vin thinks it is all right—it is just what she expected. She is thinking some of giving public readings from them, a little later. . . .

MABEL TO AUSTIN   [*Boston, 24 November 1890*]
                                   Monday, 1:30 p.m.

Your little note was found in the office this morning. It has brightened my day, and made life seem worth living.

The lecture was a grand success in every way yesterday. A great many interesting people here—about a hundred.* I send you Arlo Bates' *critique* on the *Poems*. Save it for me—& show it to Vinnie if you want to. Mrs. Louise Chandler Moulton's article upon them in the *Herald* today, goes to Vinnie. I had a long talk about them with Arlo Bates at the Mixters' the other night—& with Mr. Howells yesterday. They are making a great stir in literary circles. . . .

                                   3 Feb. [*1891*]
                                   Tuesday, 9 a.m.

A dismal rain, just freezing enough to make the cleared sidewalks treacherous beyond expression. I went down once, on my wrist. The great big black Mogul is parading on foot through the town, but that is not the kind that fall. The face was bitterly black. I never saw it so implacable.

I had a very pleasant day yesterday. There were thirteen [callers] here, comfortably distributed over several hours. I found that snake among some of my papers. I will tell you about

---

* The Todds were staying with the Andrewses, where David gave a morning lecture on his African expedition in Caro's parlor.

it [when you return from New York]—but it was in a little collection which had never been examined or copied.* . . .

Little more correspondence occurred until late summer, when David, Millicent, and Mabel visited Lydia Coonley at her summer home in western New York State, but the spring and early summer of 1891 were occupied by transcribing the remaining uncopied poems and readying 166 poems for the second volume, to be published in the fall. Mabel and Vinnie were both thoroughly enjoying the stir over the poetry. The two consulted nearly every day, and shared the back-and-forth with Higginson and Niles. As with the first book, Mabel and Colonel Higginson made changes in Dickinson's lines to accommodate public taste, but they were more restrained now that the public's ear was tuned. Poems that Mabel sent *St. Nicholas*, *The Independent*, *Youth's Companion*, and other periodicals were accepted readily, and Vinnie reaped from magazine fees and royalties the first income of her life. Mabel, meanwhile, responded to two requests to speak on Emily. She talked first in April to the Springfield Women's Club, noting the event as "a remarkable success, and very 'taking' subject." In early May she spoke to the College Alumni Club of Boston, attracting two hundred listeners, including Austin and several newspaper critics. Following Mabel on the program was Colonel Higginson, who read from Emily's letters to him. Mabel had begun to charge ten dollars plus expenses for her talks, and was earning other income from her monthly book column for *Home Magazine*, books she reviewed regularly for *The Nation*, a story on witches in January's *New England Magazine*, and the

---

* She had located, among the loose poems she was still transcribing, "A narrow Fellow in the Grass," Emily's snake poem, which had appeared twenty-five years earlier in the *Springfield Republican*. It was included in the second volume.

painting and piano pupils she still taught. She now also was copying for Austin, *sub rosa*, the minutes of the Amherst College trustee meetings, which made her privy to the confidential matters of the Gates administration.

On the darker side of life, Mabel attempted to cheer her parents, who were living separate lives. Upon his return from Africa, Eben had hoped to become the paid director of a cultural club evolving in Lynn, but nothing came of it, so he returned to his post at the Nautical Almanac Office, plagued by kidney problems and deeply embarrassed by publicity over a diamond he had been given at the Kimberley Mines, which the Navy claimed was expedition property. Molly Loomis, who would neither leave her mother nor take her to Washington, stayed on in New England, lonely and sorrowful. Mabel was servantless through the spring and summer. But for the services of Maggie Maher, spared from the Homestead on a daily basis for several months, she would not have been able to work on the poems, and as it was, she felt rebellious about any housekeeping chores that fell to her. Furthermore, Sue was being difficult, and had submitted two more of Emily's poems to a periodical, this time *The Independent*, whose editor got as confused as Higginson trying to steer among Sue, Vinnie, and Mabel. Sue again kept the fees, so riling Vinnie that at last Austin was pushed to step in more firmly with his wife.

Late in July, while she waited for proof, Mabel worked on the preface to *Poems, Second Series*, and with David's help compiled in a little leather-bound notebook an indexed listing by first line of all the remaining unpublished poems and scraps of poems, which were finally copied and would provide the contents for the "ten more volumes" Mabel and Vinnie anticipated. Decades later this list was a vital key to reestablishing the order and contents of the Dickinson fascicles. The notebook listed nearly a thousand poems.

Although August, with Sue away, was pleasant as ever, and Mabel enjoyed long carriage rides with Austin and several nights at the Evergreens, she also worked hard on proof through the month, and was tired enough at its end to be glad of the trip to Cousin Lydia's "Hillside" in Wyoming, New York, in early September, just as Sue got back to town.

AUSTIN TO MABEL   [*4 September 1891*]
                                   Friday morning, 10 a.m.

No, I can't get on without you. The rest may go, but not you, and a day by myself makes it all very vivid to me.

I came back [from taking Mabel to the train] by the same old road, for I seemed nearer to you that way, and took it leisurely, bathing in the warm sun and the humming roadsides and the wide stretch of meadow and the mountains beyond, mingled with all sorts of sweet thoughts of you.

It is clearly all right. We are not mistaken. Called at the Seelyes' that evening, as I said. Yesterday divided between my desk and the Street, about as usual. Ned arrived at half past two and the others just before 9 in the evening.

So far the status has been maintained as I would have it, with what is in my purpose. I am thought to be looking exceedingly well, and as if August agreed with me, trying as it is to the average person. August really is a favorite month with me. I wish it might run on into eternity. . . .

MABEL TO AUSTIN   Wyoming, 5 Sept. '91
                                   Saturday morning

I am getting rested—the country is lovely, the household attractive, the house immense and comfortable, the life sweet and cheerful. . . . Last week the family numbered 38! This week we are *only* between twenty-five and thirty! And all are mothers or aunts, or daughters or sons and their children. The great hall, running straight through the house from the front door, is 78 feet long. This colossal scale rather staggers me, but I like it, from its great difference. . . .

It was best for me to come, & do just this. I am more tired

than I knew, and they speak of my looking so much thinner than usual. That was a curious little thing I began to have the day I left, and it continued somewhat until yesterday.* . . .

[*Wyoming, N.Y.*] 8 Sept. '91
Tues., 4 p.m.

. . . I had your yesterday's note. It is very dear and sweet, and I know all between its lines. At the same time came some proof, which I have just finished comparing.† On Sunday evening I gave a little talk on Emily, and read my article about her, by urgent request, here in the parlor. Our family numbered about 25, among them a New York physician of much note, and an Indiana editor and politician.‡ They were all deeply interested. On Thursday night they want me to give a Japan talk to the town for the benefit of something, and to sing.

I am not very well. I wake up with a headache, and besides, I do not think I am all right in every way. But I hope I shall gain much from being here. The bell rings & I must go. P.S. 1st. . . .

AUSTIN TO MABEL

[*15 September 1891*]
Tuesday afternoon, 15th

I have just been across to Vin's, the first time I have been out today. Sunday—as I wrote you [in Wyoming]—was too much for me, but the drive [with Dwight Hills] made the special mischief. It was very warm when we started, we were dressed

---

* Mabel had begun to menstruate on the twentieth day of her cycle. This and other symptoms of ill health during this visit apparently convinced her she had suffered a miscarriage.

† Mabel had brought Emily's original poems with her so as to continue the proof work.

‡ Ten days later Susan B. Anthony was one of Mrs. Coonley's guests, fresh from a "political equality meeting" in nearby Warsaw, N.Y. "She is simple & sweet & interesting," Mabel recorded in her diary.

thinly—drove away from the wind—to be gone an hour or hour & a half. We did^{nt} get back till after six and the last hour drove against a strong cool south wind. The result being with me one of my severe colds in head and lungs—and all over. I shall be better tomorrow. I am very susceptible to a draft anyhow—and a canopy top is vastly worse in this sense than a carriage with *no* top. . . .

MABEL TO AUSTIN   [*Wyoming, N.Y., 15 September 1891*]
                              Tuesday, 14 [sic] Sept. '91

Your Monday note came this morning. The sight of your dear writing again was deep contentment, but what you say fills me with every kind of solicitude. First, that you are working and wearing yourself to death, and that God accepts so costly a sacrifice and says nothing. I do not understand Him—but still, if He is anything, so grand and noble as we have been taught, you *must* be the apple of His eye. And then, I wonder what you said in that "trying talk" [with Sue]. I must entreat you not to let it accomplish nothing. It is certainly true that you have the power in your own hands if you will *only* use it—you *must* use it—you must bring out some of your weapons and *make* them of use. It is a crisis, and you can turn it for us. I expect you to—I know you will. And yet I wish you had told me something about it. I am very lonely for you, and there has not been a day nor an hour since I came when I could not have put my head down and cried my very heart out, if I had let myself. I have not done it, but I have never been more blue and sad. I dread, inexpressibly, to come back, except for seeing you. The old burdens of pain which are always thrust upon me there seem even heavier in anticipation than when I bear them every day.

AUSTIN TO MABEL   [*21 September 1891*]
                              Monday, 5 p.m., 21st

. . . Saturday night sat with Vin a while, found D.P. over there, and he entertained us by reading your last letter to him, which in its description of the gap he had left in all hearts was almost pathetic. It really seemed as if Waterloo, or Watertown —or whatever it is—Wyoming! is the place where he is most of all needed.* He told us too of his having just received the twenty or twenty-five copies of the London paper—what you and he had sent for to distribute through the county—and which contains your life as given to Madame what do you call her†—

It occurs to me that if you can spare me a copy I can do more with it towards clearing the air of any miasma about us in a day than in all the talk I could make in a year. The great point [with Sue] has been that you claimed two men, had the best of the lives of two, but it could not but be clear to any un-prejudiced mind that so much devotion as is portrayed here to one and his every interest and aim is inconsistent with any seri-ous interest in any second.

The arrival is most opportune for our plans. It will all come right now I am sure. . . .

MABEL TO AUSTIN   [*Wyoming, N.Y.*] 22 September [1891]
Tuesday evening

I am sure you must have had a little twinge of conscience for that most cuttingly sarcastic note which I have just read from you—that is, if you have remembered it since you mailed it. If the twinge has not come already I think it will when I tell you how very deeply it hurt me. Or rather—no, it did not hurt

---

* Mabel's letter to David is missing, but her journal entry of September 20 has David putting the entire house into order, "mending & patching until it was really funny, but won everybody's heart. . . . Dear little David! Every body liked him so much—and he had such a good time! He is very gentle and lovable and manly withal. He is much sweeter and more genial every year."

† While in Chicago a year and a half earlier, Mabel had told her "auto-biography" as an astronomer's wife to her friend Laura Ormiston Chant, who was writing a series about American women for a London period-ical. Evidently it had been published.

me deeply, only sharply. I know and trust you too well for it to hurt me deeply into my heart. I know you too well, my P.S. 1st, and yours are both too real for an actual hurt to pass from one to the other. Only I never tease you—or coquette—or sharpen my wit against your gentle heart.

I am coming on Thursday night—9:30 I believe; and always and ever P.S. 1st, strong and clear and bright.

By the time *Poems by Emily Dickinson, Second Series* appeared on November 9, 1891, Mabel was eager to publish Emily's letters, no doubt encouraged by widespread interest in Colonel Higginson's *Atlantic* article of that October, which presented his correspondence with the poet. Austin thought the public exposure of his sister's letters a bit distasteful, but did not oppose Mabel's efforts to get in touch, with Vinnie's help, with the poet's numerous correspondents. Vinnie endorsed the project enthusiastically, and as Mabel embarked on the sensitive task of persuading friends and relatives who had preserved Emily's letters to allow her to borrow and transcribe them, Austin and Vinnie gradually told her many things about the Dickinson upbringing in the Homestead that illuminated the contents and aided in establishing the dates of some poems.

The project demanded enormous tact and patience, but gradually Mabel accumulated hundreds of letters, enough for a pair of volumes. Some, like those to the Norcross cousins, were gentle and intimate; in others, Emily "posed," as Austin termed it, displaying the artist's quizzical stance toward life around her. A fair amount of the poet's correspondence had already been destroyed by its recipients, and some parts of it, such as her letters to Helen Hunt Jackson, eluded diligent search, but Mabel persevered, and even discovered some letters herself. Her diary describes, for example, how in August 1892, when she was nursing Austin through an illness, she rummaged in the Evergreens attic and "found ever so many more of

[3 7 3]

Emily's letters." These were the poet's girlhood letters to her brother. On two matters relating to publication of the letters, Austin expressed himself firmly. He would not allow the 1847 daguerreotype of his sister to be used, and Sue's name, and all references to her, were to be omitted.

Preparation of the letters took Mabel three years, although as always she worked on other projects as well. With David's help she was writing a scientific book entitled *Total Eclipses of the Sun* (Roberts Brothers, 1894). Her article "An Ascent of Fuji the Peerless" appeared in the August 1891 issue of *Century*, and she was struggling with another piece for William Dean Howells about the Harvard Observatory, which she wrote and rewrote many times before it appeared in the *Century* (February 1894). By the time she pocketed a hard-earned $150, Mabel knew she much preferred to earn her income by lecturing, for the same amount was hers by way of nine talks she gave during 1892 and six more in 1893, half of them about Emily Dickinson and half about Japan. Most of her lectures were to women's clubs and church groups, but one memorable one on Emily Dickinson was given at Amherst College on June 2, 1892, before 110 faculty and other towns-people, with President Gates introducing her. More than money, she dearly loved the overwhelming appreciation that was showered upon her after each performance.

Correspondence between Mabel and Austin thinned during 1892 and 1893, even though Mabel journeyed to Bermuda for a needed rest during April 1892, and to Wyoming, N.Y., again that July. The themes she and Austin employed were so familiar as to have become a sort of shorthand between them, references to states of mind exhibited and experienced so often neither needed to spell them out for the other. The idyll now of their hours together was a search for some high location, some hilltop near Amherst, where they could build a home in which someday to look out upon the world together. An August 1893 letter to a business acquaintance in Omaha reveals that

Austin still hoped to make a break, to "get away from Amherst, where so many unpleasant associations surround me," but nothing came of it. As he raged to Mabel when she was in Bermuda, "What prevents? What? God doesn't—but I am prevented. Is it the Devil? The Devil is men and women."

The chief excitement of 1893 was the World's Fair, held in Chicago during an excessively hot summer. David seized an opportunity to set up a small Amherst College exhibit at the fair, and he, Mabel, and Millicent attended in July, staying at the magnificent new Chicago home of Cousin Lydia Coonley. Best of all, Austin came out too, and he and Mabel witnessed together exhibits and events so marvelous that, in her words, "adjectives fall powerless." Mabel and David went on to Colorado for some astronomy lectures, and also climbed Pikes Peak. Later in the summer, after the death of Grandma Wilder at the end of August, Mabel's mother came to Amherst and stayed until late October. Then Eben arrived and took her back to Washington for the first time in four years. For Mabel the year ended as the ten preceding had, in "one long struggle, and pain and unsatisfiedness and longing. And a deaf God."

MABEL TO AUSTIN   [*Chicago*] 4 July 1893
                                      Tuesday, 5:30 p.m.

Your note came—welcomely. I am glad your decision is to come, and I know David can find you plenty of airy rooms, comfortable and reasonable. . . . He will find out more tomorrow. . . . I spent yesterday at the Exposition. It is perfectly impressive and beautiful. Nothing too much has been said of it. . . . I am living in great luxury and grandeur and rather like such unusual conditions. The cousins are all lovely, and the home a delight. . . .

If you will say which station you arrive in Sunday afternoon, David will come and meet you. The P.S. 1sts are all here and rather finer than ever. . . .

I am *so* glad you are coming.

Amherst, Massachusetts, U.S.A.
[*6 July 1893*]

To _____

I rather think the Fair is monopolizing you—that is if you ever got there. The last I heard of you was from Ohio. I looked for a word yesterday morning, afternoon, evening—*this* morning and afternoon—and it is now six o'clock, and nothing yet.

Well, I go Saturday, as I wrote you last Saturday, by the Boston and Chicago Special. Out in Chicago at 3 p.m. Sunday. And shall hope to fall in with you in the course of the next day, along the Midway Plaisance, perhaps near the Chinese Theater.

7ᵗʰ July 1893
Friday noon

Your fourth of July evening note came this morning. So you are there.

Well, I am scratching with all my might to get off to-morrow, as planned.

You say if I will say what station I will arrive at on Sunday, D.P. will meet me. I dont know anything about different stations. I only know I am going to Chicago, and I supposed the train, over the route I am going, had a regular place to stop—same as in Boston and New York—and stopped there. Then I expected to get out. My train is the Boston & Chicago Special, via Lake Shore & Michigan Southern. Scheduled to reach Chicago at 3 o'c. Sunday afternoon.

Amherst, 21 July '93
Friday forenoon, to hit the noon mail

I wrote you Sunday morning before leaving Chicago—a note which you ought to have received that evening, or next morning. I wrote you again Tuesday afternoon, after my return, as you suggested, addressing to Colorado Springs—both enclosed in envelopes directed to D.P. I have heard not a word from you since we said goodbye at the corner of Hark and Randolph

Streets [in Chicago]. Perhaps you have thought the attractions of the way—and here—would suffice to fill my soul for the time without sign from you. Perhaps it ought to have occurred to me that the new sights and scenes awaiting you would suffice you, and remained mute.

I had proposed to stop with "mute"—I will not however be so unfrank, and untrue to myself as not to add that Amherst does^{nt} seem like Amherst since I got back. It is beautiful, never more so. The weather is divine. The people never so cordial, and yet it seems as if it was right after a funeral all the time, a real one. What do you suppose is the reason! Can't be a single little postscript!

MABEL TO AUSTIN   Colorado Springs, Colorado, 24 July 1893
Monday, 1:30 p.m.

I had the note in Chicago, and I could not tell in forty pages all the thoughts and comfort it gave me. Then I left there, and was thirty-six hours on the way here. Got in Wednesday morning July 19. [David's] first lecture came off, and then I was taken through the College buildings and summer school quarters, and snatched time from the various people who were showing me things to write you a note at the [Observatory] Director's desk. Then Saturday, July 22, I went to the top of Pikes Peak, and sent you a telegram from there, 14,337 feet above the sea. All its grandeur and wildness I shall tell you about when I come. . . . You ought not to try to be one bit sarcastic with me, and you would not if you could see everything. Besides, I know you are not, really. . . .

[Amherst, ca. December 1893]

You do not admit apologies, and so I will say only that the demon of distrust has access to a very small portion of the domain—in fact lives in a remote closet, and only occasionally gets his head out, but when he does wake from his usually sleeping condition, it takes all my strength to get him back and turn the key. I got him in very soon, in spite of many things I cannot understand. And in my anxiety for the welfare of your soul, do let me remind you of the religious exercise of which I spoke, and which bids fair to be largely, immeasurably largely, attended.

This is merely P.S. I.

6

The End of Austin's Life

1894 – 1895

By early 1894 Mabel was capitalizing on her gift for parlor lecturing. Responding eagerly to people and opportunities that gave full rein to her strong social inclinations, she began to experience her happiest moments away from Amherst. As she came into her full powers and Austin's health failed, the poignant tension ended with his death at age sixty-six.

MABEL TO AUSTIN   [*Brooklyn, 13 February 1894*]
                                             Tuesday, 9:30 a.m.

Perhaps you remember how soon the brilliant sunshine, which prevailed when I left you, turned to a faint gray radiance. Near New Haven it became a still, white, flying snow-storm, which grew thicker and thicker, until in New York it seemed a veritable blizzard. On the way I had pleasant talks with Mrs. Stanton, Mrs. Morris, and from Springfield to New York with Mr. Herbert Cowles. I had planned to do some errands in New

York, but of course I could not, in the blinding storm, so I came right over here, the quickest way. Some people Mrs. A[nderson] had asked to dinner could not come for the storm, so we dined quietly together, and I went very early to bed, absolutely overcome with sleepiness—and I slept ten hours; the first time I have had enough in weeks. The storm continues heavily this morning, and I shall probably not go out. I wish you were here. I wish—everything. But in this delicious storm I miss my very own *home*. But truly I never go very far from it. . . . I have had an independent literary judgement on the proof of the *Letters* this morning which fills me with joy. I will also tell you about that.* Oh, but P.S. I, every minute. I am sorry you did not come in earlier yesterday morning—I wanted to see you quietly fifteen minutes. But I remember other quiet times ═══ I already have much to tell you.

  P.S. I & P.S. I +

[*Brooklyn*] 18 Feb. 1894
Sunday noon
No. 4

I meant to write a long letter this morning, before church— my only quiet time today, but an adventure with the monkey this morning, involving yards of ruffle, caused me to be obliged to sew until the sanctuary bells rang. . . . I grudge every moment away, and yet the storms and a day of suggestive sore throat have prevented my lessening my New York list much, and I shall have to stay Monday & Tuesday anyway. I am debating a very "swell" and gorgeous lunch party on Wednesday to which

* The critique was provided by Dr. Albert Josiah Lyman, eminent minister of the South Congregational Church of Brooklyn, whom Mabel now met for the first time. Handsome, sympathetic, liberal in his views, and a clergyman of great pastoral power, he was also president of the Brooklyn Academy of Arts and Sciences and a recent widower. He and Mabel quickly became friends. After Austin died, Dr. Lyman was the one she confided in and from whom she received remarkable and unorthodox consolation.

I am urged by a stranger to me, but a leading light here, who prostrated herself to me at the Clapps'.

Sunday, later

Our guests at dinner left earlier than I expected, so I can write a little more. I am due at Mrs. Storrs' at four;* was invited to tea, but had already promised Mrs. General Barnes, so I spend two hours with dear Mrs. Storrs first. I want you to see the wonderful letter she wrote me after my talk [on Emily] at the Clapps'! She went on purpose to hear me, and went *with* me— the first place she has been, I believe, all winter. I was overpowered by invitations and attentions there, the instant I finished, but this great lunch is all I could consider. That would mean leaving in the four o'clock train Wednesday, and driving over from Northampton, or else waiting until eleven (I believe you said I could leave then) on Thursday morning, which is the latest moment I shall consent to stay, for any consideration. . . .

AUSTIN TO MABEL   [*19 February 1894*]
Six o'clock, Monday night

One word—I was up street just now, and looking into the office found your note of yesterday. I have hurriedly read it. It is lonesome and strange without you, but stay—stay—dont miss such fine opportunities as are offering—they are yours now, and we shall have them to talk over. Dont come before Thursday anyway—and dont come then if you are to miss something you ought not to. I am holding Jack to take this up.

I will write you another line tomorrow. Your note was lovely, and I send all the P.S.s there are.

MABEL TO AUSTIN   [*Brooklyn, 20 February 1894*]
Tuesday evening
No. 5

I am coming home by the 2 o'clock train on Thursday— getting back at 7:20 I believe. And now I can hardly wait for

---

* Mrs. Storrs was the wife of Richard Salter Storrs, eminent clergyman and one of Amherst College's most influential trustees.

the time. The fine lunch tomorrow which I staid for will be over, a great many new friends made, a little shopping accomplished, a very happy time well rounded out, and I, so glad to see my very own once more.

Please come over by half past eight. I shall *have* to see you. *So* much to tell. Your dear letter came today, and it warms me all over. I appreciate you—and P.S. I. Always, and more and more. P.S. I & P.S. I.

21 February 1894
Wednesday evening
No. 6

I have decided to leave New York at nine o'clock tomorrow morning, instead of two, and then I can hear Depew.* The ticket was sent on from Amherst a good many days ago, and I can just as well come as not. There is nothing special here tomorrow morning, and Mrs. Prentiss is going to send me over in her carriage [to Grand Central Station] anyway. So I am coming then. I hope you & D.P. will be there—perhaps meet me when I arrive at Northampton, or soon after. . . .

[*Brooklyn*] 12 April 1894
Thursday morning
No. 2

[*at Mrs. Prentiss's*]

Your little note is a great comfort. I shall live on it until I get another.

The great party was a brilliant success, in spite of its being the worst storm of the season—a tearing wind, pelting rain turning into heavy snow every little while. Mrs. P. said I covered myself "feet deep in glory" [talking an hour about Emily Dickinson]. Today is full too. I was invited to lunch at the Storrs' but had already promised Dr. Lyman. After, we drive to New

---

* Mabel had learned that politician Chauncey Depew was speaking at Smith College at 3 p.m. Thursday.

York to the Madison Square Garden to the famous circus which everybody is attending now, and this evening is *Uncut Leaves*, which will be about the pleasantest thing of my stay here. Tomorrow the Meridian Club luncheon.

How terrible about Bessie Seelye [dead in childbirth]! Such a thing is horribly shocking. Do write me soon again. P.S. I all the time. That is the *real*-thing, always. P.S. I and P.S. I.

AUSTIN TO MABEL   [*13 April 1894*]
Friday afternoon, just before 6

Nos. 1 and 2 both duly and safely to port [from Brooklyn], and were most welcome—as are all the numbers from that author. You are a dear, sweet, strange girl, and at the same time as simple and true to nature as daffodils and daisies. I have been differentiating you from other women a little in my leisure in your absence—and will tell you one or two of my conclusions when you return.

Should like to have seen you in your cloud of glory Wednesday night. It would have been vastly more interesting than sitting in the Agl. College Chapel listening to the twaddle I did. And tomorrow night you dazzle them again. Well that is all right, but hadnt you rather be out in the woods with me!

The weather here is as desolate and desolating as one could wish for his worst enemy. The only glimpse I have had of D.P. since you left was at Bessie Seelyes funeral this morning when he stood near me in the hall. I hope your time will go right. I want you to see the Storrs—and the Clapps. The Clapps come this way you remember. Shall send you another line tomorrow. I appreciate you to the full—and always. You may be sure—and P.S. 1st.

MABEL TO AUSTIN   [*Brooklyn*]
14 April [*1894*]
No. 3

. . . I have had, and am having, a truly brilliant time. It is certainly a "hothouse atmosphere." But, yes, I shall love the cowslips even more because of it, and the golden-rod *best of all*. You will be pleased at the appreciation I tell you of when I come. Luncheon at the Fifth Avenue Hotel yesterday, where I was guest of honor at the Meridian Club. Today my talk to the Vassar people 3 p.m.; & Twentieth Century Club tonight.* P.S. I ever, & constantly more. P.S. I. & P.S. I.

Sat., 11 a.m. Yes, it came, & I feel as if I could live again. I wish you knew how much those written words mean to me. Of course I would rather be picking arbutus with you!

AUSTIN TO MABEL   Amherst, 9 May 1894
                                                  Wednesday afternoon

I did^{nt} go to Boston yesterday and have^{nt} gone today. I did^{nt} feel up to it yesterday morning, and instead went over to see Dr. Cooper to ask him whether my constant coughing was caused by a cold, or by the tickling of my throat by my palate. He thought I should be better with the palate cut and said it was a very simple thing to do, or bear. It probably would be for most, but he used a half hour and more on me—and said when it was over—and comparatively calm—that if he had realized in advance the delicacy of my nervous organization he would^{nt} have undertaken it on me for a million dollars, that he never performed an operation which tried him so much, and that if I had^{nt} shown the most immense resolution, he could^{nt} have gone through it. I suffered greatly all night. Could^{nt} lie down and could^{nt} swallow anything. Sent to [Dr.] Seelye for some opium powders, and telephoned for [Dr.] Cooper to come over by first train this morning. He says I shall lose the week, but will be all right then. I can take only milk punch for nourishment and it almost kills me to take even this. I hate it besides, but I bear up and do it. I shall improve I suppose every day after this. I have

* Although Mabel was talking on Emily and promoting the forthcoming *Letters*, her book *Total Eclipses of the Sun* was published this week, and she also had an article, "A Half Century of Eclipses," in *McClure's*.

thought a great deal of you, and wish I could know about your ride down [to Philadelphia]—how you are located, who you have seen and see, how it goes.* . . .

MABEL TO AUSTIN   Washington, 12 May [*1894*]
                                          Saturday, 7 p.m.

Your letter is here. My heart almost breaks for your pain. I can never express to you how I suffer in your suffering, or how I ache all over to think of it. . . . In the meantime P.S. I to suffocation.

Through the summer of 1894, while Austin suffered several bouts of ill health, Mabel struggled with proof, last-minute changes and improvements, and the preface to the *Letters*. Vinnie had delayed signing a contract for the book, partly because she hated putting her "autograph," as she called it, to any business agreement, partly because she wanted full control over her sister's property. Both Mabel and Austin thought it fair that Mabel should be named recipient of half the proceeds. Vinnie wanted to be the sole recipient, then planned to share with Mabel. Thomas Niles had died in the spring of 1894, and his successor, E. D. Hardy, discovered as other editors had the difficulty of dealing with Dickinsons. Vinnie wrote him that Mabel was forcing her, but she would not submit. Mabel wrote him that Austin was convincing Vinnie otherwise. Austin wrote him that Vinnie had no business sense, or appreciation for editing, and he planned to have a talk

* During the fall of 1893 Mabel had taken charge of organizing the Amherst Women's Club, and now represented it at a three-day biennial meeting of the Federation of Women's Clubs in Philadelphia. Then she went on to Washington to collect Millicent, who had been with her grandparents since March.

with her. After a month Vinnie quietly wrote Hardy that the contract was to be in her name alone. Perplexed, Hardy sent her letter to Austin, who replied at once that the contract would speak of a divided royalty or there would be no book.

"Vinnie is an awful snake," Mabel confided to her diary, "but all the same it hurts me very much." "I am not under guardianship," Vinnie told Hardy. ". . . I can not quite understand Mrs. Todd's continued & determined hostile attitude toward me. I prefer the pleasure of extending to her *myself* an equal share in the spoils (if there is any). . . ." Austin and Mabel prevailed, and Vinnie signed their version of the contract on October 4. But the turmoil was all for naught—as Vinnie had somehow divined, there never were any spoils. *Letters of Emily Dickinson*, edited by Mabel Loomis Todd, was published November 21, and the first edition of 1,000 sold quickly, but sales were too scant thereafter to do more than cover the $400 investment in plates.

During the summer Mabel got up two new talks: "An Old Autograph Album" was her personal reminiscences of distinguished persons she had met; the other was called a "Synopsis of the Japanese-Chinese War in Corea." With them she brought the number of talks during 1894 to thirteen; the next year, having added "Eclipses" and "Five Days in Ireland" to her repertoire, she gave thirty.

The following letter is a late glimpse of Sue Dickinson, whose concern for Austin's health and whose unquenchable wit confirm her constant if relatively invisible participation in the Austin-Mabel drama.

SUE TO MATTIE   [*Young's Hotel, Boston,*
                                  ca. 8 November 1894]
                                  Wed. evening

Dear Mops this is a surprise! Papa was obliged to come down with Mr. Piper [Amherst College auditor] to look over the bonds in the vault and at breakfast Ned proposed I should come instead of staying home alone. I said "I had'nt no clothes suitable" etc. etc. but all the more I thought I'd come—it was the "pig" you know again. So at half-past two I was ready in my old black silk that tips up in front, my seal cloak for elegance and warmth as well, for it is verily cold. I fished a last winter's bonnet out of the attic and just as I left the front door I remembered that it had something on top of it last year and that the trimming was coming off. I ran back upstairs for some pins to make the bow stay on, and was off. Even tho' I do not look like your "He Vere" family. It is delicious to think how you would whip me if you were here. . . . Ned came in an earlier train. . . . We are to go home to-morrow afternoon. The real reason for my coming is to take Papa to see his specialist tomorrow between twelve and one. . . .

MABEL TO AUSTIN   Ocean Avenue [*Lynn, Mass.*]
                                            14 Nov. 1894

It is rather a brilliant visit in every way,* & a very interesting one. It is good for me to be so much appreciated. I have two or three more invitations than I expected, but I cannot accept them all. . . . The shopping is not flourishing, but I hope to do a little today. . . .

[*Boston, 16 November 1894*]

I am at the [General] Walkers' since yesterday, & until Saturday p.m., when I go home. Of course I had no idea of staying so long, and one attractive invitation after another has detained me, until I feel quite like a woman of the world. I find I know a great many people at all the teas & places, & I have had a delightful week. I shall tell you all about it in detail, but now I am starting for a long delayed shopping expedition. Pleas-

* Mabel spoke the previous day to two hundred members of the North Shore Club about Japan.

anter things have come first. Only one rainy day so far—clear & cold generally.

P.S. I, and a large one. Shall hope to see you Saturday.

Amherst, 5 January 1895
Saturday

Oh, my dear, the days are so long, and so infinitely sad, for you are sick [with pneumonia] and I cannot see you, and I miss you indescribably.

Mr. [George Washington] Cable and Colonel Higginson dined here Wednesday night, and when you did not come in, in the evening, I thought you were probably detained in some way. I never thought you might be sick. But I decided not to go to Boston on Thursday. Colonel Higginson was here until 2:36, and I had some thought of going down with him, but finally didn't. Then when I saw nothing of you Thursday afternoon, I sent over to Vinnie's to see where you might be, and learned to my infinite terror and pain that you were "very ill." From that time on I have lived in a state of suspense which you can hardly imagine. Friday I could do absolutely nothing. I have heard from you twice a day, from Vinnie or the Doctor, and I knew of Dr. Cooper coming, and the trained nurse from New York, for both of which I was glad. I gave up the Donald visit on the spot, and shall not go away at all until I hear you are on the highway to perfect health.

If I hear that tomorrow, Sunday, then I shall go to Chestnut Hill Monday. My sole hope and aspiration now is that you shall be quickly well again—every thought is merged in that prayer, which goes up with my every breath and heartbeat. I can think of nothing else. And when you are well again I will devote every power I possess to lightening and brightening *your* life, and instead of ever considering myself, I will think only of you, and of the pain and thwarting *you* have had, and make every moment while you are with me only sunshine and peace. You will understand, and you will know how I revile myself for ever making you uncomfortable for an instant. Get well right away, and you shall see how truly sweet-hearted I can be, and how much real strength at bottom I do possess. But while you are sick I am absolutely *limp*—the dazzling blue and white days are only colorless gray to me. *Do* be well! P.S. I + . . .

Monday, 4 p.m.

I really believe I have suffered more during your sickness than you have. I am completely unnerved today. The news this morning was that you are comfortable, that Dr. Cooper was over, and you are getting on all right. Yet I cannot eat or work, and I do not know what I shall do.

Of course I did not go to Boston this morning—it was raining, and I *could* not seem to start away without one more bulletin from you. It is the unhappiest time I ever lived through. I *want* you so! I want to talk it all over with you as we do everything. I want to see you out and about, and running in with the dear fresh roses in your cheeks, and your old ulster on. Oh, I miss you unutterably, and I cannot bear it rightly. If I hear tonight that you are still improving I shall try and force myself to go in the morning. But I cannot bear to think of being farther away from you—by distance. How I envy your nurse, who does things for you, and makes you comfortable and happy!* To do for you night and day, and never rest and never sleep—I should find strength like a Goliath for that. I shall write another word before I go in the morning. . . .

AUSTIN TO MABEL   [*1 February 1895*]
Friday, 5 p.m. exactly

Your line with the Brunswick envelope [from Boston] came all right this morning.† Am sorry you are not feeling better. Unless you do, you had better see a doctor. See Spaulding.

---

* A major source of anguish for Mabel any time Austin had ever been ill was the knowledge that Sue was ministering to his needs.

† Mabel was in the Boston area for four talks; one of them was to the New England Women's Club of Boston, whose president was Julia Ward Howe.

I had a short note from D.P. yesterday morning saying he had had to rush off to his sister, who was thought to be near the end.* I have just been over to the red house to see Millicent, but she was over to the Sterrets. Will go again pretty soon. . . .

5:30

Have been over again. Millicent is there and all right. Says she has written you all there is about D.P. and herself, and says she is getting on. She would have been glad to have some one stay with her, as I told her she ought to, but her father told her not to! P.S. 1 +

MABEL TO AUSTIN   [*23 April 1895*]

I have been worried to death by your non-appearance. Only today learned the facts. You *never* will take care of yourself, will you?

I am rather expecting to go tomorrow afternoon. There are several new developments, & I had better be there. It is a nasty mess.† I have greatly wanted to see you. I am delighted that you can come over tomorrow—about 11:30 if you can. I finished the Trustee book long ago. All but one or two small words. I will not send it today, though—and P.S. I, oh! yes, heartbreakingly P.S. I.

AUSTIN TO MABEL   [*17 July 1895*]
Wednesday afternoon, 4 and after

I think I am a trifle better today—but I am sick and have^{nt} the strength to walk over, as I want to do. I hope to do this tomorrow, and if there is any time when it would suit you better,

---

* Naomi Todd Compton died the following Friday.

† Mabel was embroiled in a contest over the Women's Club presidency. She wanted the club to purchase a headquarters, but many objected to her worldly aspirations and highhanded ways. The vote next day went 33–31 against her, while over one hundred members stayed home.

say so in the enclosed envelope and post in season for me to get it with my morning's mail. The P.ˢ and S.ˢ are all right.

MABEL TO AUSTIN   *[17 July 1895]*
                                Wednesday, 7:30 p.m.

I will stay in all day tomorrow, that you may come when you can most easily.

Thank you for the word, of which I was sorely in need.

But I *can* not think it right for you to be struggling on by yourself, without the aid of any good doctor. You ought to have the best one every minute. May I write to the one we spoke about in Boston, and try to get him to come here and see you?

I can not try to tell you how I have suffered in these two days. I saw you one second today. P.S. I +

Their meeting the next afternoon, at the Homestead, was their last. Austin's labored breathing and racing heartbeat alarmed Mabel. "He seems very weak & it almost broke my heart," she noted in her diary.

AUSTIN TO MABEL   *[19 July 1895]*
                                Friday morning, 11

I had a big fight for my three to four hours sleep last night, feel more natural and less nervous today and inclined to rest. Think I shall keep mainly to my bed. Anyway not dress. Shall hope and mean to see you tomorrow. Dont fail to be out of doors somewhere and somehow this beautiful afternoon.

                                   [20 July 1895]
                                Saturday morning

Dr. Bigelow pronounces me in better condition this morning than before, which he ascribes largely to my keeping very quiet yesterday, seeing no one and doing very little. He wants me to do nothing, not even notice a letter, and thinks I will then begin to improve very soon. I had a reasonably good night for me, am gaining in my breathing, am about free from nausea, hardly any appetite yet, and feel very little strength. Shall hope to see you Monday. Hardly can before. Remember how I told you you could help me most—and try to do it. Keep out a good deal this fine weather. I like Dr. Bigelow better than any one I have consulted. He has had experience in just this sort of thing, and seems intelligent and careful. Dwight Hills sickness has been of the same sort. He calls it nervous exhaustion.

This gives you some idea. The P.S.s are full to overflowing as you will later know.

Take care of yourself—and remember how you can help me.

My kindest remembrances to D.P., whose friendship and interest I can assume. You and him I do not fail to appreciate.

[*27 July 1895*]

I want to write, but I can't. My nurse begs me not to do anything requiring the least effort—says it will put me back incalculably—and keeps closest watch on me.

I have been seriously sick. It takes about all the strength I can muster to walk from my bed to my dressing room.

Dr. Cooper, who was sent for from the Rangeley Lakes, on account of his mother's ailing condition, spent an hour looking me over this forenoon. He says I must get off and into a new climate as soon as possible. Thinks I may be able to go by next Thursday—says the nurse will have to go with me, to look after me for a few days.

I shall try to get to the other house early in the week—and send for you.

Vin does^{nt} come over at all, so I have [unfinished].

All the old things and real things are solid—never more so—adamantive. You must understand—and believe.

The End of Austin's Life

My darling, my darling, I must write to you, although I am sadly sure there will be no chance to get it to you until you are enough better to see me, and then I could tell it all to you. But I will write from day to day, and perhaps hand it to you myself. I have already tried to get two notes to you. But the first one was while you were at the sickest, and Vinnie could not get at you. The other she has carried around for several days, and she professes to have no opportunity to hand it to you. So I have both here, to give you when you are better. What I have been through since the day, July 18th, when you were last out and saw me, no human being can ever know. Even you, my beloved, my king, can scarcely tell my suffering. For two weeks I could not eat, my sleep was broken constantly, and sobs choked my throat all day. I could not go out, or see anybody, and there was no sunshine or blue sky.

Then came the terrible day when I heard things that stopped my breath, and I besieged God with frantic entreaties to save you, or else kill me too. Then a sudden inspiration of help for you came into my mind, and I went at once to Boston [to a faith healer] to carry it out. To be sure I cried all the way there, but about at Wayland the sun shone out suddenly in the west, while it was raining toward Boston, and a most wonderful rainbow spanned the sky ahead. It lasted over half an hour— calm, bright, peaceful, and full of hope. It was the first time in my life that God ever spoke to me. But He did that time, and told me you would get well. I went to a friend's house for the night, and the next morning arranged to have you helped, and only then did my tears cease; but a remarkable quiet came over me. For a day or two there was said to be no special change in you. But on Tuesday, August 6th, Dr Cooper reported a distinct, and to him apparently surprising, change for the better, in your pulse and general condition. So then I knew God meant it, and showed me how to help you. And you have gained from that time—and my reason is saved.

And I have wondered—not *if*, but what, you are thinking of me, and if the time seems long to you since you held me in your arms, and if you would not like to have me come in now and kiss you, and take your dear hands in mine. I have solemnly promised God that when you are well again, and I feel your beloved arms around me again, and I know I have you safe, that from that hour I will live up to the best and highest there is in me, and make you happy as I never did before. Only God has a faint conception of how I love you—nothing human can compass such knowledge—unless you know. If you had died it would have been the utter end of my life. I could not think of any possibility, even of going on with life, much less any occupation. I know I saved your life those two days when the chances were even, and I will tell you all about it.

I have not heard from you yet this morning. I do not consider Vinnie's information trustworthy in detail, so I send to the doctor. But yesterday you saw M^r. Bowles, and had a comfortable day, so I slept better, but even then not without tossing and turning a good deal. I am not yet past the strain—and I cannot eat. I am very thin and white, but so grateful that I can only sob out my thanks for your life.

To have lived in and by and for and through you for so many years, and then to have to face the bitter possibility that you might have died, is a torment beyond the imagination of fiends. My hands tremble still, and my heart throbs and jumps. But you are getting well, oh master dear! . . .

Monday, 3:30 p.m., 12th August

"For my beloved—is mine—and I am his;
What—can—we—want—beside?" NOTHING!

But we do want that—each other. This morning three bunches of sweet peas were sent you by M^r. Parmenter—they were taken to you from here, at his request; and one of your nurses was seen, who said you were better today. *Very* slowly, but surely, oh, my heart's beloved, you are getting back, and you will be in life again. How simple for me to come in to see you, and kiss

[3 9 4]

you and love you into health! And yet China is nearer, in possibility. But my darling, get well and come back to me, and I will try not to repine at any circumstance. I belong utterly to you.

Tuesday morning, 13th August

Do you hear the crickets, *our* crickets, my beloved, at twilight? And when you hear them do you think of me? I sat on the east piazza last evening listening to them, and again in front of the house, until it seemed to me you *must* be with me. Do you hear them, sweetheart? All these fair August days I can hardly breathe without you. *Our* month, and you so ill that you are shut away from me—but only for the time, dear. You are coming back, and then I shall tell you how lonesome the lights and shadows were on the far, dim hills, and how the blue haze choked me, and blinded my eyes; and how the rich odors of corn and tobacco suffocated me with recollection and anticipation. The sunshine is hot but beautiful, the insects are wildly happy in a heaven of sizz and buzz, the warm fragrance of grass ascends to me from your dear meadow, and I see it and feel it all, yet as a stranger until you are well again. My darling, my king.

Wednesday, 14th August. Good morning, my dearest love! My heart has been with you all night, and will be all day. I am going for a little excursion today. I cannot breathe or work here, so I am going away for the day. I love you.

David and Mabel then drove to Ashfield for the day, and the next morning departed from Amherst by carriage to attend a centenary celebration in New Salem. They returned to town the next evening, August 16, just as Austin passed away.

I I I

Epilogue

The Law Suit and the Trial

1896–1898

For three days Amherst mourned the passing of its most influential and generally beloved citizen, whose death, said the *Springfield Republican*, was "due to overwork." Fifteen-year-old Millicent Todd registered in her diary the sorrow that suffused the Dell and was visible all about her. "This has been one of the saddest days that I ever passed in my life," she wrote on Sunday, August 18. "Mama has been crying all day, and Papa has cried some and has looked so sad that I have been perfectly bewildered. It seems to be a universal grief."

The next afternoon stores and businesses in the village closed for Austin's funeral, as they had twenty-one years earlier when his father died, and a throng attended the service conducted by Rev. Jonathan Jenkins at the Evergreens. "Mr. Dickinson's funeral was at three o'clock but neither Mama nor I cared to go," Millicent commented innocently, unaware that at noon that day Ned Dickinson had quietly let her mother in at a side door, while Sue and the rest of his family were at the dining table, so Mabel could say goodbye to Austin and place in his casket a token of their love.

"I kissed his blessed cold cheek today and held his tender hand," Mabel wrote that night. "The dear body, every inch of which I know and love so utterly, was there, and I said goodbye to it, but all the time I seemed singularly conscious that my own Austin himself was out in the sweet summer sunshine, more light-hearted and blithe and strong and hopeful than he has ever been before since he was a boy. . . . The whole town weeps for him. Yet I am the only mourner."

Six weeks later Mabel was still in unrelieved pain, enduring the dull anguish Emily termed "the Hour of Lead." Her diary notations attest her psychic numbness: "I cannot breathe for sorrow," "I *can not* begin again," "I try to be busy, but I cry & cry & cry," "My heart is dead & I want my body to be." She sought the seashore, had sympathetic talks with one or two understanding friends, and for hours on end read and reread Austin's beloved letters, which David carried down to her in their tin box from the bank vault, but nothing brought relief. Her plight as Austin's unacknowledged widow was exquisitely bitter, solaced only by keeping a long-ago pledge to wear mourning publicly for him, an impropriety that shocked many townspeople and could not avoid enraging Sue Dickinson. Her sole and rather absurd distraction from grief was a handsome red Columbia bicycle that was delivered at the Dell the morning following Austin's death. Mabel wanted to believe he had ordered it for her, despite his small enthusiasm for wheels, and she practiced on it single-mindedly until she learned to ride. More likely, however, the anonymous gift came from a fond admirer—the writer and reformer George Washington Cable, who had been pedaling to Amherst often that summer from Northampton to seek Mabel's contributions to a periodical he was editing.

There was another matter on Mabel's mind during these

stricken weeks: the inheritance Austin had promised her. On Friday, October 6, she ran over to the Homestead to talk to Lavinia about it, only to return upset. "I went to see Vinnie in the morning," she wrote in her diary, "and I find she is going to ignore Austin's request to her—that she shall give to me his share of his father's estate. She is, as he always told me, utterly slippery and treacherous, but he did not think she would fail to do as he stipulated in this. Oh, it is pitiful! He had an entire contempt for her, but we talked it over, and it seemed the safest way to leave it. If he knows, how sorry he must be!"

Mabel had little sympathy for the vulnerable position Austin had left Vinnie in. His will conferred his share in his father's estate—the Dickinson meadow and considerable property in stocks and bonds—to her, and also left a pair of pictures now hanging in the Evergreens to Mabel, and the Evergreens itself, together with real and personal property in his own name, to Sue. At the time he wrote the will, in early November 1887, Austin had explained to Mabel that it was "not quite as I wanted it but best for now. I have left all my share of my father's estate to Vin with the request that she turn it over to you. She has promised to do this, so you are protected in any case." Vinnie may have promised then, but she was worried now about what Sue would do if she tried to keep the promise. She was also uncertain she wanted to give Mabel anything more of the Dickinsons'. Relations between the two women had not been smooth since their altercation over the contract for Emily's *Letters* the previous summer. Vinnie was still angry that Mabel had omitted from the preface any mention of her role as Emily's sister in gathering the correspondence. On the night of Austin's death, Vinnie asked her trusted neighbor Dwight Hills, the First National Bank president, if he would be her business adviser; between her promise to Austin and all the property that was suddenly hers to manage, she felt quite helpless. She told Hills of Austin's wishes regarding

Mabel, having turned to him because of his sympathy toward that relationship. He agreed to advise her, agreed, too, to draw the necessary papers and secure legal services when she had made up her mind about the meadow, but he declined to tell her what to do, only warning that she should not take any steps without his knowledge.

Hills's deference, so different from Austin's authoritative ways, left Vinnie greatly at sea. Although she was shrewd, after sixty-two years of being protected by her father and brother in all but the simplest affairs of her life, she was too inexperienced to think much beyond immediate survival, as her numerous shortsighted and even foolish acts quickly revealed. One of her close friends and confidantes was Frances Seelye, the housekeeper for Dwight Hills and his elderly mother. Miss Seelye later described in court Vinnie's struggle throughout the autumn of 1895 to find plausible justification for Austin's extraordinary gift of patrimony to Mabel. Construing it as compensation for Mabel's work on the poems and letters, in Vinnie's eyes, gave too much weight to Mabel's role in publishing Emily's manuscripts. Construing it as anything else created more family scandal, which Vinnie was anxious to avoid. She was very upset that Mabel insisted on wearing black dresses, a black cape and hat, and a crepe veil about town. And of course anything given the Todds in Austin's name would infuriate Sue, whose wrath—with Austin no longer there as buffer—Lavinia genuinely feared. Everything considered, Vinnie had decided by October 6 to renege on her promise to Austin. However, there remained a major reason for continuing to feel ambivalent, one motive for not alienating Mabel altogether. Hundreds of Emily's poems remained to be published, and Mabel already had begun preparing the manuscript of a third volume. Without Mabel, Vinnie's dearest dream would certainly, in Emily's words, "recede unrealized."

Vinnie's quandary was exacerbated by loneliness. Relations with the house next door were not especially cordial, though Vinnie was very fond of Ned, now manfully attempting to play the Dickinson male role. For long periods after Austin's death, the Evergreens stood empty, while its occupants recovered at the Maine coast from their long, sad summer, and while they went to Geneva, New York, for the final illness, death, and funeral of Sue's sister, Mattie Gilbert Smith. In late November Ned took his mother and sister to Virginia to avoid Thanksgiving and Christmas at home. Vinnie would have been forlorn indeed had she cut off her relations with the Todds, who in many ways were more like family to her than the Evergreens residents. By the new year she had decided upon another way to please Mabel, a plan which, if cautiously carried out, would not rouse Sue. Mabel's diary for December 29, 1895, reports: "I went to see Vinnie just before tea—and had a talk with her. She is going to do one lovely thing."

The lovely thing was giving Mabel a fifty-three-foot-wide strip of the meadow that ran along the east side of the Dell, a narrow lot containing about fifty-five square rods that filled out the original plot deeded to the Todds. Austin had so long intended the Todds should have it that trees and shrubs he planted along the east side of the Dell accommodated the extra footage. One day during his last spring he and David had measured the strip, and Mabel had jotted its dimensions in pencil on a blank deed brought over for the purpose, but Austin's illness deferred completion of the paper. After Vinnie disappointed her in early October, Mabel again mentioned Austin's intentions, and undoubtedly pressed her a little. In late December, after inspecting the lot one evening by moonlight, Vinnie agreed that if Mabel would copy out the deed, she would sign it without saying anything to Dwight Hills. Why she avoided Hills is not clear. Perhaps Vinnie naïvely hoped that Mabel could draw the deed, she could sign it, and no one would be the wiser; more likely, she knew Hills would be displeased with her for evading Austin's wishes. In any event, her myopic circumvention proved to be her undoing.

Though well acquainted with Vinnie's penchant for keeping her affairs dark, Mabel knew the deed must be witnessed. Through a friend, Judge E. C. Bumpus of Boston, she learned of lawyer Timothy Spaulding of Northampton, whose Amherst antecedents and distance from town made him acceptable to Vinnie. Vinnie asked Mabel to bring him to call some evening after dark. Mabel fitted the task into her usual brisk schedule, entering in her diary on February 7, 1896: "At 6:30 Mr. Spaulding came and we went to see Vinnie—and she signed the deed before him for the piece of land 53 feet wide, and as deep as mine, adjoining mine on the east. A great weight is off my mind, to have even that, which Austin had given me, but had not finished the deed." Her description omits mention of a last-minute whispered conversation with Vinnie in the Homestead doorway. Need the deed be recorded? Vinnie fretted. Mabel said she thought she could get Mr. Spaulding to delay doing so. Neither woman wanted Sue alerted to what was, after all, a relatively inconsequential part of the original scheme. On the walk back to the Dell, Mr. Spaulding agreed to defer recording the deed until he heard from Mabel.

During late 1895 and early 1896, Mabel was busier than ever before in her life. She was giving many talks in and around Boston and New York, helping David with an astronomy textbook, writing articles for several publications, preparing the poems and preface for the third volume of Dickinson poems and correcting its proof, editing and illustrating her father's book, *An Eclipse Party in West Africa*, and editing cousin Lydia Coonley's poems, soon published anonymously as *A Cycle of Sonnets*. She also served on the state board of the Women's Club, and early in 1896 was organizing and launching Amherst's chapter of the D.A.R. Hectic activity was her antidote to despondency. Rushing about distracted her, masked her brokenhearted apathy, and restrained her urge to join Austin. By Christmas 1897, she promised herself, she would have completed her earthly tasks, particularly her last great plan of publishing her own and Austin's letters, and would then give in to her constant longing to die.

Meanwhile, she was pulled steadily into David's newest plans, another eclipse expedition to Japan, this time sailing aboard the luxurious schooner of a wealthy young New York City financier and recent Amherst College graduate, Arthur Curtiss James. The *Coronet* had already left New York in early December 1895 to take the heavier astronomical instruments around Cape Horn, and would lie in wait in San Francisco harbor until expedition members crossed the country by private railroad car in the spring. Mabel had seen the brass bed, brocade hangings, and mahogany furniture of the handsome stateroom in which she would voyage to Yezo to view the August 9 solar eclipse among the hairy Ainu. She welcomed the diversion of this trip, and made arrangements with *The Nation* and *Century* to carry her articles about it. She even painted a special set of china for use aboard the yacht. During the final days of March she replaced Austin's letters in the bank vault, packed her trunks, sent Millicent off to the Loomises, and on April 4, after a swift farewell to Vinnie, left Amherst on the mid-morning train, saddened by thoughts of other departures when Austin had been there to tend lovingly to all her unfinished tasks.

Shortly before her exodus Mr. Spaulding reminded her that Vinnie's deed must be recorded, and it evidently seemed a fitting time. Record of conveyance was made in the Registry of Deeds at Northampton on April 1, 1896. Notice appeared shortly thereafter in a Boston business publication called *Banker and Tradesman*, where some weeks later Dwight Hills, who hadn't had a conversation with Lavinia since the new year, spotted it while perusing his trade journals. He grew very angry.

Vinnie's first inkling that her secret was out occurred one May morning when the Homestead's servant, Margaret Maher, was questioned by Dwight Palmer at the village post office concerning the deed. Palmer was Sue's associate. He was a dour, unpopular merchant, always called by Austin the meanest man in town. Mabel claimed Austin had appointed him one of the executors of his estate purposely to annoy Sue, but Sue and Mr. Palmer appeared to be getting along rather well, and Vinnie trembled at finding herself at the mercy of such a formidable pair. Mr. Palmer soon went to Northampton, taking Amherst lawyer William Hammond with him, to inquire further of Timothy Spaulding about the deed. Since Dwight Hills, as he later testified, "stopped advising [Miss Dickinson] as soon as possible when I saw notice of the deed," Vinnie was very much alone in her predicament. Caught doing what she had promised Mr. Hills she wouldn't do, caught doing what she knew Sue would kill her for, Vinnie reacted like a child found with her hand in the cookie jar. She said she *hadn't* done it, which immediately got her into deeper trouble: Dwight Hills didn't believe her (he and his mother took great umbrage toward Vinnie at this point), while Susan cleverly decided to hold Vinnie to her lie and insist she get the land back.

Many observers of the debacle that followed saw it as Sue's opportunity, at long last, to wreak revenge on Mabel, and thought that Vinnie became a puppet in her sister-in-law's manipulating hands. Certainly Sue was determined the Todds should receive no part of the Dickinson estate. (Sue refused, even, to give Mabel the painted landscape and the engraving Austin had left her outright in his will, but Ned packed the pictures up and somehow got them into Mabel's possession at a convenient moment.) Nor is it likely that Vinnie on her own initiative would have gone so far as to sue Mabel, whereas Sue was eager to humiliate her enemy publicly, now that the reins of Dickinson power were in her hands. While keeping discreetly in the background, she seems to have taken advantage of Vinnie's susceptibility to male authority by using Mr. Palmer, lawyer Hammond, and even Ned as her agents to coerce Vinnie into legal action against the Todds. On May 25,

1896, the firm of Hammond and Fields drew up a Bill of Complaint in which Lavinia Dickinson accused Mabel Loomis Todd of obtaining her signature on the recently recorded deed by misrepresentation and fraud. Vinnie claimed Mabel had come to her home for a social call, bringing Timothy G. Spaulding, and had produced a paper Vinnie understood to be an agreement that no house would be placed on the land immediately east of the Todds' property. She said Mabel had falsely obtained Vinnie's signature on the deed, and had paid nothing for a piece of land worth $2,000.

The only surviving commentary on Vinnie's troubles that summer comes from a letter written by a former Amherst clergyman, Rev. Ira J. Clizbe, who while minister of the Second Congregational Church had known the Hills and Dickinson families well and was attempting to heal the breach. By then Vinnie had circulated her tale of Mabel's treachery among friends and acquaintances who called at the Homestead to be entertained by her views and vituperative wit.

24th Aug. 1896

My dear Miss Vinnie,

We received a letter from Miss Wright a few days ago telling a number of things which you had told her about your trials. We are exceedingly sorry, & have thought much about you since. After all that you have been through, it seems hard to have people try to rob you. But I cannot believe that you understand Dwight aright. From all that we have known of his & Mrs. Hills feelings toward you, & from allusions to you in his letters of late, I'm sure that he could not have meant to say that "his mother never wished to see you again."

I presume however that he was indignant when he found that you had signed a deed conveying away valuable property, without his knowledge as your business manager. He is a thorough businessman, & to such a man, having charge of your business, such an act would be very aggravating. Of course he could not understand the circumstances, & probably, being a bachelor, he cannot appreciate a woman's feelings & conduct in

[4 0 7]

such a case. I suppose it had been quite a task for him to settle up your affairs, & keep matters peaceable with the other family.

But I am sure that you have no better friends than he & his mother have been. We should be very sorry to have any unpleasantness between the two houses. Would it not be well for you to take the first step toward a better understanding? How would it do to write Dwight a note expressing regret for what you did, & asking him to come & see you. Suppose you should express to him your appreciation of what he has done for you & your sorrow for any misunderstanding between the families. I believe that he would meet you half way. You could do as much as that without any undue humiliation of yourself, & it would be the Christian way. As I grow older, I feel that it is better to go almost any length in conciliation than to have bitterness & heart burnings between old friends. According to Miss W.'s account, Mrs. Todd must be a person to be wary of. It would of course have been the right way, when she began her solicitations, to refer the matter to your business manager. But I suppose you did not think of that. . . .

Trapped by Sue, Vinnie was in no position to plead the truth with Mr. Hills. Rev. Clizbe's kind thoughts provided only the briefest respite, because a few days later Sue stormed down anew, having just learned that a third volume of poems was appearing, thanks to an advance review in the New York *Tribune* chastising Mabel Loomis Todd for further perpetuation of "mere trifles or experiments" by a "minor lyrist." Sue, vacationing with her children in Maine when she read the notice, promptly had Ned inform Vinnie of her displeasure.

South West Harbor
27th. Aug. 1896

My dear Aunt:
The morning is foggy, and allows me the opportunity to catch up a bit with my correspondence. . . .

One of our friends in the [Hotel Claremont] gave me the enclosed clipping. I hope very deeply there is no truth in it. For the sake of my Grand-Father's good name, and for the peace of my Aunt, who shunned all vulgarity, it makes me shudder to think of having the family name dragged before an unwilling public, and by a woman who has brought nothing but a sword into the family. You can tell me whether there is any truth in the suggestion. With your recent experience with these people, I can but feel that you would feel as I do about the matter. You would be held responsible naturally for any such performance, and would do more to injure any just fame that may belong to Aunt Emily, simply from a literary point of view, than any thing that could be done. Excuse my warmth on the subject, but as I am the only man left to represent the generations of strong, forceful men who have preceded me, I feel I have the right to make my protest. . . .

Please write as soon as convenient in regard to the various matters mentioned in this, and I hope I have had my annoyance for nothing. The girls [Sue and Mattie] join me in love to you, and remembrances for Maggy.

Very faithfully,
Edward Dickinson

When the Todds returned to Amherst on October 22, Mabel thrilling to the piercing autumn beauty though it provoked her agony for Austin afresh, Amherst seemed placid and welcoming. At once Mabel called on Vinnie, who hadn't answered any of her letters, but who received her as enthusiastically as ever, apparently delighted by Mabel's exotic adventures and glad of some new blue china that would be coming from Japan for the Homestead. On hearing shortly afterward that Vinnie was entering suit against David and her for fraud, Mabel was dumbfounded, as well as furious at what Vinnie had been saying about them in their seven-month absence. The whole thing seemed preposterous. Mabel went immediately to Boston to ask her friend Judge Bumpus what to do.

She had known Everett C. Bumpus, a Harvard Law School graduate and prominent member of the Boston bar, since the winter of 1889–90, which she had spent in Boston. In his career Bumpus had been a trial judge in Weymouth, a justice of the East Norfolk court, and district attorney of southeastern Massachusetts. Now, in his early fifties, he was in private practice, engaged in several large business suits in the state. Judge Bumpus assured Mabel that Vinnie had no case at all, that the Todds would win if the suit was pressed, and he urged her to countersue on the basis of her services on the poems if Vinnie persisted. When Vinnie finally filed the Bill of Complaint on November 17, Bumpus helped Mabel prepare a Defendants' Answer countering that Spaulding *had* told Vinnie she was signing a deed, which she already knew, and that there never was conversation about building houses on the lot in question.

The Answer was largely devoted, however, to a detailed account of the ten years' labor Mabel had expended in copying and publishing the Dickinson poems and letters at Vinnie's urging, for which she was paid only $200 from early royalties. Rather than Thomas Wentworth Higginson's part in the enterprise, David's helping role was stressed in order to underscore Mabel's assertion that Austin Dickinson had desired to deed the Todds the land at issue to compensate both of them for their work. When the Answer was filed, Vinnie promptly made exception to all the Todds' statements; then the case moved onto the schedule of the state Superior Court. It came up early in February 1897, but was continued to the following fall.

If Mabel and Austin's affair was long a hushed, unmentionable matter that Amherst people only whispered of, the law suit opened the floodgates. Newspapers in the region ran articles about the litigation between the two prominent families and local gossip flourished. While Vinnie's story wasn't widely believed, many in town thought the Todds had long taken advantage of her and deserved to be stopped. Others saw Sue's malevolence behind the drama and were sympathetic to the Todds. Alfred Stearns, son of the highly respected principal of the Convent, later wrote a colorful account of the town divided into social camps by the situation, but sides really had been drawn years earlier over the moral dilemma at its heart. New developments fueled partisan speculation and entertaining talk in the village for the next year. Amherst, already well acquainted with Sue Dickinson's spleen and Mabel Todd's superiorities, awaited the clash of hostilities.

It was all deeply distressing to Mabel, who held her head high through the gossip, tensions, and legal delays by rejecting the "sordid business" entirely and leaving town as often as possible. She was receiving twenty-five or thirty dollars each time she lectured now, and she gave forty-five performances during 1897. Assiduously avoiding the subject of Emily Dickinson, she worked up several new talks based on her recent travels, and launched out in 1897 with a speech on the Ainu to members of the Geographical Society of Philadelphia. "I think it was the best talk I have ever given . . . an absolute *storm* of enthusiasm," she noted afterward. The applause she received away from Amherst compensated to some extent for a dearth of it at home.

While David was angered by being publicly called a liar, Mabel resented Vinnie's ingratitude for all she had done for her and for Emily. Indignation and its corollary, a heightened sense of personal superiority, are evident in Mabel's diary throughout the winter and spring of 1897. In early April, for example, she turned down the Amherst Women's Club presidency by informing its members she was "too busy with *real* things to take up the burden of a second-rate club." A week or so later she commented, "I went downtown in Boston for a look about—and was appalled by the women shopping. Ten deep at the counters, and thronging the pavements, until I walked most of the time in the street among the cabs, as less dangerous. And in all the thousands not half a dozen *ladies*. All people who ought to have been over a washtub."

Mabel was meeting Judge Bumpus for lunch that particular day, and her inordinate disdain may have been related in unconscious ways to her friendship with him, one aspect of the Todd-Dickinson case that never came to light. Only a few weeks after Austin's death, back in late September 1895, Mabel had dined alone with the Judge while on a visit to Boston, and rubbed from her diary account of the evening are the words "but he wanted to make love to me. . . . He was very intimate." She was accustomed to shrugging off overtures of admiration from men, even married men like Judge Bumpus, and because Mabel never discouraged an admirer completely, she had continued to meet the Judge socially in Boston, then turned to him at once when the altercation with Vinnie began. Late in the spring of 1897, however, an event occurred that revealed to Judge Bumpus the true nature of Mabel's relationship with Austin Dickinson, and it is interesting that, under the circumstances, Bumpus thereafter seems to have backed off from personal involvement in the Todd suit, as if aware of the moral quicksand that might swallow up his reputation. On May 28 he was called to Northampton to conduct the cross-examination of Maggie Maher, Vinnie's chief witness, who was leaving Massachusetts for a time. William Hammond wanted a deposition taken in case Maggie didn't return before the impending trial. Maggie's testimony exposed Mabel to charges of immorality. It was never used in court, and is not included in the trial records, but was a powerful element in the drama simply by virtue of the fact that it existed.

Dwight Palmer drove the corpulent, forty-three-year-old Maggie over to the Hampshire County courthouse in his carriage. She had resided at the Homestead for twenty-nine years, and while she didn't volunteer any information about her life there, she responded cautiously to Mr. Hammond's questions, telling of hearing Mabel refer to her work on the poems as "a labor of love," and of hearing Mabel express herself satisfied with the small royalties Vinnie had shared. Maggie also described working at the Dell occasionally, so that Mabel would be able to progress with the poems. During one three-month period she had helped there every day. Then, over Judge Bumpus's repeated objections, Maggie depicted two intimate moments between Austin and Mabel she had inadvertently witnessed, and established that the pair often had been alone together at the Homestead, the Dell, and, on at least one particular occasion, the Evergreens:

> They met very frequently [at the Homestead]; probably three or four times a week, sometimes in the afternoon and sometimes in the fore-noon, either in the dining room or the library. Sometimes for three or four hours just as their consciences allowed them. They met alone; the door was shut.

Asked about the carriage drives Mabel and Austin took together, Maggie explained:

> Very often they went to ride, sometimes in the fore-noon, but generally in the afternoon. They would sometimes take a drive for a whole day. He would ask her if she was ready to take a drive such a day, and she would answer, "Yes, always ready." I heard these things myself. Mr. Dickinson asked Miss Lavinia and me to put up a lunch. We always put it up. If they went in the fore-noon, they would probably get home at six o'clock or before. Often when they went in the afternoon they didn't come back until eight or nine.

Maggie scarcely gave Judge Bumpus an opening wedge during cross-examination, barely admitting that she and Vinnie ever discussed Mabel's editing of the poems or the land question during the long hours spent together in the Homestead. Her two most enlightening admissions were that Vinnie had remonstrated with Mabel for wearing mourning in public, and that Emily had always kept her poetry fascicles in Maggie's trunk, rather than in the cherry bureau purported to have held them.

The Dickinsons had no more interest than the Todds in adding these juicy contributions to the circulating scandal, but Maggie's testimony provided them an intimidating weapon capable of ruining the Todds' reputation. Mabel might scorn such low imputations against her noble love for Austin, knowing the truth concerning the deed was on her side, but the enormous risk that Maggie's deposition would be aired at the trial appears to have given two of her supporters considerable pause. By September Judge Bumpus had persuaded the Todds to hire local attorneys and enter a countersuit against Lavinia. Mabel called the action "self-defense," explaining in her journal that Vinnie had continued to spread lies for a full year after the Todds returned from Japan, "until David decided she must be stopped. It takes him a good while to be thoroughly roused, but if he starts he is pretty forceful. . . . So we have sued her for twenty-five thousand dollars for slander, and have got her in a very tight place—for if her suit is tried, with Mr. Spaulding who witnessed the deed to say that he told her what it was and read it to her, as he did, she is bound to lose it; then mine comes on and she will be convicted of perjury if she testified to the other. Then what?" Judge Bumpus assured her she would win.

Mabel's other but equally fainthearted advocate was Dwight Hills, who early on had encouraged her to "wallop" Vinnie, and promised to testify that Vinnie talked with him many times after Austin's death about her promise to give the Todds the whole meadow. Mabel intended Hills should be her principal witness. But after he learned about Maggie's deposition he became more cautious, and eventually took to his bed through the trial. Mabel, never fully informed by Bumpus as to the specific contents of Maggie's testimony, remained unaware of these two crucial defections.

Meanwhile, an auspicious event of autumn 1897 marked a long-desired turning point in the Todds' fortunes, and in Mabel's mind augured a happy outcome for her future in general. Her mother's cousin Charles Wilder of Wellesley died, leaving fifteen thousand dollars in his will for Amherst College to buy the Clark house and adjoining land southwest of the campus for a new observatory site, and a verbal proviso from Charles's executor, his brother Herbert Wilder, stipulated that the newly purchased house should become the rent-free residence of the college astronomer. "In a way it hurts me very deeply to think of going away from this most artistic and beautiful little home," Mabel wrote of the Dell in late September.

> The [observatory] house is not half as artistic, and there are no more rooms, but it is larger, and more impressive. It is barren as to grounds . . . and my own place is now a perfect bower of beauty, with the touch of my beloved on every inch. The splendid blue spruce, the hemlocks, the white birches, forsythia, hydrangeas, magnolia, beech, chestnut, walnut, ginkgo—all the myriad lovely things he put in here are living vigorously, and it is an enchanting little place. But since Vinnie sued me for the adjoining strip of land, which she freely deeded to me after my darling died, to escape the much larger obligation which she was under promise to discharge to me, and intended to shirk, the dear meadow has pierced me. Austin's trees and beauties down here, while they are still his, have a little tang of bitterness through her wickedness so that it hurts me to look out.

The Todds moved in, late in February 1898, just a week before the trial at last began. During the intervening winter the opposed factions had battled back and forth, each jockeying to have the other's case heard first. Vinnie had won a continuance in November by producing a certificate from her physician pronouncing her heart too weak for her to appear in court, and her lawyers had also made a surreptitious effort to settle out of court, but after numerous courtroom tactics on both sides, the Dickinson equity suit was finally set for hearing on March 1.

Vinnie was an extraordinary sight when she arrived in court that Tuesday morning. She wore an outdated, none-too-tidy blue flannel dress that had served her for "best" for many years, together with yellow shoes and a long black mourning veil. Flanked on either side by her good friend Miss Vryling Buffam and the redoubtable Maggie, she sat just in front of Ned and Mattie Dickinson in the well-filled courtroom. Sue Dickinson did not attend, although Dwight Palmer was present to testify to the value of the parcel of land under dispute. Across the courtroom Mabel wore a stylish black hat adorned with two white bird wings, while the real feather in her cap, the steadfast Mrs. William F. Stearns, sat valiantly beside her. David sat on the other side with the Todd lawyers, including new counsel, John B. O'Donnell, who had been hastily brought in to replace Judge Bumpus, inexplicably called to Washington suddenly on other business. Defense witnesses Timothy Spaulding and Frances Seelye were present, although a deposition had had to be secured overnight from Dwight Hills, recently ill from nervous shock following his mother's death the previous October. Half of Amherst filled the available seats.

William Hammond opened for the plaintiff by recalling the Dickinson family's fine reputation, then rehearsed the steps by which Miss Dickinson had been tricked into signing a deed under the misapprehension that she was simply agreeing not to build on a particular piece of her property. All morning Vinnie occupied the witness stand, undergoing examination and cross-examination about her version of Mr. Spaulding's surprise social call the evening of February 7, 1896, about her relations with Mabel during publication of her sister's poems, and about her promise to Mr. Hills never to give away any property without his knowledge. Vinnie made a very lively witness, her forthright responses replete with naïve revelations about her old-fashioned, secluded life. By the noon recess she had perjured herself many dozen times. "I had never had any talk about a deed, had done nothing about a deed, and knew nothing about a deed down to that evening," Vinnie lied, with what Mabel termed "a look of her grey eyes to deceive the Elect."

> It might have been between seven and eight when Mr. Spaulding came there with Mrs. Todd [Vinnie testified]. There had been no conversation nor arrangement nor agreement between Mrs. Todd and me about his coming there. There had been no talk between Mrs. Todd and me that I wanted somebody outside of the town to witness the deed. I had not thought of making a deed. I had said nothing about it whatever. . . . Mrs. Todd asked that [Mr. Spaulding] be taken into the dining-room to see some china that he was very fond of, so she said. While there she asked me if I would sign this paper, while he was looking at this blue china in the dining-room. . . . He did not say anything to me at all. I did not see him take the paper at all. I do not remember he made any remark about it. I was simply asked if I would "sign this little paper now," and I said I would, and I did. I do not recall Mr. Spaulding's speaking to me on the subject. He did not point out the place against the seal where I should sign. Mrs. Todd pointed it out. Mrs. Todd handed me the paper and I signed it, and that is all I remember about it.

Early in the afternoon lawyer Wolcott Hamlin opened for the defense, claiming Mabel's story was so contrary to Miss Dickinson's that he wished to dwell instead upon his client's extraordinary efforts to edit Emily Dickinson's poems, for which Lavinia Dickinson had never made adequate compensation. He was interrupted by Judge John Hopkins, who pointed out that the Defendants' Answer, filed back in November 1896, had claimed it was *Austin* Dickinson's desire to compensate Mabel, not Lavinia's, so Hamlin's argument was irrelevant. Mr. Hamlin redirected himself to forging a link between Austin's wishes and Vinnie's intention to convey the strip of land in fulfillment of them. Then Mabel took the stand for three hours, making as fine a witness as Vinnie, according

[417]

to the *Springfield Republican*, although she told quite a different story. So scrupulously honest was she that many of her statements began "I think" or "I don't think" or "possibly" or "as I remember," inadvertently suggesting a tenuousness that contrasted with Vinnie's forceful, direct deceits, but Mabel was firm as she concluded giving direct evidence:

> I never committed, nor attempted to commit, any fraud upon Miss Dickinson. When Mr. Spaulding was with me that night at Miss Dickinson's I never said to Miss Dickinson or anybody that he and I came there simply for a call; I never said it. My husband, Prof. David P. Todd, never attempted in any way to defraud Miss Dickinson with reference to this land, or with reference to this deed. Miss Dickinson never said anything to me about the suit nor found fault about the signing.

No mention was made throughout the trial of Austin's original promise to Mabel of the entire Dickinson meadow, although it seemed to haunt the two days' proceedings each time the meadow was mentioned. S. S. Taft, counsel for Lavinia, focused in his cross-examination on the original meadow house lot deeded the Todds by Austin in 1886. How much had the Todds actually paid for that $1,200 parcel? he queried. In one of two instances that Mabel perjured herself, she replied she had no idea, the transaction had been entirely between her husband and Mr. Dickinson. Her other lie came shortly after—that she had met Austin Dickinson frequently "at my house and at Miss Lavinia's house, not particularly often at his own house—not at all in the past few years." Both parties knew that would be refuted if Margaret Maher took the stand.

Much of Taft's cross-examination was directed at Mabel's work on the poems and letters and her expectation of compensation. Vinnie deprecated her editorial work on the poems:

> Mrs. Todd asked the privilege of doing it. The handwriting of the poems was peculiar, but very legible to most persons,

not difficult to read, easy to read. We should not think of send-ing the original poems to the printer because they would be soiled, perhaps lost. No other reason; they might be soiled or lost in the printer's hands. I wished them copied. Mrs. Todd copied them. She copied all the little volumes. . . . I think it was three years after my sister's death before I decided to have her do it.

Mabel then had asked to edit Emily's letters. "I knew that she thought it would be for her literary reputation to do it, and it made her reputation," stated Vinnie. Neither she nor her brother had ever talked of giving Mabel land as compensation.

In large degree Mabel had created her own difficulties over compensation through her pretense that she wrote, taught, gave painting lessons, and sang publicly for the sheer pleasure of expressing her overabundant talents, whereas she sorely needed the money they earned her. Once, she lashed out at her mother on the subject: "Almost anybody can go five or six thousand dollars in debt to build a house, & teach to get money to furnish it & write & paint, I suppose. You think all these things come easily to me, because I say nothing about the debts. If you could see the pile of January bills on my desk, & know that I have drawn all the salary ahead for three months. . . . But I never talk about these things." Few in Amherst appreciated Mabel's real motives, and few had sym-pathy for her compensation dispute with Vinnie, especially after Mr. Taft elicited that Mabel kept the fees she received from her numerous Emily Dickinson talks.

Late in the afternoon David was sworn in to testify about Lavinia's December 1895 moonlight inspection of the disputed land, an event Vinnie denied ever happened, but which Pro-fessor Todd said he witnessed from an east window of the Dell. Pressed closely by Mr. Taft, he depicted Vinnie's nocturnal visit with a professional assurance that was very engaging, until Taft suddenly asked what he had paid for the lot his house stood on. "I paid nothing for it," said David. As mur-

murs of surprise filled the courtroom, Judge Hopkins quickly called for adjournment, creating what newspaper headlines termed an "abrupt pause in the case" that effectively headed off further courtroom speculation concerning compensation of the Todds by Austin Dickinson.

Truth may have been on Mabel's side, but circumstances were running against her, as she summed up many months later in her journal.

Nobody ever thought Vinnie would actually go into court, and when the day for it actually came it was a perfect amazement to see her come tripping in with every evidence of enjoyment. Everything worked badly for me. Judge Bumpus could not come on account of another case, and so old Mr. Hamlin who had been working up details of the case got Mr. O'Donnell suddenly, to do most of the court part. Of course he could not quite understand it all at so short notice, and he lost a great many points in questioning Vinnie. And Mr. Hills was sick in bed, and his deposition had to be used. But even then my side seemed absolutely certain of success. Mr. Spaulding testified that he told her it was a deed at the time she signed it, showed her where to put her name, and told her it was a warranty deed. Miss Seelye testified that she had talked to her about giving me that lot for several months before she signed the deed. Mr. Dwight Hills' deposition said that she had talked to him for months about doing it, and that he said when she got ready to do it he would have the deeds prepared. These were three disinterested witnesses. Vinnie denied everything. She said she had never talked to Mr. Hills about giving it because she never thought of giving it. That he never told her he would have the deeds prepared. That she never talked with Miss Seelye about it. That Mr. Spaulding did not show her where to sign, nor tell her it was a deed. That she had never sent me any notes to come over to her house. Twenty or more were produced. And the Judge believed at least a hundred other lies she told, in face of five reputable witnesses who contradicted her at every point. Mr. Hills says it is the most incredible case on record. So does Judge Bumpus. So even do Vinnie's friends. It is past comprehension how she could be believed. But oh! I am glad those hours of perjury are not on my soul. When I go into the great coming world, it will be as white as snow so far as this case is concerned.

Judge Hopkins's final decree, handed down on April 15, 1898, found in favor of Lavinia Dickinson. "A perversion of justice," the Todds called it, unable to understand how it could have happened. Despite his inadequacy in Mabel's eyes, counsel O'Donnell had managed to keep Maggie from testifying during the second day of the trial, and at the end had rehearsed for the court the glaringly contradictory testimony of the two opponents. How wounding to his distinguished clients, argued O'Donnell, to impute they would defraud anyone for a paltry $600 bit of property. But Taft's summation, called by the *Springfield Republican* "one of the most lucid and forceful arguments that have been heard in the Northampton court for some time," drove the Dickinson nail home. Mabel called it "mocking, insolent," a "personal abuse of me," recording that "for an hour I was hit in the face and pounded," as Vinnie's lawyers argued for the case to be settled on other grounds than the irreconcilable issue of land fraud. It should be determined instead, they advocated, by the conduct, credibility, and character of the two main witnesses.

"Miss Dickinson is a gentlewoman of about sixty years of age," expounded Mr. Taft.

She lives alone with her maid in Amherst, in the house built by her grandfather, and the house in which her father lived, the old Dickinson Homestead. Her father and brother had been members of the Hampshire Bar, and both had been treasurers of Amherst College. Until her death in 1886, her sister, Emily Dickinson the poet, lived with her and shared the Homestead with her. Emily Dickinson was a recluse, never seeing any one; and Lavinia Dickinson was very quiet, and according to the testimony of Mrs. Todd, of "retiring" disposition. She knew little of the world and nothing of business. . . . Her quiet, sincere, consistent and convincing manner of giving her evidence and of stating the way in which the defendant persuaded her to "sign this little paper which we have talked about," and sign it *then*, gives a sufficiently clear and vivid picture of the refinement and seclusion of her life as well as a connected and consistent narrative of the urgency, secretiveness and misrepresentation of the defendant.

Upon the other hand, it can be fairly claimed that the evidence, as reported, shows the defendant to be very much a woman of the world. She has not spent her life in the seclusion of the little village of Amherst. She has passed winters in the city, has been somewhat extensively upon the lecture platform, and has also traveled extensively in Europe, in the Bermudas, in the western states, and taken two voyages to Japan. She has had that business experience which one necessarily derives from extensive travel and the occupation of a public lecturer. It is a fair inference from the evidence reported that she is conversant with business affairs, and that Miss Dickinson is quite unacquainted with them.

Despite her business acumen, Mrs. Todd denied knowledge of the sum paid for her house lot, Mr. Taft pointed out, and although a facile witness, worldly and sure of herself, she had displayed peculiar hesitancy in crucial areas of her testimony, and strange vagueness in recalling certain temporal relationships. He never alluded to her friendship with Austin Dickinson.

In early May the Todds appealed the case before a September sitting of the state Supreme Court at Northampton, Justice Oliver Wendell Holmes, Jr., presiding, but that court upheld the lower court's decree, persuaded that Judge Hopkins had indeed possessed the right to make a subjective judgment. "Seldom is there a case in which the reasons for a rule that weight should be given to the expressions produced by seeing and hearing the witnesses are so strong as in this case," affirmed the high court. "*How* can a lie be endorsed and reendorsed.

And the real truth put in the wrong!" moaned Mabel. Amherst took it that Vinnie had upheld the right to change her mind. The Todds were vanquished. "That lawsuit has blackened every sunny day, has hurt the quality of every bit of work I have accomplished, has squeezed my heart, creased my forehead, and given me an unspeakable pain in every breath I draw," allowed Mabel.

Yet there was no real victory for the Dickinsons. A day after Judge Hopkins announced his verdict in April 1898, Ned was seized by angina, and died two and a half weeks later "of the Dickinson heart." Many in town felt he had been severely strained by his support of Vinnie through the trial, but there is room for suspecting that his secret support, through all the painful years, was still for Mabel. Ned's gravestone bears an erroneous death date of May 3, 1897. Perhaps this was an effort by his grieving mother and sister to disassociate his sad life from the ugly blot on the family record. Relations between the Evergreens and the Homestead were dismal and strained until Vinnie's death, only a little over a year later, on August 31, 1899. Her last bedridden months were lonely and unhappy, according to accounts of friends, but Mabel's comment on her death spared no pity. "Lavinia Dickinson died at six o'clock tonight," she noted in her diary. "I have no feeling about it, one way or the other. Only I am glad it is she and not I who has to face God with perjury to report."

At the end of 1898 Mabel closed and locked the lid on the hundreds of Dickinson poems and letters that remained in her possession. In the years following, she and David led an active life in Observatory House, teaching, writing, and raising funds for the new observatory, which was completed in 1904. Not long after they settled in their new part of town, Mabel's parents, who were also bequeathed small sums by the Wilder brothers, left Washington for good and moved into Observatory House. Molly Loomis died there in 1910 and Eben in

1912. Mabel continued to lecture extensively throughout the Northeast, and joined David on several astronomical expeditions—two to Tripoli, one to the Dutch East Indies, and one to the Andes—until in 1913, at age fifty-six, she suffered a cerebral hemorrhage from which she never regained full use of her right hand and foot. Despite this, she accompanied David to Russia a year later on an eclipse voyage that ended in chaos when World War I erupted.

During his late fifties David's behavior grew increasingly erratic, which led in 1917 to his being eased off the Amherst faculty into early retirement. The Todds' old friend Arthur Curtiss James, now a trustee of Amherst College, financed a new home, which they named Matsuba, in Coconut Grove, Florida, and there Mabel lived until her death from a second cerebral hemorrhage in 1932. David was institutionalized in 1922, and spent his last seventeen years in a series of hospitals and nursing homes. The endless schemes and designs that always preoccupied him culminated during these final years in a great plan he called "Vital Engineering," a program for eternal life.

Sue Dickinson died of a heart condition in 1913, at the age of eighty-two. Her daughter, Martha Dickinson Bianchi, who had published poetry and romances of her own from the time she was thirty, subsequently undertook to bring out the rest of her Aunt Emily's poems. From materials that had been in her mother's or Lavinia's possession, she published a string of eight volumes from 1914 to 1937, some of them in collaboration with her friend Alfred Leete Hampson, each book in turn purporting to complete the Dickinson canon. In 1945 Millicent Todd Bingham also published a book of new Dickinson poems from the manuscripts inherited from her mother.

Emily's presentation to the world would have been complicated under the best of circumstances, because of the size and unfinished condition of her poetic endeavor, not to mention the numerous poem variants that existed. But the Todd-Dickinson feud, which bred hatreds and disputes that continue today, added greatly to the complexity of her literary debut by creating controversy over ownership and rights to the manuscripts, even after those belonging to Martha Dickinson Bianchi were sold to Harvard University in 1950, and those possessed by Millicent Todd Bingham were given to Amherst College in 1956.

All three houses central to the Todd-Dickinson drama still stand today in the middle of Amherst. In 1916 the Dickinson Homestead on Main Street was sold out of the family, but was repurchased in 1965 by Amherst College and is maintained partially as a museum, open to the public on certain weekdays. The Todds' Queen Anne cottage was moved northward across Spring Street in 1907 in order to make room for a more elegant home that continues to occupy the Dell site. The Evergreens, still magnificently planted with many of Austin's trees and specimen shrubs, has been little changed by time. At this writing (1983), it is occupied by a friend of the late Martha Dickinson Bianchi.

Bibliography,
Acknowledgments,
and Index

BIBLIOGRAPHY

THE TITLES THAT follow are the sources of quotations and information cited in this book, or proved valuable to a comprehensive understanding of the Dickinsons and the Todds.

Allen, Mary Adèle, *Around a Village Green: Sketches of Life in Amherst*. Northampton, Mass.: Kranshar Press, 1939.

Amherst College Trustee Minutes, 1880–1895, Amherst College, Amherst, Mass.

Amherst Town Meeting Records, 1865–1900, Town Clerk's Office, Amherst, Mass.

Banning, Evelyn I., *Helen Hunt Jackson*. New York: Vanguard Press, 1973.

Bartlett Papers, Samuel and Mary L., Dartmouth College Library, Hanover, N.H.

Bianchi, Martha Dickinson, *Emily Dickinson Face to Face: Unpublished Letters with Notes and Reminiscences*. Boston and New York: Houghton Mifflin, 1932.

—— *The Life and Letters of Emily Dickinson*. Boston and New York: Houghton Mifflin; London: Cape, 1924. Reissued, 1930.

Bingham, Millicent Todd, *Ancestors' Brocades: The Literary Debut of Emily Dickinson*. New York and London: Harper, 1945.

—— *Eben Jenks Loomis, 11 November 1828–2 November 1912*. Cambridge: The Riverside Press, 1913.

—— *Mabel Loomis Todd: Her Contributions to the Town of Amherst*. New York: George Grady Press, 1935.

—— *Emily Dickinson's Home: Letters of Edward Dickinson and His Family*. New York: Harper, 1955.

Bingham Papers, Millicent Todd. Sterling Library, Yale University, New Haven, Conn.

Burgess, John W., *Reminiscences of an American Scholar*. New York: Columbia University Press; London: Oxford University Press, 1966.

Capps, Jack Lee, *Emily Dickinson's Reading 1836–1886*. Cambridge, Mass.: Harvard University Press; London: Oxford University Press, 1966.

Carpenter, E. W. and Morehouse, C. F., *The History of the Town of Amherst, Massachusetts*. Amherst, 1896.

Cody, John, *After Great Pain: The Inner Life of Emily Dickinson*. Cambridge: The Belknap Press of Harvard University Press, 1971.

Bibliography

Dickinson Collection. Houghton Library, Harvard University, Cambridge, Mass.

Dickinson, Susan Gilbert, "Annals of the Evergreens," published as "Magnetic Visitors," *Amherst College Alumni Magazine*, Vol. 33, no. 4 (Spring 1981).

—— "Society in Amherst Half a Century Ago," *Essays on Amherst's History*. Amherst: Vista Press, 1978.

Dickinson, William Austin, "Representative Men of the Parish, Church Buildings, and Finances," *An Historical Review: One Hundred and Fiftieth Anniversary of the First Church of Christ in Amherst, Massachusetts, November 7, 1889. Amherst, 1890.*

Franklin, Ralph W., *The Editing of Emily Dickinson: A Reconsideration*. Madison: University of Wisconsin Press, 1967.

Franklin County Court House Records, Greenfield, Massachusetts.

Frothingham Letters, unpublished (Theodore Frothingham, 1889–1921), Houghton Library, Harvard University.

Fuess, Claude M., *Amherst: The Story of a New England College*. Boston, Mass.: Little, Brown, 1935.

Hammond, William Gardiner, *Remembrance of Amherst: An Undergraduate's Diary*, 1846–1848, ed. George Frisbie Whicher. New York: Columbia University Press, 1946.

Hampshire County, Records of the Superior Court and of the Supreme Judicial Court of the Commonwealth of Massachusetts, Hampshire County Court House, Northampton, Mass., 1896–98.

Higginson, Thomas Wentworth, "An Open Portfolio," *Christian Union* (September 25, 1890).

—— "Emily Dickinson's Letters," *Atlantic Monthly* LXVIII (October 1891), pp. 444–56.

—— *Poems by Emily Dickinson*, edited by two of her friends, Mabel Loomis Todd and T. W. Higginson. Boston: Roberts Brothers, 1890.

—— *Poems by Emily Dickinson, Second Series*, edited by two of her friends, T. W. Higginson and Mabel Loomis Todd. Boston: Roberts Brothers, 1891.

Howells, William Dean, *The Rise of Silas Lapham*. Boston, 1885.

Jameson Papers, John Franklin, Library of Congress, Washington, D.C.

Jenkins, Rev. Jonathan L., "A Sermon Delivered at Edward Dickinson's Funeral," ms. in Dickinson Collection, Houghton Library, Harvard University.

Johnson, Thomas H., ed., *The Letters of Emily Dickinson*, 3 vols. Cambridge, Mass.: The Belknap Press of Harvard University Press, 1958.

—— *The Poems of Emily Dickinson*, 3 vols. Cambridge, Mass.: The Belknap Press of Harvard University Press, 1958.

King, Stanley, *A History of the Endowment of Amherst College*. Amherst, Mass.: Amherst College Press, 1950.

—— *The Consecrated Eminence: The Story of the Campus and Build-*

ings of Amherst College. Amherst, Mass.: Amherst College Press, 1951.

LeDuc, Thomas, *Piety and Intellect at Amherst College 1865–1912.* New York: Columbia University Press, 1946.

Leyda, Jay, *The Years and Hours of Emily Dickinson,* 2 vols. New Haven, Conn.: Yale University Press; London: Oxford University Press; Toronto: Burns and MacEachern, 1960.

Longsworth, Polly, *Emily Dickinson, Her Letter to the World.* New York: T. Y. Crowell, 1965.

Loomis, Eben Jenks, *An Eclipse Party in Africa.* Boston: Roberts Brothers, 1896.

—— *Wayside Sketches.* Boston: Roberts Brothers, 1894.

Marvel, Ik, *Reveries of a Bachelor.* New York, 1850.

Merriam, George S., *The Life and Times of Samuel Bowles,* 2 vols. New York, 1885.

Miller, Ruth, *The Poetry of Emily Dickinson.* Middletown, Conn.: Wesleyan University Press, 1968.

Mohr, James, *Abortion in America.* London: Oxford University Press, 1978.

Mudge, Jean McClure, *Emily Dickinson and the Image of Home.* Amherst: The University of Massachusetts Press, 1975.

Porter, David, *The Art of Emily Dickinson's Early Poetry.* Cambridge: Harvard University Press, 1966.

—— *Dickinson: The Modern Idiom.* Cambridge, Mass., and London: Harvard University Press, 1981.

Reno, "Everett Cephas Bumpus," *Memoirs of the Judiciary and the Bar of New England for the Nineteenth Century with a History of the Judicial System of New England.* Boston: The Century Memorial Publishing Company, 1901. Pp. 436–37.

Scudder, Samuel H., *The Butterflies of the Eastern United States and Canada, with Special Reference to New England,* 12 vols. Boston, 1888–89.

Sewall, Richard B., *The Life of Emily Dickinson,* 2 vols. New York: Farrar, Straus and Giroux, 1974.

—— *The Lyman Letters: New Light on Emily Dickinson and Her Family.* Amherst: The University of Massachusetts Press, 1965.

Todd, David Peck, *A New Astronomy.* New York: American Book Co., 1897.

—— *Stars and Telescopes.* Boston: Roberts Brothers, 1894.

Todd, Mabel Loomis, "An Ascent of Fuji the Peerless," *Century* (August 1891).

—— *A Cycle of Sonnets,* ed. by Mabel Loomis Todd. Boston: Roberts Brothers, 1896.

—— "The Eclipse Expedition to Japan," *The Nation* (September 1, 1887).

—— "Five Days in Ireland," *Amherst Record* (April 7, 14, 1886).

—— "Footprints," *N.Y. Independent* (September 27, 1883), *Amherst Record* (October 31, November 7, 14, 1883); Amherst: privately printed, 1883.

—— "A Great Modern Observatory," *Century* (February 1894).

—— *Letters of Emily Dickinson,* ed. Mabel Loomis Todd. Boston: Roberts Brothers, 1894.

—— *Poems by Emily Dickinson,* edited by two of her friends, Mabel Loomis Todd and T. W. Higginson. Boston: Roberts Brothers, 1890.

—— *Poems by Emily Dickinson, Second Series,* edited by two of her friends, T. W. Higginson and Mabel Loomis Todd. Boston: Roberts Brothers, 1891.

—— *Poems by Emily Dickinson, Third Series,* edited by Mabel Loomis Todd. Boston: Roberts Brothers, 1896.

—— "In September," *New York Evening Post* (September 29, 1888); *Amherst Record* (October 24, 1889).

—— "The Sexton's Story," *Amherst Record* (August 14, 21, 1889).

—— "Ten Weeks in Japan," *St. Nicholas Magazine* (December 1888).

—— *Total Eclipses of the Sun.* Roberts Brothers, 1894. (First volume in Columbian Knowledge Series, ed. David Peck Todd.)

—— "A Well-Filled Chimney," *St. Nicholas Magazine* (January 1890).

—— "The Witch of Winnacunnett," *New England Magazine* (January 1891).

Todd Papers, David Peck, Sterling Library, Yale University, New Haven, Conn.

Todd Papers, Mabel Loomis, Sterling Library, Yale University, New Haven, Conn.

Tyler, William S., *History of Amherst College During its First Half Century,* 1821–1871. Springfield, Mass., 1873. An extension of this history published in New York, 1895.

Ward, Theodora, *The Capsule of the Mind: Chapters in the Life of Emily Dickinson.* Cambridge, Mass.: The Belknap Press of Harvard University Press, 1961.

Wells, Anna Mary, *Dear Preceptor: The Life and Times of Thomas Wentworth Higginson.* Boston, Mass.: Houghton Mifflin, 1963.

Whicher, George, *This Was a Poet: A Critical Biography of Emily Dickinson.* New York: Scribners, 1938; reissued Amherst, Mass.: Archon Books, 1980.

"William A. Dickinson, Appellate, September 24, 1889–September 5, 1890," *Reports of the Supreme Judicial Court of Massachusetts,* Vol. 152. Boston: Little, Brown, 1891. Pp. 184–89.

Wright, Henry C., *Marriage and Parentage, or the Reproductive Element in Man as a means to his Elevation and Happiness.* Boston, 1854.

ACKNOWLEDGMENTS

THIS BOOK BEGAN during the seventeen years I lived in Amherst, among people raging with Dickinson fever, to many of whom I am indebted for their enthusiasm, insights, information, and penchant for conversing about Todds and Dickinsons over the vegetable bins in the supermarket. Appreciation of an earlier Amherst came through friendships with several women whose families reached back among the people in these pages—such as the late Katharine Cowles, Margaret Hitchcock Emerson, and Winifred Carpenter Gates. The late Winthrop S. (Toby) Dakin, lawyer and benefactor, whose mark on twentieth-century Amherst is as plain as Austin Dickinson's on the nineteenth, was for me a rare mentor. John William Ward, former President of Amherst College, David Porter, Professor of English at the University of Massachusetts, members of the Tuesday Club, the several authors of *Essays on Amherst's History*, and librarians at Amherst College, the Jones Library in Amherst, and the Houghton Library at Harvard University all shared sources or opened doors along the way.

The Sterling Library at Yale University, where Austin's and Mabel's letters are housed, became my home-away-from-home in 1972. Since the Todds never in their lives discarded anything, the huge collection of family papers and memorabilia that Millicent Todd Bingham gave the university in 1968 filled some three hundred Paige boxes, a rich lode of partially organized materials. I am indebted to the late Herman Kahn, formerly Associate Librarian of Manuscripts and Archives at Yale, and to David C. Maslyn, then Assistant Librarian of Manuscripts and Archives, for simply handing me a key and granting me permission to prowl the underground stacks, with its seductive rows of shelved boxes, to search out the lives of Mabel and David Todd. Over the years, as the Todd and Bingham papers became catalogued, others on the staff patiently provided invaluable assistance, particularly Judith A. Schiff, Chief Research Archivist; Mary LaFogg, Archivist for Administrative Services; and Patricia B. Stark, Principal Reference Archivist.

On the fourth floor of the Sterling was the office of Richard B. Sewall, Professor of English, who was preparing his definitive biography of the poet. By welcoming me to his "Emily Dickinson Factory," and generously sharing the love letters, journals, and diaries of Austin,

Acknowledgments

Mabel, and David, over which he then had exclusive jurisdiction, he gave this book life's breath. Without his faith and enthusiasm, the solving of mysteries and untangling of tantalizing secrets in the Todd–Bingham Collection would have been a lot less fun.

It took a move south into the eighteenth century to jolt the researcher into writing, into creating order from the rich chaos surrounding Austin and Mabel's love affair. Among those who have helped and humored me through writing and editing the manuscript, I wish to thank Jerome Bernstein, Judith Sheldon, Ladora Jackson, Emily Spencer, and my wise editor, Robert Giroux. The warmest gratitude belongs to my four daughters, Amy and Elizabeth, Laura and Annie, for their tolerance of Todd and Dickinson presences within the family, and their indulgence of a mother often *in absentia*, while the biggest thank you of all goes to my beloved husband, Chuck, who has been the book's great supporter from start to finish.

Grateful acknowledgment is made to the following for permission to use published and unpublished material in their collections: Yale University Library: The Millicent Todd Bingham Papers, Mabel Loomis Todd Papers, and the Loomis-Wilder Family Papers; The Houghton Library, Harvard University: The Dickinson Collection and The Theodore Frothingham Papers; The Trustees of Amherst College: Minutes of the Amherst College Trustees' Meetings and the Amherst College Treasurer's Reports; Dartmouth College Library: The Samuel Bartlett Papers; Library of Congress and the family of J. Franklin Jameson for the J. Franklin Jameson Papers; Yale University Press: Excerpts from *The Years and Hours of Emily Dickinson*, by Jay Leyda, 2 vol., Yale University Press, 1960; Harper and Row Publishers: Excerpts from *Ancestors' Brocades*, by Millicent Todd Bingham, Harper & Brothers, 1945.

POLLY LONGSWORTH
Williamsburg, Virginia
November 1983

INDEX

Index

Baltimore, Md., 80, 82, 85, 89, 92, 248

Banker and Tradesman, 405

Barbados, 358, 359

Barnes, Mrs. General, 381

Bartlett, Eddie, 47

Bartlett, Samuel C. and Mary L., 79, 83, 85–8, 92, 103, 106–7, 109

Bates, Arlo, 361, 364, 366

Beatrice, Princess, 228

Beecher, Henry Ward, 39, 113

Belchertown, Mass., 132, 223, 299n

Belgic, 269, 277, 279

Belgium, 232

Berkshire Mts., 254n

Bermuda, 374, 422

Bianchi, Martha Dickinson (Mattie), 6, 12, 60, 63, 86n, 112, 121, 132, 133, 139, 148, 151, 157, 160n, 178, 178n, 181, 201, 202, 207, 207n, 226, 254, 254n, 278, 307, 308, 313n, 318n, 319n, 335, 339n, 348, 352, 369, 386–7, 416, 423, 424–5

Bigelow, Dr. Orvis F., 391, 392

Bigelow, Mrs. Otis, 12n, 183n

Bingham, Millicent Todd, 6, 10, 13n, 15, 18, 18n, 23n, 25n(* †), 55, 61–2, 112n, 131, 161, 162, 170, 173, 184n, 185, 191, 203, 213n, 222n, 230, 238, 240, 245, 263n, 279, 313–16 passim, 317, 320, 322, 324, 324n, 325n, 330, 346, 364, 367, 375, 385n, 390, 399, 405, 424–5; *Ancestors' Brocades*, 6, 13n, 18n, 112n; *Emily Dickinson's Home*, 6

Birmingham, Ala., 301

Black Forest, 231

Bliss, Frederick, 207

Bliss, William, 167

Boltwood, Lucius and family, 326n

Bombay, India, 318n

Borneo, 269

Boston, Mass., 13n, 16, 19, 21, 28, 31–6, 82–3, 88, 89, 93, 100n, 139, 148, 152, 163, 164, 165, 165n, 167, 168, 169, 175, 178, 184, 190, 193, 204, 208, 209, 210, 213n, 215, 216, 219, 223, 229, 231, 235, 238, 240, 243, 245, 247, 256, 257, 261–2, 277, 278, 284, 293, 294n, 305n, 309, 310n, 312, 317, 321, 324–46 passim, 354, 355, 358, 360, 361, 362, 384, 386–7, 388, 389n, 391, 393, 404, 409, 411, 412; MLT's habitation in, 19, 31–6, 324–46; Boston Public Garden, 168, 321

Boston and Chicago Special, 376

Boston Courier, 364

Boston State House, 324

Boston Symphony, 328n, 329, 336, 340

Bowdoin College, 31

Bowles, Samuel and Mary, 110, 113, 114, 182n

Bowles, Samuel Jr., 394

Boyden Fund, 391n

Bridgeport, Conn., 248

"Bright Bits from Bright Books," *see Mrs. Logan's Home Magazine*

Brill, Mrs., 216

Brooklyn, N.Y., 39, 379–83 passim

Brooklyn Academy of Arts and Sciences, 380n

Brontë, Charlotte, *Villette*, 87

Brontë, Emily, "Last Lines," 243

Brooks, Rev. Phillips, 331

Brünig Pass, Switzerland, 234

Buffam, Miss Vryling, 416; Miss Buffam's School, 325n

Bumpus, Judge Everett C., 404, 409–10, 411–14, 416, 420

Burditt & Williams, 263, 272

Burgess, Prof. and Mrs. John W., 95n, 113–14

Burnett, Frances Hodgson, *A Fair Barbarian*, 170; *A Woman's Reason*, 146

"But Susan is a Stranger yet," *see* Dickinson, Emily

Butterflies of the Eastern United States and Canada, see Scudder, Samuel

Index

Index

Index

Index

Index

Index